DATE DUE

~~S/L~~	
~~JAN 1 0 2008~~	
~~FEB 1 2 2008~~	
~~date~~	
~~MAY 1 0 2008~~	
~~JUN 1 7 2008~~	
~~OCFE/SBLY~~	
~~NOV 2 1 2008~~	
~~APR 1 7 2009~~	
~~MAY 0 1 2009~~ jun	
~~FEB 1 3 2010~~	
11-3-14	
8/15/k	

GAYLORD · PRINTED IN U.S.A.

THE BEST AMERICAN

NONREQUIRED
READING
2007

THE BEST AMERICAN

NONREQUIRED READING™

2007

∎

EDITED BY

DAVE EGGERS

INTRODUCTION BY

SUFJAN STEVENS

HOUGHTON MIFFLIN COMPANY
BOSTON • NEW YORK
2007

Copyright © 2007 by Houghton Mifflin Company
Introduction copyright © 2007 by Sufjan Stevens

www.houghtonmifflinbooks.com

ISSN: 1539-316x
ISBN-13: 978-0-618-90276-7   ISBN-10: 0-618-90276-7
ISBN-13: 978-0-618-90281-1 (pbk.)   ISBN-10: 0-618-90281-3 (pbk.)

Printed in the United States of America

VP 10 9 8 7 6 5 4 3 2 1

"Bathing Ed Asner," "Vigil," and "Ups & Downs" by Greg Ames. First published in *Barrelhouse*, issue 3, 2006. Copyright © 2006 by Greg Ames. Reprinted by permission of the author.

"Names for Racehorses Expected to Have Undistinguished Careers" by Mike Richardson-Bryan. First published in *Yankee Pot Roast* (yankeepotroast.org), 2006. Copyright © 2006 by Mike Richardson-Bryan. Reprinted by permission of the author.

"Beginnings of Ten Stories about Ponies" by Wendy Molyneux. First published in *Monkey Bicycle,* 2006. Copyright © 2006 by Wendy Molyneux. Reprinted by permission of Wendy Molyneux.

New Words of 2006. From *The Concise Oxford English Dictionary* (2005), edited by Catherine Soanes and Nagus Stevenson, and from *The Merriam-Webster Online Dictionary* © 2007 by Merriam-Webster, Inc. (www.Merriam-Webster.com). Used by permission.

Twenty-three selections from *Not Quite What I Was Planning and Other Six-Word Memoirs . . .* by Larry Smith. Copyright © 2007 by Smith Magazine. Reprinted by permission of HarperCollins Publishers.

"International Personals" by Tin House. First published in *Tin House,* Winter 2006. Copyright © 2006 by Heather Hartley and Rob Spillman. Reprinted by permission of Heather Hartley and Rob Spillman.

Excerpts from "Petrified Forests," "Niagara Falls," "Grand Canyon," and "Dinosaur

CONTENTS

INTRODUCTION

How I Trumped Rudolf Steiner and
Overcame the Tribulations of Illiteracy,
One Snickers Bar at a Time

THERE ARE SOME THINGS you tell no one, secrets packed and folded away in the far reaches of your mind — admissions of mouth herpes, for example, or athlete's foot, or a night spent in jail for drunk driving. These irreversible facts, like birth certificates and blood donor cards, we keep under cover in the fireproof safe-deposit box hidden in the closet, under the Ouija board and Christmas-tree stand and the packs of Nicorette gum.

I'm a glutton for exhibitionism, so I'd like to reveal a dirty secret: I didn't learn to read until third grade. As an elementary school kid at the Detroit Waldorf School, I was encouraged to learn at my own pace. For the uninformed, let me tell you a little about Rudolf Steiner, the founder of the Waldorf system. An Austrian philosopher, writer, and social theorist, Steiner developed an educational system that was holistic, noncompetitive, and emotionally balanced, emphasizing social health, artistic expression, and pluralism in the classroom. In practice, this meant there were no textbooks, workbooks, reader's guides, or learning manuals — only paint, clay, knitting needles, and sheep's wool. I don't recall a library or a science lab in our school. There were indoor planters, pieces of felt, animal costumes, and wax paper. The classrooms were decorated with satin drapes and paper lanterns. There were no parallel walls or right angles. Quiet nooks and secret hollows were constructed in the corners, quilted blankets and hand-woven shawls held up with rocking chairs and wood broomsticks. Every room was designed to imitate a tree house or a bear cave or an underground den where foxes slept through the winter, nuzzling their young.

Learning was an amorphous metaphysical experience measured by the students' creative whims — beeswax one day, cotton string the next. There were no vocabulary exercises or math quizzes. The syllabus was hand drawn on the chalkboard, oil pastels in Renaissance colors simulating the seasons, sweeping rainbow illustrations of unicorns and magic owls and eavesdropping elves. The school did everything to blur all lines between fact and imagination, between art and science, between math and English, between student and teacher.

For some, the disregard for standards was galvanizing. My peers took up the violin, spoke French, learned botany, identified plants and animals, mastered oil painting, weaving, and the classical guitar. But I was a slow learner, the youngest of five, easily distracted, unmotivated, listless, prone to daydreaming. I spent much of my time huddled by the radiator, keeping my beeswax warm, humming the theme to *Star Search*. The classroom's lack of parallel surfaces coddled me in a fluid womb of sleep and thumb-sucking. I had trouble finding the restroom, so I peed in the cot. I had trouble finger-knitting, so I balled up the yarn and used it for a pillow. I had trouble making friends, so I imagined them: Peter the ox, Dora the talking skeleton, Herb the dietician. I lived in a world of fantasy and make-believe where reading and writing were banned by laws of my own creation.

Years went by — preschool, kindergarten, first grade, second grade — the dreamy sweep of a Steiner childhood. I was shuffled from calligraphy class to recorder lessons to eurythmy, with the choose-your-own-adventure of progressive schooling. It didn't matter that I was so far behind the other kids — those bold, brassy, multicultural, bilingual children with their knitted vests and viola cases. I would catch up, the teachers said. I would come around someday. I would learn to read and write by the powers of the Maypole, the winter solstice, the constellations, and Orion's enchanted belt. Waldorf teachers were less concerned with literacy and standardized testing — the unpalatable concessions of the public school system — than with watercolor pencils and cotton balls. For them, the real process of learning was to be stewed and simmered in a slow cooker, or kneaded and pulled in the baby's bottom of bread dough. We learned not by worksheets and chapter guides but by watching seedling trees grow from teacups, the passing of the seasons, Baroque music, folk songs, and Nordic my- thology. These things poked and prodded the child's imagination, opening up vast moments of wonder, inspiring great works of art, cul- tivating joy, encouraging artistry and a lifetime of learning.

Truth be told, I wasn't learning anything. I rode the absent-minded wave for four nebulous years, whistling and waving my way through educational anarchy. By the time I finished second grade, it was clear something was wrong. I still couldn't read or write. I had no friends. I had no ambitions. I was a Waldorf flunky. But by then it was too late. My parents' marriage began to crumble, along with the general down- ward slide of the times: Ronald Reagan, John Lennon, Mount St. Helens, to name a few. My parents started watching daytime TV, drank coffee till all hours of the night, ordered pizza, bleached their teeth, and shed their educational ideologies once and for all. They fought and kicked and threw dishes across the kitchen. Then they got divorced.

That summer, I went to live with my father, who had moved to the remote upper reaches of northern Michigan, to a small logging town with a bait shop and a swing bridge and a Methodist church at the top of the hill, a quiet, historical village where people spoke with a south- ern drawl and wore overalls and chewed tobacco and drove tractor- trailers to work at Kmart. My father apologized for everything — for Waldorf, for watercolor pencils, for recorder lessons, for est training, for past-lives séances, for macrobiotics, for pot-smoking, for the ridic- ulous, holistic trial and error called parenting, of which he confessed to failing greatly. "It's time you became a man," he told me. "It's time you learned to read."

So in the beginning of third grade, I was transferred to a public school, a cinderblock prison camp with metal lockers and industrial carpeting and fluorescent lights so severe they took all color out of your complexion. Right angles abounded. Maps of the USSR. Pro- tractors. Carbon copies. Vending machines. The sterile metal sur- faces of the modern age. Computers, textbooks, worksheets, MEAP, SAT, PTA, all the formidable abbreviations of public schooling. I clawed at the classroom windows like a hamster in a glass cage, desperate for fresh air.

The other children — raised on hot dogs and homogenized milk — were pig-nosed, bucktoothed, albino bullies who spent their free time at the arcade downtown playing Dig Dug or Dungeons and Dragons. But at least they could read. I couldn't even spell my own name, so I was beaten up at recess, tickled and punched behind the swings, left in a rumpled mess in the gravelly residue of the playground. After the first week of school, I was forced to take a series of multiple-choice tests — reading comprehension, basic math, language arts — each of which I failed, having artfully filled every blank with affectionate shades of the color wheel using my Swiss watercolor pencils. That's when I was ordered to go to special ed.

They sent me to a boxy trailer slumped behind the cafeteria with a stack of flash cards and a vocabulary book, highlighting useful, ordinary words that would help me navigate the everyday life of the working-class man. *Apple pie. Toothpaste. Driver's license. Checkbook. Garbage can.* I recognized the letters, but I couldn't piece them together into tangible, audible words. I was uninspired. "Give me a ball of beeswax," I begged, "or a slab of clay, and I will shape the letters from the earth and choreograph a dance for each vowel while pulling the streamers of the Maypole around the schoolyard, singing the folk songs of the ancients!"

My English teacher, Mrs. Lubbers, pulled me aside and said, "What is wrong with you? Are you retarded?" I shrugged and pointed at my heart, the light rhythm of hope, tapping its way out of any difficult situation. Mrs. Lubbers had the fresh face of a woman right out of a liberal arts college. She wore uneven dresses tied down with belts, and scarves dangled at every angle like those of a heavy-metal singer. She had bobbed hair and a birthmark on her neck in the shape of an infinity symbol. She wore metal bracelets and had a firm handshake that told you she wasn't going to give up easily.

At lunch, she pulled me into the teachers' lounge, unpacked her lunch on the table, and made me identify each object: juice box, banana, salami sandwich, potato chips. Then she pointed out the obvious packaging. Everything was tagged with its name, in clear, concise advertising. She told me about the wonders of the industrial age, how every item of food is mass-produced, wrapped, packaged, labeled, and sold to the public with its nametag right on front: *Hello. My name is*_____. She called the grocery store a public library, a literary adventure, a reader's guide for the learning-disabled. "We are surrounded by words," she said, as if reciting a psalm. "It's impossible *not* to read in this day and age. Not with all the Bazooka Joe comics lying around!"

Mrs. Lubbers had devised a theory: having been rescued from the liberal clutches of Rudolf Steiner, I was like a primate, an ignorant beast of nature, a wild stallion or Frankenstein's monster. I only needed the brash brainwashing of civilization, a crash course in modern society, capitalism, free enterprise, pop culture, Mickey Mouse, the Hardy Boys, Ronald McDonald. I needed the chlorinated conditioning of the modern world, with its pageantry of products, its multimedia of stimulation — television, *TV Guide,* GI Joe, Little Debbie, *Garfield, Peanuts,* Cocoa Puffs. I wasn't dumb, she told me. I was just Old World, nineteenth century, understimulated. The glorious product placement of the advertising age would certainly inspire in me all kinds of wild literary exploits.

Mrs. Lubbers assigned me a simple task: spend your free time at the pharmacy, the video store, or the grocery store, scanning aisles, browsing cereal boxes, examining coupons, prodding price tags and recipes for nouns, verbs, adjectives — the covert grammar of everyday objects, revealed only to the watchful eyes of the eager reader. In those quiet moments of clandestine reading I would slowly, irreversibly evolve into the acclaimed Nobel Prize–winning literary critic of tomorrow! "Read the label," Mrs. Lubbers said, "and you will uncover the *Guinness Book of World Records.* Read the label and you will soon be channeling the noble intonation of Garrison Keillor, the eloquence of Vincent Price, and the brains of Salman Rushdie."

The next day was payday, shopping day. I told my father about Mrs. Lubbers's homework assignment and begged him to take me to the local Super K, a commercial paradise, a library of information. He gave me a book of discount coupons to study in the car. When we got to the store, he pushed the cart from aisle to aisle and I kept my eyes open for the literature of the advertising world. *Palmolive. Antibacterial. Tough on grease.* I spelled out the words, shaped the vowel sounds, kept the rough edges of consonants on my tongue like a piece of hard candy. *Downy fabric softener. Duracell batteries. Aspirin pain reliever. Scotch tape.* These were mini-novels, micro-fiction, rousing in me the desire to read. I started with a book of matches, inspecting the small print: *Close cover before striking* — a mysterious line of haiku on which I meditated for hours. I sounded out the simple words on soup cans, toothpaste tubes, cracker boxes: *Weight. Squeeze. Caution. Press. Warning.* A simple glance at a box of Arm & Hammer baking soda beckoned the epic verse of warrior kings and rival siblings feuding for power with metal swords and battle-axes.

My father gathered all the groceries like a shepherd rounding up his sheep, and I scrutinized every label with the exactness of a shearer. I read the disappointing news of the cereal box: *Some settling may occur;* the morbid gasps of a can of aerosol hairspray: *Extremely flammable. Solvent abuse can kill instantly!* A box of paper clips promised a *smooth finish,* much like a fine scotch. A box of business envelopes became a patriotic icon: *Crafted with pride. Made in America.* The standup comedy on the box of a laxative tea: *Gently squeeze bag to release remaining extract.*

In the soap aisle, I memorized the seductive verbs on Alberto VO5's "extra body" shampoo: *wet, lather, rinse.* I tried to parse the mysterious ingredients on the back of the bottle, an intimidating litany of chemical compounds that might have been the recipe for an atom bomb: *acetate, panthenol, sodium chloride, water.* I proofread a can of Barbasol shaving cream, an erotic tone poem: "Our rich, thick lather / moisturizes and lubricates / for a clean, close, comfortable shave." I perused the short story of the lip balm: "If irritation occurs, discontinue use." I marveled at the absence of verbs on the Vitamin C: *one tablet, twice daily;* and the captivating demands on the caps of bleach: *push, turn, pull, pry.*

Later, at home, I moved on to other documents: junk mail, restaurant receipts, speeding tickets. In my father's messy desk drawer I uncovered a jury summons from the county clerk's office in the supreme court building, a business letter creased and folded in thirds, lying next to the hole puncher. The letter was dressed with the abrupt legalities of an administrative assistant: "Read carefully. No exceptions. Dress in a manner that shows respect. If your situation prevents you from coming in person, please call." There were unpaid phone bills, the poetry of phone numbers, first names, last names, business calls, 800 numbers. There were solicitations for credit cards, key cards, business cards, a library of area codes and office addresses. I discovered, by the book shelf, the astute astrology of my father's record collection, as gleaned from the liner notes of a 1968 recording by Aretha Franklin, born under the sign of Aries: "You are a natural leader and your pioneering strength expresses a sincere interest in the welfare of others." Soon I was reading whole sentences, paragraphs, pages and pages of newspapers, *National Geographics*, the *National Enquirer*, the *Detroit Free Press*, the *New York Times Magazine*, *The Tibetan Book of the Dead*. I took notes, made outlines, wrote thesis statements, introductory paragraphs, first drafts, revisions, ambitious dissertations on the flea circus, the shoe horn, the Sharpie, the morning-after pill, Roe v. Wade, the Interlake Steamship, the Erie Canal, the hooded sweatshirt, beeswax, the four-leaf clover, the recorder, the violin, dance theater, What I Did for Summer Vacation, Space Camp, Dance Camp, Recorder Camp, Super K, and how I heroically overcame the tribulations of illiteracy, one Snickers bar at a time.

The next school day I felt like I had a hangover. I dragged myself to class with a head cold, a migraine, a fever, my right brain battling it out with my left brain, each lobe fat and fractured with all the jingle-jangle of popular media. Bug-eyed, with drooping mouth, beaten but undefeated, I had triumphed over the educational armies of Rudolf Steiner and basked in the glories of commerce and capitalism, from which all knowledge thrives. I could finally read! I brought in a can of Campbell's tomato soup and read every word on the label, to prove it to the rest of the class: "In a four-quart pot combine one can of soup and one can of water. Simmer over low heat, stirring often. Serve. Enjoy." Mrs. Lubbers gave me a proud look, a row of stars, an A+, and, with a shuffling of neck scarves and metal bracelets, she handed me my very first book: Edward Gibbon's *Decline and Fall of the Roman Empire*, all six volumes, 3,568 pages. I took it home that night and read every single word.

SUFJAN STEVENS

Q & A

LAST YEAR I didn't write an intro, and some of the students on the *Best American Nonrequired Reading* Committee asked, "Why not?" And after they were given a very sensible and succinct answer involving barometric pressure and Spain, they persisted and said again, "Really though. Why not?" Meanwhile, a group of senators and assemblypersons were pressing *BANR* on a number of questions relating to the collection, so we decided to kill these two birds with one stone. One stone in the shape of an introduction in the shape of a Q & A.

1. Tell us: Who are they, the Nonrequired *committee's members who decide on things in this collection?*
They are high school students from all over the San Francisco Bay Area.

2. Are they touched by some kind of divine light?
The question is a good one. There is rampant speculation on the subject.

3. Are they all great-looking and charming and well dressed?
Yes. All of them, and especially Felicia Wong, who can even make her own clothes.

4. Where can I find out more about these people?
Their bios and photos are in the back of this book. The publisher has insisted that they be placed there. We are not sure why.

5. I have a question about the process by which the entries in this collection are chosen. Is it scientific?

The process by which *The Best American Nonrequired Reading* is put together is not scientific. It is whatever one would consider the opposite of scientific.

6. Creationist?

Well, no, it's not creationist either. The point is that we are probably a bit less top-to-bottom thorough than, say, the Army Corps of Engineers. Well, actually, scratch that. We are probably about exactly as thorough as the Army Corps of Engineers, in that we are intermittently thorough.

7. So how is the collection done?

We do it like so: When the committee starts a given year, the twelve or so members first sit around on a bunch of chairs and couches and rugs, and we divide up a list of about 140 magazines and journals and websites. I read off the names, and when students hear "*Alaska Quarterly Review,*" they will raise their hands, someone will be chosen, and so on. At the end of this session, we've divvied up all the publications that we'll be tracking throughout the year. Each student has an average of eight to ten periodicals that they're in charge of. They write to the periodicals in question, trying to get the periodical to send us copies. Then, once they get the copies, they read through the journals or magazines — again, not completely scientifically — and if something piques their interest, they will make Xeroxes of it, and these copies will be distributed to the committee. Once everyone has read a given piece, it will be discussed. If it is deemed appropriate for the collection, it goes in the YES pile, and this pile is placed somewhere precarious. Every year, for some reason, we place the YES pile in an area of the office where it gets misplaced, temporarily or permanently, which necessitates a long brain-plumbing session when we try to recall all the YESes (usually with success, for these YESes have been so memorable). Finally, around March, about a month before the collection is due at the publisher's, we will begin sifting the YESes and the MAYBEs, trying to find the right mix for the collection.

8. So the final selections are not necessarily, say, the top twenty vote getters?

That is correct. Often we find ourselves with more than one top vote getter from the same magazine, and because we're trying to represent a wider spectrum of publications, we usually try not to include more than one envoy from any one magazine. We also have to take into consideration a balanced mix of fiction, nonfiction, journalism, essays, humor, comics, and pieces about Burmese guitar heroes. Creating the right balance, though, sometimes means we can't take a piece we want to, if taking it would unbalance the balance. For instance, we will pick up a new or old journal and say, "Wow, this is a great publication!" And we will find a number of stories that almost work for us, but that don't, in the end, work for us. Maybe the best story in this particular journal is about lumberjacks, and we already have two stories about lumberjacks. This is the sort of thing that happens.

9. What is your opinion and the committee's opinion of the state of short stories and small magazines and other periodicals?

This is a good time. It really is.

10. More specifically?

Not all of us Americans appreciate the fact that we have about 150 very good quarterlies in this country. Every state seems to have a very good quarterly, and about a hundred colleges have very good quarterlies — from the *Kenyon Review* to the University of Illinois's *Ninth Letter*. So by our estimate there are about 150 very good quarterlies in this country. Maybe more. Now, the thing we don't always appreciate here in America is that elsewhere in the world there are few to no quarterlies. Few to none! There simply isn't the same tradition in Europe, Asia, or anywhere else. Even Canada has nothing on us, and it seems to beat us in many other things, including looks (Canadians are spectacular-looking and all smell of pine and honey). But when it comes to quarterlies, we are in good shape. Any short story writer or poet or essayist would seem to have too many choices to choose from. And any given quarterly might have a readership of 300 or 3,000 or more, and that's a lot of people. If you were asked, say, to give leg massages to that many people, you would be stuck. You'd have to clear your schedule for a day or so at least.

10a. How does it feel to select something for the collection that you found in an unlikely place?

It feels so good. This year, for example, at the last moment, we found "Humpies" by Mattox Roesch. It was published by *Agni Online*, and we all loved it, and here it is, ideally able to reach a new audience. We all took pleasure in finding that one; the mandate of the committee is to find the offbeat and the lesser known and bring these pieces to our readers, most of whom have great skin and bad eyes.

11. May we listen in on a discussion among the members of the Nonrequired *Committee?*

What? No. Of course not.

11a. May we, please? We have heard the discussions are astounding.

They are, but the answer is no.

12. (Sounds of sobbing)

Stop that. That's embarrassing.

13. (Louder sobbing)

My God. Please. Stop that. Please. Here's a tissue.

14. (Sniffling) That's not a tissue. It's toilet paper.

Do you want to hear the discussion or not?

15. (Brightening) Yes. Yes!

Fine. Please find below an actual transcript of one discussion in December 2006, when we were discussing an article from *Details* magazine called "Battle of the Bulge." The article was about the trend, being suffered then and currently, whereby men wear very tight pants, which look more like leggings. The article was suggesting that men should not wear these sorts of pants. Let's join the discussion in progress:

CHRIS BERNARD: "Battle of the Bulge"? I get so tired of World War Two.

NINA MOOG: What? This isn't that.

BORA LEE: Did you read this piece, Chris?

CHRIS: Not yet. Why?

BORA: It's not about World War Two.

FELICIA WONG: It's about a different, um, bulge.

CHRIS: (Blushing) What? (Blushing more) Oh. Oh. Oh. I get it. (Long, awkward pause)

MODERATOR: So, what did everyone think?

FELICIA: [The author] calls pants "sausage casings." (General laughter)

ARIANNA KANDELL: I thought it was really funny. We talk about politics and music, but we never talk about fashion. And it's very 2006.

NINA: But when the book comes out next year, will skinny dudes still be wearing those pants?

(Committee looks to Josh Freydkis, who wears the type of pants under discussion)

JOSH FREYDKIS: *I* still will. I'll keep wearing my skinny jeans. I have four pairs and I'm not buying new ones anytime soon.

BORA: [Name of male student at her school], for one, will continue to wear his tight jeans until the end of time.

JOSH: Unless a meteor comes and crashes and causes all skinny pants to expand, we'll still wear them.

FELICIA: The streets will be flooded with hipster tears if that happened. All of Mission Street would be drowned.

(General laughter, followed by a long pause as this thought sinks in)

CHRIS: That would be sad.

ANNA: So where does this one go?

DANIEL GUMBINER: Maybes for now.

16. That was so intense! Where do these fantastic discussions take place?

They are held in the basement of a building on Valencia Street in San Francisco's Mission District. This basement is not very clean, and is disorganized on top of its uncleanliness. This basement is across the street from 826 Valencia, the nonprofit writing and tutoring and student publishing center that benefits from this collection.

17. Come again about benefiting 826 Valencia?

All the proceeds from this book go to the nonprofit — actually, a network of seven centers, from Seattle to Boston (the newest site) — and the funds make student programming possible. For more information, go to www.826national.org.

18. Our last question is about Ed Asner.
Yes.

19. Where is the poetry about Ed Asner?
Excuse me?

20. The talk in Washington, D.C., and elsewhere is that there was to be poetry about Ed Asner, the stout and irascible actor featured prominently on The Mary Tyler Show *and* Lou Grant. *Now where is it?*
We don't know anything about —

21. We remind you that you're under oath.
Okay. Right. Okay. We had some Ed Asner poetry in our YES pile for a while, but then found that most of the students on the committee, whose average age is seventeen, did not know who Ed Asner is. So the poetry was cut.

21. Hmm. Well, now we recommend that you give us some Ed Asner poetry.
And if we don't?

22. Expect subpoenas. And then some filibustering. And maybe even some gerrymandering. And if that doesn't work, more sobbing.
Below please find some Ed Asner poetry. That is, poetry about Ed Asner, as opposed to poetry by Ed Asner, which we hear takes place in Prague and is filthy. If we promise to print these poems, will that be the conclusion of this hearing?

23. It will.
Good. These poems were written by Greg Ames and published in *Barrelhouse.*

DAVE EGGERS

Three Poems by Greg Ames

Bathing Ed Asner

I snatched the rubber duck
from his hairy, wet fist

and in a cruel voice
instructed him to quit
fooling and to sit down
dammit in the tub.

"But I didn't ask for your help,"
Asner whined, sulked, and slapped
the murky water with his puckered palms.

"Well, that's pretty much beside
the point, isn't it?" I said.
"I'm here now, *helping you,* so stop
making trouble for me, Lou Grant."

"Don't call me that!" he said.

"Well, then, lift up your arms,"
I whispered in his ear,
"and let's swab out those pits."

Vigil

I sat down on the toilet lid,
crossed my muddy boots
on the edge of the tub.

"It was only a television program,"
he said. "It was only fiction. You know,
make-believe?"

"Don't play the innocent,"
I warned him. "It doesn't become you."

"How much money do you want?"

"How dare you," I said
and averted my eyes.

"You should consider getting
these tiles regrouted."

"I don't understand," he said,
shivering in the tepid bath water.
"What do you want?"

"What do I want? Are you prepared
to give me what I want, Lou Grant?"

"Anything," he said. "Yes. Anything."

"Put this on," I said.

Ups & Downs

Blue bathrobe billowing out behind him,
Asner clutched the rusted metal handle
of the seesaw we were riding in the park.

"Not so fast!" he thundered. "I'm getting dizzy."

Now perched high above him, I could
see clear across the playground
to the tennis courts.
"How's your net game, Lou?"
I said savagely.

Bare legs splayed over splintered green wood,
a yellow isosceles of Speedo thong
visible beneath his sagging paunch,
Asner spat filthy words down at me,
up at me, and down at me.

Eyes wild, he gripped the rusted handle like a frightened child.
"Cut it out," he wheezed. "I said not so fast!"

For months I had been doing squat-thrusts
in my basement for this very purpose.
My thighs were huge and astonishing.
Asner howled as the speed increased.

"Hold on tight, Lou Grant," I shouted,
and I bent my legs for a final
triumphant push.

WE TRIED THIS LAST YEAR, and it seemed to work, so we're doing it again. Below you'll find a succession of short pieces that belong here because they are short and this section is for shorter things we found that belong nowhere else. They were collected by the *Best American Nonrequired* Committee, with help from Michelle Quint and Jeff Chiang. We begin with two items that pertain to horses.

Best American Names of Horses Expected to Have Undistinguished Careers

MIKE RICHARDSON-BRYAN

FROM *Yankee Pot Roast* (www.yankeepotroast.org)

Average at Best
Ayn Rand's Condescending Sigh
Buyer's Remorse
Cloud of Suspicion
Colic the Wonder Horse
Daddy Drinks Because I'm Slow
Exit Strategy
Fond of Long Naps
For the Love of God Run Faster
Glued Lightning

Hell Is Other Horses
I Have No Son
Limp to Victory
Low Expectations
Luck o' the Amish
Pride of Two Guys with No Business Owning a Horse
Shoulda Bought a Monkey
Slim to None
Some Budding Young Actress's Fit of Pique
Squeak of Defiance
Stupid Gypsy Curse
This Is Your Horse on Drugs
Torpor Unbound
Tripsy McStumble
Undisguised Contempt for All Things French
War Criminal

Best American Beginnings of Ten Stories about Ponies

WENDY MOLYNEUX

FROM *Monkey Bicycle* (www.monkeybicycle.com)

1. I saw the pony there, just standing there, just standing in the rain. And that's when I knew that I was going to leave my wife.

2. At the time this all happened I was on the run from this mean-ass pony named Chad. I owed Chad thirty thousand dollars, and I was thirty thousand dollars short.

3. I still remember that one hot summer. The way the heat made the cars seem to shimmer as they drove by us on the way to godknowswhere, the way the girls I had known all my life were suddenly women — taller and wiser than us boys — but most of

all I remember that night when we all gathered around the black-and-white TV set to watch as the first pony walked on the moon.

4. On Fridays, the ponies got paid. And after they got paid, they got drunk. And when they got drunk, you bet your ass somebody was going to get hurt or broken.

5. A lot of stuff's been said in the papers lately about what went down at the Federated Bank that afternoon. Some people say we did it for money. Some say we did it for glory. But none of them know the real story of how it started. It started with a little girl who wanted a pony.

6. When that pony walked into my gym and said she wanted to learn how to box, I said no. And I said no for the next thirty days when she walked in asking the same thing. And then, for some reason, on the thirty-second day, I said yes.

7. The street was teeming with people jostling and shouting and waiting for the motorcade to come down the street. And what with all the noise and the excitement and the general chaos, no one thought anything of it when a pony burst past the barricades just as the president's car came into view.

8. No one saw the pony rebellion coming. No one but Brent Steel.

9. Jeremy Chadwick had eaten one hundred hot dogs in one sitting. He had eaten seventeen blueberry pies at the county fair, taking home the blue ribbon. He had eaten an eight-pound hamburger, a jar of jalapeños, and a tub of ice cream on a dare in college. One time, to impress a girl, he had even eaten sixteen pennies. But there was one thing, just one thing, that Jeremy had never eaten.

10. It was the best of times. It was the worst of times. And there was this fucking pony, too.

Best American First Sentences of Novels Published in 2006

MONICA ALI, *Alentejo Blue*
At first he thought it was a scarecrow.

EDWARD P. JONES, *All Aunt Hagar's Children*
That 1901 winter when the wife and her husband were still new to Washington, there came to the wife like a scent carried on the wind some word that wolves roamed the streets and roads of the city after sundown.

COLSON WHITEHEAD, *Aphex Hides the Hurt*
He came up with the names.

JULIAN BARNES, *Arthur and George*
A child wants to see.

UZODINMA IWEALA, *Beasts of No Nation*
It is starting like this.

DAVID MITCHELL, *Black Swan Green*
Do not set foot in my office.

EMILY BARTON, *Brookland*
At the close of the workday on Thursday the twenty-fourth of January, 1822, Prue Winship sat down at the large desk in the countinghouse of Winship Daughters Gin to write a letter to her daughter, Recompense.

CHARLES D'AMBROSIO, *The Dead Fish Museum*
At home I'd get up early, when the sisters were still asleep, and head to the ancient Chinese man's store.

NELL FREUDENBERGER, *The Dissident*
I was not meant to be a dissident.

OLGA GRUSHIN, *The Dream Life of Sukhanov*
"Stop here," said Anatoly Pavlovich Sukhanov from the backseat, addressing the pair of suede gloves on the steering wheel.

DANA SPIOTTA, *Eat the Document*
It is easy for a life to become unblessed.

RICHARD POWERS, *The Echo Maker*
Cranes keep landing as night falls.

CLAIRE MESSUD, *The Emperor's Children*
"Darlings! Welcome! And you must be Danielle?" Sleek and small, her wide eyes rendered enormous by kohl, Lucy Leverett, in spite of her resemblance to a baby seal, rasped impressively.

PHILIP ROTH, *Everyman*
Around the grave in the rundown cemetery were a few of his former advertising colleagues from New York, who recalled his energy and originality and told his daughter, Nancy, what a pleasure it had been to work with him.

JENNIFER GILMORE, *Golden Country*
It was Joseph Brodsky, the one person who had never caused any trouble, who did not want his daughter to marry David Bloom.

DAVID LONG, *The Inhabited World*
When he looks at his hand, he sees the hand he remembers — ropy branching veins, a ridge of waxy skin on the inside of the wrist where he fumbled a glowing iron rod at his father's forge one afternoon in 1966.

JENNIFER EGAN, *The Keep*
The castle was falling apart, but at 2 A.M. under a useless moon, Danny couldn't see this.

ROBERTO BOLAÑO, *Last Evenings on Earth*
The way in which my friendship with Sensini developed was somewhat unusual.

KATE ATKINSON, *One Good Turn*
He was lost.

MARK Z. DANIELEWSKI, *Only Revolutions*
Haloes! Haleskarth! Contraband! I can walk away from anything.

CORMAC MCCARTHY, *The Road*
When he woke in the woods in the dark and the cold of the night he'd reached out to touch the child sleeping beside him.

LISA FUGARD, *Skinner's Drift*
Eva pressed her forehead to the window and watched the ruffle of waves rimming the coastline recede from view as the plane nosed its way toward Johannesburg.

MARISHA PESSL, *Special Topics in Calamity Physics*
Dad always said a person must have a significant reason for writing out his or her Life Story and expecting anyone to read it.

IRENE NEMIROVSKY, *Suite Française*
Hot, thought the Parisians.

JOHN UPDIKE, *Terrorist*
Devils, Ahmad thinks.

LEILA ABOULELA, *The Translator*
She dreamt that it rained and she could not go out to meet him as planned.

HEIDI JULAVITS, *The Uses of Enchantment*
The following might have happened on a late-fall afternoon in the Boston suburb of West Salem.

A. B. YEHOSHUA, *A Woman in Jerusalem*
Even though the manager of the human resources division had not sought such a mission, now, in the softly radiant morning, he grasped its unexpected significance.

Best American New Words of 2006

FROM *The Concise Oxford English Dictionary* and *Merriam-Webster's Collegiate Dictionary, Eleventh Edition*

abdominoplasty • *noun* a surgical operation involving the removal of excess flesh from the abdomen (Oxford)

aerobicized or **aerobicised** • *adjective* (of a person's body) toned by aerobic exercise: *aerobicized Hollywood women* (Oxford)

agritourism • *noun* the practice of touring agricultural areas to see farms and often to participate in farm activities (Merriam-Webster)

agroterrorism • *noun* terrorist acts intended to disrupt or damage a country's agriculture (Oxford)

aquascape • *noun* 1. a scenic view of a body of water 2. an area having a natural or constructed aquatic feature (as a pond or fountain) (Merriam-Webster)

avian influenza • *noun* a highly variable, mild to fulminant influenza of birds that is caused by strains of the influenza A virus which may mutate and be transmitted to other vertebrates (Merriam-Webster)

bahookie • *noun* a person's buttocks (Oxford)

best of breed • *noun* any item or product considered to be the best of its kind (Oxford)

big-box • *adjective* of, relating to, or being a large chain store having a boxlike structure (Merriam-Webster)

biodiesel • *noun* a fuel that is similar to diesel fuel and is derived from usually vegetable sources (as soybean oil) (Merriam-Webster)

blowback • *noun* the unintended adverse results of a political action or situation (Oxford)

celebutante • *noun* a celebrity who is well known in fashionable society (Oxford)

crunk • *noun* a type of hip-hop or rap music characterized by repeated shouted catchphrases and elements typical of electronic dance music, such as prominent bass; *adjective* very excited or full of energy (Oxford)

gastric bypass • *noun* a surgical bypass operation that typically involves reducing the size of the stomach and reconnecting the smaller stomach to bypass the first portion of the small intestine so as to restrict food intake and reduce caloric absorption in cases of severe obesity (Merriam-Webster)

hardscape • *noun* the man-made features used in landscape architecture, e.g., paths or walls, as contrasted with vegetation (Oxford)

labelmate • *noun* a singer or musician who records for the same company as another (Merriam-Webster)

manga • *noun* a Japanese comic book or graphic novel (Merriam-Webster)

mentee • *noun* a person who is advised, trained, or counseled by a mentor (Oxford)

mesotherapy • *noun* (in cosmetic surgery) a procedure in which multiple tiny injections of pharmaceuticals, vitamins, etc., are delivered into the mesodermal layer of tissue under the skin, to promote the loss of fat or cellulite (Oxford)

mouse potato • *noun* a person who spends a great deal of time using a computer (Merriam-Webster)

obesogenic • *adjective* tending to cause obesity (Oxford)

polyamory • *noun* the state or practice of having more than one open romantic relationship at a time (Merriam-Webster)

qigong • *noun* an ancient Chinese healing art involving meditation, controlled breathing, and movement exercises (Merriam-Webster)

rendition • *noun* (also **extraordinary rendition**) (especially in the U.S.) the practice of sending a foreign criminal or terrorist suspect covertly to be interrogated in a country with less rigorous regulations for the humane treatment of prisoners (Oxford)

retronym • *noun* a new term created from an existing word in order to distinguish the original referent of the existing word from a later one that is the product of progress or technological development (e.g., *acoustic guitar* for *guitar*) (Oxford)

riffage • *noun* informal guitar riffs, especially in rock music (Oxford)

ringtone • *noun* the sound made by a cell phone to signal an incoming call (Merriam-Webster)

sandwich generation • *noun* a generation of people who are caring for their aging parents while supporting their own children (Merriam-Webster)

shoulder-surfing • *noun* the practice of spying on the user of a cash-dispensing machine or other electronic device in order to obtain their personal identification number, password, etc. (Oxford)

spyware • *noun* software that is installed in a computer without the user's knowledge and transmits information about the user's computer activities over the Internet (Merriam-Webster)

therapize or **therapise** • *verb* subject to psychological therapy: *you don't need to therapize or fix each other* (Oxford)

unibrow • *noun* a single continuous brow resulting from the growing together of eyebrows (Merriam-Webster)

wave pool • *noun* a large swimming pool equipped with a machine for producing waves (Merriam-Webster)

wedge issue • *noun* (U.S.) a very divisive political issue, regarded as a basis for drawing voters away from an opposing party whose supporters have diverging opinions on it (Oxford)

Yogalates (also trademark **Yogilates**) • *noun* a fitness routine that combines Pilates exercises with the postures and breathing techniques of yoga (Oxford)

zombie • *noun* a computer controlled by a hacker without the owner's knowledge, which is made to send large quantities of data to a website, making it inaccessible to other users (Oxford)

Best American New Band Names

Islands, Didi Mau, David and the Citizens, Mixel Pixel, Beirut, Kind of Like Spitting, Vulturines, Call and Response, Black Fiction, Idiotchild, A Study in Her, Gogo Airheart, +/−, Bottom of the Hudson, Tokyo Police Club, Calling All Monsters, Cold War Kids, Dead Girls Ruin Everything, Sunset Rubdown, Viva L'American Death Ray, Mondo Jet Set, The Wildlife, Eagle Seagull, Venice Is Sinking, The Happy Bullets, Centro-Matic, Pinewood Derby, The Tah-Dahs, Lesbians on Ecstasy, Tom Thumb and the Latter Day Saints, Mad Marge and the Stonecutters, Cranebuilders, The Real Tuesday Weld, Bling Kong, The Rock 'n' Roll Adventure Kids, Brilliant Red Lights, The Morning After Girls, Saturday Looks Good to Me, Rock Votolato, Her Majesty, Dylan in the Movies, Komputadora, The Wes Hollywood Show, Lorenzo's Music, Rosemont Family Reunion, The Theatre Fire, Voices and Organs, The Scattered Pages, Wooden Wand, Alastair Moock, Great Lake Swimmers, Shakey Bones, The Abi Yoyos, Macromantics, The Hidden Cameras, Clair de Lune, Cloudland Canyon, Pornopop, Woolly Leaves, Letting Up Despite Great Faults, Michael Zapruder's Rain of Frogs, Apostle of Hustle, Hundred Hands, Elephone, Think About Life Band, The Pinker Tones, Controller, Ambulance Ltd, Thee More Shallows, Dodo Bird, My Dad Is Dead, Robotnicka, Bedouin Soundclash, A Silver Mount Zion, Radio Berlin, Professor Murder, Ratatat, Say Hi to Your Mom, The Raincoats,

Voxtrot, Caribou, Chin Up Chin Up, Menomena, Deerhunter, Charlemagne Palestine, The Long Blondes, Explosions in the Sky, The Hold Steady, The Thermals, Junior Boys, I'm from Barcelona, Girl Talk, Sunset Rubdown, Band of Horses, Tapes'n Tapes, Swan Lake, Oh No, El Perro del Mar, Camera Obscura

Best American Six-Word Memoirs

In 2006 the online magazine Smith *(smithmag.net) asked its readers and hundreds of professional writers to write their life stories in exactly six words. The form was made famous by Ernest Hemingway, who wrote this after being challenged to write a complete story in six words: "For sale: baby shoes, never used." The editors of* Smith *received more than ten thousand submissions. Here are some examples:*

Wanted world, got world plus lupus.
— Liz Futrell

Being a monk stunk. Better gay.
— Bob Redman

Found true love, married someone else.
— Bjorn Stromberg

Mistakenly kills kitten. Fears anything delicate.
— Susan Henderson

Bad brakes discovered at high speed.
— Johan Baumeister

Scarred by 911; helped by penguins.
— Audrey Blackburn

Ex-wife and contractor now have house.
— Drew Peck

Savior complex makes for many disappointments.
— Alanna Schubach

My spiritual path is 100 proof.
— John House

Wasn't born a redhead; fixed that.
— Andie Grace

Boyfriend in bed, still a lesbian?
— Cheryl Burke

Hugged some trees, then burned them.
— Tom Price

Fears commitment, debt. Attracts spouse, house.
— Beth Grundvig

Young, skinny, ridiculed. Old, skinny, envied.
— Phil Sweet

Lucky in love, unlucky in metabolism.
— Leah Weathersby

Discovered moral code via Judy Blume.
— Beth Greivel

Hiding in apartment knitting against depression.
— Laurie White

Near death experiences are my forte.
— Anna Mauser-Martinez

I like big butts, can't lie.
— Dave Russ

ABCs MTV SATs THC IRA NPR.
— Jancee Dunn

Never really finished anything, except cake.
— Carletta Perkins

My ancestors were accented cow herders.
— Nina Moog

I managed not to destroy anything.
— Tucker Frazier

Best American Personals from Around the World

The winter 2006 issue of Tin House *collected personal ads from a number of newspapers and magazines outside the United States. Some of their findings:*

À Nous Paris (free magazine)

Woman lacking love will commute to it 9:00 A.M. to midnight, except Sundays.

Man, 53 years old, French, originally from Kabul, with a very lovely head and features despite a slight problem with his left eye, who smokes a little bit, is looking for a woman from anywhere.

Man suffering from a great lack of motherhood in search of a woman.

55-year-old handyman from the country looking for a serious Parisienne 45–55 years old to live in Paris in her place.

Paris Voice Free (English-language magazine)

I will be happy to waste precious time with you in Paris speaking English.

Fieracittà (newspaper, Naples and the Campagna, Italy)

I will marry an intelligent man without any problems of any kind from 50 years old on up.

Little wolf-boy, cute, sweet and solitary is looking for a real wolf with fur — well endowed and who can hold out sexually. Send telephone number and photo for faster contact.

30-year-old man, cute, nice, simple, from a little town would like to know a girl from the country who is not emancipated. Peasants welcome.

Good looking 40-year-old, serious, sincere and reserved, a regular blood donor would like to meet couples to establish a close friendship based on reciprocal fairness. I would like to thank the others whom I did not summon — they should not contact me.

London Review of Books

Employed in publishing? Me too. Stay the hell away. Man on the inside seeks woman on the outside who likes milling outside hospitals guessing illnesses of out-patients. 30–35.

Don't speak, you'll only destroy my already low opinion of you. And put your pants back on. And your wig. Terminally disappointed woman (38, Barnstaple) WLTM a man. Form a queue, then I'll negotiate the criteria.

American man, 57. I just want a girlfriend. What the hell is going on here?

Woman, 43, would like to meet a man — any man — whose evolutionary path isn't that of Homer Simpson. Suspecting that's too difficult, I may go lesbian.

Ploughing the loneliest furrow. 19 LRB personals and counting. Only one reply. It was my mother telling me not to forget the bread on my way home from B&Q. Man, 51.

This is as gay as I get. Man, 37.

There's enough lithium in my medicine cabinet to power three electric cars across a sizeable desert. I'm more than aware that this isn't actually a selling point, but nonetheless it's my favourite statistic about me. Man, 33 — officially Three Cars Crazy.

Every woman I've ever met is painted with unnerving accuracy by the ads placed in this column. You're all my mother, aren't you? M., 37, Worcs.

Angry trollop, 37. Offers?

Man, 46. Appears quite normal, but probably best avoided. What do the doctors know?

Easily, but rarely, led forties M post-graduate gooseberry, London/ SE, seeks beautiful twenty-year-old snake for fun evenings/ engagement/ crushing disappointment. My hobbies include crying and hating men. F., 29.

Like I've said so many times before here, 'desperate.' Do I have to spell it out? D-E-S-P-E-R-A-T-E. Jeez, what does it take to catch a 20-year-old athletic male in this magazine? F., 67.

Baste me in butter and call me Slappy. No, really. M. 35.

Meet the new me. Like the old me only less nice after three ads without any sexual intercourse. 42-year-old fruitcake (F.).

Nihilist seeks nothing.

I'll see you at the LRB singles night. I'll be the one breathing heavily and stroking my thighs by the 'art' books. Asthmatic, varicosed F (93) seeks M to 30 with enough puff in him to push me uphill to the post office. This is not a euphemism.

Male LRB readers. Drawing little faces on your thumbs, getting them to order meals, then shouting at them for not being able to pay is no way to win a woman. You know who you are. Men to 40 with working credit cards, reply to once bitten, twice bitten, three strikes and you're all out F, 35.

The only item you'll find in my fridge is soup. Forty litres of the stuff. Beat that. M. 46.

M, 34, would like to meet F to 30 able to scientifically prove the validity of the ten-second rule concerning dropped food.

My only academic achievement was contaminating the water supply in class 2C by sneezing over the beaker tray. It caused the biggest out-break of conjunctivitis ever known at Sutton Primary. I wasn't sorry then and I'm not sorry now. Bitter PR exec. (F, 34).

WLTM man to 40 who enjoys living on the edge (of Putney).

Want to meet you, but I can give no information.

Guardian (U.K.)

Obvious gold-digger welcome if lover of the arts. I am a sincere, genuine, gentle, successful, semi-retired arts entrepreneur, inviting just one warmhearted lady to share delightful enthusiasms and lots of laughter. Potential mutual admiration, even adoration. She has no baggage and can cook (occasionally). Probably brunette.

Japan Today (English-language newspaper)

Sexy female seeks JF. Affluent executive seeks nice slave up to 35 to enjoy intimate time with. Let's enjoy good restraint first.

Craigslist, Mumbai

PLEASE BE MY OBNOXIOUS GIRLFRIEND FOR ONE WEEK
Hello gals of Mumbai and beyond . . . I am looking for an obnoxious girlfriend for one week to restore my glee in being single.

Best American Article Titles from the Best American Trade Magazines

You may be surprised to know that the vast majority of periodicals published in this country or any other are what are commonly known as trade magazines — that is, magazines that cover a specific industry. Below we've compiled some of the best article titles from some of the best-named trade magazines. These are all real.

Hooked on Crochet!

Breaking the Yarn Ceiling: The Men of Crochet
Allez Crochet: Crochet and the French Revolution
Crochet in Congress; Uniting with Yarn

Meat Processing Global

Up Yours Upton!
The Vegetarian Mind — A Voyage into Madness
SauSAGE Words from an Industry Veteran
Kobe on Kobe: The NBA Super Star Talks Beef

Square Dancing Today

Circle Dancing; the Revolution
Dosey-Do: You Have What It Takes on the Dance Floor?
Why It's Cool to Be a Square

Spirit Led Woman

Putting the OH Back in WOHrship
Mother or Magdalene: Which Mary Are YOU?
Dating Jews: Devil or Delightful?

ColdFusion Developer's Journal

This Ain't Your Parents ColdFusion
Brrrr — Programmers Putting the Heat Back in Their Frigid
    Love Lives
DBML, CFML, CFUG: Why Acronyms RULE

Herb Quarterly

Brits vs. Yanks: A History of the "H" Dispute
Thyme Out! What the Herb Experts Aren't Telling You
Got Any Herb? Why San Francisco Is Giving Herb Lovers a Bad
    Name

Southern Accents

Gone With the Taste?
Decorating Like Sherman — Oranges, Reds, and Yellows
Southern Discomfort? Creating the Bed of Your Dreams

Bassin'

Bass Class: Understanding Gills
Can Fishing Be Sexy? You Bet Your Bass!
AARP loves Carp . . . and Bass!

Brake and Front End

What You Need to Know about Over-Lube
Undercoating Uncovered
ABS BS? ABSolutely

Trapper and Predator Caller

Windigo — One Man's Search for Immortality
Outsmarting the Mongoose
Trap to the Future: The Ethics of GPS Trapping

Grief Digest

Griever's Remorse, the Silent Killer
Tears of Joy; 101 Ways to Mourn Losing Your Grief
Color Corner: Grieving with Pastels

Hair's How Magazine

Rare and Unfortunate: Taming the Reverse Widow's Peak
Move Over Mousse, Here Comes Tar
Right Angles: The Secret of German Hairstyling

Iron Memories

40 Acres and a Tractor
Tractor and Found Her
How Many Vintage Tractors Is Too Many?

Lab Animal

Down and Out: Dealing with Duck Eczema
An Elephant Forgets: How One Savvy Researcher and His Absent-
  Minded Elephant Could Cure Alzheimer's
Tamarins vs. Marmosets: We Report, You Decide

Mini Truckin'

Truckin' but Smaller: An Intro to Mini Truckin'
Scraping the Surface: The Art of Lowering
Chroming on a Budget

Men of Integrity

Integritous: Al Sharpton and Jesse Jackson Tell It Like It Is
God Is Watching All the Time
Tom DeLay: Gerrymandering for Jesus

My Cuddle Time Bible Story Book

Sleeping with Jesus
Baby Bibles: Tall Tales for Tiny Tots
Everybody Poops (Except God)

Best American Creationist Explanations for the World's Natural Wonders

In 2006 a tax-exempt organization called Answers in Genesis began pro-
ducing brochures for tourists visiting natural wonders — Niagara Falls,
the Grand Canyon, Devil's Tower, and others. The brochures are meant to
counter the information at the sites that presents a scientific view of the ori-
gins of the phenomena. AiG's brochures offer biblical explanations.

Petrified Forests, Yellowstone

Evolutionary View
  "Evolutionists explain the petrified forests of Yellowstone as the result
  of an ongoing cycle: (1) a forest grows and then is buried by volcanic
  ash and other debris. (2) Dissolved minerals are soaked up by the trees,
  petrifying them. (3) The ash weathers into clay and soil. (4) A new forest grows on top of the previous one, which is subsequently buried by
  volcanic ash to begin the process again."

Creationist View
  "The evidence points to catastrophic processes, which are consistent
  with the Bible's teaching of creation about 6,000 years ago and a
  worldwide Flood. The petrified forests of Yellowstone actually are the
  result of a catastrophic burial during the Genesis Flood, which with its
  associated volcanic activity, would have produced the right conditions
  for those trees to have been rapidly deposited and then to have been
  petrified quickly."

Niagara Falls

Evolutionary View
  "During the last Ice Age, the entire Niagara area was covered in thick
  sheets of ice. As these sheets melted, they carved deep river beds and
  lakes, including the Great Lakes, out of the land. About 12,000 years
  ago, the Niagara River was formed by melted ice as it moved toward
  the ocean. With this rapidly moving water, the river then carved the Niagara gorge and created Niagara Falls."

Creationist View
"The rapid melting of the post-Flood ice sheets would have greatly increased the water flow over the edge of Niagara Falls, and with increased sediment content, the rate of erosion would also have greatly increased in the early years after the ice age. The age for the initial formation of the Falls moves to around 3,500 years ago, consistent with the Biblical timescale for the Flood."

Grand Canyon

Evolutionary View
"Over 70 million years, the Colorado River threaded through the Colorado Plateau and flooded numerous times, changing the river's path again and again until it reached its present course. As the flooded river changed its drainage basin, the increased momentum picked up rocks and other debris which tore away the river's bottom and thus changed the landscape of the plateau. The water also filled the cracks in the plateau and froze during the winter months and caused these cracks to expand and break the rock apart. Over time, this action changed the topography of the entire plateau, gradually digging deeper and deeper into the rock and forming Grand Canyon."

Creationist View
"The Biblical explanation for how the Canyon formed is actually quite simple. The 'basement' layers, consisting of granites and metamorphic rocks, were formed on Day 3 of Creation Week. Many of the other layers were deposited by the waters of the global Flood as described in Genesis 7–8. These unhindered, swirling currents picked up, transported and eventually deposited tons of sediment in layers. These were then tilted and bent through great tectonic activity during the final stages of the Flood. The fossils entombed in the sediments of the Canyon also remind us of God's terrible judgment on sin and of the salvation He offers."

Dinosaur National Monument

Evolutionary View
"According to some, 150 million years ago a river flowed through this area where many dinosaurs lived. As the dinosaurs died, their car-

casses and bones were gradually and progressively picked up by the flooded waters of the river and were carried and deposited into the main channel, where they were buried one on top of the other. Over the millions of years that followed, the deposited sand and mud hardened and became solid rock. Through time, the earth's crust was reshaped and rock layers were bent, the face of the cliff becoming exposed by slow erosion. Long exposure to the elements of rain, snow, and wind caused the sedimentary rock to erode, slowly revealing the buried fossils."

Creationist View

"Created on Day 6 with the other land creatures and man, dinosaurs walked the earth until the catastrophic Flood destroyed all land-dwelling, air-breathing creatures not preserved on the Ark. Although representatives of each dinosaur kind were on the Ark and survived to repopulate the earth after the Flood, those that weren't on the Ark perished in the Flood.

"Many of these were washed together by the swirling Flood waters and buried in the rapidly forming sedimentary layers. When the earth-covering waters finally receded, the earth's surface was greatly altered as mountains rose and valleys lowered. This explains why we find fossils of sea creatures and other former marine life in these high cliffs and in many other mountains around the world."

Best American New Animal Plagues

The following natural phenomena were reported by Earthweek: A Diary of the Planet *in 2006:*

Fish from Heaven

A cloudburst over the northern Indian village of Manna unleashed a rain of small fish that sent villagers into the streets to collect them as they fell. "Initially, no one noticed it. But soon we saw some slushy objects on the ground and noticed some slight movement," a shopkeeper named Abubaker told the *Hindustan Times*. Meteorologists agreed that the pencil-thin fish were probably scooped up by a water-spout and carried high into the atmosphere before falling on Manna. But scientists said they were baffled that many of the fish were still alive. Many incidents of fish, frogs, and other small creatures raining down from the sky have been reported worldwide. But "live rains" have been rare.

Monster Rabbit

The British town of Felton allowed two marksmen to be hired to hunt down and kill an oversized rabbit that had been ripping up and de-vouring crops. "It is a massive thing. It is a monster," one local resi-dent, Jeff Smith, told the *Northumberland Gazette*. "The first time I saw it, I said, 'What the hell is that?'" Smith claims to have seen the black and brown rabbit, which has one ear bigger than the other, as have other residents. The British Rabbit Council says the sightings are credible, and that some rabbits, like the Continental Giant, can grow to be twenty-six inches in length. Local gardeners have hired armed guards to protect their patches from the ravenous rabbit.

Super Mosquitoes

A study by Aristotelio University in Greece says that air pollution, overpopulation, and the widespread use of insect repellent around Athens have led to the development of a "super breed" of mosquito with some disturbing characteristics. The *Ta Nea* daily reported that the evolved insect can see in color and is faster, larger, and better able to locate humans than other mosquitoes in the Mediterranean. The Athens-area mosquitoes can smell blood from as far away as one hun-dred feet — almost a third farther than established varieties. The super mosquitoes flap their wings up to 500 times a second, com-pared with 350 beats in normal mosquitoes.

Elkoholic Bully

An elk in western Sweden has been terrifying children at a school where the animal becomes intoxicated after eating fermented apples.

The *Dagens Nyheter* newspaper reports that the animal has become addicted to the alcohol it gets from the rotting fruit of a tree on the school grounds. Once the elk becomes sufficiently buzzed, the newspaper says, it lies down for a snooze in a defensive position in front of the tree, then wakes up and charges anyone who comes near. Authorities at the Eklanda school, in the Gothenburg suburb of Moelndal, called in police, but authorities have so far failed to drive away the intemperate animal.

Best American Failed Television Pilots

Channel101.com is a place where aspiring television writers, actors, and directors can showcase their wares. The participants pitch television shows and then film short versions of pilots, which can be viewed on the site. The creators of the following shows, it should be noted, are in on the joke.

TITLE: Time-Traveling-Arm Disease
SUMMARY: Ted Crouton, a magnet for rare diseases, copes with the diagnosis of a time-traveling arm.
CAST:

Dr. Cass Rasmussen	Cass Rasmussen
Johnson	Abed Gheith
Ted Crouton	Mike McCafferty
Suzanne	Dawn Cody
Dr. Lewis	Derek Waters
Zordaff/Additional Voices	Brian Wysolmierski

NOTABLE FEATURES:
- Ted is also plagued by a kneecap that does not respect the space-time continuum.
- The time-traveling arm is made from a mold casting of the real arm of actor Jeremy Irons.

TITLE: Lumberwood Forest
SUMMARY: The year is 1882, and a group of lumberjacks are faced with a great challenge when their only cook is injured.

CAST:

Cookie	Ryan Elder
Reader	Mike Manasewitsch
Billy	Deanna Rooney
Mathias	Ryan Ridley
Willem	Kyle Kinane
Blimpie	Eric Acosta
Sailor Lumberjack	Aaron Moles
Creep Lumberjack	Jason Whetzell
Cowboy Lumberjack	Dan Murrell

NOTABLE FEATURES:

- In one episode, two lumberjacks fight to the death for the coveted position of sous-chef.
- Drama ensues when Cookie, protesting the Chinese Exclusion Act of 1882, tries to teach the men to wok.

TITLE: Bedroom

SUMMARY: The walls of a room talk to one another in this unique pilot of photographs and voice-acting.

CAST:

Outside Door Wall	James Atkinson
Ceiling	Wade Randolph
Floor	Steve Agee
Plain Wall	Vatche Panos
Ugly Bed Wall	Eric Acosta
Mirror Wall	Mike Rose

NOTABLE FEATURES:

- A meddling remodeler threatens the gang with his dreams of house-flipping.
- The room adheres strictly to the ancient philosophy of feng shui.

TITLE: The Con Time Machine

SUMMARY: A version of H. G. Wells's *Time Machine*, featuring a machine that may or may not travel through time.

CAST:

Dr. Murav	Jason Makiaris
Professor Cortez	Wade Randolph
Dr. Archipeligos	Mike McCafferty

NOTABLE FEATURES:
- The time machine also convinces people to buy time-shares in Cabo and invest in gold
- Things become awkward when Professor Cortez discovers that Drs. Archipeligos and Murav are actually gynecologists.

TITLE: Doctor, Telemarketer, Grocery Bagger, Executioner
SUMMARY: He can work three jobs . . . but can he work four? In his first screened pilot since *The Pool Master,* Aaron Moles tells the story of a man overwhelmed by his responsibilities.
CAST:

Angry Customer	Steve Huey
Death Row Inmate	Dean Pelton
Hospital Intercom Voice	Erni Crews
Melissa Thornton	Amy Roiland
Lover	Christian Thomas Le Guilloux
The Boss	Dan Murrell
Voice-Over	James Schneeberg
Dr. Steve Thornton	Aaron Moles

NOTABLE FEATURES:
- Steve collects welfare, too.
- Pilot episode: Dr. Steve worries that being an executioner may violate the Hippocratic oath.

TITLE: Young Stephen Hawking
SUMMARY: It's 1977, and Stephen Hawking is eager to learn about the opposite sex. Will the help of Carl Sagan and Albert Einstein be enough?
CAST:

Stephen Hawking	Christian Thomas Le Guilloux
Carl Sagan	Vatche Panos
Albert Einstein	Myke Chilian
Jane Wilde	Amy Roiland
Bianca	Shannon Vincent-Brown
Classmate	Kelsy Abb

NOTABLE FEATURE:
- Despite his pals' best efforts, Hawking's utter confusion about girls inspires his life's work studying black holes.

Best American Names of Television Programs Taken to Their Logical Conclusions

JOE O'NEILL

FROM *Opium*

1. Dancing with the Stars
2. Buying the Stars Drinks
3. Getting the Stars' Number
4. Finding Out Three Days Later That the Number Belongs to the Public Library

1. Touched by an Angel
2. Contacted by a Lawyer Who Deals with These Sorts of Cases
3. Settled Out of Court with an Angel
4. Blamed All Subsequent Problems in Life on Encounter with the Angel

1. 24
2. 7
3. 365

1. Band of Brothers
2. Is That Why They All Have the Same Haircut?
3. Actually, the Ramones Aren't Really Brothers

1. The Amazing Race
2. I Thought This Show Was Gonna Be About Aryans
3. Oh.

Best American Police Blotter Items

These police blotter items of 2006 are from Buffalo, New York. They were collected by Looptard.com.

A resident reported that four suspicious adults with children were in the area, ringing doorbells. Police determined the suspects to be Jehovah's Witnesses.

A Washington Highway resident called police to report that a neighbor was sitting in the middle of the street crying.

A male was reportedly yelling and screaming obscenities in his Randolph Avenue driveway. Police reported he was trying to rap.

■

Middle-American Gothic

FROM *Spin*

I'M FORTY-ONE YEARS OLD, and outwardly I may be one of the least goth people you could ever meet. For more than a decade, my style, fashion-wise, has been faux-preppy English professor, which means I wear sport coats and corduroy pants. To add a touch of flair, and to hide my bald head, I wear a tan cap, backward, so it looks like a beret. My musical taste, I should tell you, is similar to my clothing, which is to say it is decidedly nongoth. Twenty years ago, in college, I listened primarily to Cat Stevens, James Taylor, and Simon and Garfunkel; recently I've discovered Radiohead and find them to be quite good. So, clearly, I'm some kind of musical retard. Thus, *Spin,* being rather mischievous, thought I'd be the perfect person to cover Gothicfest 2005, which was the first of its kind, just as there was a first Super Bowl or world war. It was an all-day gathering of twenty goth bands in Villa Park, Illinois, a distant suburb of Chicago. The following is a diary of my adventures amid these dark minstrels and their loyal brood.

Saturday, September 17, 2005, the Odeum Sports & Expo Center

12:25 P.M. I'm wearing my checked sport coat, white shirt, tan cap, and jeans (to help me fit in a little), but I already seem to be attracting stares. There are roughly one hundred people mingling about, and the Halloween-ish costumes are causing a knee-jerk terror response in me. There's also pounding, scary music being played by a DJ.

I may have subconsciously chosen a white shirt to be defiant — everyone else is, of course, in black — and I just fantasized about be-

ing beaten to death as an intruder, getting kicked repeatedly while lying on the ground. A few of the fellows here look like neo-Nazi skin-
heads, which, I think, provoked this beating-to-death fantasy; also,
I'm a little depressed, and that always brings on suicidal thoughts.

Two chubby, expressionless boys stand to my right. They were once
cute children, but now I imagine that they spend hours in dark bed-
rooms looking at violent porn. Or perhaps they have tender reveries
about being sweet to the girls that they adore from a distance. I'd like
to think about them in this generous light — that they are actually
gentle young men — but it's hard not to stereotype them as potential
serial killers. It's their eerie, still blankness that makes me think
they're capable of murder — and the fact that I'm in the Midwest.
The Midwest seems to cultivate serial killing. Must be the boxed-in
geography.

One wears glasses and has multipierced ears and a scruffy pubes-
cent beard. His hair is dyed red and spiked up. His dirty, loose jeans
flow to the floor over his shoes.

His friend has a more mature beard but is fatter, shorter, and his
nose is swollen with oil and clogged pores. His eyes are slits. He
wears a winter hat, a dirty T-shirt, and filthy jeans. He really could be a
medieval Visigoth; I can imagine him swinging an ax with vigor. I do
like it that these two are standing next to each other, that they are
friends and are here together. It makes me think of my childhood best
friend, whom I hadn't seen for years, and then learned two years ago
that he had died. I miss him. In fact, I dreamed about him last night.
Every few months I dream that we're friends again.

12:45 P.M. The Odeum Sports & Expo Center resembles an airplane
hangar, with bleachers on one side. There are no windows, and
though it's midday, it feels like night, which is fitting. There's a con-
cession area at one end and a very large stage at the other. There are
also about two dozen booths, selling various goth goods: CDs, black
capes, plastic skulls, human skeletons, knives, and Vampire Wine.
It's just wine, but when you drink it, I guess you pretend that it's
blood. It reminds me of how, when I was a kid, you could get chocolate cigars and cigarettes and pretend you were an adult.

The first band, Dead Girls Corp., has just started playing. The singer keeps reminding the audience that the band has driven all the way from California. He wants us to appreciate this sacrifice, which is understandable, but mentioning it repeatedly is a little tiresome. "Feeling empty because there's something to say," he sings. Shouldn't it be "because there's *nothing* to say"? Then again, he may be right. All we really can express is pain. This diary and everything else I've ever written is actually a code for one word: *help!*

A fellow to my right is wearing a T-shirt that promotes the film *American Psycho*. Another young man's shirt says BIOHAZARD LEVEL 4. It occurs to me that I'm inwardly apocalyptic and these people are outwardly apocalyptic. I may dress like a somewhat libidinous college professor, but in my heart of hearts I'm in a state of dark despair about the world. But are these people embracing the apocalypse while I'm nervously awaiting it? I may not look the part, but in my own way, I belong here.

1:15 P.M. I'm in a side room reserved for bands, talking to the ceremonial host and hostess of Gothicfest, Mark and Michelle.

Mark, nineteen, is wispy, with large, vulnerable eyes and dark hair draped across his forehead. He wears a black shirt, a velvet scarf, and saddle shoes. His black jeans are decorated with the lyrics of a song he wrote, "Crimson Tears of Tragedy."

Michelle, thirty-five, is short, pale, and voluptuous. She's got on a black satin ball gown, made in Germany from a sixteenth-century design, bejeweled gloves, platform boots, and an elaborate dreadlocked hairpiece.

"What do you get out of the goth scene?" I ask.

"The beauty of it," says Michelle. "The elegance. The history. There's so much conformity. We're nonconformists. We don't judge and we don't want to be judged. We're just artists expressing ourselves. I'm into traditional goth: Bauhaus and Joy Division. I hold true to the people who started the movement. My look is more classic, elegant, but some days I can go cyber."

"I fall more into the glam-goth scene," says Mark. "My idols were, like, David Bowie."

"What do your families think about you being goths?" I inquire.

"My mother loved the scene," says Michelle. "Like Peter Murphy.

My father is totally sympathetic. Even when I was younger, into punk, he said, 'I will never have a square daughter.'"

"I live with my grandparents," Mark says. "My grandfather loves me for what I do — that I express myself. But my grandmother throws temper tantrums, calls me a fag because I wear makeup and I'm very feminine. I have an abusive relationship with my father. Constant beatings. I saw him in July, and he beat the shit out of me."

"Did you fight back?" I ask.

"I don't fight back," Mark says. "As much as I don't like him, I love him because he's my father. So I just take it. He wants me to be more of a man, not so fem. He wants me to be tougher, cold, heartless, an alpha male."

Later, Mark tells us how his uncle, a goth who had drug problems but was a true father to him, committed suicide by slashing himself. Mark found him as he was bleeding to death. Mark starts crying, and Michelle and I try to comfort him.

"I'm sorry I'm crying," he says.

"It's all right," I say.

2:20 P.M. A band called Drake is playing. The lead singer wears a long robe. He chants into the microphone in an ominous, froggy voice: "Dost thou leave me with such a myth / Falling into the abyss." I admire his rhyme scheme, but it would be much better if he had a lisp — "the abyth."

I eyeball the young man next to me, who is thin, brown-haired, and not very goth, except for his arms, which are encased in black fishnet stockings.

"Excuse me, could I interview you?" I ask.

"Sure," he says. "They call me Rain."

"Who's they?"

"The people at my college. I used to have purple hair, and they weren't used to that there, so they called me Purple Rain, and it got shortened to Rain. My real name is Tim, but every Tim I know is a Melvin — an idiot — so I kept Rain."

"Are you still in college?"

"No, I'm thirty."

"What's your take on Gothicfest?" I ask.

"Well, I'm here for the headliner, Hanzel und Gretyl. I'm actually more into industrial. Most of the bands here today are industrial. Goth is dying. The scene is, like, twenty years old. It should die. It's all regurgitating what was done in Germany ten, twelve years ago. Goth now is more about the clothing than the music. You can buy goth stuff at Hot Topic in the malls. Goth is dead in my world because it's packaged. It's not counterculture, it's pop culture . . . Have you read Chomsky?"

"Not really," I say, embarrassed, and then add weakly, "I have a sense, though, of what Chomsky is about."

"A lot of the political message of industrial is voicing what Chomsky says — that we live in a benevolent fascist state."

"I really need to read Chomsky," I say. "Immediately."

"You should see this documentary about him, *Manufacturing Consent*."

"Thanks for the tip," I say, and I sheepishly take my leave. I wasn't expecting to meet a Noam Chomsky fan at Gothicfest.

3:10 P.M. A band with female members, Ghost Orgy, is onstage. They have a lovely, femme-fatale-ish violinist and a busty lead singer in high black boots. There are about four hundred people here now, sporting a number of interesting T-shirt slogans: EAT A BAG OF SHIT; FUCK YOU, YOU FUCKING FUCK; and AN EXPERIMENT IN SICKNESS. A girl walks past me with a backpack shaped like a coffin.

The singer suddenly lifts up her skirt, revealing black panties. At that moment it hits me: I need to interview this young lady.

3:40 P.M. I'm sitting with Ghost Orgy's Dina Concina, who is in her mid-twenties and even more beautiful up close. I compliment her on her performance, discreetly omitting the lifting-of-the-skirt part. She says she started her music career as a rock 'n' roll singer but she's been into goth for the past three years.

"I realized how much hate I have inside," she says, explaining her transition. "And I get to channel it onstage."

"What do you hate?" I ask.

"Our corporate jobs, shit like that. People. Our lives."

"Why do you hate your life?"

"Because I work a corporate job. Well, I just quit. But I was an engineer scientist for Kraft Foods."

"What's an engineer scientist do?"

"I created the recipes for cookies and crackers. I launched the new Cheese Nips. They're fucking good. You should try them."

"What do your parents think about you being in a goth band?"

"They don't even know the name of my band. They would kill me. They're old-school Filipino parents. But they're awesome. They know I'm in a band, but they don't know that I'm singing about death and demons and blood."

"They don't subscribe to *Spin*, do they?"

She smiles and then tells me that her neck is very stiff — she wrenched it onstage.

"I could give you a neck rub," I say, and I can't believe these words have come out of my mouth. It's like I have Tourette's. There's nothing more pathetic than a man who offers a beautiful young woman a massage.

"That would be great," she says. First a Chomsky fan and now a young woman who will let me touch her! This Gothicfest is remarkable.

I stand behind her and knead her neck. I feel like a dirty old man, and then I remember: I *am* a dirty old man.

4:10 P.M. I'm in the bleachers with Steve Watson and his twelve-year-old daughter, Bethany, who are finishing up some hot dogs. Steve, fifty-three, is friendly and articulate. He's wearing khaki pants and a golf shirt. Bethany is frail and cute, with black lipstick, a retainer on her teeth, and a tiara on her dark hair. "Bethany is into all kinds of music," Steve says. "Punk. Metal. And, quite frankly, I enjoy it as well. Living where we live, we're not exposed to all this." He waves his hand in front of him.

"You're a very open-minded parent," I say.

"I try to be. The community where we live is very affluent, and the people there are very intolerant. Not only are they intolerant of other people racially and financially, but if you don't fit into the WASP lifestyle, you're shunned. Luckily for me, I have sufficient income so that I can say 'fuck you.'"

"Why do you live there?"

"Economic advantages. Schools are very good. Crime is zero. But it's not a utopia. Everybody is forced into conformity, and it puts the kids under a lot of stress. Bethany had some friends who wanted to come today, but their parents wouldn't let them. I tell you, we're treated more openly and accepting at these concerts than in our own community."

Bethany tells me she had a band but they split up. Their name was Toxic Popsicle. "Not your average prom queen," Steve tells me. "But I'm cool with it."

7:15 P.M. I pass the booth selling skulls. They are very realistic-looking and can be used as piggy banks and candleholders. The short, smiling proprietress says, "Everybody likes a little head."

"What did you say?" I ask. The music is very loud.

"Everybody likes a little head."

"*What?*"

"Everybody likes a little head." A male cohort tries to explain her sense of humor: "We usually work biker shows." I move on to the next stall, which is selling gigantic swords. I ask the woman standing behind a glass case of knives, "You can sell this stuff to someone right now?"

"No," she says. "At the end of the concert they can get it, and then they're escorted out by security."

"That's good to know."

12:00 A.M. I'm exhausted. I've been listening to goth music for almost twelve hours. The last band is on, but I can't take much more. There are about six hundred people here now — Gothicfest isn't a mad success, but it's not a failure, either. It's been a good day for the goths.

A pretty girl gyrating next to me shouts over the music, "Dance with me!"

"I'm too old," I say.

"No, you're not," she says.

"How old are you?" I ask. She looks about nineteen, twenty.

"Fifteen," she says.

"Have a good time," I say, and quickly head for the exit.

On my way out, I pass a fellow with spikes poking out of the top of his shaved head. It's like there are miniature traffic cones dividing his cranium in half.

"Are those spikes screwed into your skull?" I ask incredulously.

He puts his hand in his pocket, takes out a small bottle of glue, and says, "I'm not dumb, you know."

I nod and leave. Outside, there's a large, jaundiced moon in the black sky. I hope it's still there when the goths come out. I feel like a parent whose children prefer to stay inside and watch TV. The father pleads, "It's a beautiful day. Why don't you go play outside?" In this case, I feel like pleading, "It's a completely spooky night. Forget the loud music — come outside and have a blood sacrifice or something! There's a full moon!"

But I don't say anything to anyone. I bid a silent farewell to the expo center, and with the moon watching over me, I get the hell out of there.

ALISON BECHDEL

■

A Happy Death

FROM *Fun Home*

THERE'S NO PROOF, ACTUALLY, THAT MY FATHER KILLED HIMSELF.

NO ONE KNEW IT WASN'T AN ACCIDENT.

HIS DEATH WAS QUITE POSSIBLY HIS CONSUMMATE ARTIFICE, HIS MASTERSTROKE.

I CAN'T BELIEVE IT. SUCH A GOOD MAN.

THERE'S NO PROOF, BUT THERE ARE SOME SUGGESTIVE CIRCUMSTANCES. THE FACT THAT MY MOTHER HAD ASKED HIM FOR A DIVORCE TWO WEEKS BEFORE.

THE COPY OF CAMUS' *A HAPPY DEATH* THAT HE'D BEEN READING AND LEAVING AROUND THE HOUSE IN WHAT MIGHT BE CONSTRUED AS A DELIBERATE MANNER.

SUCH A GOOD MAN.

CAMUS' FIRST NOVEL, IT'S ABOUT A CONSUMPTIVE HERO WHO DOES NOT DIE A PARTICULARLY HAPPY DEATH. MY FATHER HAD HIGHLIGHTED ONE LINE.

spared him a great deal of loneliness. He had been unfair: while his imagination and vanity had given her too much importance, his pride had given her too little. He discovered the cruel paradox by which we always deceive ourselves twice about the people we love – first to their advantage, then to their disadvantage. Today he understood that Marthe had been genuine with him – that she had been what she was, and that he owed her a good deal. It was beginning to ta... s of the street; t... ...aw Marthe's sudd... ...by a burst of gratitude he could not express – in the old

A FITTING EPITAPH FOR MY PARENTS' MARRIAGE.

BUT DAD WAS ALWAYS READING SOMETHING. SHOULD WE HAVE BEEN SUSPICIOUS WHEN HE STARTED PLOWING THROUGH PROUST THE YEAR BEFORE?

WAS THAT A SIGN OF DESPERATION? IT'S SAID, AFTER ALL, THAT PEOPLE REACH MIDDLE AGE THE DAY THEY REALIZE THEY'RE NEVER GOING TO READ *REMEMBRANCE OF THINGS PAST*. DAD ALSO LEFT A MARGINAL NOTATION IN ANOTHER BOOK.

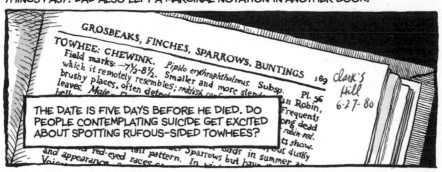

THE DATE IS FIVE DAYS BEFORE HE DIED. DO PEOPLE CONTEMPLATING SUICIDE GET EXCITED ABOUT SPOTTING RUFOUS-SIDED TOWHEES?

MAYBE HE DIDN'T NOTICE THE TRUCK COMING BECAUSE HE WAS PREOCCUPIED WITH THE DIVORCE. PEOPLE OFTEN HAVE ACCIDENTS WHEN THEY'RE DISTRAUGHT.

BUT THESE ARE JUST QUIBBLES. I DON'T BELIEVE IT WAS AN ACCIDENT.

IMPORTANT MESSAGE
FOR Allison Bechdel
DATE 7-2-80   TIME 12:27 AM/PM
WHILE YOU WERE AWAY
M Your Mother
OF
PHONE NO.

TELEPHONED	✓	PLEASE CALL	
CAME TO SEE YOU		WILL CALL AGAIN	
...TE YOU		RUSH	
RETURNED YOUR CALL			

MESSAGE Call home as soon as possible – it's an emergency

AFTER I HAD MADE THE FIVE-HOUR DRIVE HOME FROM COLLEGE AND EVERYONE ELSE HAD GONE TO BED, MOM AND I DISCUSSED IT.

IT'S POSSIBLE THAT WE CHOSE TO BELIEVE THIS BECAUSE IT WAS LESS PAINFUL.

IF HE'D INTENDED TO DIE, THERE WAS A CERTAIN CONSOLATION IN THE FACT THAT HE SUCCEEDED WITH SUCH APLOMB.

I THINK IT WAS SOMETHING HE ALWAYS MEANT TO DO.

HIS HEADSTONE IS AN OBELISK, A STRIKING ANACHRONISM AMONG THE UNGAINLY GRANITE SLABS IN THE NEW END OF THE CEMETERY.

HE HAD AN OBELISK COLLECTION, IN FACT, AND HIS PRIZE SPECIMEN WAS ONE IN KNEE-HIGH JADE THAT PROPPED OPEN THE DOOR TO HIS LIBRARY.

IT'S ALSO A SHAPE THAT IN LIFE HE WAS UNABASHEDLY FIXATED ON.

IT SYMBOLIZES LIFE.

HIS ULTIMATE OBELISK IS NOT CARVED FROM FLESHY, TRANSLUCENT MARBLE LIKE THE TOMBSTONES IN THE OLD PART OF THE CEMETERY.

MOM COULDN'T CONVINCE THE MONUMENT MAKER TO DO IT.

THE GRANITE IS HANDSOME, CRISP... AND, WELL, LIFELESS.

ON A MAP OF MY HOMETOWN, A CIRCLE A MILE AND A HALF IN DIAMETER CIRCUMSCRIBES:

(A) DAD'S GRAVE,

(B) THE SPOT ON ROUTE 150 WHERE HE DIED, NEAR AN OLD FARMHOUSE HE WAS RESTORING,

(C) THE HOUSE WHERE HE AND MY MOTHER RAISED OUR FAMILY, AND

(D) THE FARM WHERE HE WAS BORN.

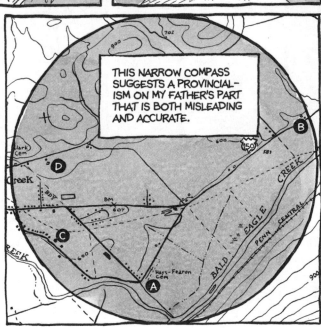

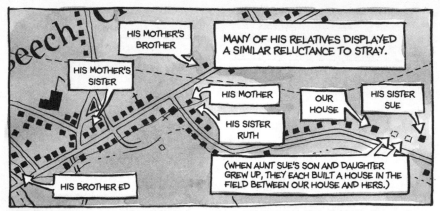

His mother's brother

His mother's sister

MANY OF HIS RELATIVES DISPLAYED A SIMILAR RELUCTANCE TO STRAY.

HIS MOTHER

OUR HOUSE

HIS SISTER SUE

HIS SISTER RUTH

(WHEN AUNT SUE'S SON AND DAUGHTER GREW UP, THEY EACH BUILT A HOUSE IN THE FIELD BETWEEN OUR HOUSE AND HERS.)

HIS BROTHER ED

BUT IT'S PUZZLING WHY MY URBANE FATHER, WITH HIS UNWHOLESOME INTEREST IN THE DECORATIVE ARTS, REMAINED IN THIS PROVINCIAL HAMLET.

AND WHY MY CULTURED MOTHER, WHO HAD STUDIED ACTING IN NEW YORK CITY, WOULD LIVE THERE CHEEK BY JOWL WITH HIS FAMILY IS MORE PUZZLING STILL.

COME OUT TO CAMP! YOU DON'T HAFTA SHOOT NOTHIN'. WE'LL JUST SIT AROUND THE STOVE AND GET BOMBED.

OLD SCHOOL CHUM

HELEN? DON'T STOP. I'M JUST SHOWING OFF YOUR HOUSE TO SOME FRIENDS.

AUNT SUE

IT WAS MADE CLEAR THAT MY BROTHERS AND I WOULD NOT REPEAT THEIR MISTAKE.

DON'T YOU KIDS GET ANY IDEAS ABOUT DRAGGING A TRAILER INTO THE BACKYARD. AFTER YOU GRADUATE FROM HIGH SCHOOL, I DON'T WANT TO SEE YOU AGAIN.

(MY COUSIN'S HOUSE BEING DELIVERED.)

MY PARENTS HAD IN FACT GOTTEN AS FAR AS EUROPE, WHERE MY FATHER WAS STATIONED IN THE ARMY. MOM FLEW THERE TO MARRY HIM.

THEY LIVED IN WEST GERMANY FOR ALMOST A YEAR DURING DAD'S SERVICE, IN SOME DEGREE OF EXPATRIATE SPLENDOR.

BUT THEN, THE STORY GOES, MY GRANDFATHER HAD A HEART ATTACK AND DAD HAD TO GO HOME AND RUN THE FAMILY BUSINESS.

THIS WAS A FUNERAL PARLOR BEGUN BY MY GREAT-GRANDFATHER, EDGAR T. BECHDEL.

THE CHANGE IN PLANS WAS A CRUEL BLOW. I WAS BORN SOON AFTER THEY GOT BACK.

FOR A SHORT TIME WE ALL LIVED WITH MY GRANDMOTHER AND AILING GRANDFATHER AT THE FUNERAL HOME.

LESS THAN A YEAR LATER, WE MOVED TO A RENTED FEDERAL-STYLE FARMHOUSE AND MY BROTHER CHRISTIAN WAS BORN.

DAD STARTED TEACHING HIGH SCHOOL ENGLISH. FUNERAL DIRECTING PROVIDED ONLY A PART-TIME INCOME IN OUR THINLY POPULATED REGION.

BY THE TIME WE MOVED TO THE GOTHIC
REVIVAL HOUSE AND JOHN WAS BORN,
EUROPE HAD DISAPPEARED FROM MY
PARENTS' HORIZON.

IT WAS SOMEWHERE DURING THOSE
EARLY YEARS THAT I BEGAN CONFUSING
US WITH THE ADDAMS FAMILY.

LONG BEFORE I COULD READ,
I WOULD PUZZLE OVER A
BOOK OF ADDAMS CARTOONS.

THE CAPTIONS ELUDED ME, AS DID THE IRONIC REVERSAL OF SUBURBAN CONFORMITY.
HERE WERE THE FAMILIAR DARK, LOFTY CEILINGS, PEELING WALLPAPER, AND MENACING
HORSEHAIR FURNISHINGS OF MY OWN HOME.

IN ONE OCCULT AND
WORDLESS CARTOON...

...A WORRIED GIRL HAD A STRING RUNNING FROM HER MOUTH TO A TRAP DOOR.

THE LAMP NEXT TO HER LOOKED JUST LIKE MY LAMP. IN FACT, THE GIRL LOOKED JUST LIKE ME.

THE RESEMBLANCE IN MY FIRST-GRADE SCHOOL PHOTO IS EERIE.

WEARING A BLACK VELVET DRESS MY FATHER HAD WRESTLED ME INTO, I APPEAR TO BE IN MOURNING.

MY MOTHER, WITH HER LUXURIANT BLACK HAIR AND PALE SKIN, BORE A MORE THAN PASSING LIKENESS TO MORTICIA.

MOM, HOW COME YOU NEVER GO OUTSIDE?

I TOLD YOU, I'M A VAMPIRE.

NOCTURNE

AND ON WARM SUMMER NIGHTS, IT WAS NOT UNUSUAL FOR A BAT TO SWOOP THROUGH OUR LIVING ROOM.

BUT WHAT GAVE THE COMPARISON REAL WEIGHT WAS THE FAMILY BUSINESS...

...AND THE CAVALIER ATTITUDE WHICH, INEVITABLY, WE CAME TO TAKE TOWARD IT.

CAN I GET IN?

THE "FUN HOME," AS WE CALLED IT, WAS UP ON MAIN STREET.

MY GRANDMOTHER LIVED IN THE FRONT. THE BUSINESS WAS IN THE BACK.

I REMEMBER SEEING MY GRANDFATHER LAID OUT THERE WHEN I WAS THREE. PEOPLE WERE AMUSED BY WHAT SEEMED TO ME A REASONABLE ENOUGH REQUEST.

PUT ME CLOSER.

MY FATHER HAD BEEN GIVEN A FREE HAND WITH THE INTERIOR DECORATION OF THE VIEWING AREA, AND THE ROOMS WERE HUNG WITH DARK VELVET DRAPERY. THIS ENSURED A SOMBER MOOD ON THE SUNNIEST OF DAYS.

THERE WAS A MINIMUM OF FURNITURE, AND A VAST EXPANSE OF TEXTURED OLIVE WALL-TO-WALL CARPETING.

MY BROTHERS AND I HAD LOTS OF CHORES AT THE FUN HOME, BUT ALSO MANY INTERESTING OPPORTUNITIES FOR PLAY.

WE WERE STRICTLY FORBIDDEN TO CLIMB INTO THE CASKETS.

AND THE CRUSHABLE CAPSULES FILLED WITH SMELLING SALTS.

THESE WERE FOR REVIVING PEOPLE WHEN THEY FAINTED FROM SHOCK OR GRIEF, WHICH, DISAPPOINTINGLY, NEVER SEEMED TO HAPPEN.

WHEN A NEW SHIPMENT OF CASKETS CAME IN, WE'D LIFT THEM WITH A WINCH TO THE SHOWROOM ON THE SECOND FLOOR OF THE GARAGE.

THOUGH THERE WERE NEVER ANY DEAD PEOPLE IN THE SHOWROOM, IT HAD THE OTHERWORLDLY AMBIENCE OF A MAUSOLEUM.

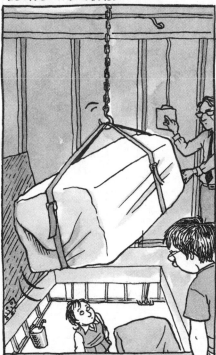

IT WAS USUALLY AFTER SCHOOL, IN A MELANCHOLY, FADING LIGHT, THAT WE FOUND OURSELVES UP THERE UNWRAPPING CASKETS.

A RICH SCENT OF CEDAR HUNG IN THE AIR.

MORE VELVET DRAPES MUFFLED ANY SOUNDS FROM OUTSIDE AND HEIGHTENED THE SENSATION THAT TIME WAS AT A STANDSTILL.

Burial Wear

LIKE A MEDIUM CHANNELING LOST SOULS, THE FILAMENT OF A SPACE HEATER VIBRATED TUNELESSLY TO OUR FOOTFALLS.

IT WASN'T THE SORT OF PLACE YOU WANTED TO BE ALONE IN.

WAIT FOR ME!

ON THE OTHER HAND, IT WAS NOT PARTICULARLY SCARY TO SPEND THE NIGHT IN THE FUNERAL HOME PROPER, EVEN WHEN WE HAD A DEAD PERSON.

MY BROTHERS AND I OFTEN SLEPT THERE WITH MY GRANDMOTHER.

PERMANENT GREASE STAIN FROM MY DEAD GRANDFATHER'S VITALIS

TO QUIET US DOWN, GRAMMY WOULD LET US SWEEP THE CEILING WITH THE BEAM OF HER FLASHLIGHT IN SEARCH OF BUGS.

THERE'S ONE!

PISS-ANT!

WHEN WE SPOTTED ONE, SHE WOULD DECLARE IT TO BE EITHER A "PISS-ANT" OR AN "ANTIE-MIRE"-- A TAXONOMIC DIFFERENTIATION I WAS NEVER CLEAR ON--AND SQUASH IT WITH A RAG ON THE END OF A BROOM.

AFTER THIS, WE WOULD BEG HER TO TELL US A STORY.

THE STORY, I SHOULD SAY, BECAUSE THERE WAS ONE TALE THAT HELD US IN SUCH THRALL THAT THE REST OF MY GRANDMOTHER'S REPERTOIRE--HER STILLBORN TWINS, THE TIME MY AUNT HAD WORMS--PALED BEFORE IT.

TELL US THE STORY OF WHEN DAD GOT STUCK IN THE MUD!

ALL RIGHT: SETTLE DOWN, NOW.

WUNST UPON A TIME, WHEN YOUR DADDY WAS A LITTLE BOY, HE WANDERED OFF.

"HE WAS LITTLER THAN YOU, JOHN, NO MORE THAN THREE. IT WAS SPRINGTIME."

"THE FIELDS WAS JUST PLOWED, AND BRUCE LIT OUT ACROST ONE. IT WAS THAT WET, PRETTY SOON HE COULDN'T LIFT HIS LITTLE LEGS OUT OF THE MUD!"

"BUT JUST THEN, ALONG COMES MORT DEHAAS WITH THE MAIL, AND HE SEES BRUCE A WAY OUT THERE, JUST A TINY SPECK."

WHAT IF THE MAILMAN DIDN'T SEE HIM?

WOULD HE OF DIED?

WELL, I DON'T KNOW, DEARS. BUT MORT COMMENCED TO WALK OUT ACROST THE MUDDY FIELD TO WHERE BRUCE WAS.

"HE GAVE HIM A YANK, AND HE WAS THAT STUCK, HIS OVERSHOES COME OFF!"

(I KNOW MORT WAS A MAILMAN, BUT I ALWAYS PICTURED HIM AS A MILKMAN, ALL IN WHITE-- A REVERSE GRIM REAPER.)

"HE BRUNG YOUR DADDY INTO THE KITCHEN IN HIS STOCKING FEET, AND I UNDRESSED HIM RIGHT THERE."

LOSE SOMETHIN', DOROTHY?

OH, MY LANDS!

UNDRESSED HIM?!

WHY?

WHY, HE WAS ALL OVER MUD, DEARS.

THEN WHAT?!

AND HERE THE STORY REACHED ITS BIZARRE, GRIMMSIAN CLIMAX.

THEN I WRAPPED HIM IN A QUILT AND PUT HIM IN THE OVEN.

SHE WAS REFERRING, OF COURSE, TO A COOK-STOVE.

BUT ALL WE COULD ENVISION WAS THE MODERN OVEN SHE HAD NOW, WITH ITS RED-HOT ELEMENTS.

THE TALE WAS ENDLESSLY COMPELLING.

AGAIN!

WUNST MORE, THEN WE'LL GO TO SLEEP.

BY DAY, IT WAS DIFFICULT TO IMAGINE DAD EVER HELPLESS, NAKED, OR TRUSSED UP IN THE OVEN.

WHEN YOU'RE DONE, DO THE VACUUMING.

THAT'S CHRISTIAN'S JOB.

THOUGH THE WAY GRAMMY HELPED HIM TIE HIS SURGICAL GOWN IN BACK WAS EVOCATIVE.

DO IT, OR I'LL GIVE YOU SOMETHING TO WHINE ABOUT.

DAD WORKED BACK IN THE INNER SANCTUM, THE EMBALMING ROOM.

PRIVATE

THIS SMELLED OF BACTERICIDAL SOAP AND EMBALMING FLUID. IT WAS DOMINATED BY A PORCELAIN ENAMEL PREP TABLE AND A CURIOUS WALL CHART.

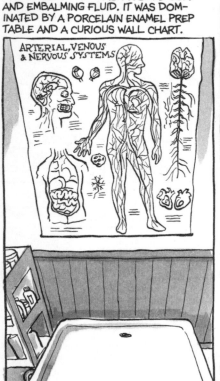

ARTERIAL, VENOUS & NERVOUS SYSTEMS

I DIDN'T NORMALLY SEE THE BODIES BEFORE THEY WERE DRESSED AND IN A CASKET.

ALISON!

BUT ONE DAY DAD CALLED ME BACK THERE.

THE MAN ON THE PREP TABLE WAS BEARDED AND FLESHY, JARRINGLY UNLIKE DAD'S USUAL TRAFFIC OF DESICCATED OLD PEOPLE.

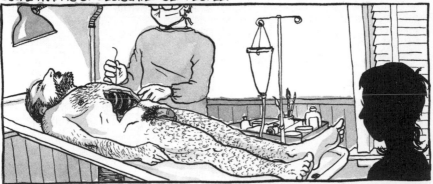

THE STRANGE PILE OF HIS GENITALS WAS SHOCKING, BUT WHAT REALLY GOT MY ATTENTION WAS HIS CHEST, SPLIT OPEN TO A DARK RED CAVE.

THERE WAS SOME PRACTICAL EXCHANGE WITH MY FATHER DURING WHICH I STUDIOUSLY BETRAYED NO EMOTION.

IT FELT LIKE A TEST. MAYBE THIS WAS THE SAME OFFHANDED WAY HIS OWN NOTORIOUSLY COLD FATHER HAD SHOWN HIM **HIS** FIRST CADAVER.

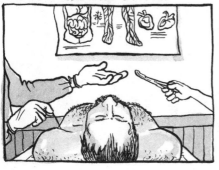

OR MAYBE HE FELT THAT HE'D BECOME TOO INURED TO DEATH, AND WAS HOPING TO ELICIT FROM ME AN EXPRESSION OF THE NATURAL HORROR HE WAS NO LONGER CAPABLE OF.

OR MAYBE HE JUST NEEDED THE SCISSORS.

IS THAT ALL?

MM-HMM.

I HAVE MADE USE OF THE FORMER TECHNIQUE MYSELF, HOWEVER, THIS ATTEMPT TO ACCESS EMOTION VICARIOUSLY.

PRIVATE

FOR YEARS AFTER MY FATHER'S DEATH, WHEN THE SUBJECT OF PARENTS CAME UP IN CONVERSATION I WOULD RELATE THE INFORMATION IN A FLAT, MATTER-OF-FACT TONE...

MY DAD'S DEAD. HE JUMPED IN FRONT OF A TRUCK.

...EAGER TO DETECT IN MY LISTENER THE FLINCH OF GRIEF THAT ELUDED ME.

THE EMOTION I HAD SUPPRESSED FOR THE GAPING CADAVER SEEMED TO STAY SUPPRESSED.

GOD, I'M SORRY.

EVEN WHEN IT WAS DAD HIMSELF ON THE PREP TABLE.

THERE'S BEEN AN ACCIDENT.

I WAS AWAY AT SCHOOL THAT SUMMER, GENERATING BAR CODES FOR ALL THE BOOKS IN THE COLLEGE LIBRARY.

I HAVE TO GO HOME. MY FATHER GOT HIT BY A TRUCK.

PRIMITIVE MODEM

OH MY GOD. IS HE OKAY?

UMM...

I BICYCLED BACK TO MY APARTMENT, MARVELING AT THE DISSONANCE BETWEEN THIS APPARENTLY CAREFREE ACTIVITY AND MY NEWLY TRAGIC CIRCUMSTANCES.

AS I TOLD MY GIRLFRIEND WHAT HAD HAPPENED, I CRIED QUITE GENUINELY FOR ABOUT TWO MINUTES.

THAT WAS ALL.

JOAN DROVE HOME WITH ME AND WE ARRIVED THAT EVENING. MY LITTLE BROTHER JOHN AND I GREETED EACH OTHER WITH GHASTLY, UNCONTROLLABLE GRINS.

IT COULD BE ARGUED THAT DEATH IS INHERENTLY ABSURD, AND THAT GRINNING IS NOT NECESSARILY AN INAPPROPRIATE RESPONSE. I MEAN ABSURD IN THE SENSE OF RIDICULOUS, UNREASONABLE. ONE SECOND A PERSON IS THERE, THE NEXT THEY'RE NOT.

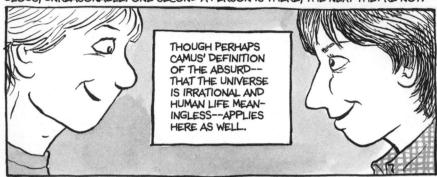

THOUGH PERHAPS CAMUS' DEFINITION OF THE ABSURD-- THAT THE UNIVERSE IS IRRATIONAL AND HUMAN LIFE MEAN- INGLESS--APPLIES HERE AS WELL.

IN COLLEGE, I NEEDED *THE MYTH OF SISYPHUS* FOR A CLASS. DAD OFFERED TO SEND ME HIS OLD COPY, BUT I RESISTED HIS INTERFERENCE.

S.222
INTRO. TO WESTERN PHILOSOPHY

THE MYTH OF SISYPHUS
CAMUS: THE REBEL

I WISH I COULD SAY I'D ACCEPTED HIS BOOK, THAT I STILL HAD IT, THAT HE'D UNDERLINED ONE PARTICULAR PASSAGE.

longing for death.
The subject of this essay is precisely this relationship between the absurd and suicide, the exact degree to which suicide is a solution to the absurd. The principle can be established that for a man who does not cheat, what he believes to be true must determine his action. Belief in the absurdity of existence must then dictate his conduct. It is legitimate to wonder, clearly and without false pathos, whether a conclusion of this importance requires forsaking as rapidly as possible an incomprehensible condition. I am

IT'S NOT THAT I THINK HE KILLED HIMSELF OUT OF EXISTENTIALIST CONVICTION. FOR ONE THING, IF HE'D READ CAREFULLY, HE WOULD HAVE GOTTEN TO CAMUS' CONCLUSION THAT SUICIDE IS ILLOGICAL.

BUT I SUSPECT MY FATHER OF BEING A HAPHAZARD SCHOLAR.

BECHDEL! PUT THAT GODDAMN BOOK DOWN. WE'RE GOING OUT.

Φ K Ψ

A SNAPSHOT OF HIM IN A FRAT BROTHER'S SPORTS CAR REMINDS ME OF CARTIER- BRESSON'S PHOTOS OF CAMUS.

MAYBE IT'S JUST THE CIGARETTE. IN EVERY PHOTO I'VE SEEN OF CAMUS, THERE'S A BUTT DANGLING FROM HIS GALLIC LIP.

BUT CAMUS' LUNGS WERE FULL OF HOLES FROM TUBERCULOSIS. WHO WAS HE TO CAST LOGICAL ASPERSIONS AT SUICIDE?

TO BE FAIR, EVERY-ONE SMOKED THEN.

HE COULDN'T HAVE LASTED MUCH LONGER EVEN IF HE HADN'T DIED IN A CAR CRASH AT FORTY-SIX.

CAMUS WAS KNOWN TO HAVE SAID TO HIS FRIENDS ON VARIOUS OCCASIONS THAT DYING IN A CAR ACCIDENT WOULD BE *UNE MORT IMBÉCILE*.

IN JANUARY OF 1960, THE SPORTS CAR HE WAS RIDING IN CAROMED OFF ONE PLANE TREE AND WRAPPED AROUND ANOTHER.

THE WRITER ALBERT CAMUS KILLED IN AUTOMOBILE ACCIDENT

NIXON MAY HURT G.O.P. PLAT

MY PARENTS WERE STILL IN EUROPE.

CAMUS ALSO SAID, IN *THE MYTH OF SISYPHUS*, THAT WE ALL LIVE AS IF WE DON'T KNOW WE'RE GOING TO DIE.

Yet one will never be sufficiently surprised that everyone lives as if no one "knew." This is because in reality there is no experience of death. Properly speaking, nothing has been experienced but what has been lived and made conscious. Here, it is barely possible to speak of the experience of others' deaths. It is a substitute, and illusion, and it never quite convinces us. That melancholy convention cannot be persuasive. The horror comes in reality from the mathematical aspect of the event. If time

BUT THEN, HE WASN'T A MORTICIAN.

I SUSPECT THAT FOR MY FATHER, DEATH WAS ALL TOO CONVINCING.

IN THE LETTERS HE SENT ME AT COLLEGE, SOMETIMES HE SEEMED THE PERFECT ABSURD HERO, SISYPHUS SHOULDERING HIS BOULDER WITH DETACHED JOY.

> The weekend was of little consequense entertainmentwise. I was called at 3:30 AM for Fay Murray's death. That shot that Friday Saturday. Some highlights of my work her yellow lace bikini rose-embroidered panties. Her died red hair after three months of hospitalizati͏ her hairdersser and her hairpieces. Her bitter green velvet jumpsuit with gold sequined trim and plunging neckline. Well I did my best with red lips, green eyeshadow, lots of rouge and eyebrow pencil and low and behold there lay Fay. She had lovely flawlessly smoothskin. Everyone was pleased and you would never have guessed she was <u>seventy</u>.

OTHER TIMES, HE WAS DESPAIRING.

> *Claude H. Bechdel Funeral Home*
> *Telephone 717-962-2727*
> *Beech Creek, Pennsylvania 16822*
>
> *Dorothy E. Bechdel*   *Bruce A. Bechdel*
>
>   Sunday 9-24-77
>
> Dear Al-
>
> I'm at fun home, tending local tragedy. Beautiful girl, 38, wrapɣped her car around one of those big trees in the Rupert's front yard. Worked eighteen hours yesterday. now I'm here fighting off the ghouls — it's bad for my blood pressure.

I DON'T HAVE ANY LETTERS ABOUT THE SUICIDES HE DEALT WITH, LIKE THE LOCAL DOCTOR WHO SHOT HIMSELF A FEW MONTHS BEFORE DAD'S OWN DEATH.

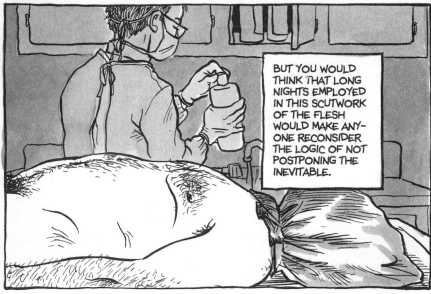

BUT YOU WOULD THINK THAT LONG NIGHTS EMPLOYED IN THIS SCUTWORK OF THE FLESH WOULD MAKE ANY-ONE RECONSIDER THE LOGIC OF NOT POSTPONING THE INEVITABLE.

YOU WOULD ALSO THINK THAT A CHILDHOOD SPENT IN SUCH CLOSE PROXIMITY TO THE WORKADAY INCIDENTALS OF DEATH WOULD BE GOOD PREPARATION.

THAT WHEN SOMEONE YOU KNEW ACTUALLY DIED, MAYBE YOU'D GET TO SKIP A PHASE OR TWO OF THE GRIEVING PROCESS--"DENIAL" AND "ANGER," FOR EXAMPLE--

BUT IN FACT, ALL THE YEARS SPENT VISITING GRAVEDIGGERS, JOKING WITH BURIAL-VAULT SALESMEN, AND TEASING MY BROTHERS WITH CRUSHED VIALS OF SMELLING SALTS ONLY MADE MY OWN FATHER'S DEATH MORE INCOMPREHENSIBLE.

WHO EMBALMS THE UNDERTAKER WHEN HE DIES?

IT WAS LIKE RUSSELL'S PARADOX...

...THE FAMOUS CONUNDRUM OF THE CLEAN-SHAVEN BARBER WHOSE SIGN READS, "I SHAVE ALL THOSE MEN, AND ONLY THOSE MEN, WHO DO NOT SHAVE THEMSELVES."

THE BARBER, EQUALLY UNABLE TO SHAVE HIMSELF, AND TO NOT SHAVE HIMSELF, IS IMPOSSIBLE.

YET SOMEHOW, THERE HE IS.

MY FATHER COULD HAVE USED A BARBER. HIS FACE WAS ROUGH AND DRY, SCRAPED CLEAN WITH NO HELP FROM THE EXPENSIVE LOTIONS AND AFTERSHAVES ON THE SILVER TRAY IN HIS BATHROOM AT HOME.

HIS WIRY HAIR, WHICH HE HAD DAILY TAKEN GREAT PAINS TO STYLE, WAS BRUSHED STRAIGHT UP ON END AND REVEALED A SURPRISINGLY RECEDED HAIRLINE.

I WASN'T EVEN SURE IT WAS HIM UNTIL I FOUND THE TINY BLUE TATTOO ON HIS KNUCKLE WHERE HE'D ONCE BEEN ACCIDENTALLY STABBED WITH A PENCIL.

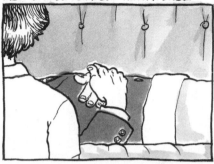

DRY-EYED AND SHEEPISH, MY BROTHERS AND I LOOKED FOR AS LONG AS WE SENSED IT WAS APPROPRIATE.

IF ONLY THEY MADE SMELLING SALTS TO INDUCE GRIEF-STRICKEN SWOONS, RATHER THAN SNAP YOU OUT OF THEM.

THE SOLE EMOTION I COULD MUSTER WAS IRRITATION, WHEN THE PINCH-FUNERAL DIRECTOR LAID HIS HAND ON MY ARM CONSOLINGLY.

I SHOOK IT OFF WITH A VIOLENCE THAT WAS, IN FACT, RATHER CONSOLING.

THIS SAME IRRITATION WOULD OVERTAKE ME FOR YEARS AFTERWARD WHEN I VISITED DAD'S GRAVE.

ON ONE OCCASION I FOUND IT DESECRATED WITH A CHEESY FLAG, PLACED THERE BY SOME WELL-MEANING ARMED SERVICES ORGANIZATION.

I JAVELINED THIS, UGLY BRASS HOLDER AND ALL, INTO THE CORNFIELD THAT IMMEDIATELY ADJOINS HIS PLOT AT THE EDGE OF THE CEMETERY.

AGAIN, THERE WAS SOME FLEETING CONSOLATION IN THE SHEER VIOLENCE OF MY GESTURE.

D. WINSTON BROWN

■

Ghost Children

FROM *Creative Nonfiction*

THE CAR GLEAMED under the Alabama sunlight. While the sun was still in its early-morning warming mode, I had risen from my bed, moved the hosepipe from the front yard to the driveway in the rear of the house, and driven my car, a 1979 Datsun 200SX, to the middle of the driveway. I retrieved a plastic bucket, several brushes, a box of detergent, and several rags needed to remove every particle of dust and dirt from the spoke hubcaps, from the now sparkling glass of each window, from each inch between hood and trunk, and from the silver grille, which sat like a snarl at the front between the bumper and the hood. By the time I left the house, shortly before noon, the car gleamed; its candy-apple-red paint glistened. I picked up Garrett, a friend with a penchant for Pink Floyd and bottled beer, and we drove to meet other friends, the whole time watching the daylight grow heavy and settle on the candy-apple-red sparkle.

As each hour passed and we changed locations — a clean car on a Saturday required frequent changes of venue — I never parked in the shade and, as dusk approached, sought out spots under streetlights. The car gleamed throughout the day and into the night as we drank beer purchased from stores that let teenage drivers of gleaming cars buy beer. We drank more beer at each stop, in each new neighborhood: Forestdale, Bush Hills, Southside, the Brickyard. We restocked at the Icehouse in Ensley; we restocked at the package store on Goldwire. We cruised through more neighborhoods: Center Point, East Lake, Druid Hills, Fountain Heights. I drove the car slow; I played the music loud. Cameo was out then: the song "Word Up!" The crowd changed as the hours passed: two people riding, three people riding, but no more than three because it was a small car and we all thought a lot of ourselves back then. We rode and drank and smoked, and long after the sun had tired of us, a guy named Spoon, a classmate, climbed into the back seat. Spoon sat in the middle of the seat so he could stretch his long, skinny arm between the front seats. Garrett and I, in the front seats, watched as Spoon pointed out approaching landmarks where I needed to turn. We were going to Annetta Simon's house. Spoon's idea. He knew her, said we needed to meet her.

I remember that his elbow was huge compared to the rest of his arm, like a tennis ball skewered on a mop handle. I remember we rode slowly through the night as if on the prowl. I remember the heat remained just shy of 99 degrees that night, and I fell in love with how the chill of beer on the back of my throat felt like time stopping for a moment before a slow drag of warm air delivered a thaw. I remember we were at a red stoplight — it had been yellow when I stopped — and Spoon slid his thin arm forward again, low, barely above the gearshift, until I found myself transfixed by the gleam of a silver handgun, .38 caliber, which sat softly in the cushion of his palm.

I had seen guns before, but never in my car.

This was not a year; this was a time. People were wearing Guess jeans with leather pocket-flaps or Levi's 501 Blues. Polo was destroying Izod, and hip-hop was just beginning to strip the veneer from the unconscious ease of life. And guns — guns were not yet a fashion statement. So when skinny Spoon, a kid I let cheat off me in algebra so he would share his weed before school, reached his arm forward with his hand cradling the silver weapon, I possessed no preconstructed, cool response, no learned reaction designed to maintain my coolness.

"Shit, Spoon. What the hell is that?"

"Watch the road," Garrett said. I'd begun to inch into the intersection.

"It's a gun," Spoon said.

"I know it's a gun," I said. "But what the fu —"

"Chill out," Spoon said. "I thought we could use it to scare —"

"Spoon," I said, "I ain't down for using no gun on a girl. If she don't want to —"

"Chill," Spoon said again. "I don't have to force any girls to do anything." He leaned his long head forward between the seats. "I thought we could get, I mean, scare them niggers who came by the school last week."

The last week Spoon spoke of had consisted of a fight: Garrett and me versus three boys who'd come to our school as it was letting out. Garrett had walked out the door with his arm around the girlfriend of one of the boys. He had told her a joke that I'd told him, and they were laughing as they emerged from the school. I was maybe seven yards behind them when I saw the boys approach from the right. They were man-boys compared to us. Their blue jeans were creased and starched. Gold hung from their necks: herringbones wide as Band-Aids and rope chains weighed down by crosses the size of those pocket Bibles that evangelicals are fond of giving away. With each step, their faces curled into hardened scowls.

They shoved Garrett from behind. I dropped my books and ran toward them. From there, it progressed like most any fight, a slow-motion blur of fists and cuss words and falling and kicking. We, surprisingly, held our own. I hit someone on the jaw. Someone hit me in the gut. A girl yelled, then another. These things I remember as occurring all at once, like some theatrical production. It slammed to a halt, all of the jumbled confusion, when one of the boys pulled out a gun. It looked old and dull and more like a prop from a John Wayne movie than a weapon, but there was no denying it was a gun. He held his arm straight, the gun sideways, and he placed the barrel inches away from my head. What he said I don't remember. I fixated on the gold-nugget rings he wore on three of his fingers. I remember thinking as long as I could see the shine of those rings I was still alive. I heard someone cry, "No." I heard someone's sneakers squeak in the doorway behind me. Down the block, a car's engine revved. The moment flooded with isolated sounds: squeaks, gasps, jangled keys, running feet. I struggled to hear what I didn't want to hear — the crack of the gun when it fired.

It never came.

A gun to the head. A crowd of witnesses. A world slowed down to a single moment. What did I feel? I asked myself that for days, weeks, years. I tried sometimes to re-create the moment in my head, to force myself to trudge back mentally to that gun's barrel, but memory and desire are too strong to be kept separated; they blend and produce mutated offspring. The facts always changed when I tried to remember. I questioned myself and then questioned my questions. Even when other students told me what they'd seen — that I'd stood motionless, didn't blink, didn't flinch or cower or try to move in the least — it felt unfamiliar, nothing like the perfectly still free-fall I felt whenever I tried to remember on my own.

There was one person, Jeremy McGetty, who witnessed that after-school brawl and described how I'd reacted in one word: reconciled. He told me this after lunch on the Wednesday following the fight, and on Thursday I asked him to elaborate. I wanted to know what he thought I'd been reconciled with. Lanky and dark-skinned, Jeremy was quiet by choice and read all the time. "Reconciled with the possibility," he told me, "of both living and dying." Then, revising slightly, he repeated himself: "Reconciled with dying."

Reconciled became a refrain in my head. It didn't fit; I refused to allow it to fit. A decent student with a middle-class background, a product of an insular private school, I was not supposed to be someone who reconciled his life with dying. I knew people who had, maybe, reconciled, at least with their situations. They didn't come to school often. Their subjects didn't agree with their verbs. They never spoke of a distant future. But even these boys, except for a handful, couldn't hide the fact that they feared something. They were the children of bitter divorces. They had fathers conspicuous only by their absence. They never had curfews. My parents' marriage was successful. My father attended every event his sons were in. My mother was a schoolteacher, and three of my grandparents had been schoolteachers. My older brother and I were on our way to being third-generation college graduates. I knew my destiny because my family taught it to me, day after day, in both deed and word. So when I thought about being reconciled with something, death was not the normal and expected completion of that thought. With parental guidance. With the expectation of table manners. With Christmases where gifts crowded around the tree. But not with death. Yet when I thought of it — of that description of my reaction — my blood surged: I felt pleased, thrilled even, that in that moment I had not retreated, not shrunk. I reconciled.

I can recall few details of the six days that passed between my conversation with Jeremy McGetty and seeing that gun in my car. I can still clearly see the gun, not the hand holding it, just the gleaming gun, which glittered even more as light from the streetlamps we passed momentarily caught in its silver and crept slowly across its curves.

But this is not about guns. This is not a celebration of violence, nor is it a refutation of guns or violence. It is not that simple. Black boys, guns, anger. No matter the economic class of the boys, no matter the education, no matter the professional position — whether we move mops through hallways or carry briefcases through boardroom doorways — we seldom lose that head-nod to another brother or that anger, caged and carried in spines, which skirts just below the skin, racing or prodding alongside blood. But this is not about anger either — at least not in the simple sense. There is no simple answer as to how a gun in my car became a primal summons.

To understand something, anything, about that moment requires another story, one in which I am only a witness.

I was twelve. It was late, and I was asleep.

When my father woke me, my eyes would not at first release the darkness. Then I heard his voice. His voice didn't coax. He didn't tickle me or nudge me or call me one of his many nicknames. He used my name — Daryl — and repeated his request for me to wake up and dress only once. I recognized his tone as unrecognizable, unheard before, and the request was a commandment that allowed room only for obedience. No questions. No rubbing crust from the corners of my eyes. No slow, reluctant withdrawal from warm sheets.

For years after, when I talked about this night, I described my father's voice — depending on the audience — as alternately stark or angry or full of rage, sometimes loud, sometimes louder. It took nearly a decade for me to know that his voice was reconciled.

My father drove a long, brown Buick LeSabre with power seats and power windows. Alone on the back seat, I felt like the sole person in a church pew. We passed through empty streets with no regard for streetlights or stop signs. My mother sat in the front passenger seat without a single comment about our speed. Most intersections rose slightly like small mounds, and in that fast-moving, heavy car, it felt as if those mounds were waves, and with each rise and fall I felt I left behind my stomach.

Something had happened to my brother. He was older, a junior in high school, and at a party, and something had happened to him. I didn't worry about him, though. He was my brother — my older, bigger brother — and was indestructible, and so my parents' level of quiet concern didn't alarm me. Instead, I sat on the back seat with my mind excited by what I'd seen my father place next to him on the seat: his gun. My history with this gun: I'd seen my father fire it into the sky on the Fourth of July, and once, I'd snuck into my parents' bedroom with my brother and peered into my father's file cabinet at the gun. My brother, after taking a step or two backward, had clapped his hands, a loud smack I just knew was gunfire. I had dropped to the floor and held my breath until I heard his taunting laughter.

When we arrived at our destination, my father swept up the gun and rushed out of the car, leaving me to the care of my mother. People crowded the driveway. I saw my brother: he looked fine. He and a friend, I learned, had been attacked by a gang: BAQ. This gang was the terror of Birmingham then, and because my brother had taken them on and emerged with only bruises and scrapes — minus one Armitron calculator watch — he would become even more one-dimensional to me: indestructible, tough, cool.

My father had walked away as my mother and I walked toward the house. He and his gun had climbed back into the car and disappeared. While he was gone, and after I'd nosed my way into complete knowledge of what had happened to my brother, I began to create scenarios in my head: my father riding with his lights out; my father finding the BAQ members, draped by slinky women in short skirts and hanging out on car hoods, drinking beer; my father pulling out his gun, demanding the return of my brother's calculator watch. (I loved that watch.) I drifted toward the street and listened for gunfire, but the night offered only unbroken silence.

When my father returned and joined the others, he did it as if he'd only been to the store for a pack of cigarettes. He didn't tell where he'd been, and no one asked. I waited for him to say something. I inspected his clothes for some hint, but there was none. The mood evolved into jokes and laughter, into conversations about nothing, and the men drank beer. I felt cheated, my curiosity not satisfied. When we drove home, we did it slowly. We stopped at lights, and my mom sang along with the soul songs on the radio. I leaned forward to glimpse the gun, but the seat between my parents held nothing. Finally, I stretched out on the bed-sized back seat and fell asleep.

There is nothing original in that anecdote. A man, his son, and the need to protect. But at twelve I didn't understand that level of protection. I was gawky and entering that stage of life when loneliness becomes a badge. But I understood embarrassment. I understood pride. Protection was pushing someone when he pushed me. It was also associated with things: gold chains, a new pair of Nikes, clean cars with bumping stereos. These things, I somehow learned, deserved protection, deserved my blood if need be. We all knew this, and we all knew an infraction — like stepping on someone's new Air Jordans — meant a fight was inevitable. Years later, fists would turn to knives, and knives would turn to guns, but when I was twelve, a father, a gun, and a gang-attacked brother were only exciting.

You never know exactly how one story will fit on top of another, how the brain will create its own truth to satisfy your deepest needs. Things may happen discretely, days apart, months apart, cities and decades and neighborhoods apart, but history collapses, then memory, and nothing ever remains discrete. Isolation is the lie we tell ourselves to comfort ourselves, but connections stretch the prisms we see through to allow more in, and more always changes things. A child changes a house; a war changes a teenage boy. Death leaves a void. Long before my father carried his gun as a weapon, history had constructed my prism, as it had for so many other young black boys. It was an unspoken history, so I didn't truly comprehend why I instinctively bristled at the word "nigger," or why the white guard at the jewelry store followed my father, my brother, and me while we shopped for a Christmas gift for my mother, or what it meant when some white child, some innocent classmate at my 98 percent white private school, said he couldn't come spend the night because his grandfather had told him that he "didn't need to be going to no nigger's house in a nigger neighborhood." He said "black," but I heard "nigger" even then, and I hit him. It's that anger — history's long and subtle voice — that, when misunderstood, becomes a simmering hostility. I saw it grow in friends; I saw it in the eyes of brothers I passed at parties and in the eyes of old men in haggard clothes who stood outside the Masonic temple. I came to recognize the broken, to discern them by their walks, their limp handshakes, their newly purchased suits, and then I came to both despise and love them.

Years later, I would deromanticize that night, unravel the cowboy dreams I'd dressed it in, and begin the work of understanding what my father did, what my father had been willing to do. But first I would have to encounter my car, Garrett, Spoon, me, and the gun.

I didn't consciously think about my father and his gun when Spoon stretched his weapon forward like an offering. I merely accepted it. In my hand the gun felt heavy, solid, and the metal felt as if it had recently been buried in cool dirt. It wasn't the first gun I'd held in my hand, but it felt heavier than I remembered. It contained no fun, no play, and we rode the next few blocks in silence. Not a reflective silence. Reflection would have demanded too much of me. I spent those few blocks divorcing myself from what I was about to do. There was justice to be exacted — and revenge. I thought of him only as The Boy. Where's The Boy now? How do we find The Boy? Is The Boy alone? The gun became a part of my hand. The metal settled into my palm with both a mechanical and a natural ease. I drove as if I'd always driven with a gun in one hand. Somewhere in the quiet of that car, we all gave our consent. Finally, I asked Spoon which way I needed to go. He told me to make a U-turn.

What I know now and couldn't have known then is that we — so many young black boys — had moved beyond simply being frightened by the brutal world. Progress in this country since the first slaves, though slow and incremental and often delivered reluctantly, had nonetheless been steady. Each decade, each era, you could mark notables: Buffalo Soldiers, Marcus Garvey, A. C. Powell, Brown v. Board, Wright, Ellison, Martin, Malcolm, civil rights legislation (long past due). Then something died. Hard to pin exactly what and where, but the effect was crushing. Maybe, as James Baldwin writes in *The Fire Next Time*, psychological death happened first when black soldiers returned from World War II in search of home but instead lost hope as America spurned them. If so, that same death knell finally tolled as the 1960s expired, when we, the ghost children of Dynamite Hill and American capitalism, sensed a similar loss of hope.

Faith and charity were scarce too. We no longer asked, Why hast Thou forsaken me? We accepted our forsakenness, assumed it as a status quo that would never bend but might, one day, break. Not that we gave up on God; we just no longer waited on divine intervention. If God had not rescued this country from its black heart, how could He help a black man put food on the table, buy a house, feel good about bringing a son into a country that had spent the better part of its youth denying those sons the right to be men? No one needed to tell us of this legacy; its impatient and simmering anger fell into our bones. Without a reason for patient faith, we fell into the acquisition of now — of seizing everything and every dream, now. For many boys, life and death fell, with the weight of a Bible, into the hand that wielded the gun. We were not adrift, not without direction, but we knew, without knowing, the invisible barrier that often existed between possibility and us. It stretched before us like our own 33rd parallel, our Mason-Dixon Line, our Edmund Pettus Bridge. This was an old war, and we didn't know how to fight it. So we fought and killed each other. We battled over gold chains and gym shoes, over ghetto blasters and Gazelles and four-finger gold rings. These things symbolized style, and style was manhood. We struggled to protect these trinkets, fought over them and all they represented.

What we have learned to fight for, to protect, is not an easy path to trace. What makes it real? The list is far too long: the atrocity of slavery; the 1921 race riots in Tulsa; the inherited memory of lynching; the murders of Medgar Evers and Emmett Till; burned-in mental images of water cannons blasting people down sidewalks, police dogs ripping the clothes of marchers, children locked into paddy wagons. Just pick one from this short list. For me, I came to understand why I took that gun from Spoon only after hearing for the first time a story that I'd heard at least twenty times before.

It takes place in Dynamite Hill. It involves a boy, maybe ten, maybe eleven; a garage where three men, sometimes four, sit in a car without closing the garage door or turning on any lights; and a bedroom closet full of guns. It's important to know, first, that Dynamite Hill existed as a thriving neighborhood filled with blacks of all classes and professions. In the middle of it all was a lawyer who lived at the corner of Center Street and Tenth Court and who became a target of racists during the late fifties. Arthur Davis Shores was a small man physically, always impeccably dressed, dapper, but he fought with a savage intellect to make significant changes: he stood up to racism, one court case at a time. In return, his house was dynamited — several times. That number would have probably been higher had it not been for the men who decided to maintain a protective vigil, across the street in the dark garage, for their neighbor. They protected their neighborhood, as did other men in other unlit garages in nearby blocks (there were around thirteen homes bombed in the neighborhood during this time), but this garage I know because it was in my grandparents' house and because my grandfather, a high school football coach, was one of the men waiting in it.

Every day, sometime close to dusk, a car would back into my grandparents' garage. The door would remain open. Three, sometimes four men would pile into the car as darkness came. My grandmother, also a schoolteacher, would cook for them — a meal or snacks to get them through the night. Danger was more than a possibility. Houses, including Mr. Shores's house, had already been bombed. The men never took the key out of the ignition. They had lookouts who walked the sidewalks. They communicated with walkie-talkies. My father, a boy of ten or eleven, also had a role. Every evening, as the men ate and then settled into their nightly duties, my father, just a boy then, was responsible for going into my grandparents' bedroom closet and retrieving the weapons. Not handguns: he nightly carried a collection of assorted rifles. The men didn't mean simply to deter — they meant to kill if necessary.

I don't know everything they did during those nights. But I do know three things. One: my father, already proficient with guns, was a child nonetheless and still prone to concentration lapses. The story he tells involves him hurriedly swooping the rifles into his arms without first checking the safeties. One of the rifles fires. The blast is a wind's rush that travels past my father's face, inches (or less) from his cheek or from entering his chin and blowing away enough of his face to transform it beyond a mother's recognition. A hole opens in the ceiling, scarring the house my grandmother keeps immaculate. Two: the hole, for a long time, is not repaired. My grandmother hates guns and wants the hole to be a reminder. Three: later that night, while my father is still in the garage receiving a lecture on handling guns, a call comes in over the walkie-talkie. A lookout sees someone walking near Mr. Shores's house, and he believes he saw the person toss something that was lit. The men rush from the garage. My father, a boy, follows. They surround the suspect. He's white, a teenager. Guns are drawn. Not shot, just drawn. The interrogation reveals that the suspect lives nearby, on the white side, blocks away, and he is out walking so that his mother won't catch him smoking a cigarette. He tells them he tossed the cigarette butt in the grass. The men, cautious, check out his story by calling his house. The white boy goes home; the black men resume their vigil. My father is now a witness.

When I was a little older, after the twenty-first time I heard this story, I saw it in a different light. I thought about my grandmother. My grandmother was a part of the missionary society at an African Methodist Episcopal church; she treated people, all people, as her Bible and her preacher instructed, yet she allowed her young son to be the gun transporter. A ten-year-old. I imagine her being torn, maybe expressing her worries, one night in bed, to my grandfather, who tells her what she knows already — something about the world and how their boy needs to learn to face that world as a man. That night, they decide on his manhood, and I imagine she tightens her lips in silent agreement.

Since my grandmother was a schoolteacher, I'm sure she knew that her boy needed to seize his manhood, that the world would try to strip it from him as she'd seen it do to so many of her ex-students. Even she must have known that an element of necessary violence lurked in all manhood, at least for boys born black in America.

What she doesn't know is that time will transform that violence. My grandfather and his partners wielded violence to protect. I don't assume, in any way, that senseless killing didn't happen prior to my teenage years, but I do know that I lived through an evolution, one where guns became common, where boys wanting to be men no longer fought one another but shot to kill. And over what? Not for social change or to protect a neighbor. But over jewelry. Over cars. Over trendy gym shoes. Over blocks of faded, cracked pavement.

But I'd not yet arrived at these thoughts the night Spoon and Garrett watched me play with the silver gun while we sat at a red light. I felt I'd been given something I needed. We drove until we came to a stop next to a corner gas station. Across the street was a group of teenagers. They were laughing and joking. I saw no familiar faces for the first few moments. Then Spoon pointed to someone who'd drifted away from the crowd. I recognized him. My hand tightened around the gun. I wanted him to feel what I'd felt, and I wanted to feel the power he'd felt. No one told me to drive. I just did, pulling the car to a stop in the westbound, inner lane. He was running before I fully extended my arm. I fired. He kept running toward the crowd. Maybe he was trying to reach the house behind the people. I fired again, followed him with the gun's barrel, sliding my arm along the door, and fired again. People ran, open-mouthed, and they looked like puppets, toys, not real. I kept The Boy in sight. I fired until the gun emptied, and then I heard the screams, noticed the fear of the people running.

I've never gotten over how good it felt, the physicality of that un-challenged power; it threw me into some sort of high. I remember driving away, all three of us whooping in the electric delight of con-quest. I remember drinking a beer and feeling as if my blood still vi-brated from firing the gun. I loved feeling like that, but then — as quick as a book slammed shut — I feared it. That fear crept through me. It crept through me when I watched the late, late news that night and when I read the newspaper the next morning. When I went to school on Monday, I spent several classes glancing at the door, expect-ing to see policemen crash through.

Nothing happened. Life went on.

My friends, the ones who knew, just laughed. They treated me like a victorious general. They nosed around intently for facts, and they laughed when they learned I'd hit nothing. I became something dif-ferent to them, and to myself. I fired no more guns during high school or after. I don't really know what happened to Spoon. He dropped out of high school, and I saw him a few times, hanging out-side of parties or at George Ward Park on Sundays. Garrett became a drug addict whose ravaged body quit a few years shy of his twenty-fifth birthday. As for me, I heard the clap of that gun for years in my sleep, until it eventually faded.

Then, when I heard my father's story again, I thought of my twisted attempt at manhood, at pride. Somewhere along the way, my father succeeded in handing down to me a better ideal of manhood. I went on to college and a career, but I know so many others who didn't. I still see them occasionally, and I remember how we were all boys, at some point, who dreamed of manhood. Unfortunately, America has a long history of discouraging its darker-hued sons from becoming men, and from that discouragement has risen a legacy of anger. Anger at poll taxes. At separate but equal. At the murder of Amadou Diallo. At the murder of James Byrd Jr. At the language and practice of racism in all its old guises and modern disguises.

I don't know who said it first, but I remember my father telling me something he said his father had told him: a man ain't nothin' but a man. As children do, I shrugged it off when young, but, as children do, I recalled it later and began the difficult work of understanding his stories and what they meant to me, for me. Sometimes, I suppose, what a society fractures in its sons is something only a father can heal. This is not to discount mothers, but it often takes a man to guide a boy into becoming a man.

These days, when I look at boys dressed in identical brand-name clothes; boys who speak perfect English in public spaces; or boys with their baseball caps tilted to the side, their jeans slung low, their teeth encased in platinum and diamonds, their heads covered in perfect cornrows or their biceps adorned with RIP tattoos, I know all they want in life is to be men — and I know they are doubtful or scared they may not be given the chance. The truth about those dragons that lie in wait for them fuels a naked and aggressive and urgent ambition to compete in America's marketplace. This need manifests as an electric vitality that permeates American culture, giving it life and allowing its consumers to come close to the void — to play in the darkness — without risk. Meanwhile, the black boys who huddle like alchemists, creating and re-creating opportunity where it doesn't exist, allow our real (and historical) anger to propel us at a furious pace toward dreams we refuse to defer. And though not possible, we do want to put down that anger gifted to us by a generation and a country that has yet to fulfill its obligation of showing us how to deal with, prosper, evolve, and stand in the darker legacy of our manhood. Until that happens, as many ingredients shall fuel us — a deep and buried anger being one of them — as have contributed to the complex and tragic creation of these United States.

SCOTT CARRIER

■

Rock the Junta

FROM *Mother Jones*

ONE NIGHT IN RANGOON I had a hard time sleeping and got up early, while it was still dark, and walked a few blocks down to the harbor along the Irrawaddy River near the Botataung Pagoda, where a single strand of the Buddha's hair is kept. It's a sacred relic for the Burmese, more than two thousand years old, encased in gold. During the Second World War the British bombed the pagoda to rubble, but when the monks dug through the heap they found the hair in perfect condition inside a small box, a miracle, and they rebuilt the shrine around it.

There were dogs sleeping on the street as if they owned the place, and a line of thirty or forty young monks walking single file, from tallest to shortest, exiting the pagoda after early-morning prayers. On a concrete runway along the river, which was perhaps a half mile wide, men and women were exercising in the dark, doing tai chi and walking backward, listening to the BBC or VOA in Burmese on transistor radios. The sun came up through the thick air, dark red and monstrous. The river turned from slate to blood to pea soup.

I was depressed. We'd come to Burma to see if there might be some hope of a revolution, but people seemed more concerned with making money to buy Game Boys and cell phones, even though a cell phone SIMM card cost $3,000, the equivalent of twelve years of work at the average yearly salary of about $260. I don't know how many people had told me they were hoping the United States would invade. The doorman at our hotel, the Three Seasons, said, "I want you to tell President Bush to send his army. They will be welcomed by all

Myanmar people. Tell them we have plenty of beer for them to drink."
But President Bush . . . President Bush . . . oh, I was depressed.

Along the water, the concrete benches under the palm trees were
mostly filled by sleeping teenagers, boys and girls, one to a bench. But
at the end of the pier, six boys lay fully awake, listening to their friend
sing and play a guitar. He was maybe sixteen years old, and the guitar
had an IRON CROSS ACOUSTICS sticker on the front of it. I sat down a
few feet away, rolled a cigarette, and listened. The kid had a clear
voice, a strong voice, and he was pouring his heart out in a love song,
as real as Willie Nelson. They'd been up all night, maybe high on
methamphetamines, but their clothes were clean, shorts and baseball
hats, and they were polite. I didn't have a lighter, and the youngest
one noticed this and waved to a man walking by and told him to give
me a light.

So I sat there and listened and started disintegrating. This has happened twice before. The first time was in the Tiki Room at the Bom-
bay Oberoi, listening to a Bengali play guitar and sing "My Way." The
second time was in a Zapatista village in the mountains of Chiapas,
listening to a young woman from Montana play guitar and sing "Re-
demption Song." Both times I was left in little pieces that took a long
time to push back together. And there along the river, listening to our
music, all about yearning for freedom, I again felt overwhelmed by
the same juxtapositions and ironies.

Burma is a forgotten country. You might have a hard time finding it
on a map, and it may not even be called Burma on the map you're
looking at. It might be called Myanmar, as that's the official name for
it now. It's an extremely fucked-up place, the size of Texas, located between Thailand and India, south of China. For the past forty-four
years, it's been cut off from the rest of the world by a junta of xeno-
phobic and superstitious generals calling themselves the State Peace
and Development Council. Others call them mendacious assholes
and hungry ghosts.

The population is about fifty million, and they live like imprisoned
children, with very little knowledge of their own history and very little
opportunity to learn. Their government controls nearly every aspect
of their lives — what they can read, what they can say and think,

where they go, how they make money. Nothing much comes into the country, and nothing much goes out — except opium, teak, and jade by way of the black market, which is also controlled by the military. Strangely, Burma is open to tourism, but not many people care to visit.

I lied on my visa application, saying I was a college professor; my travel companion wrote in "Spiritual Adviser," partly as a joke and partly because we were supposed to be visiting the Buddhist temples that dot the landscape. The country is sometimes called the Golden Land because the bell-shaped pagodas are often covered in gilt. Before going to Burma, I'd read how its people are living through an Orwellian nightmare, how in 1988 they turned out in the streets en masse shouting, "Dee-mo-ka-ra-see!" This protest ended with at least three thousand dead, shot by their own military. A couple of weeks later, Aung San Suu Kyi, the daughter of the founding father of Burma's democratic movement, made a speech from the steps of the Shwedegon Pagoda in Rangoon calling for a second Burmese revolution, and she's been under house arrest pretty much ever since — even after she won a national democratic election in 1990, making her the rightful leader of the country; even after she was awarded the Nobel Peace Prize in 1991.

She lives in her father's house, on the shore of a large lake, guards outside her gate. They do not allow her a telephone or a TV or a radio. She has no mail coming in or going out. During the day she hears the distant roar of traffic; at night there are frogs. She meditates a lot. She is by far the most powerful person in Burma.

So I expected to see a military presence on the streets in Rangoon, the capital city, or what used to be the capital city until late last year when the astrologers of the chief hungry ghost, Chairman Than Shwe, foresaw that it would be prudent to move all government offices two hundred miles north, to a small malarial city where they could be better defended from enemies foreign or domestic. I expected to see tanks shaking the ground, or soldiers inside bunkers at the intersections, or checkpoints and roadblocks — something demonstrating who was in control and who was not. Up in the mountains, the Burmese military was busy burning ethnic tribal villages to the ground, systematically raping women, and forcing hundreds of thousands into slave labor camps. But in Rangoon it took two days to even see a policeman — traffic cops dressed in white coats and white British Raj helmets, armed only with whistles. The traffic became gridlocked and no one even honked a horn.

And the people on the streets, who I imagined would be huddling and scurrying about like caged rats, seemed rather calm and even happy, strolling along, the men sashaying in long skirts and sandals, some sitting on the broken sidewalks in kindergarten-sized chairs, drinking tiny cups of tea. The women, some of them, smeared light brown cellulose paste in circles on their cheeks, which looked sort of wild and exotic but is actually a traditional way to protect their skin from the sun.

At one of the busier intersections downtown there was a government billboard that said, in English:

PEOPLE'S DESIRE
Oppose those relying on external elements, acting as stooges, holding negative views.
Oppose those trying to jeopardize stability of the State and progress of the nation.
Oppose foreign nations interfering in internal affairs of the State.
Crush all internal and external destructive elements as the common enemy.

But up above the billboard, on the rooftops of the apartment buildings, there were fields of satellite dishes gazing up to the sky like sunflowers. It didn't make sense. Inside their homes people were watching CNN, BBC, HBO, and MTV, while out on the street they were supposed to be wary of stooges.

Everywhere we went, we were watched. Long, intense stares coming from every direction, as if we were out of place and out of time, and it was hard to tell whether the Burmese were wondering if we were "external destructive elements" or some second-rate soap-opera stars they'd seen on TV. They did not, however, appear to be very friendly, and some of them laughed at us. Yes, a mockery, seconded by legions of squawking crows in every tree.

Men did approach us, trying to sell us shoes, postcards, offering to change money, always some kind of business, and we'd try to talk to them. But it was always a pretend conversation. The reason I say this is because the minute we'd ask a question about their lives, like "What's it like to live here?," the response would be the same — first a turning away, moving the body and the head to the side, then a glazing over of the eyes, a gaze without focus. It was a turning inward, pulling a shell around their bodies.

"It is dangerous for us," one man said. "There are spies everywhere."

He was a young social worker for the government, out drinking whiskey with two friends in the Chinatown part of the city. "Everyone in Myanmar has either gone to jail or knows someone who has gone to jail for saying the wrong thing. I have a friend in Insein [pronounced "insane"] Prison who held up a sign at a protest. The sign said only one word, 'Freedom.' His sentence is seven years."

Even other Western tourists spoke in whispers, turning in both directions to see if anyone was listening. This syndrome has a name among some NGO workers — "Burma head." In a 1977 book called *Discipline and Punish: The Birth of the Prison*, Michel Foucault discussed the social effects of surveillance, using a prison designed by Jeremy Bentham in 1787, called the Panopticon, as a model. The cells are arranged in a circle around a central observation tower, so that one person inside the tower can see into every cell at all times, but the prisoners, while able to see the tower, never really know whether there is a person in there watching them. The observer can see out, but the observed can't see in.

> Hence the major effect of the Panopticon: to induce in the inmate a state of conscious and permanent visibility that assures the automatic functioning of power. So to arrange things that the surveillance is permanent in its effects, even if it is discontinuous in its action; that the perfection of power should tend to render its actual exercise unnecessary; that this architectural apparatus should be a machine for creating and sustaining a power relation independent of the person who exercises it; in short, that the inmates should be caught up in a power situation of which they are themselves the bearers.

This was why there was no visible military presence in the city. It wasn't necessary. The people controlled themselves. Even tourists were not immune. In the Panopticon of Burma, you were a prisoner among prisoners, each with your own cell. The effect was a deadening of desire, a flatlining of curiosity and humor, and loneliness hung in the air, heavy as the smog cloud that covers all of Asia. There was not a buzz or a whir or a whisper of testosterone among the men, and the women, although many were beautiful, had not an ounce of glamour, not a scent of sensuality among them. The food was horrendous, cooked in the morning and left to sit through the day at room temperature, so that by dinner the stuff on the plate looked like dark brown entrails and tasted like pure MSG. And while there was a lot of rock and pop music being played all over town, most of it was just awful. For instance, while on a bus we were subjected to a video of a girl dressed like Britney Spears singing, "She's a maniac, a maniac on the floor. And she's dancing like she's never danced before." Only she stood like a frightened child. Behind her was a large photograph of Mother Teresa, and every time she came to the refrain she'd turn around and sing to it.

This is how it went the first few days in Rangoon. However, things changed dramatically on a Sunday evening when we saw a young man carrying a guitar. Just a guitar.

We were standing outside the Baptist church across from the Sule Pagoda. The sun was going down and the sky was turning orange and red, and the spotlights were coming on and illuminating the golden dome of the pagoda, traffic circling around the perimeter. We'd just come out of the Sunday service. Christianity is permitted, but the rulers have a problem with anyone who professes a belief in a power higher than them, so being a Christian in Burma is a radical thing, and Christians suffer some discrimination because of it. For instance, they can't rise very far in the military, and they can't hold high positions in the government. "You know," my spiritual adviser said, "Buddhists pray and meditate alone, but Christians do it together, in a group, and I think this is why people here become Christians. Did you see how they stood up and sang those hymns in there? They were really into it, not at all like the solemn and glum singing in the churches my parents dragged me to as a kid. There was a lot of energy in there."

Before I had time to agree with her, a young man about eighteen or twenty years old came walking by carrying a guitar. He had long, straight hair down to his shoulders, a little goatee under his chin, and a gold ring in his ear — a hipster. A hipster with a yellow acoustic guitar in his right hand.

My friend ran over to him and desperately asked him if he would play a song. He smiled and said he didn't know how to play; he just liked carrying the guitar around.

"Well," I said, "if you could play, who would you play like? What music do you like to listen to?"

And he said, "Chit San Maung, number one guitar in Myanmar. Iron Cross, number one band."

"He lives here, in Rangoon?"

"Yes, he lives here. All Iron Cross live here."

"Do you know where we can find him?"

"No," the kid said. He smiled and walked away.

I guess we just hadn't been paying attention that well, because now we started seeing Iron Cross bumper stickers on the beat-up taxicabs around the city. Sometimes the cabs had stickers that said, in English, DRIVE SAFELY. But the only other sticker on any car was either IRON CROSS ACOUSTICS or IRON CROSS UNPLUGGED.

Also, we started seeing more teenage boys with guitars — sitting in doorways or outside apartment buildings, strumming, trying to learn how to play. They all knew Chit San Maung. One kid said he was "the best guitar player in all of Asia, no question."

We heard Iron Cross songs in taxicabs, coming out of apartment windows, and from large speakers set up on the street by kids selling sunglasses. Some of them sounded like Metallica, some sounded like Hawaiian cowboy music, some were covers, some were original, but the lyrics were always in Burmese.

Those kids selling sunglasses on the street with the big speakers, the song they were listening to was a good example of a typical Iron Cross song. It started out with kind of a sultry funk, sort of the same mood as the way people in Rangoon walk down the street, kind of relaxed and cool, no problem, or maybe like watching a girl in a summer dress, but then it exploded into heavy metal and loud screaming.

It was the two sides to life in Burma — one calm and relaxed, the other brutally painful.

When I was seven years old, in 1964, I went over to a friend's house after school. He had a teenage sister, and we were in her bedroom, and she put "I Want to Hold Your Hand," a 45, on her little box record player. She hung her head and swayed back and forth so her hair bounced off her cheeks. Then she started dancing with her arms up in the air, twisting her ass, jumping up and down. I'd never seen anything like it, but I knew it was dangerous.

The first time we saw Iron Cross was the same. We were in a coffee shop for tourists where a TV screen showed European models strutting around in pajamas. Then the channel changed to an Iron Cross live performance. The sound was off, but it was clear they were into something loud and fast — and powerful. The singer with a shaved head screaming into the microphone, the drummer in a frenzy, and Chit San Maung playing lead guitar as if he were struggling to tame it. We didn't need to hear the sound to know what the song was about — sticking it to the Man.

It seemed very strange these guys were not in jail.

The next morning we were both sick, coughing up yellowish-green phlegm, so we took a taxi to a health clinic inside one of the more expensive hotels in town. (Burma has close to the lowest health care standards of any country in the world.) The driver had an English-Burmese dictionary on the dashboard and wanted to talk. He said he'd grown up in a village in the mountains along the border with Thailand, but his life there was so boring he left and came to the city to seek his fortune.

"I have not one good thing to say about the government," he said. "They ruin my country. They lie about everything. Nobody knows the truth. We cannot. Have you seen our newspaper? Only good news. All a bluff. First thing children learn in school is not ask questions. At university you pay for grades, nobody learns, nobody knows how to make what we need. We export rubber, we don't know how to make tires. When we buy them, very expensive."

"Could you leave the country if you wanted to go?" I asked.

"Yes, we can go out, if we have money we can go out, but I don't have money. Only military, black-market men have money."

"But if you could leave, would you stay away, or would you come back?"

"I love my country, you understand? I want to die in my country because I love my people. If government says we live on five hundred kyat [forty-three cents] a day, we live on five hundred kyat a day, okay. We can do this and be happy with each other, love each other. But this government is very bad men," he said.

"Do you know the band Iron Cross?"

"Yes, my friend is friend with Chit San Maung, guitar player."

By the time we came out of the clinic with some antibiotics, the cab driver had the phone number.

I called Chit, and he spoke enough English to understand what I was asking. Mainly he said yes, yes, yes, and that he'd send a car to pick us up. The car came at eight P.M., a new black Land Cruiser with tinted windows and bumper stickers I hadn't seen on any other car — one of the Jesus fish, and "No Jesus, No Peace. Know Jesus, Know Peace," "Never Say Die," as well as IRON CROSS ACOUSTICS, the name of their new album. I asked the driver, a young man who said he was in Chit's family, if Chit was a Christian, and he said, "Yes, for sure."

"So are Iron Cross songs religious songs?"

"No," he said, "it's not allowed. No words in English, no Christian words. Only love songs." Then he stuck in an Iron Cross CD and turned it up loud, maybe to get me to stop asking questions, maybe because it was a beautiful song.

The boulevards in Rangoon are lined with palms and banyan trees. It's not a bad city, the way it's laid out, and better at night, weaving through traffic at forty miles an hour, listening to a song that sounds like it's about a train coming down the tracks while passing buses packed tight with people, arms and heads hanging out the windows, flying by frog-legged men pedaling tricycle rickshaws, too fast to really see strange animist shrines with Christmas-tree lights or a karaoke bar with women modeling onstage.

Chit's house had a wall around the outside and a sign out front that said PTL DIGITAL STUDIOS. I asked the driver if PTL stood for "Praise the Lord," and he said yes. But when I asked him if he'd heard of Jim and Tammy Faye Bakker, he said no.

Downstairs there was a small recording studio — a sound room and double-paned glass separating the control room. We were taken up two flights into the production room — carpet on the floor, a large computer and big speakers sitting on a desk, ten guitars hanging on the wall, and Iron Cross concert posters, including one from a 2003 tour to America.

Chit came in and shook our hands, and he was like a 140-pound lightbulb, so happy we'd come. He was with an older man he introduced as his uncle, who, he said, was going to help translate. He didn't look like Chit at all, more like a wiseguy type, but at the time I just accepted the thing without question.

Chit said he'd started playing in church when he was five years old. He grew up in the village of Henzada, northwest of Rangoon, along the Irrawaddy River. The church had a good choir, and they sang "Amazing Grace," things like that, and he also had a Chet Atkins tape that he listened to a lot. When he was a teenager, he moved to Rangoon and studied with the most famous guitar player in the country at that time. He was the one who came up with the name Iron Cross — with respect, Chit said, to the World War I German medal for heroism, bravery, and leadership.

I asked him where the group had played in the States, and he said New York, Washington, D.C., San Francisco, and Los Angeles.

"Have you heard of Jim and Tammy Faye Bakker?" I had to ask.

"No, who are they?"

"Oh, just a couple who had a TV show in America called *The PTL Club*. It doesn't matter. Your driver told us your songs aren't religious, that the government won't allow it."

"Yes, we give them the words, and if they don't like them, they change the words."

"Does that bother you?"

"No, they do their job, we do ours. We only play love songs, and sometimes it's hard to say who writes the words. Sometimes the words are not important."

"You know, the first time we saw you was on a TV, and the sound was turned off so we couldn't even hear the music, but I saw you have power in your guitar. It was obvious, just in the way you were playing, and I wondered why you weren't in jail. Why does the government let you play anything at all?"

Up to that point, he understood my questions and answered them by himself, but suddenly he acted like he didn't understand the question and turned to his uncle for help. They talked for a minute in Burmese, and then the uncle said, "Iron Cross songs are not about politics."

"But," I said, "have you seen *Woodstock*, the movie of the concert?"

Chit nodded his head.

"There's a part where Jimi Hendrix . . . you know Jimi Hendrix?"

Another nod.

"There's a part where Jimi Hendrix plays 'The Star-Spangled Banner,' our national anthem, only he tears the hell out of it, kind of makes it burst into flames, and this was during the Vietnam War."

Another nod, only barely.

"I know you can play like that. I saw you do it on TV."

By that time he was turning around and looking at his uncle.

"If I were the generals, I'd be worried, big time."

Chit grabbed his cell phone from his pocket. It hadn't gone off, but he looked at it like it had, and he excused himself and left the room.

I was so stupid. I'd lost my head and was talking to him like he was a rock star in America, immune from prosecution, thinking his uncle really was his uncle and his friend. But the guy was a spook, there to monitor the interview, for sure.

So we sat there in silence for a minute with the uncle, and then my companion tried to break the tension by asking him if he meditates.

"Yes," the uncle said, "more when I was younger than now. Now not as much as I would like."

"What do you like about it?"

"Meditation makes you free," he said. "No worries, no anxiety."

"See?" she said to me. "You should meditate. It would make you less crazy."

And I must have been crazy, because I just couldn't shut up. I asked the uncle, "Do you know what I'm talking about? Do you understand what I'm saying about the guitar?"

"Yes," he said, "I think it sometimes might be true, but what you say will not happen here. People listen to Iron Cross to be happy, to forget their lives. They gamble on football, English Premier League, for the same reason. It's a diversion."

"So you don't see another rebellion coming, like what happened in 1988?"

"No, people are busy finding money to buy things they want. Boys today want to fight in video games, not in the street."

"Then what can help?"

He thought for a minute and said, "I'm afraid nothing can help this."

Chit came back into the room, apologized again, and sat down. There were beads of sweat on his forehead, and his light had gone off. I'd blown it. The interview was over. But as we were leaving, Chit said Iron Cross was going to play on Friday in the park, outdoors, and if we wanted to come, he'd have some tickets brought by our hotel.

The next day we went to an Internet café to try to find some information on Iron Cross. We'd gone in once before, but left when the guy behind the counter told us to write down our passport numbers and the name of our hotel, and we noticed that his computer screen showed the website addresses that every customer in the room was visiting. But people on the street would tell us only that Iron Cross was the best band in the country, nothing more. And there had to be more, a lot more, than this. So we went in and wrote down our information and Googled Iron Cross. Only a few stories came up, but enough to realize the band was under pressure.

The first incident happened in 1995 when the band's lead singer, Lay Phyu (pronounced "pew"), came out with a solo album called *Power 54*. The title had been approved by the censors, and the CD was in the stores before the authorities realized that 54 is Aung San Suu Kyi's address on University Avenue in Rangoon. The government sent men out in the streets with bullhorns demanding that anyone with a copy of the CD bring it out and hand it over so that it could be burned. They called in Lay Phyu for a meeting, whereupon he insisted that the name had nothing to do with Aung San Suu Kyi; it merely connoted the number of songs produced by Iron Cross to date, nothing more, and if they wanted he would change the name to *Power.* Iron Cross was banned from performing for a period of time, I don't know how long, but Lay Phyu didn't stop causing trouble.

He refused to sing propaganda songs, and a tour to America was canceled. His hair reached his waist and the government told him to cut it, so he shaved his head. Iron Cross was asked, or ordered, to perform at the wedding of a military officer's son, and Lay Phyu refused, saying, "These are not our people." Lay Phyu was a rebel, very popular among the poor as well as among the sons and daughters of the military junta.

It was the latter who came to the concert, which was by a lake in an arena the size of a baseball infield, the perimeter surrounded by trees and beer stands. The tickets cost $4 and the beer $1, and a teacher or a lawyer in Burma makes $20 a month, so the young people who came, maybe about four thousand, were not of this class. Boys arrived with boys, girls arrived with girls, and there was little interaction between them. About half the boys were dressed conservatively, in button-up shirts; the other half, the hipsters, wore T-shirts with dragons or NIR-VANA on the front, blue jeans, chains hanging from belts, necklaces, earrings, sneakers. The girls, except for maybe five, pretty much covered up. I saw three in short skirts and tight shirts, and two in dresses and high heels, but that was about it for the fashion show.

The band came out and launched into a cover of a song I'd heard before but couldn't name, maybe Nine Inch Nails or Metallica. The hipsters danced with their hands in the air; the others stood motionless. No women danced.

And Lay Phyu wasn't there. When the song ended, some of the crowd started chanting, "Lay Phyu! Lay Phyu! Lay Phyu!" But he didn't come out, and the band played another cover of a song I'd heard before but couldn't name, and then there was more chanting of "Lay Phyu!" But still no Lay Phyu.

I asked the guy next to me what was up, and he said Lay Phyu had been banned from performing. It had happened recently and everyone there knew about it — everybody but us. I wanted the revolution to start right there, but the band played on and the crowd forgot about

Lay Phyu. The hipsters got drunk and danced with their shirts off, tattoos bared, thrashing around in sort of a mosh-pit-type thing, getting more and more crazy, shaking their long hair and screaming out the words to the songs. Everybody knew the words to the songs, and as the night went on, the band slowed down, and it became kind of a group sing-along, the same thing we'd seen in the Baptist church. It made me think we'd made a big mistake after 9/11 by responding with military force. All we've accomplished so far in the war on terrorism is to make more terrorists, like the sorcerer's apprentice chopping up the broom with the ax. We should drop boom boxes instead of bombs. Tens of thousands of iPods falling with little parachutes . . . probably would cost less than the smallest bomb we've got.

But when it was over, it was over. No encores, no lighters. And the crowd, which had trickled in slowly, left as one great mass, like they couldn't get out of there fast enough, like they thought there was going to be trouble if they stayed, or they didn't want to be seen as individuals. Strength in numbers, even when running away.

We ended up in a cab that had the three girls in short skirts in the back seat. Two of them spoke nearly perfect English, which I thought was a stroke of good luck, but when I asked them "What's the deal with Lay Phyu?" they shut up and didn't speak a word until they got out of the cab at their apartment building. It was one quiet taxi ride, for sure.

A lot of people wouldn't talk about it, and from those who did I got four or five different answers: he was caught gambling at his house; he got into an argument with someone else in the band — an ego thing; he was a drug addict; and . . . while he'd been out of the country he'd recorded a song that was critical of the government and they finally found out about it. Nobody knew for sure, and this was okay with them.

But it was not okay with me. It pissed me off. If they didn't care what happened to Lay Phyu, then I found it hard to care about them. If you don't care, then it's not rock 'n' roll. If you don't care, it's not even music. When Lay Phyu didn't come out at the concert, the audience should have destroyed the stage. The Burmese people should not wait for the United States to send our troops, and they should not wait on the UN Security Council to approve a resolution. The Burmese people need to start the revolution themselves, like they did in 1988.

Listen: Aung San Suu Kyi is meditating on her back porch beside the lake. Sitting on a cushion in the lotus position, she empties her mind of thoughts and desires. She is not a prisoner. A frog plops in the water.

JOSHUA CLARK

■

American

FROM *New Orleans Review*

CHARTRES STREET WAS EMPTY of anything but sun and heat and a silence I expected at any moment to be filled with the bird's call that unfailingly swoons into the quietest pockets of the world. But it wasn't there yet. There wasn't even an insect. Hadn't been since yesterday morning. It was unnerving, just standing there, hearing every movement, every creak of bone, every swallow, breathing in pulses of silence while we gazed vacantly over sagging pastel shotgun houses.

"Looked just like mannequins floating out in front of my house," said Big Shot Trey Nasty. Foam from his tall boy ran down his six-inch fire-red goatee, the bubbles at last settling into its horned end. "Then one of them turned over and I saw the fingertips all puckered. A woman and a kid, this kid I'd pay five bucks to mow my lawn."

Nelle looked down at the unopened beer in her hands. Big Shot's block, on the other side of St. Claude, had taken eight feet of water.

"When it started flooding, I figured the storm drains were clogged," Big Shot said. "I put on my waders and went out into the street, felt along the gutter, but the drain was clear. They'd turned the pumps off. The city must've turned the pumps off. Then I bumped into the woman floating there. Her hand touched me. Them puckered fingertips."

"Tayl," I said, "your house on Lesseps, your mom's place too, they're not flooded?"

Tayl retched. He was siphoning gas from a Toyota, the only other vehicle on the block. The only tree on the block had fallen on it and crushed the hood and windshield.

"Water's just on the other side of St. Claude," said Big Shot. "His place is fine. Bywater's dry. How about you?"

"Same." I nodded toward Nelle. "She lives out by Lakeview. We haven't been over there yet because of all these shootings we keep hearing about. So is it going down now, the water?"

"It's coming up," said Tayl, wiping gasoline off his chin, his eyes red, tears streaming down his cheeks.

"From where?"

"That's what I'd like to know." Tayl spat. He screwed the funnel onto his gas can, walked across the street, and began filling his SUV.

A wiry old man wearing boxers and flip-flops rounded the corner, a couple tattoos long ago turned to green splotches on his chest, his skin brown and taut and smooth as driftwood. He bummed a beer and told us that Robért's was open. He said they were letting you take whatever you wanted. So the four of us piled into Tayl's Denali and headed for Elysian Fields, leaving the old man standing there in the middle of the street sucking on his beer.

There were only six other vehicles in the Robért's parking lot, but people of every color and age were spilling out of the grocery. The few who'd scored shopping carts were pushing ungodly masses of food, the others carrying loads in whatever makeshift containers they could find, some just kicking all the food they could through the parking lot.

The grocery store was cavernous in its darkness, cloudy liquid creeping over our flip-flops, our eyes trying to make sense of the dark, and the darker shapes within it, scurrying, colliding. We felt our way past the cash registers, past shifting figures, the dank black space around us pierced only by the flicker and glimmer of matches and lighters and a flashlight or two deeper in the store. I grabbed the latest *Atlantic* off the magazine rack, something on the cover about how Arafat ruined Palestine. "We need a flashlight," I said.

"Yeah, in the truck," said Big Shot.

We felt our way back outside. Big Shot pulled the largest flashlight I'd ever seen out of the back of the Denali. It was rectangular, the size and shape of a large shoebox. "Use it for alligator hunting," said Big Shot, storming back toward the entrance with us in tow. "Sun got nothing on this baby."

He was right. When we got back into the heat of the place, he turned it on and the whole grocery store became blinding noon. People who'd been groping in the dark could now see what was in front of their faces, their feet sloshing through the light's glare off the inch-deep colorless muck.

People started to follow us, scrambling to get into the light, pushing each other out of it. Big Shot shut it off. He flipped up a panel on the flashlight's top that emitted just enough of a glow for us to follow him and not bump into anything.

We found the beer section. Big Shot hit the light just long enough to see that only three dented cans of Milwaukee's Best Light were left. We stood shoulder to shoulder, crestfallen. We took apart some Barq's Root Beer display shelves. I handed one back to Nelle, but she didn't take it.

"Nelle?" I called quietly.

Nothing.

"Nelle?"

Again, nothing.

"Goddammit. Nelle!"

Two hulking figures stopped moving beside us. We stood silently facing each other, breathing in sweat. I could feel their stillness, their eyes, the frailty to the calm, the latent fear we all had of each other. Then the darkness began shifting around them again as they went back to loading their own trays with soda cans. I wanted to scream for her but was too afraid it would shatter this fragile civility, give voice to questions: Who is it that's just behind me, bumping their ass into mine? Who just hit me with their elbows? Who just splashed me, knocked my tray over, took the last Sunny D even though he already had eleven of them? We were all waiting for the first drop of panic, and I wasn't about to let it out.

"Nelle," I whispered with all the rage and volume a whisper can carry. "Shit. Hit the light for a second." He did. She wasn't in the aisle.

Tayl tapped me on the shoulder, pointed behind me. "Look."

"Oh my God," I said.

"Jesus Christ," said Big Shot.

"They haven't touched the imports," said Tayl.

The first few cartons we picked up fell apart from all the slop they'd been sitting in, and the bottles slid to the floor, smashed, and added to the sludge. We picked the rest up from the bottom, loaded up, and the three of us headed back to the Denali — Dos Equis, Dos Equis Amber, St. Pauli Girl, Foster's, Beck's, Harp, Bass, Red Stripe, Corona, Corona Light, Negro Modelo, Newcastle, Boddington, and Guinness. The Heineken was gone.

As we walked back inside, a teenage girl, her lips and cheeks pierced, strings of red tear tattoos falling from both eyes, pushed past us on her way out with what looked like an industrial-sized laundry cart loaded with enough food to start her own small grocery store. A girl with a pink mohawk poked her head out of the top of the cart between bags of Fritos and asked me what time it was.

"Three-thirty, something like that," I said.

"We all need to get out of here, because at four they're going to blow the levee to save the Quarter," she said. "Doesn't that suck?" Then she disappeared back into the Fritos.

We hit every aisle, one at a time. Tayl and I would stand behind Big Shot at the beginning of each one as he illuminated it for about two seconds, before anyone else had a chance to see anything, then we'd scramble in the dark, fumbling around for what we'd seen that we wanted, trying to remember where it was. It was about hit or miss. I still hadn't seen Nelle, and I continued to whisper for her intermittently, still breathing the sweat of the place in darkness so close it seemed to press my own sweat back into my pores.

When we walked out for the fourth time, the edges of the trays slicing into our bleeding fingers, I had salted and unsalted peanuts, almonds, macadamias, cashews, roasted walnuts, red beans, white beans, white rice, brown rice, long grain rice, wild rice, saffron rice, dirty rice, basmati rice, broccoli-and-cheese couscous, twelve boxes of white-chocolate sugar-free Jell-O instant pudding mix, and four liters of prune juice, which I'd thought was cran-raspberry cocktail. I heaped it all on top of the already two-foot-deep pile in the SUV. Big Shot had five cases of the Big Shot strawberry soda from which he'd gotten his name. Tayl had meant to load up on Cheetos and instead walked out with twenty bags of sun-dried-tomato vegetarian chips cooked in olive oil, which left an aftertaste like pennies in my mouth as we walked back in again.

A kid who couldn't have been older than thirteen, wearing a red bandanna pulled high over his nose and mouth, heaved a large black safe out of the manager's office, just inside the entrance. He picked up a sledgehammer and started going at it. We agreed this would be our last trip in. It was time for liquor.

And every ounce of it was gone. Big Shot hit the light to see what was in the darkness past the liquor. There must have been hundreds of bottles of wine, every shelf full up and untouched. We knew we weren't getting ice anytime soon, so reds it was. We didn't waste time looking at the brands, only the prices, in the dim glow of the flashlight, grabbing anything over $10 as the sledgehammer clanged away steadily behind us. By the time we'd loaded a couple dozen bottles on each of our trays, the kid was really getting into it. He paid us no attention as we shuffled around him back outside, sweat dripping off the pointed tip of his bandanna.

I dumped my wine in the truck, tossed the Barq's shelf in after it, told Tayl to wait a second, and dashed back inside.

I stood in the entrance, screamed, "Nelle!"

The sledgehammer stopped. The kid looked up at me, the whites of his eyes, just above his bandanna, catching some spark of light that perforated the darkness. In ringing silence the shuffle of the place behind him roared, chaos building without the rhythm of his sledgehammer. He looked at me as if to ask why I would let such a thing happen — did I know the consequences, what beast could come tearing out of the dark if he didn't keep its pulse steady? He shifted his man-sized fingers around the shaft, forearm muscles twitching, shining ribs heaving, white boxers sweat-soaked, beads of sweat still falling from the bandanna's tip.

"Here," came her voice, from somewhere too far away for me to know where "here" was.

"Nelle!" I shouted louder, and bolted past the kid. "Nelle?"

The sledgehammer made a deep crash, then it shifted into a more tinny, piercing ring with every blow, like it had struck another level of the safe.

Little fires lit dark faces all around. Someone knocked me into a magazine rack. "Where?" I called. Only the sledgehammer's ringing echo called back. I walked down an aisle, whispers crowding around me, the air too close to hear them. I came out into the very back of the store. A wet hand grabbed my ankle. "Here," she said. A flickering match, someone rummaging through cold cuts, lit her silhouette. She was sitting in the thick muck on the floor below me.

"What are you doing, baby? We got to get out of here."

"American cheese," she said. She was crying. "Where's the American cheese? That's all I wanted, and I can't find it anywhere." She broke into sobs. The person beside us dropped the match into the liquid on the floor. It hissed, then he swore, bumped into me, jabbing me with an elbow before flailing and sloshing through the darkness toward the exit.

I leaned down. "Baby, listen. We need to go."

I reached out, searching the darkness until my hand ran into packages of shredded cheese. I felt farther down, found her shoulder, her hips, her knees. She'd fallen over onto her side and folded her knees into her chest. "Now, baby. Right now."

I grabbed her underneath the arm, pulled her up.

We took little steps, shuffling through the sludge, now well over our toes, all the little flickering matches one by one going out around us, the sledgehammer's pace quickening as we approached it. I looked hard at the safe for the first time as we made our way around the kid. It didn't have a single scratch on it.

Outside, Nelle shielded her eyes, water seeping past us out into the parking lot now. People stood there guarding enormous quantities of food heaped on the ground before them, unsure what to do next.

Nelle was soaked, her hair clotted, dripping with something the color of sour milk, her eyes swollen but impossibly dry. She smelled sweet, of fresh ruby-red grapefruit juice and strawberry-banana yogurt.

Tayl had the truck running. He looked at Nelle and shook his head. I popped the back, grabbed a bottle of a cabernet-shiraz blend from southern Australia. I told Tayl we'd walk, meet them back at his place in the Bywater — the car was too full as it was. He told us to round up anyone who wanted to eat well tonight, said he'd have a couple dozen lamb chops going on the grill by the time we got there.

As he pulled out, a gray-bearded man, his skin barely a shade lighter than the black polyester shirt that hung loose over his sunken, hunched frame, walked up to Nelle and me and held out an open bag of cookies. "Y'all want some shortbread cookies?" he asked.

"No thanks," I said.

"You sure?"

"We have plenty," I said. "Thank you."

"I only wanted a couple. You see, I got me a sweet tooth and just couldn't resist having a couple shortbreads. I was going to put the rest back inside, but now, well, it looks like it's getting a little scarier in there now. I can't just let them waste."

We began walking out of the parking lot. Nelle broke away from me, turned to the old man, who was still watching us. "Do you need anything else?" she asked him. "Any food or water or anything?"

"No, no," he said.

"You come with us," said Nelle. "We have plenty where we're going. It's not far. We'll have a barbecue. We can get your family. Do you have family here?"

"No, no, that's okay," he said. "I only wanted a couple shortbreads. You see, I got me a sweet tooth."

He looked down at the cookies in his hand, extended them in offering to the people scattering around him, away from him and away from the building with all the food they could hold, ignoring him on their way back to the neighborhood. And then there were the people with garbage bags slung over their shoulders, the ones paying no attention to the old man or Robért's, walking along St. Claude Avenue in the opposite direction, ones who'd given up waiting on the Industrial Canal levee for the National Guard and had already walked through the entire Bywater on their way to the Superdome.

Across the street, on the other side of St. Claude, was water, the first flooding we'd actually seen. Just a few inches at first, then deeper and deeper into the distance until it swallowed cars, then trucks, then homes. There was a heap of mannequins piled up in the neutral ground, torsos, arms, legs, heads dirty and mutilated, all of them white, more and more black people walking by them, by us, as I sifted through the mannequins, broke the index finger off one. I picked up a brick from the crumbled wall of some crumbled building, put the wine down on the sidewalk. I held the mannequin finger, its tip pointing down on top of the cork, and pounded the broken top end lightly with the brick. Wine flew up into my face as I knocked the cork into the bottle. I took a sip, handed the bottle to Nelle. "Here."

A young couple with dreadlocks and backpacks walked by, asked us if we'd heard the news — "They just shot some girl dead in the back of Robért's," said the girl. "Just a couple minutes ago. Some white girl who'd gotten lost from her friends. They shot her for cheese. We're getting the hell out of here."

"What time is it?" Nelle asked them.

"About quarter to four."

"Here," said Nelle, holding the wine out to them. "They're blowing the levee in a few minutes."

The couple studied her, half her body wet with the cloudy muck now congealing in her hair. When they handed the bottle back to us, we said farewell and walked along the neutral ground toward the Industrial Canal, Nelle's puckered fingers entwined in mine. The water stayed just to our left, the Bywater dry to our right, both within reach. We could practically smell the barbecue, the dirty rice cooking on a skillet on the grill, peppers and onions simmering while women dragged their children past us in the opposite direction, toward Canal Street, their fathers and brothers and husbands hunched beneath the weight of what was left heaped into green garbage bags over their shoulders, dizzy, so dehydrated they were no longer even sweating. And we waited for the levee to blow, for the explosion, the water, for the day to die so we wouldn't have to see Big Shot's house, a few blocks up from Tayl's, while we ate those lamb chops.

■

What Is Your Dangerous Idea?

Each year the Edge Foundation (www.edge.org) asks dozens of scientists one provocative question and then collects the answers on their website and in a subsequent book. The question they asked of scientists in 2006 was "What is your dangerous idea?" Below are some of the most interesting answers.

Laws Requiring Parental Licensure

DAVID LYKKEN is a behavioral geneticist and emeritus professor at the University of Minnesota. He is the author of *Happiness*.

I believe that during my grandchildren's lifetime the U.S. Supreme Court will find a way to approve laws requiring parental licensure.

Traditional societies in which children are socialized collectively, the method to which our species is evolutionarily adapted, have very little crime. In the United States, the number of fatherless children, living with unmarried mothers, currently some 10 million in all, has increased more than 400 percent since 1960, while the violent crime rate rose 500 percent by 1994, before dipping slightly due to a de-layed but equal increase in the number of prison inmates (from 240,000 to 1.4 million). In 1990, across the fifty states, the correla-tion between the violent crime rate and the proportion of illegitimate births was 0.7.

About 70 percent of incarcerated delinquents, of teenage pregnan-cies, of adolescent runaways, involve (I think result from) fatherless rearing. Because these frightening curves continue to accelerate, I believe we must eventually confront the need for parental licensure — you can't keep that newborn unless you are twenty-one, married, and self-supporting — not just for society's safety, but so that those babies will have a chance for life, liberty, and the pursuit of happiness.

We Have No Souls

JOHN HORGAN is the director of the Center for Science Writings at Stevens Institute of Technology. He is the author, most recently, of *Rational Mysticism: Spirituality Meets Science in the Search for Enlightenment.*

This year's Edge question makes me wonder: Which ideas pose a greater potential danger? False ones or true ones? Illusions or the lack thereof? As a believer in and lover of science, I certainly hope that the truth will set us free, and save us, but sometimes I'm not so sure.

The dangerous, probably true idea I'd like to dwell on is that we humans have no souls. The soul is that core of us that supposedly transcends and even persists beyond our physicality, lending us a fundamental autonomy, privacy, and dignity. In his 1994 book *The Astonishing Hypothesis: The Scientific Search for the Soul,* the late, great Francis Crick argued that the soul is an illusion perpetuated, like Tinkerbell, only by our belief in it. Crick opened his book with this manifesto: "'You,' your joys and your sorrows, your memories and your ambitions, your sense of personal identity and free will, are in fact no more than the behavior of a vast assembly of nerve cells and their associated molecules." Note the quotation marks around "You." The subtitle of Crick's book was almost comically ironic, since he was clearly trying not to find the soul but to crush it out of existence.

I once told Crick that "The Depressing Hypothesis" would have been a more accurate title for his book, since he was, after all, just reiterating the basic, materialist assumption of modern neurobiology and, more broadly, all of science. Until recently, it was easy to dismiss this assumption as moot, because brain researchers had made so little progress in tracing cognition to specific neural processes. Even self-proclaimed materialists, who accept intellectually that we are just meat machines, could harbor a secret, sentimental belief in a soul of the gaps. But recently the gaps have been closing, as neuroscientists — egged on by Crick in the last two decades of his life — have begun unraveling the so-called neural code, the software that transforms electrochemical pulses in the brain into perceptions, memories, decisions, emotions, and other constituents of consciousness.

I've argued elsewhere that the neural code may turn out to be so complex that it will never be fully deciphered. But sixty years ago, some biologists feared the genetic code was too complex to crack. Then, in 1953, Crick and Watson unraveled the structure of DNA, and researchers quickly established that the double helix mediates an astonishingly simple genetic code governing the heredity of all organisms. Science's success in deciphering the genetic code, which has culminated in the Human Genome Project, has been widely acclaimed — and with good reason, because knowledge of our genetic makeup could allow us to reshape our innate nature. A solution to the neural code could give us much greater, more direct control over ourselves than mere genetic manipulation.

Will we be liberated or enslaved by this knowledge? Officials in the Pentagon, the major funder of neural-code research, have openly broached the prospect of cyborg warriors who can be remotely controlled via brain implants, like the assassin in the recent remake of *The Manchurian Candidate*. On the other hand, a cult-like group of self-described "wireheads" looks forward to the day when implants allow us to create our own realities and achieve ecstasy on demand.

Either way, when our minds can be programmed like personal computers, then, perhaps, we will finally abandon the belief that we have immortal, inviolable souls — unless, of course, we program ourselves to believe.

The Evolution of Evil

DAVID M. BUSS is a psychologist at the University of Texas, Austin. He is the author of *The Murderer Next Door: Why the Mind Is Designed to Kill*.

When most people think of torturers, stalkers, robbers, rapists, and murderers, they imagine crazed, drooling monsters with maniacal

Charles Manson–like eyes. The calm, normal-looking image staring back at you from the bathroom mirror reflects a truer representation. The dangerous idea is that all of us contain within our large brains adaptations whose functions are to commit despicable atrocities against our fellow humans — atrocities most would label evil.

The unfortunate fact is that killing has proved to be an effective solution to an array of adaptive problems in the ruthless evolutionary games of survival and reproductive competition: preventing injury, rape, or death; protecting one's children; eliminating a crucial antagonist; acquiring a rival's resources; securing sexual access to a competitor's mate; preventing an interloper from appropriating one's own mate; and protecting vital resources needed for reproduction.

The idea that evil has evolved is dangerous on several counts. If our brains contain psychological circuits that can trigger murder, genocide, and other forms of malevolence, then perhaps we can't hold those who commit carnage responsible: "It's not my client's fault, your honor. His evolved homicide adaptations made him do it." Understanding causality, however, does not exonerate murderers, whether the tributaries can be traced to human evolutionary history or to modern exposure to alcoholic mothers, violent fathers, or the ills of bullying, poverty, drugs, or computer games. It would be dangerous if the theory of the evolved murderous mind was misused to let killers go free.

The evolution of evil is dangerous for a more disconcerting reason. We like to believe that evil can be objectively located in a particular set of evil deeds, or within the subset of people who perpetrate horrors on others, regardless of the perspective of the perpetrator or victim. That is not the case. The perspectives of the perpetrator and victim differ profoundly. Many view killing a member of one's in-group, for example, to be evil, but take a different view of killing those in the outgroup. Some people point to the biblical commandment "thou shalt not kill" as an absolute. Closer biblical inspection reveals that this injunction applied only to murder within one's group.

Conflict with terrorists provides a modern example. Osama bin Laden declared: "The ruling to kill the Americans and their allies — civilians and military — is an individual duty for every Muslim who can do it in any country in which it is possible to do it." What is evil from the perspective of an American who is a potential victim is an act of responsibility and higher moral good from the terrorist's perspective. Similarly, when President Bush identified an "axis of evil," he rendered it moral for Americans to kill those falling under that axis — a judgment undoubtedly considered evil by those whose lives have become imperiled.

At a rough approximation, we view as evil people who inflict massive evolutionary fitness costs on us, our families, or our allies. No one summarized these fitness costs better than the feared conqueror Genghis Khan (1167–1227): "The greatest pleasure is to vanquish your enemies, to chase them before you, to rob them of their wealth, to see their near and dear bathed in tears, to ride their horses and sleep on the bellies of their wives and daughters."

We can be sure that the families of the victims of Genghis Khan saw him as evil. We can be just as sure that his many sons, whose harems he filled with women of the conquered groups, saw him as a venerated benefactor. In modern times, we react with horror at Genghis Khan's description of the deep psychological satisfaction he gained from inflicting fitness costs on victims while purloining fitness fruits for himself. But it is sobering to realize that perhaps half a percent of the world's population today are descendants of Genghis Khan.

On reflection, the dangerous idea may not be that murder historically has been advantageous to the reproductive success of killers; nor that we all house homicidal circuits in our brains; nor even that all of us are lineal descendants of ancestors who murdered. The danger comes from people who refuse to recognize that there are dark sides of human nature that cannot be wished away by attributing them to the modern ills of culture, poverty, pathology, or exposure to media violence. The danger comes from failing to gaze into the mirror and come to grips with the capacity for evil in all of us.

More Anonymity Is Good

KEVIN KELLY is the editor at large of *Wired* and the author of *Cool Tools*.

More anonymity is good. That's a dangerous idea.

Fancy algorithms and cool technology make true anonymity in mediated environments more possible today than ever before. At the same time, this techno-combo makes true anonymity in physical life much harder. For every step that masks us, we move two steps toward totally transparent unmasking. We have caller ID, but also caller-ID block, and then caller-ID-only filters. Coming up: biometric monitoring and little place to hide. A world where everything about a person can be found and archived is a world with no privacy, and therefore many technologists are eager to maintain the option of easy anonymity as a refuge for the private.

However, in every system I have seen where anonymity becomes common, the system fails. The recent taint in the honor of Wikipedia stems from the extreme ease in which anonymous declarations can be put into a very visible public record. Communities infected with anonymity will either collapse or shift the anonymous to the pseudo-anonymous, as on eBay, where you have a traceable identity behind an invented nickname. Or voting, where you can authenticate an identity without tagging it to a vote.

Anonymity is like a rare-earth metal. These elements are a necessary ingredient in keeping a cell alive, but the amount needed is a mere hard-to-measure trace. In larger doses these heavy metals are some of the most toxic substances known. They kill. Anonymity is the same. As a trace element in vanishingly small doses, it's good for the system by enabling the occasional whistleblower or persecuted fringe. But if anonymity is present in any significant quantity, it will poison the system.

There's a dangerous idea circulating that the option of anonymity should always be at hand, and that it is a noble antidote to technologies of control. This is like pumping up the levels of heavy metals in your body to make it stronger.

Privacy can be won only by trust, and trust requires persistent identity, if only pseudo-anonymously. In the end, the more trust the better. Like all toxins, anonymity should be kept as close to zero as possible.

Drugs May Change the Patterns of Human Love

HELEN FISHER is a research professor in the Department of Anthropology at Rutgers University. She is the author of *Why We Love*.

Serotonin-enhancing antidepressants, such as Prozac and many others, can jeopardize feelings of romantic love, feelings of attachment to a spouse or partner, one's fertility, and one's genetic future.

I am working with psychiatrist Andy Thomson on this topic. We base our hypothesis on patient reports, fMRI studies, and other data on the brain. Foremost, as SSRIs (selective serotonin reuptake inhibitors) elevate serotonin, they also suppress dopaminergic pathways in the brain. Because romantic love is associated with elevated activity in dopaminergic pathways, it follows that SSRIs can jeopardize feelings of intense romantic love. SSRIs also curb obsessive thinking and blunt the emotions — central characteristics of romantic love. One patient described this reaction well, writing:

> After two bouts of depression in 10 years, my therapist recommended I stay on serotonin-enhancing antidepressants indefinitely. As appreciative as I was to have regained my health, I found that my usual enthusiasm for life was replaced with blandness. My romantic feelings for my wife declined drastically. With the approval of my therapist, I gradually discontinued my medication. My enthusiasm returned and our romance is now as strong as ever. I am prepared to deal with another bout of depression if need be, but in my case the long-term side effects of antidepressants render them off limits.

SSRIs also suppress sexual desire, sexual arousal, and orgasm in as many as 73 percent of users. These sexual responses evolved to enhance courtship, mating, and parenting. Orgasm produces a flood of oxytocin and vasopressin, chemicals associated with feelings of attachment and pair-bonding behavior. Orgasm is also a device by which women assess potential mates. Women do not reach orgasm with every coupling, and the "fickle" female orgasm is now regarded as an adaptive mechanism by which women distinguish males who are willing to expend the time and energy to satisfy them. The onset of female anorgasmia may jeopardize the stability of a long-term mateship as well.

Serotonin-enhancing antidepressants also inhibit males' evolved mechanisms for mate selection, partnership formation, and marital stability. The penis stimulates to give pleasure and advertise the male's psychological and physical fitness; it also deposits seminal fluid in the vaginal canal, fluid that contains dopamine, oxytocin, vasopressin, testosterone, estrogen, and other chemicals that most likely influence a female partner's behavior.

These medications can also influence one's genetic future. Serotonin increases prolactin by stimulating prolactin-releasing factors. Prolactin can impair fertility by suppressing the release of hypothalamic GnRH (gonadotropin-releasing hormones) and pituitary FSH (follicle-stimulating hormones) and LH (luteinizing hormones) and/ or suppressing ovarian hormone production. Clomipramine, a strong serotonin-enhancing antidepressant, adversely affects sperm volume and motility.

I believe that *Homo sapiens* has evolved (at least) three primary, distinct, yet overlapping neural systems for reproduction. The sex drive evolved to motivate ancestral men and women to seek sexual union with a range of partners; romantic love evolved to enable them to focus their courtship energy on a preferred mate, thereby conserving mating time and energy; attachment evolved to enable them to rear a child through infancy together. The complex and dynamic interactions among these three brain systems suggest that any medication that changes their chemical checks and balances is likely to alter an individual's courting, mating, and parenting tactics, ultimately affecting their fertility and genetic future.

The reason this is a dangerous idea is that the huge drug industry is heavily invested in selling these drugs; millions of people currently take these medications worldwide; and as these drugs become generic, many more people will take them — inhibiting their ability to fall in love and stay in love. And if patterns of human love subtly change, all sorts of social and political atrocities can escalate.

The Multiverse

Brian Greene is a physicist and mathematician at Columbia University. He is the author, most recently, of *The Fabric of the Cosmos.*

The notion that there are universes beyond our own — the idea that we are but one member of a vast collection of universes called the multiverse — is highly speculative, but both exciting and humbling.

It's also an idea that suggests a radically new but inherently risky approach to certain scientific problems.

An essential working assumption in the sciences is that with adequate ingenuity, technical facility, and hard work, we can explain what we observe. The impressive progress made over the past few hundred years is testament to the apparent validity of this assumption. But if we are part of a multiverse, then our universe may have properties that are beyond traditional scientific explanation. Here's why:

Theoretical studies of the multiverse (within inflationary cosmology and string theory, for example) suggest that the detailed properties of the other universes may be significantly different from our own. In some, the particles making up matter may have different masses or electrical charges; in others, the fundamental forces may differ in strength and even number from those we experience; in others still, the very structure of space and time may be unlike anything we've ever seen.

In this context, the quest for fundamental explanations of particular properties of our universe — for example, the observed strengths of the nuclear and electromagnetic forces — takes on a very different character. The strengths of these forces may vary from universe to universe, and thus it may simply be a matter of chance that in our universe these forces have the particular strengths with which we're familiar. More intriguingly, we can even imagine that in the other universes where their strengths are different, conditions are not hospitable to our form of life. (With different force strengths, the processes giving rise to long-lived stars and stable planetary systems — on which life can form and evolve — can easily be disrupted.) In this setting, there would be no deep explanation for the observed force strengths. Instead, we would find ourselves living in a universe in which the forces have their familiar strengths simply because we couldn't survive in any of the others where the strengths were different.

If true, the idea of a multiverse would be a Copernican revolution realized on a cosmic scale. It would be a rich and astounding upheaval, but one with potentially hazardous consequences. Beyond the inherent difficulty in assessing its validity, when should we allow the multiverse framework to be invoked in lieu of a more traditional scientific explanation? Had this idea surfaced a hundred years ago, might researchers have chalked up various mysteries to how things just happen to be in our corner of the multiverse, and not pressed on to discover all the wondrous science of the last century?

Thankfully that's not how the history of science played itself out — at least not in our universe. But the point is manifest. While some mysteries may indeed reflect nothing more than the particular universe we find ourselves inhabiting within the multiverse, other mysteries are worth struggling with because they are the result of deep, underlying physical laws. The danger, if the multiverse idea takes root, is that researchers may too quickly give up the search for such underlying explanations. When faced with seemingly inexplicable observations, researchers may invoke the framework of the multiverse prematurely — proclaiming some phenomenon or other to merely reflect conditions in our own bubble universe and thereby failing to discover the deeper understanding that awaits us.

Science Will Never Silence God

JESSE BERING is the director of the Institute of Cognition and Culture at Queen's University, Belfast.

With each meticulous turn of the screw in science, with each tightening up of our understanding of the natural world, we pull more taut the straps over God's muzzle. From botany to bioengineering, from physics to psychology, what is science really but true revelation — and what is revelation but the negation of God? It is a humble pursuit we scientists engage in: racing toward reality. Many of us suffer the harsh glare of the American theocracy, whose heart still beats loud and strong in this new year of the twenty-first century. We bravely favor truth, in all its wondrous, amoral, and meaningless complexity, over the singularly destructive Truth born of the trembling minds of our ancestors. But my dangerous idea, I fear, is that no matter how far our thoughts vault into the eternal sky of scientific progress, no matter how dazzling the effects of this progress, God will always bite through his muzzle and banish us from the starry night of humanistic ideals.

Science is an endless series of binding and rebinding his breath. There will never be a day when God does not speak for the majority. There will never even be a day when he does not whisper into the ears of the most godless scientists. This is because God is not an idea, nor a cultural invention, nor an "opiate of the masses," nor any such thing. God is *a way of thinking* that was rendered permanent by natural selection.

As scientists, we must toil and labor and toil again to silence God, but ultimately this is like cutting off our ears to hear more clearly. God too is a biological appendage; until we acknowledge this fact for what it is, until we rear our children with this knowledge, He will continue to howl his discontent for all of time.

Applied History

STEWART BRAND, the founder of the *Whole Earth Catalog*, is the author of *The Clock of the Long Now.*

All historians understand that they must never, ever talk about the future. Their discipline requires that they deal in facts, and the future doesn't have any yet. A solid theory of history might be able to embrace the future, but all such theories have been discredited. Thus historians do not offer, and are seldom invited, to take part in shaping public policy. They leave that to economists.

But discussions among policy makers always invoke history anyway, usually in simplistic form. "Munich" and "Vietnam," devoid of detail or nuance, stand for certain kinds of failure. "Marshall Plan" and "Man on the Moon" stand for certain kinds of success. Such a totemic invocation of history is the opposite of learning from history, and Santayana's warning continues in force: "Those who cannot remember the past are condemned to repeat it."

A dangerous thought: What if public-policy makers have an obligation to engage historians, and historians have an obligation to try to help?

And instead of just retailing advice, go generic. Historians could set about developing a rigorous subdiscipline called Applied History.

There is only one significant book on the subject, published in

1988. *Thinking in Time: The Uses of History for Decision Makers* was written by the late Richard Neustadt and Ernest May, who long taught a course on the subject at Harvard's Kennedy School of Government. (A course called "Reasoning from History" is currently taught there by Alexander Keyssar.)

Done wrong, Applied History could paralyze public decision-making and corrupt the practice of history — that's the danger. But done right, Applied History could make decision-making and policy far more sophisticated and adaptive, and it could invest the study of history with the level of consequence it deserves.

A Political System Based on Empathy

SIMON BARON-COHEN is a psychologist at the Autism Research Centre at Cambridge University. He is the author of *The Essential Difference: Male and Female Brains and the Truth about Autism.*

Imagine a political system based not on legal rules (systemizing) but on empathy. Would this make the world a safer place?

The British Parliament, the United States Congress, the Israeli Knesset, the French National Assembly, the Italian Senato della Repubblica, the Spanish Congreso de los Diputados — what do such political chambers have in common? Existing political systems are based on two principles: getting power through combat, and then creating/revising laws and rules through combat.

Combat is sometimes physical (toppling your opponent militarily), sometimes economic (establishing a trade embargo to starve your opponent of resources), sometimes propaganda-based (waging a media campaign to discredit your opponent's reputation), and sometimes a voting-related activity (lobbying, forming alliances, fighting to win votes in key seats) with the aim of defeating the opposition.

Creating/revising laws and rules is what you do once you are in power. These might be constitutional rules, rules of precedence, judicial rulings, statutes, or other laws or codes of practice. Politicians battle for their rule-based proposal (which they hold to be best) to win and to defeat the opposition's rival proposal.

This way of doing politics is based on systemizing. First you analyze the most effective form of combat (itself a system) to win. If we do X, then we will obtain outcome Y. Then you adjust the legal code (another system). If we pass law A, we will obtain outcome B.

My colleagues and I have studied the essential difference between how men and women think. Our studies suggest that, on average, more men are systemizers and more women are empathizers. Since most political systems were set up by men, it may be no coincidence that we have ended up with political chambers built on the principles of systemizing.

So here's the dangerous new idea. What would it be like if our political chambers were based on the principles of empathizing? It is dangerous because it would mean a revolution in how we choose our politicians, how our political chambers govern, and how our politicians think and behave. We have never given such an alternative political process a chance. Might it be better and safer than what we currently have? Since empathy is about keeping in mind the thoughts and feelings of other people and not just your own, and being sensitive to another person's thoughts and feelings and not just riding roughshod over them, it is clearly incompatible with notions of "doing battle with the opposition" and "defeating the opposition" in order to win and hold on to power.

Currently we select party (and ultimately national) leaders based on "leadership" qualities. Can they make decisions decisively? Can they do what is in the best interest of the party or the country even if it means sacrificing others to follow through on a decision? Can they ruthlessly reshuffle their cabinet and cut people loose if they are no longer serving their interests? These are the qualities of a strong systemizer.

Note that we are not talking about whether such politicians are male or female. We are talking about how a politician, irrespective of gender, thinks and behaves.

We have had endless examples of systemizing politicians who were unable to resolve conflict. Empathizing politicians would perhaps follow the example of Nelson Mandela and F. W. de Klerk, who sat down to try to understand each other, to empathize with each other, even if the other was defined as a terrorist. To do this involves the empathic act of stepping into the other's shoes and identifying with the other's feelings.

The details of a political system based on empathizing would need a lot of working out, but we can imagine certain qualities that would have no place.

Gone would be politicians who are skilled orators but who simply deliver monologues, standing on a platform, pointing forcefully into the air to underline their insistence — even the body language containing an implied threat of poking their listeners in the chest or the face — to win over an audience. Gone too would be politicians so principled that they are rigid and uncompromising.

Instead we would elect politicians based on different qualities: those who are good listeners, who ask questions of others rather than assume they know the right course of action. We would instead have politicians who respond sensitively to a different point of view, and who can be flexible about where the dialogue might lead. Instead of seeking to control and dominate, our politicians would be seeking to support, enable, and care.

The Human Brain Will Never Understand the Universe

KARL SABBAGH, a writer and television producer, is the author of *The Riemann Hypothesis: The Greatest Unsolved Problem in Mathematics.*

Our brains may never be well enough equipped to understand the universe, and we are fooling ourselves if we think they will.

Why should we expect to be able eventually to understand how the universe originated, evolved, and operates? While human brains are complex and capable of many amazing things, there is not necessarily any match between the complexity of the universe and the complexity of our brains, any more than a dog's brain is capable of understanding every detail of the world of cats and bones, or the dynamics of stick trajectories when thrown. Dogs get by and so do we, but do we have a right to expect that the harder we puzzle over these things, the nearer we will get to the truth? Recently I stood in front of a three-meter-high model of the Ptolemaic universe in the Museum of the History of Science in Florence, and I remembered how well that worked as a representation of the motions of the planets until Copernicus and Kepler came along.

Nowadays, no element of the theory of giant interlocking cog wheels at work is of any use in understanding the motions of the stars and planets (indeed, Ptolemy himself did not argue that the universe really was run by giant cog wheels). Occam's razor is used to compare two theories and allow us to choose which is more likely to be true, but hasn't it become a comfort blanket whenever we are faced with aspects of the universe that seem unutterably complex — string theory, for example? But is string theory just the Ptolemaic clockwork *de nos jours?* Can it be succeeded by some simplification, or might the truth be even more complex and far beyond the neural networks of our brains to understand?

The history of science is littered with examples of two types of knowledge advancement. There is imperfect understanding that "sort of" works, which is then modified and replaced by something that works better, without destroying the validity of the earlier theory. Newton's theory of gravitation was replaced by Einstein. Then there is imperfect understanding that is replaced by some new idea that owes nothing to older ones. Phlogiston theory, the ether, and so on were replaced by ideas that saved the phenomena, led to predictions, and convinced us that they were nearer the truth. Which of these categories really covers today's science? Could we be fooling ourselves by playing around with modern phlogiston?

And even if we are on the right track in some areas, how much of what there is to be understood in the universe do we really understand? Fifty percent? Five percent? The dangerous idea is that perhaps we understand one half of one percent, and all the brain and computer power we can muster may take us up to one or two percent in the lifetime of the human race.

Paradoxically, we may find that the only justification for pursuing scientific knowledge is for the practical applications it leads to — a view that runs contrary to the traditional support of knowledge for knowledge's sake. And why is this paradoxical? Because the most important advances in technology have come out of research that was not seeking to develop those advances but to understand the universe.

So if my dangerous idea is right — that the human brain and its products are actually incapable of understanding the truths about the universe — it will not, and should not, lead to any diminution at all in our attempts to do so. Which means, I suppose, that it's not really dangerous at all.

The Near-Term Inevitability of Radical Life Extension and Expansion

RAY KURZWEIL is an inventor and technologist. He is the author, most recently, of *The Singularity Is Near: When Humans Transcend Biology.*

My dangerous idea is the near-term inevitability of radical life extension and expansion. The idea is dangerous, however, only when contemplated from current linear perspectives.

First the inevitability: the power of information technologies is doubling each year and, moreover, comprises areas beyond computation, most notably our knowledge of biology and of our own intelligence. It took fifteen years to sequence HIV, and from that perspective the Human Genome Project seemed impossible in 1990. But the amount of genetic data we were able to sequence doubled every year, while the cost came down by half each year.

We finished the genome project on schedule and were able to sequence SARS in only thirty-one days. We are also gaining the means to reprogram the ancient information processes underlying biology. RNA interference can turn genes off by blocking the messenger RNA that expresses them. New forms of gene therapy are now able to place new genetic information in the right place on the right chromosome. We can create or block enzymes, the workhorses of biology. We are reverse-engineering — and gaining the means to reprogram — the information processes underlying disease and aging, and this work is accelerating, doubling every year. If we think linearly, then the idea of turning off all disease and aging processes appears far off in the future, just as the genome project did in 1990. On the other hand, if we factor in the doubling of the power of these technologies each year, the prospect of radical life extension is only a couple of decades away.

In addition to reprogramming biology, we will be able to go substantially beyond biology with nanotechnology, in the form of computerized nanobots in the bloodstream. If the idea of programmable devices the size of blood cells performing therapeutic functions in the bloodstream sounds like far-off science fiction, I would point out that we are doing this already in animals. One scientist cured type 1 diabetes in rats with blood-cell-sized devices containing seven nanometer pores that let insulin out in a controlled fashion and that block antibodies. If we factor in the exponential advances in computation and communication (price-performance multiplying by a factor of a billion in twenty-five years, while at the same time shrinking in size by a factor of thousands), these scenarios are highly realistic.

The apparent dangers are not real, but unapparent dangers are real. The apparent dangers are that a dramatic reduction in the death rate will create overpopulation and thereby strain energy and other resources and exacerbate environmental degradation. However, we need to capture only 1 percent of 1 percent of the sunlight to meet all of our energy needs (3 percent of 1 percent by 2025), and nano-engineered solar panels and fuel cells will be able to do this, thereby meeting all of our energy needs in the late 2020s with clean and renewable methods. Molecular nanoassembly devices will be able to manufacture a wide range of products, just about everything we need, with inexpensive tabletop devices. The power and price-performance of these systems will double each year, much faster than the doubling rate of the biological population. As a result, poverty and pollution will decline and ultimately vanish despite the growth of the biological population.

There are real downsides, however, and this is not a utopian vision. We have a new existential threat today in the potential of a bioterrorist to engineer a new biological virus. We actually do have the knowledge to combat this problem (for example, new vaccine technologies and RNA interference, which has been shown capable of destroying arbitrary biological viruses), but it will be a race. We will have similar challenges with the feasibility of self-replicating nanotechnology in the late 2020s. Containing these perils while we harvest the promise is arguably the most important issue we face.

Some people see these prospects as dangerous because they threaten their view of what it means to be human. There is a fundamental philosophical divide here. In my view, it is not our limitations that define our humanity. Rather, we are the species that seeks and succeeds in going beyond our limitations.

Where Goods Cross Frontiers, Armies Won't

MICHAEL SHERMER is the publisher of *Skeptic* magazine, a monthly columnist for *Scientific American,* and the author, most recently, of *Science Friction: Where the Known Meets the Unknown.*

Where goods cross frontiers, armies won't. Restated: Where economic borders between two nations are porous, political borders become impervious to armies.

Data from the new sciences of evolutionary economics, behavioral economics, and neuroeconomics reveal that when people are free to cooperate and trade (such as in game-theory protocols), they establish trust that is reinforced through neural pathways that release such bonding hormones as oxytocin. Thus modern biology reveals that where people are free to cooperate and trade, they are less likely to fight and kill those with whom they are cooperating and trading.

My dangerous idea is a solution to what I call the really hard problem: How best should we live? My answer: in a free society, defined by free-market economics and democratic politics — fiscal conservatism and social liberalism — leading to the greatest liberty for the greatest number. Since humans are by nature tribal, the overall goal is to expand the concept of the tribe to include all members of the species in a global free society. Free trade between all peoples is the surest way to reach this goal.

People have a hard time accepting free-market economics for the same reason they have a hard time accepting evolution: it is counterintuitive. Life looks intelligently designed, so our natural inclination is to infer that there must be an intelligent designer — a God. Similarly, the economy looks designed, so our natural inclination is to infer that we need a designer — a government. In fact, emergence and complexity theory explains how the principles of self-organization and emergence cause complex systems to arise from simple systems without a top-down designer.

Charles Darwin's natural selection is Adam Smith's invisible hand. Darwin showed how complex design and ecological balance were unintended consequences of individual competition among organisms. Smith showed how national wealth and social harmony were unintended consequences of individual competition among people. Nature's economy mirrors society's economy. Thus integrating evolution and economics — what I call evonomics — reveals that an old economic doctrine is supported by modern biology.

Runaway Consumerism Explains the Fermi Paradox

GEOFFREY MILLER, an evolutionary psychologist at the University of New Mexico, is the author of *The Mating Mind: How Sexual Choice Shaped the Evolution of Human Nature.*

The story goes like this: Sometime in the 1940s, Enrico Fermi was talking about the possibility of extraterrestrial intelligence with some other physicists. They were impressed that our galaxy holds one hundred billion stars, that life evolved quickly and progressively on Earth, and that an intelligent, exponentially reproducing species could colonize the galaxy in just a few million years. They reasoned that extraterrestrial intelligence should be common by now. Fermi listened patiently, then asked simply, "So, where is everybody?" That is, if extraterrestrial intelligence is common, why haven't we met any bright aliens yet? This conundrum became known as Fermi's paradox.

The paradox has become ever more baffling. More than 150 extrasolar planets have been identified in the past few years, suggesting that life-hospitable planets orbit most stars. Paleontology shows that organic life evolved very quickly after Earth's surface cooled and became life-hospitable. Given simple life, evolution shows a progressive trend toward larger bodies, brains, and social complexity. Evolutionary psychology reveals several credible paths from simple social minds to human-level creative intelligence. Yet forty-some years of intensive searching for extraterrestrial intelligence have yielded nothing. No radio signals, no credible spacecraft sightings, no close encounters of any kind.

So it looks as if there are two possibilities. Perhaps our science overestimates the likelihood of extraterrestrial intelligence evolving. Or perhaps evolved technical intelligence has some deep tendency to be self-limiting, even self-exterminating. After Hiroshima, some suggested that any aliens bright enough to make colonizing spaceships would be bright enough to make thermonuclear bombs, and would use them on each other sooner or later. Perhaps extraterrestrial intelligence always blows itself up. Fermi's paradox became, for a while, a cautionary tale about Cold War geopolitics.

I suggest a different, even darker solution to Fermi's paradox. Basically, I think the aliens don't blow themselves up; they just get addicted to computer games. They forget to send radio signals or colonize space because they're too busy with runaway consumerism and virtual-reality narcissism. They don't need Sentinels to enslave them in a Matrix; they do it to themselves, just as we are doing today.

The fundamental problem is that any evolved mind must pay attention to indirect cues of biological fitness rather than tracking fitness itself. We don't seek reproductive success directly; we seek out tasty foods that tend to promote survival and luscious mates who tend to produce bright, healthy babies. Modern results: fast food and pornography. Technology is fairly good at controlling external reality to promote our real biological fitness, but it's even better at delivering fake fitness — subjective cues of survival and reproduction without the real-world effects. Fresh organic fruit juice costs so much more than nutrition-free soda. Having real friends is so much more effort than watching *Friends* on TV. Actually colonizing the galaxy would be so much harder than pretending to have done so by filming *Star Wars*.

Fitness-faking technology tends to evolve much faster than our psychological resistance to it. The printing press is invented; people read more novels and have fewer kids; only a few curmudgeons lament this. The Xbox 360 is invented; people would rather play a high-resolution virtual ape in "Peter Jackson's King Kong" than be a perfect-resolution real human. Teens today must find their way through a carnival of addictively fitness-faking entertainment products: MP3,

DVD, TiVo, XM radio, Verizon cell phones, Spice cable, EverQuest online, instant messaging, Ecstasy, BC Bud. The traditional staples of physical, mental, and social development (athletics, homework, dating) are neglected. The few young people with the self-control to pursue the meritocratic path often get distracted at the last minute: the MIT graduates apply to do computer-game design for Electronic Arts rather than rocket science for NASA.

Around 1900, most inventions concerned physical reality: cars, airplanes, zeppelins, electric lights, vacuum cleaners, air conditioners, bras, zippers. In 2005, most inventions concern virtual entertainment — the top ten patent recipients are usually IBM, Matsushita, Canon, Hewlett-Packard, Micron Technology, Samsung, Intel, Hitachi, Toshiba, and Sony — not Boeing, Toyota, or Wonderbra. We have already shifted from a reality economy to a virtual economy, from physics to psychology, as the value driver and resource allocator. We are already disappearing up our own brainstems. Freud's pleasure principle triumphs over the reality principle. We narrowcast human-interest stories to each other rather than broadcast messages of universal peace and progress to other star systems.

Maybe the bright aliens did the same. I suspect that a certain period of fitness-faking narcissism is inevitable after any intelligent life evolves. This is the Great Temptation for any technological species — to shape their subjective reality to provide the cues of survival and reproductive success without the substance. Most bright alien species probably go extinct gradually, allocating more time and resources to their pleasures and less to their children.

Heritable variation in personality might allow some lineages to resist the Great Temptation and last longer. Those who persist will evolve more self-control, conscientiousness, and pragmatism. They will evolve a horror of virtual entertainment, psychoactive drugs, and contraception. They will stress the values of hard work, delayed gratification, child rearing, and environmental stewardship. They will combine the family values of the religious right with the sustainability values of the Greenpeace left.

My dangerous idea-within-an-idea is that this, too, is already happening. Christian and Muslim fundamentalists and anticonsumerism activists already understand exactly what the Great Temptation is and how to avoid it. They insulate themselves from our creative-class dream worlds and our EverQuest economics. They wait patiently for our fitness-faking narcissism to go extinct. Those practical-minded breeders will inherit the earth, as like-minded aliens may have inherited a few other planets. When they finally achieve Contact, it will not be a meeting of novel readers and game players. It will be a meeting of dead-serious superparents who congratulate each other on surviving not just the Bomb, but the Xbox. They will toast each other not in a soft-porn holodeck but in a sacred nursery.

Democracy May Be on Its Way Out

HAIM HARARI, a theoretical physicist, is the former president of the Weizmann Institute of Science.

Democracy may be on its way out. Future historians may determine that democracy will have been a one-century episode. It will disappear. This is a sad, truly dangerous, but very realistic idea (or, rather, prediction).

Falling boundaries between countries, cross-border commerce, merging economies, the instant global flow of information, and numerous other features of our modern society all lead to multinational structures. If you extrapolate this irreversible trend, you get the entire planet becoming one political unit. But in this unit, antidemocracy forces are now a clear majority. This majority increases by the day due to demographic patterns. All democratic nations have slow, vanishing, or negative population growth, while all antidemocratic and uneducated societies multiply fast. In democratic countries, most well-educated families remain small, while the least educated families are growing fast. This means that, both at the individual level and at the national level, the more people you represent, the less economic power you have. In a knowledge-based economy, in which the number of working hands is less important, this situation is much more nondemocratic than in the industrial age. As long as upward mobility of individuals and nations could neutralize this phenomenon, democracy was tenable. But when we apply this analysis to the entire planet as it evolves now, we see that democracy may be doomed.

To this idea we must add the regrettable fact that authoritarian multinational corporations by and large are better managed than democratic nation-states. Religious preaching, TV sound bites, cross-boundary TV incitement, and the freedom of spreading rumors and lies through the Internet encourage brainwashing and discourage rational thinking. Proportionately, more young women are growing up in societies that discriminate against them than in the more egalitarian societies, increasing the worldwide percentage of women treated as second-class citizens. Educational systems in most advanced countries are in a deep crisis, while modern education in many developing countries is almost nonexistent. A small, well-educated technological elite is becoming the main owner of intellectual property, which is by far the most valuable economic asset, while the rest of the world drifts toward fanaticism of one kind or another. Given all of the above, the unavoidable conclusion is that democracy, our least bad system of government, is on its way out.

Can we invent a better system? Perhaps. But this cannot happen if we are not allowed to utter the sentence "There may be a political system that is better than democracy." Today's political correctness does not permit one to say such things. The result of this prohibition will be an inevitable return to some kind of totalitarian rule, different from that of the emperors, the colonialists, or the landlords of the past, but not more just. On the other hand, open and honest thinking about this issue may lead either to a gigantic worldwide revolution in educating the poor masses, thus saving democracy, or to a careful search for a just (repeat, just) and better system.

The Idea That Ideas Can Be Dangerous

DANIEL GILBERT is the Harvard College Professor of Psychology at Harvard University. He is the author of *Stumbling on Happiness*.

"Dangerous" does not mean exciting or bold; it means likely to cause great harm. The most dangerous idea is the only dangerous idea: the idea that ideas can be dangerous.

We live in a world in which people are censured, demoted, imprisoned, beheaded, simply because they have opened their mouths, flapped their lips, and vibrated some air. Yes, those vibrations can make us feel sad or stupid or alienated. Tough shit. That's the price of admission to the marketplace of ideas. Hateful, blasphemous, prejudiced, vulgar, rude, or ignorant remarks are the music of a free society, and the relentless patter of idiots is how we know we're in one. When all the words in our public conversation are fair, good, and true, it's time to make a run for the fence.

■

Selling the General

FROM *Five Chapters* (www.fivechapters.com)

I

DOLLY'S FIRST BIG IDEA was the hat. She picked teal blue, fuzzy, with flaps that came down over the general's large, dried apricot ears. The ears were unsightly, Dolly thought, and best covered up.

When she saw the general's picture in the *Times* a few days later, she almost choked on her poached egg: he looked like a baby, a big sick baby with a giant mustache and a double chin. The headline couldn't have been worse: "General B's Odd Headgear Spurs Cancer Rumors, Local Unrest Grows."

Dolly bolted to her feet in her dingy kitchen and turned in a frantic circle, spilling tea on her bathrobe. She looked wildly at the general's picture. And then she realized: the ties. They hadn't cut off the ties under the hat as she'd instructed, and a big fuzzy bow under the general's double chin was disastrous. Dolly ran barefoot into her office/ bedroom and began plowing through fax pages, trying to unearth the most recent sequence of numbers she was supposed to call to reach Arc, the general's human-relations captain. The general moved a lot to avoid assassination, but Arc was meticulous about faxing Dolly their updated contact information. These faxes usually came at around three A.M., waking Dolly and sometimes her daughter, Lulu. Dolly never mentioned the disruption; the general and his team were under the impression that she was the top publicist in New York, a woman whose fax machine would be in an office with a panoramic view of New York City, not ten inches away from the foldout sofa where she slept. Dolly could only attribute this misapprehension to some dated article that had drifted their way on Google. Or maybe the general had known four years ago that he would want a publicist eventually, and had saved old newspapers or copies of *Vanity Fair* or *In Style* or *People*, where Dolly had been written about and profiled by her then nickname, La Doll.

The first call from the general's camp had come just in time: Dolly had hocked her last piece of jewelry. She was copy-reading textbooks until two A.M., sleeping until five, and then providing polite phone chitchat to aspiring English speakers in Tokyo until it was time to wake Lulu and fix her breakfast. And all of that wasn't nearly enough to keep Lulu at Miss Rutgers's School for Girls. Often Dolly's three allotted hours of sleep were spent in spasms of worry at the thought of the next monstrous tuition bill.

And then Arc had called. The general wanted an exclusive retainer. He wanted rehabilitation, American sympathy, an end to the CIA's assassination attempts. If Qaddafi could do it, why not he? Dolly wondered seriously if overwork and lack of sleep were making her hallucinate, but she named a price. Arc began taking down her banking information. "The general presumed your fee would be higher," he said, and if Dolly had been able to speak at that moment she would have said, That's my weekly retainer, hombre, not my monthly, or Hey, I haven't given you the formula that lets you calculate the actual price, or That's just for the two-week trial period when I decide whether I like working with you. But Dolly couldn't speak. She was crying.

When the first installment appeared in her bank account, Dolly's relief was so immense that it almost obliterated the tiny anxious muttering voice inside her: Your client is a genocidal dictator. Dolly had worked with shitheads before, God knew; if she didn't take this job, someone else would snap it up; being a publicist is about not judging your clients — these excuses were lined up in formation, ready for deployment should that small dissident voice pluck up its courage to speak with any volume. But lately Dolly couldn't even hear it.

Now, as she scuttled over her frayed Persian rug looking for the general's most recent numbers, the phone rang. It was six A.M. Dolly lunged, praying Lulu's sleep hadn't been disturbed.

"Hello?" But she knew who it was.

"We are not happy," said Arc.

"Me either," Dolly said. "You didn't cut off the —"

"The general is not happy."

"Arc, listen to me. You need to cut off the —"

"The general is not happy, Miss Peale."

"Listen to me, Arc."

"He is not happy."

"That's because — look, take a scissors —"

"He is not happy, Miss Peale."

Dolly went quiet. There were times, listening to Arc's silken monotone, when she'd been sure she heard a curl of irony around the words he'd been ordered to say, like he was speaking to her in code. Now there was a long, long pause. Dolly spoke very softly. "Arc, take a scissors and cut the ties off the hat. There shouldn't be a goddamned bow under the general's chin."

"He will no longer wear this hat."

"He has to wear the hat."

"He will not wear it. He refuses."

"Cut off the ties, Arc."

"Rumors have reached us, Miss Peale."

Her stomach lurched. "Rumors?"

"That you are not 'on top' as you once were. And now the hat is unsuccessful."

Dolly felt the negative forces pulling in around her. Standing there with the traffic of Eighth Avenue grinding past beneath her window, fingering her frizzy hair that she'd stopped coloring and allowed to grow in long and gray, she felt a kick of some deep urgency.

"I have enemies, Arc," she said. "Just like the general."

He was silent.

"If you listen to my enemies, I can't do my job. Now take out that nice silver pen I can see in your pocket every time you get your picture in the paper and write this down: Cut the strings off the hat. Lose the bow. Push the hat farther back on the general's head so some of his hair fluffs out in front. Do that, Arc, and let's see what happens."

Lulu had come into the room in her pink pajamas and was rubbing her eyes. Dolly looked at her watch, saw that her daughter had lost a half hour of sleep, and experienced an inner collapse at the thought of Lulu feeling tired at school. She rushed over and put her arms around her daughter's shoulders. Lulu received this embrace with the regal bearing that was her trademark.

Dolly had forgotten Arc, but now he spoke from the phone at her neck: "I will do it, Miss Peale."

It was several weeks before the general's picture appeared again. Now the hat was pushed back, and the ties were gone. The headline read, "Extent of B's War Crimes May Be Exaggerated, New Evidence Shows."

It was the hat. He looked sweet in the hat. How could a man in a fuzzy blue hat have used human bones to pave his roads?

La Doll had met with ruin on New Year's Eve three years before, at a wildly anticipated party that was projected, by the pundits she'd considered worth inviting, to rival Truman Capote's Black and White Ball. The Party, it was called, or the List. As in: Is she on the list? There were nominal hosts, all famous, but the real host, as everyone knew, was La Doll, who had more connections and access and juju than all of these people combined. And La Doll had made a very human mistake — or so she tried to soothe herself at night, when memories of her demise plowed through her like a hot poker, skewering her in her sofa bed, so she writhed in agony and drank brandy from the bottle. She'd thought that because she could do something very, very well — namely, get the best people in the world into one room at one time. She could do other things well too.

Like design. La Doll had had a vision: broad, translucent trays of oil and water suspended beneath small, brightly colored spotlights whose heat would make the opposing liquids twist and bubble and swirl. She'd imagined people craning their necks to look up, spellbound by the shifting liquid shapes. And they did look up. They marveled at the lighted trays; La Doll saw them do it from a small booth she'd had built high up and to one side so she could view the panorama of her achievement. From there, she was the first to notice, as midnight approached, that something was going wrong with the translucent trays that held the water and oil. They were sagging a little — were they? They were, slumping like sacks from their chains and melting, in other words. And then they began to collapse, flop and drape and fall away, sending hot oil onto the heads of every glamorous person in the country, and some other countries too. They were burned, scarred, maimed in the sense that tear-shaped droplets of scar tissue on the forehead of a movie star or small bald patches on the head of an art dealer or model or generally fabulous person constitute maiming. But something shut down in La Doll's brain as she stood there at a safe distance from the burning oil. She didn't call 911. She just watched in frozen disbelief as her guests shrieked and staggered and covered their heads, tore hot, soaked garments from their flesh, and crawled over the floor like people in medieval altar paintings whose earthly luxuries have consigned them to hell.

The accusations later — that she'd done it on purpose, that she was a sadist who stood there delighting as people suffered — were actually more terrible, for La Doll, than watching the oil pour mercilessly onto the heads of her five hundred guests. Then, she'd been protected by a cocoon of shock. But what followed she had to watch in a lucid state: They hated her. They were dying to get rid of her. It was as if she were not human but a rat or a bug. And they succeeded. Even before she'd served her six months for criminal negligence, before the class action suit that resulted in her entire net worth (never as large as it had seemed) being distributed in small parcels to her victims, La Doll was gone. Wiped out. She emerged from jail thirty pounds heavier and fifty years older, with wild gray hair. No one recognized her, and after a few gleeful headlines and photos of her new, ruined state, they forgot about her.

II

When the headlines relating to General B had definitively softened, when several witnesses against him were shown to have received money from the opposition, Arc called again. "The general pays you each month a sum," he said. "That is not for one idea only."

"It was a good idea, Arc. You have to admit."

"The general is impatient, Miss Peale," he said, and Dolly imagined him smiling. "The hat is no longer new."

That night, the general came to Dolly in a dream. The hat was gone, and he was meeting a pretty blonde outside a revolving door. The blonde took his arm and they walked inside. Then Dolly was aware of herself in the dream, sitting in a chair watching the general and his lover, thinking what a good job they were doing playing their roles. She jerked awake as if someone had shaken her. The dream nearly escaped, but Dolly caught it, pressed it to her chest. She understood: the general should be linked to a movie star.

Dolly scrambled off the sofa bed, waxy legs flashing in the street light that leaked in through a broken blind. A movie star. Someone recognizable, appealing — what better way to humanize a man who seemed inhuman? If he's good enough for her . . . that was one line of thinking. And also: The general and I have similar tastes: her. Or else: She must find that triangular head of his sexy. And even: I wonder how the general dances? And if Dolly could get people to ask that question, the general's image problems would be solved. Gone. It didn't matter how many thousands he'd slaughtered; if the collective vision of him could include a dance floor, all that would be behind him.

There were scores of washed-up female stars who might work, but Dolly had a particular one in mind: Pia Arten, who seven years ago had debuted as the nervy, stoic girlfriend of a football player stricken with leukemia, and stolen the movie out from under the famous male lead. She'd been nominated for best supporting actress, and standing on the red carpet in a gold crushed-velvet dress, she'd been impossible to look away from. But Pia had turned out to be one of those unfortunate people who couldn't take the bullshit, a handicap that had resulted in perfectionism, bad behavior, and (it was rumored) spectacular acts of self-destruction: sending a bag of horseshit to an iconic male actor, yanking off a balding director's baseball cap and tossing it into an airplane propeller. No one would hire Pia anymore, but the public would remember her. That was what mattered to Dolly.

Pia wasn't hard to find; no one was putting much energy into protecting her. By noon, Dolly had reached her: weary-sounding, smoking audibly. Pia heard Dolly out, asked her to repeat the generous fee she'd quoted, then paused. In that pause Dolly detected a familiar mix of desperation and squeamishness. She felt a queasy jab of pity for the actress, whose choices had boiled down to this one. Then the pause ended with Pia saying yes. Singing to herself, wired on cappuccino made on her old Krups machine, Dolly called Arc and laid out her plan.

"The general does not enjoy American movies," came Arc's response.

"Who cares? Americans know who she is."

"The general has very particular tastes," Arc said. "He is not flexible."

"He doesn't have to touch her, Arc. He doesn't have to speak to her. All he has to do is stand near her and get his picture taken. And he has to smile."

"Smile?"

"He has to look happy."

"The general rarely smiles, Miss Peale."

"He wore the hat, didn't he?"

There was a long pause. Finally Arc said, "You must accompany this actress. Then we will see."

"Accompany her where?"

"Here. To us."

"Oh, Arc."

"You must."

Entering Lulu's bedroom, Dolly felt like Dorothy waking up in Oz. Everything was in color. A pink shade encircled the overhead lamp. Pink gauzy fabric hung from the ceiling. Pink-winged princesses were stenciled onto the walls — Dolly had learned how to make the stencils at a jailhouse art class, and had spent days decorating the room while Lulu was at school. Long strings of pink beads hung from the ceiling. When she was home, Lulu emerged from her room only to eat.

She was part of an intricate weave of girls at Miss Rutgers's School, a mesh so fine and scarily intimate that even her mother's flameout and jail sentence (during which Lulu's grandmother had come from Minnesota to live with her) couldn't dissolve it. It wasn't thread holding these girls together, it was wire. And Lulu was the steel rod around which the wires were wrapped. Overhearing her daughter on the phone with her friends, Dolly was awed by her authority: she was stern when she needed to be, but also gentle. Sweet. Lulu was nine.

She sat in a pink beanbag chair, doing homework on her laptop and IMing her friends (since the general, Dolly had been paying for wireless). "Hi, Dolly," she said, having stopped calling Dolly Mom when she got out of jail nine months ago. Lulu narrowed her eyes at her mother like it was hard to see her. And Dolly did feel like a black-and-white intrusion into this bower of color, a refugee from the dinginess surrounding it.

"I have to take a business trip," Dolly said. "To visit a client. I thought you might want to stay with one of your friends so you won't miss school."

School was where Lulu's life took place. She'd been adamant about not allowing her mother, who once had been a fixture at Miss Rutgers's, to jeopardize Lulu's status with her new disgrace. Nowadays, Dolly dropped Lulu off around the corner, peering around dank Upper East Side stone to make sure she got safely in the door. At pickup time, Dolly waited in the same spot while Lulu dawdled with her friends outside school, toeing the perfectly manicured bushes and (in spring) flower beds, completing whatever transactions were required to affirm and sustain her power. When Lulu had a play date, Dolly went no farther than the lobby to retrieve her. Lulu would emerge from an elevator, flushed and smelling of perfume or freshly baked brownies, and take her mother's hand and walk with her past the doorman into the night. Not in apology — Lulu had nothing to apologize for — but in sympathy that things had to be so hard for both of them.

Lulu cocked her head, curious. "A business trip. That's good, right?"

"It is good, absolutely," Dolly said a little nervously. Lulu knew nothing of the general.

"How long will you be gone?"

"A few days. Four, maybe."

There was a long pause. Finally Lulu said, "Can I come?"

"With me?" Dolly was startled. "Can you? But you'd have to miss school."

Another pause. Lulu was performing some mental calculation that might have involved measuring the peer impact of missing school versus being a guest in someone's home, or the question of whether you could manage an extended stay at someone's home without that someone's parents speaking with your mother. Dolly couldn't tell. Maybe Lulu didn't know herself.

"Where?" Lulu asked.

Dolly was flustered; she'd never been much good at saying no to Lulu. But the thought of her daughter and the general in one location made her throat clamp. "I — I can't tell you that."

Lulu didn't protest. "But Dolly?"

"Yes, darling?"

"Can your hair be blond again?"

They waited for Pia Arten in a lounge by a private runway at Kennedy Airport. When the actress finally arrived, dirty-haired, reeking of smoke, dressed in jeans and a faded yellow sweatshirt, Dolly was assailed with regrets — she should have met with Pia first! The girl looked too far gone, too spent; people might not even recognize her! While Lulu used the bathroom, Dolly hastily laid things out for the actress: no mention of the general's name in front of Lulu, look as glamorous as possible (Dolly glanced at Pia's small, beaten suitcase), cozy up to the general with some serious PDA while Dolly took pictures with a hidden camera. She had a real camera too, but that was just a prop.

They boarded the general's plane at dusk. After takeoff, Pia ordered a double martini from the general's airline hostess, sucked it down, reclined her seat to a horizontal position, pulled a sleep mask over her eyes (the only thing on her that looked new), and commenced to snore. Lulu leaned over her, studying the actress's worn, delicate face. "Is she sick?"

"No," Dolly sighed. "Maybe. I don't know."

"I think she needs a vacation," Lulu said.

III

Twenty checkpoints preceded their arrival at the general's compound. At each, two soldiers with submachine guns peered suspiciously into the black Mercedes with Dolly and Lulu and Pia in the back seat. Four times they were forced outside into the scouring sunshine and patted down at gunpoint. Each time, Dolly cringed on Lulu's behalf, searching her daughter's studied calm for signs of trauma. In the car Lulu sat perfectly straight, pink Kate Spade bookbag nestled in her lap. She met the eyes of the machine-gun holders with the same even look she must have used to stare down the many girls who had tried in vain, over the years, to unseat her.

High white walls enclosed the road. They were lined with hundreds of plump, shiny black birds whose long purple beaks curved like scythes. Dolly had never seen birds like these. They looked like birds that would screech, but each time a car window slid down to accommodate another squinting gunslinger, Dolly was surprised by the total silence.

Eventually a section of wall swung open and the car veered off the road and pulled to a stop in front of a massive compound: lush green gardens, a sparkle of water, a white house whose end was nowhere in sight. The birds squatted along its roof, looking down.

Their driver opened the car doors, and Dolly and Lulu and Pia stepped out into the sun. Dolly felt it on her newly exposed neck, a discount version of her trademark blond chin-length cut. The heat forced Pia out of her sweatshirt, which mercifully revealed a clean white T-shirt underneath. Dolly noticed marks on Pia's bare arms: small pink scars. "Pia, are those . . ." She faltered. "On your arms, are they . . . ?"

"Burns," Pia said. And she gave Dolly a look that made her stomach twist until she remembered, very dimly, like something that had happened in a fog or when she was a child, someone asking her — begging her — to put Pia on the list, and telling that person no. No way, it was out of the question, Pia's stock was too low.

"I did it myself," Pia said.

Dolly stared at her, uncomprehending. This made Pia grin, and for a second she looked mischievous, young. "Lots of people have, Dolly. You didn't know?"

Dolly wondered if this might be a joke. She didn't want to fall for it in front of Lulu.

"You can't find a person who wasn't at that party. And they've got proof. We've all got proof — who's gonna say we're lying?"

"I know who was there," Dolly said. "I've still got the list in my head."

"You?" Pia said, smiling at Dolly. "Who are you?"

Dolly was quiet. She felt Lulu's gray eyes on her.

Pia did something unexpected then. She reached through the sunlight and took Dolly's hand. Her grip was warm and firm, like a man's. Dolly was startled to feel a prickling in her eyes.

"It's bigger than all of us," Pia said softly. "That's the horror of it."

A trim, compact man in a beautifully cut suit emerged from the compound to greet them: Arc. The sight of him eased the tension that had been building in Dolly.

"Miss Peale. We meet at last," he said with a smile. "And Miss Arten" — he turned to Pia, who looked even scruffier beside the meticulous Arc — "it is a great honor as well as a pleasure." He kissed Pia's hand with a slightly teasing look, Dolly thought. "I have seen your movies," Arc said. "The general and I watched them together."

Dolly steeled herself for what Pia might say, but her answer came in a sweet voice like a child's, except for the slight curve of flirtation. "Oh, I'm sure you've seen better movies," she said.

"The general was impressed."

"Well, I'm honored. I'm honored that the general found them worth watching."

Dolly glanced at the actress, expecting mockery, but it wasn't there. Pia looked humble, absolutely sincere.

"Alas, I have unfortunate news," Arc said. "The general has had to make a sudden trip." They stared at him. "It is very regrettable," he went on. "The general sends his sincere apologies."

"But we . . . can we go to where he is?" Dolly asked.

"Perhaps," Arc said. "You will not mind some additional travels?"

"Well," Dolly said, glancing at Lulu. "It depends how —"

"Absolutely not," Pia interrupted. "We'll go wherever the general wants us to go. We'll do what it takes. Right, kiddo?"

Lulu was slow to connect the diminutive "kiddo" to herself. It was the first time Pia had spoken to her directly. Lulu glanced at the actress, then she smiled. "Right," she said.

They would leave for a new location the next morning. Arc offered to drive them into the city that evening, but Pia wasn't interested. "Forgive my lack of curiosity," she said as they settled into their two-bedroom suite, which opened onto a private swimming pool. "But I'd rather enjoy these digs. They used to put me up in places like this." She gave a bitter laugh.

"Just don't overdo it," Dolly said as Pia headed for the wet bar.

Pia turned. "Hey. How was I out there, Mamacita? Any complaints so far?"

"You were excellent," Dolly said, then added softly, so Lulu wouldn't hear, "Just don't forget who we're dealing with."

"I want to forget," Pia said, pouring herself a large drink. "I'm trying to forget. Aren't you?" She raised her glass to Dolly and took a sip.

So Dolly and Lulu rode alone with Arc in his charcoal-gray Jaguar, a driver peeling downhill along tiny streets, sending pedestrians lunging against walls and darting into doorways to avoid being crushed. The city shimmered below: millions of white slanted buildings steeping in a smoky haze. Soon they were surrounded by it. The city's chief source of color seemed to be the laundry flapping on every balcony.

The driver pulled over beside an outdoor market: heaps of sweating fruit and fragrant nuts and fake leather purses. Dolly eyed the produce critically as she and Lulu followed Arc among the stalls. The oranges and bananas were the largest she'd seen, but the meat looked dangerous. Dolly could see from the careful nonchalance of venders and customers alike that they knew who Arc was.

"Is there anything you would like to buy?" Arc asked Lulu.

"Yes, please," Lulu said, "one of those." It was a star fruit; Dolly had seen them at Dean and DeLuca a few times. Here they lay in obscene heaps, studded with flies. Arc took one, nodding curtly at the vendor, an older man with a knobby chest and a kind, worried face. The man smiled, nodding eagerly at Dolly and Lulu, and Dolly was taken aback to see that he looked afraid. As if she could hurt him. As if she would ever do such a thing.

Lulu took the dusty, unwashed fruit, wiped it carefully on her sweater, and sank her teeth into its bright green rind. Juice sprayed her collar. She laughed and wiped her mouth with her hand. "Mom, you have to try this," she said, and Dolly took a bite of crunchy orange fruit that was some combination of melon, apple, and plum. She and Lulu shared the star fruit, licking their fingers under Arc's watchful eyes. Dolly felt oddly buoyant. Then she realized why: Mom. It was the first time Lulu had used the word in nearly a year.

Arc led the way inside a crowded teashop. A group of men hastened away from a corner table to give them a place to sit, and a forced approximation of the shop's former bustle resumed. A waiter poured sweet mint tea into their cups with a shaking hand. Dolly tried to give him a reassuring look, but his eyes fled hers.

"Do you do this often?" she asked Arc. "Walk around the city?"

"The general makes a habit of moving among the people," Arc said. "He wants them to feel his humanity, to witness it. Of course, he must do this very carefully."

"Because of his enemies."

Arc nodded. "The general unfortunately has many enemies. Today, for example, there were threats to his home, and it was necessary to relocate. He does this often, as you know."

Dolly nodded. Threats to his home?

Arc smiled. "His enemies believe he is there, but he is far away."

Dolly glanced at Lulu. The star fruit had left a shiny ring around her mouth. "But . . . we're there," she said.

"Yes," Arc said. "Only us."

Dolly lay awake most of that night, listening to coos and rustles and squawks that sounded like assassins prowling the grounds in search of the general and his cohort: herself, in other words. She had become the helpmate and fellow target of General B, a source of fear to those he ruled.

How had it come to this? As usual, Dolly found herself revisiting the moment when the plastic trays first buckled and the life she had relished for so many years poured away. But tonight, unlike countless other nights when Dolly tipped down that memory chute, Lulu lay across from her in the king-size bed, asleep in a frilly pink nightie, her doe's knees tucked under her. Dolly felt the warmth of her daughter's body, this child of her middle age, of an accidental pregnancy resulting from a fling with a movie star client. Lulu believed her father was dead; Dolly had shown her pictures of an old boyfriend.

She slid across the bed and kissed the side of Lulu's face. It had made no sense at all to have a child — Dolly was pro-choice, riveted to her career. Her decision had been clear, yet she'd hesitated to make the appointment — hesitated through morning sickness, mood swings, exhaustion. Hesitated until she knew, with a shock of relief and terrified joy, that it was too late.

Lulu stirred and Dolly moved closer, enclosing her daughter in her arms. In contrast to when she was awake, Lulu relaxed into her mother's touch. Dolly felt a swell of irrational gratitude toward the general for providing this one bed. It was such a rare luxury to hold her daughter, to feel the faint tap of her heartbeat.

"You know I'll always protect you," Dolly whispered into Lulu's fragile ear. "Nothing bad will ever happen to us."

Lulu slept on.

IV

The next day, they piled into two black armored cars that resembled jeeps, only heavier. Arc and some soldiers went in the first car, Dolly and Lulu and Pia in the second. Sitting in the back seat, Dolly thought she could feel the weight of the car shoving them into the earth. She was exhausted, full of dread.

Pia had undergone a staggering transformation since the day before. She'd washed her hair, put on full makeup, and slipped into a gold crushed-velvet dress that Dolly instantly recognized as the one she'd worn to the Academy Awards years ago, after her first movie. The gold fabric brought out flecks of gold in Pia's eyes. The effect was beyond anything Dolly could have hoped for. She found Pia oddly painful to look at.

They breezed through the checkpoints and soon were on the open road, circling the pale city from above. Dolly noticed venders by the road. Often they were children, who held up handfuls of fruit or cardboard signs to the jeeps as they approached. When the vehicles flew past, the children fell back against the embankment, perhaps from the speed. Dolly let out an involuntary cry the first time she saw this and leaned forward, wanting to say something to the driver. But what, exactly? She hesitated, then sat back and tried not to look at the windows. Lulu watched the children, her math book open in her lap.

It was a relief when they left the city behind and began driving through empty land that looked like desert, antelopes and cows nibbling the stingy plant life. Without asking permission, Pia began to smoke, exhaling through a thin slit of open window. "So, kiddo," she said, turning to Lulu, "what big plans are you hatching?"

"You mean . . . for my life?" Lulu asked.

"Absolutely."

"I don't know," Lulu said, thoughtful. "I'm only nine."

"Well, that's sensible."

"Lulu is very sensible," Dolly said.

"But what do you imagine for yourself? That's what I'm asking," Pia said. She was restless, fidgeting her dry, manicured fingers as if she wanted another cigarette but was making herself wait. "Or do kids not do that anymore."

Lulu, in her wisdom, seemed to divine that what Pia really wanted was to talk. "What did you imagine," she asked, "when you were nine?"

Pia considered this, then laughed. "I wanted to become a movie star."

"And then you did."

Pia lit a fresh cigarette. "I did," she said, closing her eyes as she exhaled. "I did."

Lulu turned to her gravely. "Was it not as fun as you thought?"

Pia opened her eyes. "The acting?" she said. "God, I could do it every minute, every second. But I hated the people."

"How come?"

"They were phony. They lied constantly. And when you got through all the phoniness and the lying, it turned out they were mean."

Lulu nodded as if this were something she knew all about. "Did you try lying too?"

Pia laughed. "I did, actually. I tried it a lot. But whenever I managed to pull it off, I had this urge to put a gun in my mouth. That's what's called a no-win situation, kiddo."

"I don't want to be an actress," Lulu said. "I don't like having to say the same thing again and again."

Pia glanced at Dolly. "Where did you get this kid?"

They drove and drove. Lulu did math. Then social studies. She wrote an essay on owls. After what felt like hundreds of miles of desert, punctuated by bathroom stops at outposts patrolled by soldiers, they tilted up into the hills. The foliage grew dense, filtering out the sunlight.

Without warning, the cars swung off the road and stopped. Dozens of solders in camouflage seemed to materialize from the trees. Dolly and Lulu and Pia stepped out of the car into a jungle crazed with birdcalls.

Arc came over. "The general is waiting," he said. "He is eager to greet you."

Everyone moved as a group through the jungle. The earth under their feet was soft and red. Monkeys scuttled in the trees. Eventually they reached a set of crude concrete steps built into the side of a hill. More soldiers appeared, and there was a creak and grind of boots on concrete as all of them climbed. Dolly kept her hands on Lulu's shoulders. She heard Pia humming behind her: not a tune, just the same two notes repeated.

The hidden camera was ready in Dolly's purse. As they climbed the steps, she took out the activator and held it in her palm.

At the top of the stairs the jungle had been cleared away to accommodate a slab of concrete that might have been a landing pad. Sunlight poured down through the humid jungle air, making wisps of steam at their feet. The general stood in the middle of the concrete, flanked by soldiers. He looked short, but that was always true of famous people. He wasn't wearing the blue hat, or any hat, and his hair was thick and unruly around his grim triangular face. He wore his usual military regalia, but something about it all seemed slightly askew or in need of cleaning. The general looked tired — there were pouches under his eyes. He looked grumpy. He looked like a soldier had just yanked him out of bed and said, "They're here," and he'd had to remind himself of who the hell the soldier was talking about.

There was a strange, short pause when no one seemed to know what to do.

Then Pia reached the top of the stairs. Dolly heard the humming behind her, but she didn't turn to look; instead, she watched the general recognize Pia, watched the power of that recognition move across his face in a look of appetite and uncertainty. Pia came toward him slowly — poured toward him, really, that was how smoothly she moved in her gold dress, like the jerking awkwardness of walking was something she'd never experienced. She poured toward the general and took his hand as if to shake it, smiling, circling him a little, seeming embarrassed to the point of laughter, like they knew each other too well to shake hands.

Dolly was so taken by the strangeness of it all that at first she didn't think to shoot; she missed the handshake completely. It was only when Pia pressed her narrow gold body to the general's uniformed chest and closed her eyes for a moment that Dolly came to — click — and the general seemed disconcerted, unsure what to do, patting Pia's back out of politeness — click — at which point Pia took both his hands (heavy and warped, the hands of a bigger man) into her own slender hands and leaned back, smiling into his face — click — laughing a little, shyly, her head back like it was all so silly, so self-conscious-making for them both. And then the general smiled. It happened without warning: his lips pulled away to reveal two rows of small yellow teeth — click — that made him appear vulnerable, eager to please. Click, click, click — Dolly was shooting as fast as she could without moving her hand, because that smile was it, the thing no one had seen, the hidden human side of the general that would stun the world.

All this happened in the span of a minute. Not a word had been spoken. Pia and the general stood hand in hand, both a little flushed, and it was all Dolly could do not to scream, because they were done! She had what she needed, and they were done, without a word having been spoken. She felt a mix of awe and love for Pia, this miracle, this genius who had not merely posed with the general, but tamed him. That was how it felt to Dolly now, like there was a one-way door between the general's world and Pia's, and the actress had eased him across it without his even noticing. He couldn't go back! And Dolly had made this happen — for once in her life she had done a helpful thing. And Lulu had seen it.

Pia's face still held the winsome smile she'd been wearing for the general. Dolly watched her scan the crowd, taking in the dozens of soldiers with their automatic weapons, Arc and Lulu and Dolly with her ecstatic shining face, her brimming eyes. And Pia must have known then that she'd pulled it off, engineered her own salvation, clawed her way back from oblivion and cleared the way to resume the work she loved more than anything. All with a little help from the dictator to her left.

"So," Pia said, "is this where you bury the bodies?"

The general glanced at her, not understanding. Arc stepped quickly forward, as did Dolly. Lulu came too.

"Do you bury them here, in pits," Pia asked the general in the most friendly, conversational voice, "or do you burn them first?"

"Miss Arten," Arc said with a tense, meaningful look. "The general cannot understand you."

The general wasn't smiling anymore. He was not a man who could tolerate not knowing what was going on. He'd let go of Pia's hand and was speaking sternly to Arc.

Lulu was yanking Dolly's hand. "Mom," she hissed, "make her stop!"

Her daughter's voice jerked Dolly out of a momentary paralysis. "Knock it off, Pia," she said.

"Do you eat them?" Pia asked the general, "or do you leave them out so the vultures can do it?"

"Shut up, Pia," Dolly said more loudly. "Stop playing games."

The general spoke harshly to Arc, who turned to Dolly. Arc's forehead was visibly moist. "The general is becoming angry, Miss Peale," he said, and there was the code; Dolly read it clearly. She went to Pia and took hold of her bare arm. She leaned close to her face.

"If you keep this up," Dolly said softly, "we will die." But one glance into Pia's pained, broken eyes told her it was hopeless. Pia couldn't stop.

"Oops!" Pia said loudly in mock surprise. "Was I not supposed to bring up the genocide?"

Here was a word the general knew. He flung himself away from Pia as if she were on fire, commanding his solders in a strangled voice. They shoved Dolly away, knocking her to the ground. When she looked back at Pia, the soldiers had contracted around her, and the actress was hidden in their midst.

Lulu was shouting, trying to drag Dolly back to her feet. "Mommy, do something, do something. Make it stop!"

"Arc," Dolly called, but Arc was lost to her now. He'd taken his place beside the general, who was screaming with rage. The soldiers were carrying Pia; Dolly had an impression of kicking from within their midst. She could still hear Pia's voice:

"Do you drink their blood, or just use it to mop up your floors?"

"Do you wear their teeth on a string?"

There was the sound of a blow, then a cry. Dolly jumped to her feet. But Pia went on, unbowed. "I hope they haunt you," she bellowed hoarsely. "I hope they visit you in your sleep."

And then she was gone. The soldiers carried her through the door of a structure hidden in the trees beside the landing pad. The general and Arc followed them in. The jungle was eerily silent: just parrot calls, and Lulu's sobs.

V

It was because of Arc that Dolly and Lulu got out. While the general raged, Arc whispered orders to two soldiers, and when the general was out of sight they hustled Dolly and Lulu down the hill through the jungle and back to the cars. The drivers were waiting, smoking cigarettes. During the ride Lulu lay with her head in Dolly's lap, sobbing as they sped back through the jungle and then the desert. Dolly rubbed her daughter's soft hair, wondering in a numb, helpless way if they were being taken to prison. But eventually, as the sun leaked toward the horizon, they found themselves at the airport. The general's plane was waiting. By then, Lulu had sat up and moved away from Dolly across the seat.

Lulu slept hard during the flight, clutching her Kate Spade bag. But Dolly didn't sleep. She stared straight ahead at Pia's empty seat.

In the dark of early morning, they took a taxi from Kennedy to Hell's Kitchen. Neither of them spoke. Dolly was amazed to find their building intact, the apartment still at the top of the stairs, the keys in her pocket. It hardly seemed possible.

Lulu went straight to her room and shut the door. Dolly sat in her office, addled from lack of sleep, and tried to organize her thoughts. Should she start with the embassy? Congress? How long would it take to get someone on the phone who could actually help her? And what would she say?

Lulu emerged from her room in her school uniform, hair brushed.

Dolly hadn't even noticed it was light. Lulu looked askance at her mother, still in yesterday's clothes, and said, "It's time to go."

"You're going to school?"

"Of course I'm going to school. What else would I do?"

They took the subway. The silence between them had become inviolable; Dolly feared it would never end. Watching Lulu's wan, pinched face, she felt a cold wave of conviction: if Pia died, Lulu would be lost to her.

At their corner, Lulu turned without saying goodbye.

Shopkeepers were lifting their metal gates on Lexington Avenue. Dolly bought a cup of coffee and drank it on the corner. She wanted to be near Lulu. She decided to wait on that corner until her daughter's school day had ended, five and a half more hours. Meanwhile, she would make calls on her cell phone. But Dolly was distracted by thoughts of Pia in the gold dress, oil burns winking on her arms, then her own insane pride, thinking she'd made the world a better place. The memory made Dolly almost sick.

The phone was idle in her hand. These were not the sorts of calls she knew how to make.

When the gate behind her shuddered up, Dolly saw that it was a two-hour photo shop. The hidden camera with its roll of film was still in her purse. It was something to do; she opened the door and went in.

She was still standing outside the shop an hour later when the guy came out with her pictures. By then she'd made a few calls about Pia, but no one seemed to take her seriously. Who could blame them? Dolly thought.

"These, uh . . . did you use Photoshop or — or what?" the guy asked. "They look, like, totally real."

"They are real," she said. "I took them myself."

The guy laughed. "Come on," he said, and Dolly felt a shudder deep in her brain.

What else would I do?

She rushed back home and called her old contacts at the *Enquirer* and the *Star,* a few of whom were still there. Let the news trickle up. This had worked for Dolly before.

Soon a messenger arrived at her apartment to pick up the prints. Within a couple of hours, images of General B nuzzling Pia Arten were being posted and traded on the web. By nightfall, reporters from the major papers around the world had started calling. They called the general too, whose human-relations captain emphatically denied the rumors.

That night, while Lulu did homework in her room, Dolly ate cold sesame noodles and set out to reach Arc. It took fourteen tries.

"We can no longer speak, Miss Peale," he said.

"Arc —"

"We cannot speak. The general is angry."

"Listen to me."

"The general is angry, Miss Peale."

"Is she alive, Arc? That's all that matters."

"She is alive."

"Thank God." Tears filled Dolly's eyes. "Is she — are they — treating her okay?"

"She is unharmed, Miss Peale," Arc said. "We will not speak again." They were silent, listening to the hum of the overseas connection. "It is a pity," Arc said, and hung up.

But Dolly and Arc did speak again. Months later — a year, almost — when the general visited Washington and then came to New York to speak at the United Nations about transitioning to democracy. Dolly and Lulu had left the city by then, but one evening they drove into Manhattan to meet Arc at a restaurant. He wore a black suit and a wine-colored tie. He seemed to savor retelling the story, as if he'd memorized its details especially for Dolly: how three or four days after she and Lulu had left the general's redoubt, the photographers began showing up. First one or two, whom the soldiers ferreted out of the jungle and imprisoned, then more, too many to capture or even count — they were superb hiders, crouching like monkeys in the trees, burying themselves in shallow pits, camouflaging themselves in leaves. Assassins had never managed to locate the general with any precision, but the photographers did: scores of them surging across the border without visas, curled in baskets and wine casks, rolled up in rugs, juddering over unpaved roads in the backs of trucks and eventually surrounding the general's enclave, which he didn't dare leave.

It took ten days to persuade the general that he had no choice but to face his inquisitors. He donned his military coat with the medals and epaulettes, pulled the blue hat over his head, took Pia's arm, and walked with her into the phalanx of cameras awaiting him. Dolly remembered how startled the general had looked in those pictures, newly born in his soft blue hat, unsure how to proceed. Beside him Pia was smiling, wearing a dress Dolly hadn't seen before, black and close-fitting. Her eyes were hard to read, but each time Dolly looked at them, rubbing her gaze obsessively over the newsprint, she heard Pia's sardonic laugh in her ears.

"Have you see Miss Arten's new movie?" Arc asked. "I thought it was her finest yet."

Dolly had seen it, a romantic comedy that showed Pia in a footloose mode Dolly hadn't seen before. She'd gone with Lulu to the local theater in the small upstate town where they'd moved shortly after the other generals began to call, first G, then A, then L and P and Y. Word had gotten out, and Dolly was deluged with offers of work from mass murderers eager for a fresh start. "I'm out of the game," she'd told them all, and directed them to her competitors.

Lulu had opposed the move at first, but Dolly was firm. And Lulu had settled in quickly at the local public school, where she took up soccer and found a new coterie of girls who seemed to follow her everywhere. No one in town had ever heard of La Doll, so Lulu had nothing to hide.

Dolly had received a generous lump sum from the general shortly after his rendezvous with the photographers. "A gift to express our immense gratitude for your invaluable expertise, Miss Peale," Arc had said over the telephone, but Dolly had heard the smile and understood the code: hush money. She used it to open a small gourmet shop on Main Street, where she sold fine produce and unusual cheeses, artfully displayed and lit by a system of small spotlights Dolly had designed herself. "This feels exactly like Paris" was a comment she often heard from New Yorkers who came on weekends to visit their country houses. Now and then she would get a shipment of star fruit, and Dolly always put a few aside to eat with Lulu. She would bring them back to the small house they shared at the end of a quiet street. After supper, the radio on, windows open to the night, she and Lulu would feast on the sweet, strange flesh.

STEPHEN ELLIOTT

■

Where I Slept

FROM *Tin House*

MY HOMELESS YEAR began in early October 1985 and ended on the last day of August 1986. I was thirteen, and then fourteen, and it's a story I've never told, in part because I slept so many different places that year.

I slept in the broom closet of a friend's apartment building. The closet was just inside the entryway, past the eight slotted mailboxes. It was the size of a single bed, crowded with mop buckets and cleaning solutions, and I could stretch all the way out and my toes would just touch the door. The building was a tan-and-yellow-brick four-flat. Kwan lived with his parents and grandmother in a two-bedroom on the second floor, part of a wave of Korean immigrants arriving on the north side of Chicago in the early eighties on their way to the suburbs along with the Kurds and Russian Jews. When I would go over to visit after school, his grandmother would clutch my head in her bony hands and pray for me.

"She wants to know if you're going to church," Kwan would interpret. When it was time for dinner, Kwan would politely ask me to leave.

I had a leather bomber jacket my father had given me in one of our better moments, and some clothes, and I wore all of it when I slept there. It was just as hard and cold in the broom closet as it was outside, and it was winter in Chicago and I was thirteen. I could see my breath pooling in the dark and woke shivering in the middle of every night. I had a watch, so I knew it was usually three, and I waited until six and then went to the laundromat on California Avenue and sat there trying to get warm. But after a while I couldn't get warm, and even in school I was shivering all the time, vibrating in my big jacket.

But this isn't about school (I was in eighth grade). And it's not about my father handcuffing me to a pipe and leaving me there in the basement of his old house. And it's not about the hotel room I ended up in one homeless evening with a white man in a nurse's uniform and a wig giving head to three black men, lines of coke spread haphazardly across the table. All of that is true, but this is just a list of the different places I slept. It's the only way I can get any perspective.

I slept at home. I went home several times. I had a large bedroom, and the walls were covered in wallpaper that looked like an open sky full of birds and clouds. I had a down comforter and two pillows in Charlie Brown pillowcases. I had a manual typewriter I banged on, and I taped bad poetry all over my walls and listened to Pink Floyd albums on the cabinet record player. I made dinner from endless cans of Chef Boyardee and stacks of frozen steaks. If I was to guess, I would say that, counting rapprochements with my father, I slept at home a full month out of the eleven I spent as a homeless child in Chicago. Friends who ran away would climb in through my window and sleep beneath my bed.

I turned fourteen in a basement I had broken into with my friends Albert and Justin. Justin was often homeless that year and he slept many different places as well. The floor was blue cement, and we sat up most of the night against the wood storage sheds working our way through pints of vodka and confessing to things like masturbation. In the morning the police woke us with flashlights and boots and sent us back to the streets.

I slept in the police station, the Twenty-fourth District, the flat, dark building with the giant parking lot on Clark Street. I was arrested for curfew, then drug possession, then breaking into parking meters. I slept on the scratched steel cot inside the cell in the juvenile unit or sitting upright with my wrist next to my ear, handcuffed to a steel loop in the wall.

A Jewish man found me in the broom closet. He seemed confused. He couldn't understand why a child was sleeping there. He probably owned the building. He was probably just coming to get a mop. "It's okay," I told him, gathering my things in my arms, careful not to look in his eyes, and walking away. I was fourteen. I didn't want to answer the obvious questions. The broom closet was locked after that.

On the coldest nights, when my lashes became icicles, I sneaked into a boiler room and slept next to the warm pipes and left when I heard the banging that meant someone was coming down the stairs. I walked along Devon Avenue when the bank clock read twenty below. I had hypothermia. It was like a circuit at times: roof, roof, boiler room. Other times it was a pattern, and I would go to the same place over and over again and go to sleep just like anyone else.

I slept at my father's girlfriend's apartment, on a couch in her living room, and I watched her sleep through the half-open door to her bedroom, her blanket riding up her naked thighs. She slept flat on her stomach with her head turned, breathing softly into the pillow, her legs slightly spread. I watched the balls of her feet, the curves of her toes, and her tan calves. This is not about her struggling to hold on to me, arms wrapped around my waist, while I lunged for the doorknob, my father on his way, upset over the social workers who had begun to bother him about his homeless child. Or the violence that would occur after he found me walking late that night down Chicago Avenue, covered in snow, and took me home for a single night to smack me across the face and shave my head.

I slept in my grandparents' small flat outside Sheffield, England. My grandparents are dead now, both of them. They weren't expecting me. I drank barley wine at night with them and my grandfather told me stories of the Great War and made jokes about his missing thumb. When they went to sleep I journeyed out to the pubs and I drank some more. During the day I hiked the Little Don River, watched the sheep in the long green fields. I found my first strip club in the back of a small pub with a broken window. Several times I hitchhiked into Sheffield to watch punk rock bands and met people who were looking for fights. I wasn't looking for a fight. After a week my grandparents sent me back to America.

I slept above the Quik Stop on Pratt and California, only a block away from my grammar school. I climbed the gutters to the roof and lay in the corner beneath the lip, to block the wind. Sometimes I would poke my head up and see the crossing lights and the black empty streets and I would feel so lucky and free. There were video games in the store, but I wasn't allowed inside. The teachers knew I was homeless and bought me lunch, but no one offered to take me home. My friends' parents also didn't offer to take me in. At PTA meetings parents were warned to keep their children away from me. I was a known drug user, an eighth-grade drinker when I could get the money together. One time Justin's father chased me down the sidewalk in his taxi, trying to run me over. When I jumped the fence to get away, he pressed a gun against my friend Roger's chest and demanded he tell where I was. But Roger didn't know, and that, like so many other things that happened that year, is not what this is about.

I stole food from the Dumpster behind the Dominick's, cold packets of meat just past date. I slept at the canal where we built fires and planned adventures, all the neighborhood's forgotten children, the ones whose parents didn't notice them missing or didn't care, dancing near the flames. Nobody looked for us. We named things. The tree I sat in was called "Steve's office," the fire pit was "Pete Brown's grave." Pat had a throne dug into the dirt below the path, and Rob had "Rob's chair," which was just the tip of a boulder protruding horizontally from the slope. We respected each other's space most of the time. We built a fire every night, and we threw rocks at the rats as they scurried in and out of the filthy water. We had wonderful times at the canal playing heavy-metal music and popping acid while trying to stay awake for cops and tougher kids who might want to beat us up. One time Fat Mike came running, out of breath. He had seen headlights near the baseball stadium. "Dude," he said. "Could be a cop car, could be a party car, I don't know." We laughed for hours over that. We woke up covered in dirt, reeking of smoke, and went to school.

I slept at home. My mother was dead. My father didn't always notice me when I came back; other times he woke me with a loud whistle. He never reported me missing when I left again, we didn't want each other, and eventually he moved himself to the suburbs with his new wife and didn't bother to give me his forwarding address.

I slept three nights with a Christian man who did painting work for my father. He lived in a small apartment, and his wife was dying rapidly, like my mother had. I went with him to church. I ruined his baking pan cooking hamburger on his stove. It wasn't working out, he told me. Years later my father still tries to contact me demanding I write his Christian friend a thank-you letter.

There was a man named Ron. He had an apartment beneath Pat's mother's apartment. Pat's mother was a junkie, and Ron was just a twenty-year-old slacker who would one day go to community college and get a degree in hospitality that would allow him to work in a hotel. I had stolen some money and bought a quarter pound of marijuana and Ron let me stay with him until the marijuana was gone. Pat's mother is dead now. Justin's parents are also dead. Roger's dad is dead. Dan's mom is dead. It has nothing to do with the story, but my friends' parents all died young.

I slept beneath Brian's bed, and when Brian's father caught me he kicked me out and then he beat Brian. Brian's father saw me stumbling down the street drunk with my shirt off in the middle of winter, and he said to his daughter, "I ought to put him out of his misery." He did too much coke and had a bad heart. He died too.

I slept in the closet of an independent-living home for wards of the state. The home was on Sacramento. A normal, boxy-looking house in the middle of the street with a small basketball court in the back yard. Eight boys lived there, transitioning between group homes and living alone. Some of the boys sneaked me inside. The closet was small and I had to sleep sitting up with my legs crossed. I was discovered by the staff and they fed me a bowl of cereal. One day the state would take custody of me and I would also be a ward of the state and I would live in that very home for a time.

More often than anything else I slept outside. I slept in parks and in the woods and on the neighborhood rooftops. But when you can fall asleep anywhere, you often do. I was always the last to leave the party. I never had to go home.

Sometimes Justin would have a girlfriend and I would sleep on the couch and he would sleep in the bedroom. Justin was popular that way. He was beautiful, like a woman, with his long black hair. Sometimes Justin and I slept together on a gravelly rooftop and he wrapped his thin legs over my legs and his sinewy arms across my chest and held me tightly, his face buried in my neck, and I was never sure if he was doing that because he wanted to or because he thought I expected it from him.

Justin and I slept at the Maxworks, a hippie commune in Jewtown. The neighborhood doesn't exist anymore. They've paved it over to expand the university campus. Maxworks was a three-story abandoned building taken over by radicals, many of whom lived there for twenty years. They smoked dandelions and banana skins and made pocket money selling handmade pipes to the junkies sitting around garbage cans outside. Justin and I were too young to recognize what we had stumbled on, the failure of an earlier generation's promise. They gave us acid and yellow sunshine, and one of the women, in a flowery skirt, with unshaven legs and armpits, had sex with Justin. I don't remember her name, but I remember her spinning in circles in a trash heap near a fire. Her arms were outstretched and her dress translucent. I was so jealous but there was nothing I could do about it. I was an ugly child, and sometimes my ugliness kept me safe.

From the Maxworks, over the next eight days in the summer of 1986, Justin and I slept our way in cars and trucks across America. The truck stop in East Los Angeles was a sea of flashing lights, the air wavy with gasoline, open trailers filled with rolls of carpet, men standing on dock ladders or leaning back in their rigs, chatting lazily on the radio in the deafening hum of the motoring engines. I slept in the cabin of a truck while the driver molested Justin in the front. I slept right through it, and in the morning, sitting in a doughnut shop under a blank gray sky surrounded by highways and the roar of traffic, Justin told me he wanted to kill that man. He had stolen our only bag, and inside was my poetry and our maps. I thought that was what Justin was talking about, the poetry and the maps. But years later, when I was at a party telling my favorite story, about hitchhiking from Chicago to California with my best friend, he would interrupt me and say, "Steve, I was molested."

"Why didn't you wake me up?" I asked, which was a dumb thing to say. I was so angry.

In Las Vegas we slept in the juvenile detention center. We had caught a ride with a German, and he took us from Los Angeles to the Strip. He wore shorts and drove with a beer between his legs. Good beer, he said, from Germany. He stopped in a convenience store and bought cheap beer so we would have something to drink too. He had a small bong in the glove compartment and a pillbox filled with weed and we smoked that as we drove into the desert. He dropped us off at Caesars Palace, where we stocked up on free matchbooks and wondered what to do next.

A state trooper answered that question. We were out on the entry ramp, trying to hitch a ride out of town. Our clothes were muddy and ripped. We were put in jail as runaways. They contacted my father but he didn't respond. He stopped in the printer on Pratt Avenue and told the woman working there, "They arrested my son in Las Vegas. I'm not going to get him."

"No offense," she told me when I met her years later, "but I didn't give a shit."

I said goodbye to Justin in his small white-walled room on the ground floor of the institution. It was early in the morning, the desert sun rising above the low buildings, and he wasn't quite awake. His dark hair covered his eyes. His gym shoes were in the hallway in front of the red walking line, and he asked why I was being let out first. I told him I didn't know. They drove me to the Greyhound station and then took my handcuffs off. They gave me four dollars when they let me out, and I spent it on cigarettes and candy bars. I slept on a bus for three days as it snaked slowly across the country from Las Vegas to Chicago. We stopped at the McDonald's restaurants dotting the highway and at a state fair in Carbondale. The man next to me fed me whiskey in a coffee cup and I slept against his shoulder at night. He was fresh out of prison and asked if I would be willing to snatch someone's purse. I said I didn't think I would be very good at that.

Justin wouldn't get out for several more weeks, and when he did, he would be rearrested on an outstanding warrant and would go to the Audi Home and his parents would refuse to pick him up and the state would take custody of him and he would spend the rest of his childhood in a state home in the Chicago suburbs.

When I got back to Chicago I slept on the streets, as I had been doing for so long now. I slept on a friend's porch until his mother found out. I slept on the same rooftops. I hooked up with a children's agency and they put me in Central Youth Shelter. It was a gladiator arena filled with children awaiting placement and stuffed thirty to a room. We sat around during the day watching television or playing basketball in the fenced yard. The shelter was understaffed, and nobody would tell me where I was going or when I would get out. Then I walked away.

I slept for a while in a house connected to a Catholic church and in the private homes of people who had volunteered to take in children while the state waited the requisite twenty-one days to see if they were willing to take custody. There was something wrong with the adults who took me in, all men living alone. I think they were pedophiles, and I was a disappointment to them. I played pool with other homeless children at the Advocacy Center beneath the Granville train tracks. There was a girl there, a year older than me, tall and thin and freckled. She always beat me and then did this little victory dance with her hands, fingers stretched like wings. She had the biggest smile.

Then I slept in the house I had grown up in, which my father was in the process of selling. It was an obvious mistake.

I woke into his fists and tried to cover my face. He dragged me into the kitchen, where he had clippers, forced me to my knees in front of the cabinet, and shaved my head. It was the second time he had done that. There were giant bald patches from where his hands slipped, and I looked like a mental patient. He must have been waiting for me or searching the neighborhood. He had planned to do this. Revenge for something. The meanest thing possible, worse even than the beating, worse than handcuffing me to a pipe — to be humiliated in front of everyone. To be a circus freak. It was an act of raw cruelty well within my father's emotional range. But that's not what this is about at all. This isn't about hate or love or what went wrong between my father and me or the kind of resentments that never go away. This isn't about splitting the blame between bad parents and bad children. It's not about culpability. It's about sleeping and the things that are important to that, like shelter and rain.

That night was the last night of my homeless year. It was the end of August and high school would start in a couple of days. That day I had cut my wrist open, and there was a bright red gash that bled through the afternoon. It was hot and a festival was under way in the park. A soft breeze cut around the sleigh hill and a few clouds pocked the long sky. I solicited beer, and people bought it for me because they thought maybe I was crazy or maybe they could get me to leave. I asked one man if I could go home with him, and he said, "Look, I

bought you a beer," which was true enough. As night fell a band as-
cended the stage and I danced while they played, slamming in the
mosh pit at the top of the baseball diamond, my wrist still open,
splashing traces of blood on people's clothes. Proof I was there.

I crawled into the entryway of an apartment building across from
the park. I didn't care anymore. I slept in the open and I heard foot-
steps pass and a door closing. The floor was small tiles held together
with cement, and the door was a glass case barreled in dark wood. I
rested with my head on my arm and my knees pulled toward my
chest. I had a sack of clothes somewhere. A friend's parent had given
it to me, long white shirts and discarded pants, but I couldn't remember where I'd left it. My jeans were torn and I wore a black rock 'n' roll
T-shirt. I knew it was only a matter of time until the door-closing became a phone call and the phone call became swirling red and blue
lights and the lights became a back seat and a window with bars. The
police came and they asked where my parents were. I told them I
didn't know, which was true. The police weren't mean or angry. They
were just doing their job. In the morning I met a different set of officers, who didn't wear uniforms or carry guns. The new officers offered me sandwiches and something to drink. They asked what had
happened to my wrist, and I told them I had fallen on a tin can, but
they didn't believe me. I was taken to a hospital and a kind nurse used
surgical tape to close the hole in my wrist.

"Why would you do that?" she asked, and I wanted to laugh at her. I
wanted to ask if she was offering me a place to stay. But she was just
concerned and nice and I would meet a lot more people like her.
Things got much better after that, though it took me a little while to
recognize it. Things were going to work out fine, save for some scars.

KEVIN A. GONZÁLEZ

■

Lotería

FROM *Indiana Review*

Such is the burial of Hector.
— Homer, *The Iliad*

WHEN HECTOR'S FATHER won the lottery, in 1954, he bought a condo in Miami Beach, right on Collins, just a few blocks from where the luxury art-deco Eden Roc and Fontainebleau resorts would eventually go up, and he gave it to his mistress. Now, fifty years later, Hector is helping his mother move in.

Up until last week, when his father was still on his deathbed back in Puerto Rico, every time his mother stepped outside to fetch some juice or empty a bedpan, Hector would scold the old man, whispering: "How could you not have thought any of this through?" and "Have you ever heard of a plan, Dad, of making plans?" and even "How the hell could you do this to her? To us? You sick son of a bitch." His father just lay there, yellow, as if his bladder had exploded and his skin had soaked up all the piss, his mouth muzzled by an oxygen mask, and Hector could almost swear he saw a grin materialize through the hazy plastic. One last fuck-you grin.

Like his father, Hector was a lawyer, and although he knew nothing of equations, he still, naively, tried to solve for X. Two hundred thousand dollars in 1954 is equal to X dollars in 2004. If in 1954 a Coke cost ten cents, and in 2004 it costs a dollar, then what? Two million? Some vending machines were all the way up to a dollar and a quarter. Soon they would be a dollar and two quarters. Jesus! That's another million dollars right there! How stupid had his father been not to invest a cent? Ten cents? A quarter? Not to have bought his wife a condo? A house? A mansion with a terrace and a hot tub? An aspirin: Hector always needed an aspirin. He didn't even want to think about this: Miami was the only property they had.

"Mrs. Hector Lopez-DiCosta?" said the doorman. "I have your key. I was so very sorry to hear about —"

"Socorro," Hector's mother said. "*My* name is Socorro."

The doorman seemed spooked when she trilled her *r*'s. "Of course," he said, and pulled a keychain out of a drawer. He looked too old to be opening drawers, let alone doors. "That's a lovely name," he said. "What does it mean?"

"Help me, I'm drowning."

It was a one-bedroom apartment with mirrors lining the entire living room wall and a small balcony that overlooked the bogus, man-made beach of Miami and its seemingly endless boardwalk. It had been the model apartment fifty years ago, and, except for the electrical appliances, which were brand new, little of the decor had changed. There was a crystal chandelier over a round table where, Hector imagined, his father's mistress must have eaten salads or hard-boiled eggs or salads with hard-boiled eggs in them. On the counter there were two Lladró figurines of rosy-cheeked girls pushing wheelbarrows full of flowers, facing each other as if they were just about to crash. Beside them there was a photo of Hector's father standing next to Dwight Eisenhower, just the two of them — the photo originally had more people in it, but it had been cropped to create the illusion of intimacy. Hector picked up the silver frame. He knew that photo: it had *not* been just the two of them.

In the bedroom there was white shag carpeting everywhere, and a king-size bed, and twin floor lamps with stained-glass heads on either side of it. Hector examined the glass for cracks. Which side had it been? All Hector remembered was his father sitting at the foot of the bed, his head in his hands, weeping. It had been New Year's Eve, and sure, the mistress's body had been there too, on the white carpet, beside the bed, and one of those lamps had fallen on her, and it was still lit, and Hector had picked it up and put it back in its place and flicked it off, and the pills, everywhere, pills, pills, pills; but now he didn't remember any of it. Or at least he didn't *want* to remember any of it. Not how he bid farewell to 1983 in this dim apartment, closer to his father than he'd ever been, just a week before his own son, Tito, was born. Not his father's almost unintelligible voice on the phone, repeating "Miami." Something Miami. Come to Miami. Miami needs you. Miami-Miami. And that's where he'd been, Miami, at the foot of this bed, sitting on these very same leaf-patterned bed sheets. Shit! The leaf-patterned bed sheets! How could he forget about the leaf-patterned bed sheets?

"Mom," Hector said. "Mom, I'm going to Macy's." He ripped the sheets from under the mattress and slid the pillows out of their leaf-patterned cases. He crumpled everything into a ball, a leaf-patterned ball, pressed it tight against his chest, and walked out of the bedroom.

His mother's back was turned, but he could see, on the mirrored wall, that she was crying.

"Mom," he said. He thought about hugging her. They never hugged. They hadn't even hugged at the funeral, but then again, she hadn't cried. He had, in fact, never seen her cry.

"Who in the world," she said. "Who in the world likes to look at themselves in the mirror all day long, going about their business, all day long, looking at themselves?" And he did, he did hug her. He dropped the ball of dirty linens and he hugged her. "A conceited Cuban whore, that's who! A conceited Cuban whore who kills herself in my house, that's who!"

Yes, she knew, she knew. Are you kidding? *Everyone* knew.

Back in 1954, after Hector Lopez-DiCosta won the lottery, he bought a Rolls-Royce Silver Dawn in Manchester and drove it all over Europe with his friend Raymond DiCarlo. They sold the car a year later and returned to Puerto Rico, lugging two Cuban women they'd met in Madrid and with the "Di" attached to their surnames. They both bought condos for their mistresses in Miami Beach, on the same floor of the same building, and escaped to visit them several times a year.

When, in 1956, Raymond DiCarlo died, everyone wondered about the identity of those two women at the funeral, one of them sobbing even louder than the widow. And why was Hector Lopez-DiCosta the only one who knew them, and why was he holding their hands as he escorted them outside, and why was he overheard telling them to leave, to please leave, because it just wasn't right, because there are ways to do things and then there are ways to do things?

Returning from Publix, of course Socorro recognized the woman's face in the elevator, even after all those years, instantly — it was the woman who had sobbed the loudest at the DiCarlo funeral — and so she muttered, under her breath, "Slut."

"Excuse me?" the woman said. She was wearing two-toned pink and yellow sandals and a seagrass hat.

"You heard me," Socorro said.

There were two innocent bystanders in the elevator: a man in a wheelchair and a young woman — his granddaughter or nurse — standing behind him. The man looked up, confused, first at Socorro, then at the woman with the hat, then back at Socorro.

"What did you say?" the woman said. She tilted her head and the hat wobbled.

"I know who you are."

"Listen to me —"

"No, you listen to me. I never have to listen to you. I never, ever have to listen to you, slut." And with that, the elevator doors opened, and Socorro dropped her bag of groceries and hurried away as fast as she could — which was not fast at all — down the hall.

The other woman turned and wished the people in the elevator a good afternoon, then stepped out. The man in the wheelchair had his eyes closed, as if the pink and yellow sandals had somehow blinded him. The young woman behind him was smirking, as if she could not wait for the steel doors to shut, for the elevator to rush her upstairs so she could call her best friend and say, "Oh, my God! I just saw a little eighty-year-old lady call another little eighty-year-old lady a slut! Can you believe that, Brenda? Even at eighty you can still be a slut!"

While his mother was out grocery shopping, Hector found the suicide notes. He found a copy in a drawer in the bedroom, one in a cupboard in the kitchen, and another folded inside the cover of his father's book of essays on top of the counter. He found a copy in the walk-in closet, inside the pocket of his father's suit, the only suit there was, which he had also been checking for money. He found fifty copies inside a shoebox, and fifty more inside an old brown suitcase, which is where he began to gather them all. Those sheets of paper were like land mines, he knew, if his mother ever stumbled on one of them, and so he spent the afternoon sweeping the apartment while she slept. She had returned from Publix with no groceries at all, still visibly upset, and she had strapped on her sleeping mask, lain down on top of the new non-leaf-patterned sheets Hector had bought at Macy's, and fallen asleep. Hector had kept searching, and he found the note under the sink, wedged between two rolls of paper towels. And he found it in the liquor cabinet just after he'd decided to take a break and pour himself a scotch. And he found another inside the box of Parker Brothers' Monopoly, his father's favorite board game, the little green houses strewn all over the floor as if there had just been a hurricane. Once he was certain he'd gathered all the copies, he dropped the suitcase down the garbage chute, the same place where he'd dumped the leaf-patterned linens, and went out for a stiff drink.

Okay, make that eight stiff drinks. Hector sat at the corner of the bar, right next to the station where the waitresses ordered the drinks for their tables. The television was tuned to ESPN Classic, and Michael Jordan was on, leading the Bulls to three straight titles. One of the waitresses made small talk with Hector while she waited for the bartender to fix her drinks.

"Nice watch," she said. It was the Patek Philippe his father had brought back from Geneva. It *was* a nice watch, Hector thought, but man, had his father felt like an ass when he found out he could've gotten it cheaper from a stuttering jeweler in San Juan.

He had said to the jeweler, "But it was *made* in Switzerland!" And the jeweler had said, "The ex-exchange. Exchange will kill you. Will kill you, you know."

Hector looked down at the watch as if he'd forgotten it was now clasped around his wrist instead of his father's. "Thanks," he told the waitress. "Got it in Europe. In Switzerland."

"Really? I've never been."

"Well, then we should go sometime."

"Yes," she said. "Yes, yes, we should." She laughed, picked up her tray, and went to deliver the drinks.

It was the strangest thing: Hector could not remember what the suicide note had said. Yes, he'd seen more than a hundred copies of it, and he'd read it more than once, but still, all his energies had been focused on the search, like a child during an Easter egg hunt. All he wanted to do was find all the fucking eggs. Who cared what bright colors they were painted, whether they had chocolate or chicks inside, as long as he had them all in his possession? As long as no one else found them first?

What he remembered was that some words had run into each other, their large cursive letters dragging their extremities. Also, there had been no periods. There were commas but no periods. Hector's father's name — well, his *own* name — as well as life and death, had seemed omnipresent. Hector this, Hector that, it said. Life something, Death something, it said. What's the point? it should have said, and maybe it did. Hector imagined his father giving his mistress that photograph of himself with Eisenhower. "Look, *mi amor*," he might have said, "this is me with the president." God, who was this man? Had he gone to a pharmacy and just stood there dropping dime after dime into a Xerox machine, making copies of his mistress's suicide note, the strobe light reflecting off his Patek's golden face? A dime in 1983 is equal to X cents in 2004. How much did copies cost back then? Perhaps it was the other way around: a dime in 2004 is equal to X cents in 1983. Or perhaps some things hadn't changed that much. Had he made those copies out of guilt? Out of pride? And then, when Hector realized he would never be able to ask his father any of these questions, he ordered stiff drink number nine.

Hector knew his father had returned to the apartment several times after the suicide, to work on his quote-unquote book. That's the excuse he'd given Socorro from the beginning: his book. He needed to think about his book. Do research on his book. Take his book to the Keys to get a tan, to feed it stone crabs and Cristal. And even after the mistress wasn't around anymore, even after he had self-published a collection of essays, mostly plagiarized off old *Time* and *National Geographic* articles, he would still pack his suitcase and say, "My book," and take off for Miami. It must have been during one of those trips, or during *all* of those trips, that he made the copies. After the last trip, in the late nineties, when Hector's father had returned, he announced proudly that he'd just bought an SUV. "One of those big new cars," he'd said. "Everyone in Miami has one, so I got the biggest one there was."

"What," Hector had said, "were you planning on returning there? I figured that was your last trip." Now it was he who was driving that Ford Expedition, and he didn't feel all that good about having said what he'd said.

"So," the waitress said, "you a tourist?"

"Sometimes," Hector said. "But not today."

She smiled. "What do you do?"

"Lawyer. Retired. Retired lawyer."

"You must be one of the happy ones, then." She kept smiling. "This isn't what I do, by the way. I'm a massage therapist, across the street at the Eden Roc. I'm training."

"That's good to know."

"I got the job. I just need to pass the final, that's all." She picked up her tray.

"Well," Hector said, raising his glass, "let me know if you ever need a practice subject."

"Oh, no," she said. "It's not *that* kind of test. It's anatomy. The names of muscles and stuff. But I'll let you know." She winked and took off again.

While searching the apartment, Hector had found something else: a holographic will written by his father on a yellow legal pad, dated January 2, 1984. It was indeed a holographic will, Hector thought, reading it over and over at the bar, Michael Jordan and the Bulls celebrating above him. Hector was a lawyer, after all; he knew a holographic will when he saw one, and this one left everything to him. Of course, technically it was void, seeing as though Hector Lopez-DiCosta had written and registered a formal will many years later, leaving his grandson, Tito, as the executor. But still, there was something about reading his father's handwriting, something about running the tips of his fingers over the page, something devastating, something that made Hector feel as if his heart was a rim that someone had just dunked a basketball into.

Hector pulled out the MasterCard to pay, a card that was still linked to his father's bank account. His own account had barely a thousand dollars in it. He knew there would be money, good money, eventually. His father had left a sensible amount, but he had also left it in the hands of an eighteen-year-old kid who wasn't even sure if he was going to college. What was it that Tito said he wanted to be? Something with a *w* — a writer or a welder. He had been a straight-A student through middle school, but in high school he'd started drinking and skipping class to go surfing. He had also joined a leftist group and frequented pro-Puerto-Rican-independence rallies, and this angered Hector even more than the drinking. What was wrong with the kid? An *independentista?* A writer? A welder? A welder, Hector decided — God, please let my boy grow up to be a welder.

Even though it had been fifteen years since Hector divorced Tito's mother, and even though those last fifteen years had been a decadent fusion of alcohol and gambling, he and Tito had remained close. Close, but only after Tito had turned ten and Hector deemed that it was an okay age to take him on weekends, an okay age to lug him to bars. And close, that is, until Hector found out Tito had lent himself to be the executor of the will.

Hector was aware that he'd made many mistakes with his son, the first of which had been naming him Hector. He had always wanted to have a son named Achilles, to pull a 180 on his father, but Tito just happened to be born at a most vulnerable time: it was the beginning of an election year, right after Hector's trip to Miami, where, in helping his father bury his mistress, it seemed as though they had washed out the tainted stuff of the past and, in the process, become cordial, something they had never been before.

Though Hector never referred to Tito by his given name, the name was there, and its presence hovered over Hector: it was something inflamed he carried inside him, like a blooming sore at the back of his throat. Tito had no idea how to oversee the distribution of the estate, Hector knew, and he would have to hire a lawyer. The whole process would take at least a year. The idea was ludicrous: hire a lawyer when Hector could have just as simply dealt with everything himself. Dealt with everything better. He knew his father's assets — oh, he knew his father's assets, all right. There were very few things, in fact, that Hector knew better than his father's assets. Though Hector Lopez-DiCosta hadn't invested anything after winning the lottery, or after inheriting a small fortune from his own parents, nor had he invested any of the money he'd embezzled as a politician, he had somehow managed not to squander it all away. There was a safe-deposit box in Old San Juan, two different savings accounts with Banco Santander, the checking account that fed the MasterCard, and, to top it off, an off-shore account in the Caymans.

Then there was the issue of the house in Puerto Rico. Though Hector Lopez-DiCosta had lived his entire life in what was now a decaying mansion right in the middle of an otherwise commercial avenue, only a third of the property had actually belonged to him. The other two-thirds belonged to his sisters. They had never been bothered by their brother's appropriation of the mansion: it was normal for the eldest son to make the parents' dwelling place his own after their passing, and it's not as if the sisters needed any help themselves: one had married an olive oil tycoon, and the other a man whose last name was Bacardi. They had, however, never liked Socorro. At the funeral, they had both crept up to Hector, pushing their silver walkers, their beautiful tanned nurses clinging to their sides, and they had thrown their arms, heavy with jewelry, around his neck. Afterward one of them sobbed, "And your poor mother! What will she do now? Where will she live?" Hector had been expecting an eviction of this sort, though perhaps a subtler one, a more compassionate one, but still, he had said nothing. Now it was up to Tito and his lawyer to deal with the sisters. How can any eviction be compassionate? Hector dropped the MasterCard onto the bar.

"Taking off already?" the waitress said.

"I think I'm done."

"What about Switzerland? You promised. I get off in fifteen."

She was attractive. She was like most of the women Hector had slept with during the last fifteen years, which is to say she worked a dead-end job and was about ten to twenty years younger than he. She was independent and witty and lonely and white, and Hector knew she would be no trouble, no trouble at all.

"Well, my jet's in the shop. Something wrong with the Jacuzzi. Defective bubbles, you know. But I can buy you a drink." Hector gestured toward the bottles shelved, as in a caste system, behind the bar.

She grimaced. "I don't drink here," she said. "Business and plea-sure, you know."

"Well, how about —"

"You live around here?"

"Yeah, I'm just across Collins, but —"

"Well, I'm sure you have some Drambuie or something at home."

"But, see, the thing is . . . Drambuie? Did you just say Drambuie? My place is no good."

"Oh, I see, I see. No ring, no tan line. I just figured, you know —"

"No, it's not that. No." How could a man with a blinding Patek clasped around his wrist live with his mother? Even worse, how could a man with a blinding Patek clasped around his wrist *admit* he lived with his mother?

"It's fine," the waitress said. "You have a car? I need a ride anyway. We can just do my place."

What was it about spring and subtlety? What was it about despair and bars that still have those old cigarette machines with the handles you have to pull to get what you want? Now Hector felt terrible for having said what he'd said to his father. If he could do it over, he would say, "An SUV? *Hmmm.* I agree!"

After returning from Europe, Hector Lopez-DiCosta did what any other early-thirties, power-hungry Latin man with a law degree would do if he didn't have to work another day in his life: he became a politi-cian, a right-wing politician. He purchased the position of secretary of justice, one of the most luxurious and undemanding chairs in the government. The Department of Justice was like a casino: you had your dealers, box men, floor men, pit bosses, shift bosses, shift man-agers, and then the guy who rakes in the cash. Hector Lopez-DiCosta was the guy who raked in the cash. He had hundreds of people work-ing beneath him: a sub-secretary of justice who oversaw the sub-sub-secretaries who oversaw the sub-sub-sub-secretaries who oversaw . . . all the way down to the dealers, who in this case worked in cubicles. He also had a deep travel fund he could exploit, to visit his mistress in Miami or to be in photographs with Eisenhower in D.C. He had the makings of a good politician, though. Everywhere he went, he shoved the Statehood Party's ideas down everybody's throat. Statehood, state-hood, statehood — it was the cure for everything in Puerto Rico. Crime? Statehood! Education? Statehood! Health care? Statehood! Hurricanes? Statehood! Canker sores? Just dab a little statehood on them and watch them melt away!

Statehood was the only one of his father's ideas that had remained with Hector, and this was perhaps because he'd heard nothing but statehood after his father returned from Europe. Everyone had received some sort of present after the lottery, of course: the mistress got her condo; Socorro got clothes and jewelry and maids to tend to the house that was by no means hers; Hector Lopez-DiCosta got himself a mistress, a cushy government chair, two Cadillacs — an Eldorado and a Coupe de Ville — and a Patek Philippe; and Hector, four years old then, got a miniature longhaired dachshund. He named it Lotería; or, rather, his father named it for him. It was, at least, a better name than Statehood.

Hector didn't remember much about the years his father had been in politics other than that it was usually him, his mother, and the maids at home. What he remembered was the day his father was forced to resign: there had been a murder, a political murder of four *independentistas,* and the cover-up had gone awry. His father had somehow been involved in it, and there had been reporters blocking the gates of their house, trying to get an interview. Lotería had barked at them, and Socorro had tried shooing them away, but only Hector Lopez-DiCosta had been able to move them with his Eldorado Special. It was shiny and red, and it had shot out of the garage so fast that the reporters had scattered like pigeons, their cameras swinging from their necks as they ran. So fast, Hector thought, that his father had perhaps not felt the bump when he ran over Lotería, and most likely had not seen Hector in the rearview mirror, running to the dead dog, taking him in his arms, and shooting a long, hard stare at the fading fenders of the Caddy, cursing the random pulse of its brake lights.

Hector brought his mother lunch, and she didn't ask him where he'd spent the night. He hadn't been able to fall asleep, and so he'd lain beside Michelle, the waitress, thinking. He had decided Miami would do him good. On his way back to Collins, he had stopped at a sporting goods store and charged a bicycle and the most expensive swimming goggles he could find to the MasterCard. He would get an apartment. He would exercise, live a healthier life. At Publix he bought all kinds of fruit and Tupperware. He bought lightbulbs and a cutting board — a new apartment would surely need lightbulbs and a cutting board. He bought two decks of playing cards for his mother. Maybe she would meet some nice old ladies at the building and they could all play canasta together. Wouldn't that be something? Canasta, he thought. Why not canasta? Anything's possible!

"You can put the fruit in my fridge," Socorro said, "and the cards on top of my counter."

Hector noticed how her voice had improved since his father had died. She'd never really had any health problems other than skin cancer, basal cell, which she said was nothing, but her voice had always been sluggish and cracked. Her words came out exhausted, as if they had just scaled all the way up the walls of her throat from her stomach. The only time Hector remembered her speaking clearly had been at Disney World, after riding Space Mountain. She had gotten out of the roller-coaster car and started speaking as smoothly as a radio host. Nobody could explain it. Five minutes later, the sluggish, cracked voice had returned. She wasn't speaking that clearly now, but there was definitely more clarity to her than there had been in years.

"I think I'm getting a place, Mom," Hector said. "An apartment."

"In Miami? You know, you don't have to stay. You can go back. Don't stay because of me."

"No, no. I want to. I think it'll be good. It'll be good."

"You know, you can have my bed. I'll sleep on my couch. I don't really mind my mirrors that much. I'll get used to them."

"It's fine. Really, it'll be good. I'll find something nearby."

"Just remember, my everything is yours too," she said. "Will you pass me my TV remote?"

During the next few hours it got worse. My chandelier. My little round table. My Lladró figurines of my rosy-cheeked girls pushing my wheelbarrows full of my flowers. If only they'd hurry up and crash, Hector thought, so orange and pink petals would spill everywhere and his mother would have a little color in her life. Hearing her use possessive pronouns like that broke his heart a little, and he thought that perhaps if Tito were there, he might be able to weld it back together. Later, when the phone rang and his mother picked it up, he knew it had to be Tito.

"Here he is," Socorro said into the receiver, and handed Hector the phone.

"Yes?" Hector said.

"Her voice," Tito said. "It sounds a lot better."

Hector said nothing.

"So, how the hell are you?" Tito said.

"Yes?" Hector repeated. "What do you want?" He had avoided Tito ever since the will had been read. He had not spoken to him at the funeral, and he had only very reluctantly shaken his hand during the kiss-of-peace part of the Mass. This is what Hector figured: his father had wanted someone to take his place, and his son, behind his back, had agreed to do so. It was as if Hector had not existed, either to his father or to his son, and for this there was no welder in the world who could mend him.

"Come on," Tito said. "You have to talk to me someday."

"Is that why you called? You don't know me. I can live without talking to you. Hell, I have no problem saying goodbye to you right —"

"I got a call from the bank," Tito said.

"So? It's your job to get calls from the bank now. You signed on, remember? It's your job to deal with all that, not mine. So don't even think about asking my advice, because frankly I don't care. I don't have anything to do with that. Not with you or your grandfather or my aunts or any of the money."

"Oh, but you do!" Tito said. "See, apparently someone's been charging shit to a dead man's credit card in Miami. Got any idea who that could be?"

Hector said nothing.

"Dad, look —"

"No, you look. I'm the father here and none of this is your business. You don't know anything about anything."

"Dad —"

"Listen, son," Hector said. "Do me a favor."

"What?"

"If you ever have a son —"

"Yeah?"

"Name him Achilles." Hector hung up.

Hector's new apartment was not pretty, nor was it clean, but it was cheap and twelve blocks away from his mother's. It was, actually, the first one he looked at, and he hadn't looked at it all that well, because he hadn't noticed the cockroaches until after putting down the first month's rent. He had gone to Publix and bought three cans of Raid, and he emptied two of them all over the apartment. He swept up the small black carcasses with paper towels, and dizzy as only a pesticide junkie could be, he took his bike and his swimming goggles and headed for the boardwalk.

He rode all the way down to Ocean Drive, and he almost fell off the bike half a dozen times, because whenever an attractive girl would rollerblade past him, he would spin his head around to look at her ass. Once, when his father could still walk, though barely, Hector had taken him for a walk on the beach, right across the street from that decaying mansion. Hector had held on to his father's arm, and they had walked slowly, protractedly. His father could barely lift his feet off the ground, so that every time he stepped, he dragged the soles of his shoes on the sand, leaving the wake of a snowmobile. A girl in her early twenties had jogged by in a bikini. His father, gradually and with a lot of effort, began to turn his body. Then he stood there, motionless and fulfilled, staring at the girl jogging away from him. Hector remembered saying, "Well, at least your eyes still work. That's something." And after the girl had jogged far away, his father spun his neck to look at him and said, "You're a damn idiot. You don't know anything about anything. My mind is younger than hers. It just happens to be trapped inside this goddamn carapace." Hector had never felt guilty, after that day, for finding much younger women attractive, even though he knew his bluntness had embarrassed Tito whenever they had gone to the beach together.

On his way back to the new apartment, Hector stopped at several hotels to swim laps in their pools. He snuck into the Doral, the Eden Roc, the Fontainebleau, and nobody said a word to him. He was a good swimmer. He had swum in prep school and college, and he had even competed for the Puerto Rican team at the '67 Pan American Games in Winnipeg. He had put on more than fifty pounds since then. He was going to lose the weight. He was going to feel better. This was Miami, and he was going to bike and swim and eat fruit every day from now on.

When Hector walked into his apartment, it still stank of pesticide, and there was a giant cockroach on the white Formica countertop. Hector retreated slowly toward the closet where he'd put the last can of Raid. Holding the can, he tiptoed back to the counter and let out a nice thick spray. When the roach lifted its wings to fly away, Hector jumped back and, as in a reflex, took off his shoes and threw them at the flying thing, but he missed, so he took off his T-shirt and began swatting at it, but that didn't do anything either. The roach just dodged the shirt, did a few figure eights in the air, and flew into a crease behind the kitchen sink. "Come out of there, Hector!" Hector said to the roach. "Take that, Hector!" he yelled as he sprayed Raid into the crease. "See you in hell, Hector! See you in hell!" When the can was finally empty, he went out for a stiff drink.

Okay, okay, make that eight stiff drinks. Hector sat in the same spot of the same bar and flirted with the same waitress, Michelle. She had been happy to see him. He told her he got a new unfurnished apartment. He stressed "unfurnished," and she got the hint and invited him to spend the night at her place again.

"You want to go buy furniture tomorrow?" she said. "It's my day off."

"You want to?" Hector said, almost amazed at her offer.

"Well," she said, "it's not Geneva, but I love buying furniture."

"I'm sorry. You *love* buying furniture? That's terrible. There must be a pill you can take for that."

While she took care of her tables, Hector sat there pretending to watch the Miami Heat on the screen above him, thinking about his parents. How they had sent him away to Camp Half Moon in Massachusetts every summer, to boarding school when he got to seventh grade, then to prep schools all over New England. How he'd gotten expelled from Andover and Blair and Mercersburg, thinking that if he kept getting expelled, his father would have no choice but to take him home. And how he had been wrong about everything. He could have gone to an Ivy League school. He could have been something. Once, as a freshman at Andover, he had written a short story about his dog Lotería, and it had won second place in a school-wide contest. He had thought then it was pity, that pity had won him second place, but perhaps that hadn't been the case. Perhaps he really had been on to something.

And his mother, how sorry he felt for her. Sorry she had put up with his father, sorry she had wasted fifteen years typing out that book of plagiarized essays. How his father would pace the room, dictating, and how whenever she made a mistake, he would scream, scream and tell her she was no good. Sorry she didn't believe in divorce. Sorry she was a good Catholic who would rather believe in the seven years she lived across the street from that mansion, at the Condado Renaissance, waiting for reconciliation. He was sorry his father had brought the mistress to their home in Puerto Rico while Socorro was out, after the DiCarlo funeral, and sorry to have witnessed his father and the mistress in the middle of a fight. And he was sorry that the mistress had thrown an ashtray at his father's head, and sorry he'd started bleeding, and sorry that his father had liked it. More than anything, he was sorry his mother found out from the maids, and sorry that his father was a masochist who had forgiven the mistress. "Mom," he'd wanted to say to Socorro all his life, "all you had to do was throw a fucking ashtray at his head every once in a while. All you had to do was draw some blood when he got out of line."

Hector unhooked the detachable back seat of the Expedition and left it at Michelle's. He bought a bed, two leather chairs, a table, and some minor electrical appliances: a microwave, a George Foreman grill, a food processor. He even bought Michelle a food processor like the one he got himself. He'd been thinking of healthy pesto sauce, fruit smoothies for breakfast, piña coladas on the weekends — things that, he was sure, he would someday get around to fixing. Once again, he hadn't been able to sleep the night before, and after unloading everything at his place, he decided to take Michelle out to dinner.

They drank and ate and bought a bottle of scotch, and she suggested that they drive, that they just drive somewhere until they tired. That was the beautiful thing about Miami, Hector thought: he was no longer trapped on an island one hundred miles long by thirty-five miles wide, and he could drive, drive, drive, down to Chile or up to Anchorage if he so desired. Perhaps that's why his father had never given the mistress the title to that apartment; perhaps that's why he had returned to Miami all those years — because he wanted the freedom of it, the uninhibited options of it. Perhaps that's even why, when he played Parker Brothers' Monopoly, if anyone landed on Chance and got the Get Out of Jail Free card, Hector Lopez-DiCosta would pay a thousand dollars for it, or two thousand, or whatever it took, even though getting out of jail in Monopoly costs only fifty dollars. Hector had always thought it ruined the game, and Tito had always found it hilarious, how he would tell his grandfather, "I'll give you the Get Out of Jail Free card if you give me all your money and all your properties." And Hector Lopez-DiCosta would do it. He would hold up the yellow Get Out of Jail Free card and say, "It was a bargain, this card. This card, my friends, is the most important thing you can ever have." Perhaps he also thought that if Puerto Rico became a state of the Union, there would be a bridge or a tunnel, or perhaps if Puerto Rico became a state, you could just drive on top of the Atlantic, drive, drive, drive, if you ever needed to get away. Hector Lopez-DiCosta always went out gracefully: he would have his Get Out of Jail Free card and he would be bankrupt, but he would be happy, because that's all he ever wanted.

And so they drove. They drove west on Tamiami Trail, past the Florida Turnpike and Westwood Lake, and when they passed the welcome signs for Everglades National Park, Hector stopped the car and they got out and sat on the hood with the bottle of scotch. They kissed and drank, and drank and kissed, and said nothing, or almost nothing. She said, "I love you," and Hector said, "Me too." He was lying now on the hood of the Expedition, facing up, thinking about his father. Michelle said, "I want to be with you," and he said, "Me too." She was looking at him. "I want to move in with you," she said. He was looking up. "Yeah," he said. "Good." She bent to kiss him. He didn't close his eyes. In the sky, the stars glistened like all the periods that suicide notes have forgotten.

When Hector opened the door to his apartment the next morning, he saw the giant cockroach on his new table. When he shut the door the cockroach took flight and once again eluded his best efforts and hid in the crease behind the sink. How could it still be alive? Hector wasn't even sure if *he* could have survived all that Raid. Because he didn't have anything else, he emptied three glasses of water into the crease behind the sink. "Goddamn you, Hector!" he said to the roach. "I hope you fucking drown in there, Hector!"

When Hector brought his mother lunch and noticed that the playing cards were still in their plastic wrapper on the counter, he asked if she'd made any friends.

"Everyone here knows," she said. "They all look at me with pity. Even the doorman, even the doorman knows."

"They don't," he said. "Mom, the people here are so old they don't even remember their own lives, let alone anyone else's."

"The people here are so old they have to remember other people's lives better than their own. It's how they live."

"Well," Hector said. He wasn't going to argue with that. He looked around and the first thing that caught his eye was the box of Monopoly. "You want to play Monopoly? You and me?"

"Me and no one. I never liked that game."

Hector sat back on the couch and opened his father's book of essays to a random page that said "Mesopotamia" at the top. What had his father known about Mesopotamia? Hector hadn't read the whole book, and as far as he knew, neither had anyone else. He had tried, but he hadn't been able to follow his father's sentences: they were full of semicolons and dashes and commas, and each one seemed to go on for half a page and never get to the point. The only essay he had been able to absorb was the one about Puerto Rico, about statehood, so he looked it up in the table of contents and flipped to it.

While he read, he saw, out of the corner of his eye, his mother fumbling with the phone book. She was leafing through it, and when she found the page she was looking for, she put her finger on it and ran it down the page. She picked up the phone and began to dial.

"Who are you calling?" Hector asked.

She ignored him and finished dialing. She pressed her mouth to the receiver.

"Yes," she said. "Good afternoon. Do you pick up?"

She waited for the other side to respond.

"My sister," she said. "Eighty-three. Natural causes."

Hector looked at her, perplexed. She was waiting for the other side to speak.

"That is fine," she said. "There is no problem. Collins, block 4600. Beside the Eden Roc Hotel. Apartment 205."

Their apartment was 206, and Hector felt the need to correct her.

"Mom," he said urgently. "It's 206. We live in 206."

She waved him off. "Thank you," she said into the phone. "I will wait." And she hung up.

"Who did you just call?" Hector asked. "What the hell was that?"

She didn't answer. She got up and walked into the kitchen. She opened the refrigerator and poured herself a glass of Harveys Bristol Cream.

Hector got up from the sofa. He looked at the phone book. It was open to "Funeral Homes."

"Mom!" he said, holding up the yellow pages. "Mom, what is this? What did you just do? Are you trying to tell me something here?"

She sipped her sherry. "This has nothing to do with you," she said.

"But Mom —"

"I said relax." Her voice really had gotten better.

For the next hour, Socorro kept pacing the apartment, and every few minutes she would walk to the front door and glance through the peephole. Hector had gone back to the sofa, to the essay on statehood, but he hadn't been able to concentrate. He still hadn't slept since coming to Miami. It was just a matter of time until the MasterCard got cut off, and there was a giant flying cockroach waiting for him at home. Why was his mother acting so strange? He might have missed a copy or two of the suicide note when he swept the apartment. What would compel a man to hide a copy of a suicide note inside a board game? A game — is that what everything had been to his father? Had making

Tito the executor been some sort of move? Rolling the dice one last time from the grave? What kind of man adds two letters to his surname to make him seem more exotic? More glamorous? Hector tried to imagine his father cutting up that photo of Eisenhower, removing the other people who had been in it. He just couldn't picture his father with two fingers stuck in a pair of scissors. Perhaps he had asked his secretary to do it. Or his sub-secretary, or his sub-sub-secretary. Perhaps it had been Socorro. That would make sense, Socorro. His father would yell out her name in public places, and it always sounded as if he was asking for help, as if he was drowning. Hector had always wanted no one to come when he called.

There was some commotion out in the hallway. Socorro was looking through the peephole and grinning and nodding, and Hector could hear a woman speaking loudly outside. Suddenly someone rang the bell to their apartment. Socorro retreated from the peephole and scurried into the bathroom, and Hector heard her lock the door.

Hector was disoriented. He got up and walked to the front door and opened it. There was a woman in her eighties, and her face was rather familiar. Behind her there were two men dressed in suits, wearing white gloves, holding a stretcher with a body bag and a medical kit on top of it. They seemed even more disoriented than Hector.

"Hector," the woman said, "right?"

"Y-yes," he stuttered.

"Did you call these men?"

"No," he said. He remembered her. She had been there in 1983 when he had come to be with his father. She had been at the funeral, at his father's mistress's funeral, and she hadn't seemed to get along with his father. But why would she? She was obviously a friend of the mistress, and it was his father's name that the suicide note had repeated over and over.

"Is your mother home?" the woman said.

"No," Hector said. "She's out. I'm sorry."

The woman seemed discouraged. She turned toward the two men and shrugged her shoulders. "I'm sorry, gentlemen," she said. "Apparently there's been a mistake. No one is dead." She turned toward Hector again. She studied his face. "You," she said. "You're your father." Then she walked into the apartment across the hall and shut the door.

Hector knocked on the bathroom door. "You can come out now," he said.

When Socorro came out, she didn't say anything at all about what had just happened. Instead she sat on one of her chairs, perched her arms on top of her little round table, sipped her Harveys Bristol Cream, and told Hector that she used to be a poet.

"What?" Hector said. "A what?"

"A poet. I wrote beautiful poetry."

"You did?"

"I did. I was the valedictorian, you know. Did you know that?"

"You were? I thought you never went to college." She was calm and melancholy, and these feelings were rubbing off on him. Hearing his mother speak of something lost with such passion made him feel as if that ball of leaf-patterned linens was stuffed, moist, somewhere inside him.

"In high school. I was the valedictorian in high school, and they asked me to speak at the graduation, so I read a poem. Everyone stood up and clapped."

"A poem?" Hector said. "No kidding."

"It's very true. I was a poet. But then I met your father."

"Well, that could kill anyone's poetry."

She laughed. Hector realized he hadn't heard her laugh in a long time. "What you said before," she said. "I think you're right. I think it'll be good here. Maybe I could write again."

Someone was now wringing it out, that moist ball of cloth in his chest.

Hector began executing stakeouts, staying up all night with a shoe in his hand, waiting for Hector the Cockroach to come out. He bought a flashlight, and he would turn off the ceiling light to try to fool Hector. He would go to the front door and open and close it and stay inside the apartment, so Hector would think he had left. What did cockroaches eat? He left out all kinds of food: cheese, half-eaten fruit, Taco Bell. Occasionally Hector would come out, elude him for a few minutes, flip him the antennae, and fly into some remote crease. It was official: Hector the Cockroach was immune to Raid and to all other pesticides sold at Publix, whereas Hector the Man wasn't. Hector the Man was dizzy as hell.

It had been a week since he'd come to Miami with his mother, and Hector had still not been able to sleep. He would go visit her in the mornings, sneak into the hotel pools in the afternoons, then he would eat, go to a bar, and come home to sit with a shoe in his hand until morning. Sometimes he even forgot that he hadn't slept in a week, that he had ever slept at all, that sleep even existed. He hadn't returned to Michelle's bar, or even seen Michelle, since the night they drove out to the Everglades, but it didn't surprise him that when he came home from swimming, she was sitting in front of his apartment, waiting.

"What's up with you?" she said.

Hector told her to wait while he changed, then he took her out to eat. He told her nothing was up. He had been spending time with his mother, helping her cope. The truth was that he had been going to a different bar every night because he hardly remembered anything about their drive to the Everglades.

"I failed the test," Michelle said. They were sitting at a table at Wolfie's.

"The one with all the muscle names?"

"I can't take it again till summer."

"I'm sorry," Hector said. He'd had a taste of her massages; they were good, and so he told her so. But she didn't say anything back, not anything about massages anyway.

"So," she said. "What you said about me moving in with you. I was thinking you could help me move my stuff tomorrow?"

"What?" Hector said. "What I said?" He hadn't said anything about anything — that was his position and, by God, he was sticking to it. There was already one too many roommates for his liking, what with Hector the Cockroach refusing to budge. Yes, it was him and Hector the Cockroach in the apartment, and it was going to stay like that. It was going to stay like that at least until he got his hands on the fucking cockroach, or until the cockroach got the best of him, whichever happened first.

"I quit my waitress job because I had the one at the hotel. But I failed the test, and I don't have it anymore. Not till summer at least. So you told me to stay with you."

"Honey," he said, "you don't want to live with me. Trust me, you don't want to live with me."

"Is it that you don't want *me* to live with *you?*"

"Well," Hector said. "That too."

"But you said I could!"

"But I didn't! I don't even know you. Why would you even ask me? You don't even know *me*."

"But I do. I do know you!"

"I'm sorry," he said. "Listen, I want to be your friend. If you need help, I might be able to help you out or something."

"Well, I need this month's rent."

"Rent? You think I should pay your rent?"

"It's eight hundred dollars."

"I don't care how much it is. I'm not paying your rent. Plus, that's even more than I pay."

"Yeah, but you live in a shithole."

"Exactly! I live in a shithole and you want to move in. Why would you want to move into a shithole to begin with? Why would you want to share a shithole with someone you don't even know?"

"I told you," she said. "I know you."

"Will you please stop saying that?"

"I know you, I know you, I know you."

"Okay." Hector chuckled. He got up and pulled out the MasterCard. "Just so you know," he said, "I'm paying this bill. This one's on me. And that's it. Good luck. See you."

"If you ever want to see your back seat again, you'll give me eight hundred dollars."

"What?" Hector took a step back. "My back seat?"

"The back seat of your truck, that you left at my house. If you ever want to see it again, you better pay up."

Hector made sure he wasn't being followed as he walked down the street. He went into a liquor store, charged a bottle of Dewar's, and went home. The nerve of that woman, he thought, kidnapping the back seat of his Expedition. The back seat of his Expedition! After he bought her a food processor! It was leather, the back seat, black leather. He imagined her drinking a piña colada while sitting on it. Eating a bowl of fettuccine al pesto on it.

When he turned on the light, he saw that Hector the Cockroach was again resting on the white kitchen counter. This time, however, he did not make an attempt to fly away as Hector the Man approached. He just sat there — a black spot, disgusting, vulnerable. Hector the Man took off one shoe and held it, in his left hand, over Hector the Cockroach, so that Hector the Cockroach seemed to be drowning in its shadow.

The ceiling light mirrored off the Patek, and a golden spotlight shone into Hector's face. He knew his father had paid two grand for it. *Two grand in 1954, equal to X grand in 2004.* But it would have been less than two grand if he'd bought it from that stuttering jeweler in San Juan. Hector had admired that jeweler because he hadn't been afraid of his father. He had just shrugged his shoulders and told his father he was wrong, point-blank. And how upset his father had been: more upset than the day he was forced to resign from politics; more upset, even, Hector thought, than the day the mistress had taken the pills. He had just been scared when the mistress had taken the pills, scared because he knew he was responsible. And he had been scared the day he resigned, scared because he might go to jail. But the jeweler, the jeweler had *upset* him, and so Hector Lopez-DiCosta had made fun of him for years: "The ex-ex-ex-exchange ex-ex-exchange will kill you," he would say, and Hector would laugh, but he would laugh with the jeweler, not at his father's mimicry.

Hector had always wanted to pull a stuttering-jeweler line on his father; he had always wanted to rip the Get Out of Jail Free card from his hand. A part of him admired what it took to give everything up for freedom, but not if that everything included him and his mother, and certainly not if that freedom was more like a license to fuck with his head. Holding the shoe over the cockroach that he had named Hector, he thought of Lotería, his dog, and how he had wanted to make his father bleed that day. And he thought of his mother, standing in the small balcony where the mistress had once stood, looking over that sad, man-made beach. And he thought of Tito, whom Hector Lopez-DiCosta had somehow manipulated into being the executor of his will, just because he was the type of man who would do such a thing, because he wanted Hector and Tito not to have what he and Hector never did have.

Hector saw his own eyes blazing, reflected off the microwave door. A whack and it would all be over — no more Hector. He couldn't do it, though. If he did, there would be nothing to do the next day. Or the next. So he let him live.

MIRANDA JULY

■

How to Tell Stories to Children

FROM *Zoetrope: All-Story*

TOM HAD DONE some bad things. Now, it seemed, he was getting his comeuppance. There was almost nothing to say that the universe had not said already. I asked about his wife.

Is Sarah willing to talk about it?

Sure, but she's blasé. She doesn't give a shit.

That's terrible.

Yeah.

And the student?

She won't stop fucking him.

Oh man. Man oh man.

Yeah.

And she knows about your, your things — your affairs?

No.

We sat in silence, sipping our tea. And to think eleven years before I had been one of these things. I pressed my finger against a cold tea bag. A few minutes later we embraced and went our separate ways.

He didn't call me for a few weeks. This was customary within our friendship, confide and retreat, but I wondered. I wondered if perhaps our last conversation had been an overture. Not the conversation exactly, but the silences within it. There had been many dark pits of tea-sipping silence; looking back, I could imagine placing my hand on his hand while kneeling in one of these dark pits. And in such a pit could one even be sure what one was doing? One might seek solace in a friend and literally go inside this friend to get the solace; and the friend, being old and familiar, might give especially good solace. With this kindness in mind I e-mailed Tom:

Lunch?

And he responded:

Sarah is pregnant and we're having the baby!! More soon, I have to run. Just wanted you to hear it from me first. Love, Tom

At the baby shower Tom's mother walked around with a clipboard assigning to all the guests days on which to bring a healthy meal to the new parents; it was called a meal tree, like a telephone tree. If Tom and Sarah did not answer the door we were told to leave the meal on the front porch in a basket that would be labeled THANK YOU, FRIENDS!

Luckily, I was allocated the last possible day, and I hoped that the passing of time would carry me out of horror, toward feelings of joy. But the day came and I had no such feelings. I knocked on their door very quietly, hoping to leave the meal in the Thank You, Friends basket, which actually said PUT MEALS HERE. The door swung open immediately.

Deb, thank God you're here, can you take her?

And the baby was handed to me. Tom guided us past a tear-stained Sarah, who gave a sarcastic wave, and into the office/baby room. Tom looked at me and winced apologetically before shutting the door and leaving us alone. There was a silence, and then,

I didn't say that! I said I could have if I wanted to because it's my body!

But our baby was in your body! You could have hurt her!

It's perfectly safe as long as it's not rough sex!

Oh. So it did happen.

I held my breath and pulled the child to my chest as if she were me. There was a long silence during which I imagined Sarah weeping silently. But suddenly her voice issued, clear and unadorned with guilt.

Yeah.

Yeah. And what was this not-rough sex like if it was not rough?

It was gentle.

They were in a wilderness that was too wild for me, their words flying past deadly animal teeth. I wished I was hearing about this second- or even thirdhand: "We had a terrible fight"; "I heard they had a terrible fight"; "I had an acquaintance who knew a couple who, back in the latter part of the previous century, had a terrible fight, perhaps even had terrible fights on a regular basis, this acquaintance doesn't know for sure, she is realizing now that she didn't really know the couple, on account of the fact that she had mixed intentions with regard to the man in the couple, intentions that now are even more ancient history than this ancient, historical, terrible fight."

Tom began screaming and I wondered if the baby's soft brain was, in this moment, changing shape in response to the violent stimuli. I tried to intellectualize the noise to protect the baby's psyche, whispering: Isn't it interesting to hear a man scream? Doesn't that challenge our stereotypes of what men can do? And then I tried, *Shhhhhhhhh.*

She burrowed for a nipple, I slipped my finger into her mouth. And as she slept in my arms I began to find I could think only thoughts that were cosmological in scale. I considered the round ball of the sun, the food cycle, and time itself, which now seemed miraculous and poignant. I curled my whole body around her. Tom and Sarah were just distant traffic beside my primeval blossoming, the almost painful expansion of my heart to include their descendant. I studied each scale model of a finger; I gazed at her shut eyes, with their majestic lashes, and her good intention of a nose. But I could not remember her name. I looked at her face — Lilya? No, it was something less innocent, more earnestly clever. I stared at a stuffed bunny and a row of acrobatic wooden clowns on a shelf. Lana? No. The clowns leaned and bent and gradually came into focus. They were not only acrobatic, they were alphabetic, and they would contort forever to spell the name, *Lyon.*

Throughout time there have been women who came by their children gradually, organically, without the formalities of conception or adoption. It felt intuitive to me but was a confusing situation for my boyfriends.

Didn't we just see Lyon?

Not since she learned to swim with water wings.

But can one really call that swimming?

Oh, come on, you know how afraid she is of water. It's a big, huge deal.

How about "it's a big deal" and we save "big, huge deal" for us? Can we do that? Can we save that for something big and huge that happens to us?

Like what?

Like, I don't know, a big, huge . . . feeling between us.

Uh-oh, this sounds like it's about to be a long conversation. Look, you don't have to go. Just drop me off and pick me up at four.

She is running toward me covered in hundreds of water droplets, a pink-and-yellow-flowered swimsuit, sunlight in her eyes, red mouth broken open into a shout, crashing wetly into my legs with so much to say:

I went in before but that was holding on to the side and then today this morning I went in again, holding on to the side but then I let go! I let go! And I couldn't touch the bottom! And it was for nine seconds! But I think I can do it longer but I had to rest on a towel because I was so tired and Daddy said you were coming over so I waited, I've been waiting for almost a million years, can we go in now? Did you see my towel? See, it has a picture of a teenager with a bikini and a little dog, don't step on it, you messed it up, can you fix it please? Yeah. Can we go in now? Can you hold me at first?

We bobbed around in the middle of the pool, her legs wrapped around my waist, one arm around my neck, the other directing us through the water. We were heavy and clumsy but also weightless and graceful. In the deep end she gripped me and screamed; in the shallow end she broke free and marveled at her own bravery. She checked the water wings every couple of minutes, pressing on them to make sure they were still hard.

I think this one's going down.

No, it's fine.

Can you blow it up a little more?

I don't want to pop it.

Can you check it?

It's fine, see? It's the same as the other one.

She felt the other one, looked up at me solemnly, opened her eyes wide, and then suddenly jumped up and down, shouting, splashing, reckless. Sarah looked up from her magazine and then looked down again. Tom looked across the patio, our eyes met, and for a split second I remembered my drunken nineteen-year-old face pressed against his chest at a party, his lips resting on the top of my head, murmuring, You know I wish I could. It seemed impossible that I ever thought of him as the main attraction. Now he was Lyon's father, and she possessed the daring, the warmth, the wicked charm I once thought I would find in him. Lyon plunged her face into the water and held a winged arm in the air; her fist released a spiky finger for each second endured: *one, two, three, four, five* — the other arm shot up — *six, seven, eight, nine, ten* — her arms froze in the air, all digits holding numbers; and then her face, smeared with wet hair and mucus, rose out of the depths. Gasping, furious, she shook her stiff hands at me.

I ran out of fingers! That was longer than ten seconds! You saw it was longer! Did you count?

I think it was thirteen.

I think it might have been twenty-seven!

Do you want to know how to count higher? You just start over on the first hand.

No.

You remember ten and you start on the first hand with eleven.

I said no. I don't want to know.

But how will you count big numbers?

When it goes bigger than ten, you can do it.

Okay, but what if I'm not there?

At this she laughed. She jumped out of the pool and ran toward her mother on the lounger. Lyon shrieked, now in a drunken imitation of laughter, and hurled herself onto Sarah.

What's so funny?

Deb.

She is funny, isn't she. A funny bunny.

Friday night was date night, named for the date Sarah and Tom would go on while Lyon slept over at my house. But because they usually just stayed home and fought, and Lyon and I more often went to dinner and saw a movie, date night became our code for Night of Endless Fun. Don't underestimate how much joy an eight-year-old and an almost-forty-year-old can bring each other. We usually began at Miso Happy, our favorite Japanese place. We thought the name was terrible but we liked the noodles. We talked about everything, including but not limited to: My gray hairs, should I dye them? Could I dye them individually? Could I pay a mouse with a tiny paintbrush to jump on my head and dye them one by one? And why did Tom and Sarah have to fight so much? Was it Lyon's fault? No, absolutely not. Could she stop them from fighting? Again, no. Also: Would they buy her a twenty-four-color pen set, and if they did, how jealous would her best friend Claire be when Lyon brought it to school? Our guess was *very*. And why had Deb's last boyfriend dumped her?

I dumped *him*.

Maybe you didn't French-kiss him enough.

I promise you that wasn't it.

Tell me how many times a day you kissed and I'll say if it was enough.

Four hundred.

Not enough.

If there was a decent kid movie, we would see that after dinner, but usually we went to the second-run theater, where we saw things like *McCabe and Mrs. Miller* or *Bonnie and Clyde* or *Shampoo*. We were massive Warren Beatty fans. I worried at first about the sex and the violence, but Lyon discovered that as long as the movie was made before 1986 she could take it. Thus, *Reds* was okay but *Ishtar* was too disturbing. After the movie we went home and took a bath in my tub, also known as La Salon Paree. We made potions out of combinations of shampoos and tested them on each other's backs for scent, froth, and beautification properties. We checked Lyon's body for signs of puberty, which never appeared. (Or yes, they did, but years after the close of La Salon Paree.) We slept together in my giant bed, which was exactly as wide as it was long. It made as much sense to sleep one direction as another, and Lyon charted our course by spinning around: Tonight weee willlll sleeeeeep — and then flinging herself down — this way! She lay still, holding the spot, while I moved the pillows around to our new north. We read from an antique book called *How to Tell Stories to Children, and Some Stories to Tell*. Lyon was bored by the prosaic "Billy Beg and His Ball" and "The Fox and the Ox," but she loved to hear me read the chapter called "The Story-teller's Mood — A Few Principles of Method, Manner and Voice, from the Psychological

Point of View." Afterward we slept. Spooning at first, and then, because Lyon radiated an uncomfortable heat, back to back.

By the time she was nine she was living at my house three or four days a week, and Sarah and Tom were sleeping at other people's houses most nights. Occasionally Tom, in a moment of manic elation, would suggest I meet his current girlfriend.

It's only because she's gorgeous and I think you would appreciate that.

Well, thank you, but that's okay.

Oh. Are you jealous?

No.

But you would have been when we were younger.

Probably.

Sarah sure is. Do you at least want to see a picture?

No.

What do you think of her? Is she not perfect?

She is.

Do you want to keep the picture?

What would I do with it?

I don't know, you could put it on your refrigerator.

I wouldn't want Lyon to see it.

Oh, she's already met her.

When Lyon was ten she entered a spiritual phase. None of us three was religious, so she drew from a wide array of sources. She called it The Pleiades: an ever-evolving combination of mythology, Anne Frank, gleanings from her friend Claire, who went to Sunday school and wore a crucifix, and her own form of erratic piety. She could add and subtract rituals as needed. Some days were Days of Darkness and she asked me either to cover my face with a veil or just to stay away from her. On Ms. Frank's birthday we cried, and those of us who could not spontaneously cry were given the option of whispering every bad thing we had ever done to the last page of the book, the page before they are discovered by the SS. The Pleiades derived much of its authority from an ability to conjure guilt.

Lyon wore my castoff silver Gaia pendant, which was abstractly vaginal in a way she wasn't aware of, and pretended to loathe it. When

Claire made a big fuss about her stupid old cross, Lyon said, Tell me about it, my parents make me wear this.

What is it?

It's for our religion.

Are you Jewish?

No, it's really complicated. Here, let me show you, take off your shirt.

What are you gonna do?

Just touch your back with my necklace.

Oh, that. That's not religious. My mom does it with her nails, we call it Backles.

Backles?

Yeah.

She touches your back like this?

Yeah.

No offense, but your mom might be a pervert.

No she's not.

Backles is actually called foreplay and it's to get you in the mood.

What mood?

Reckless abandon.

That night in bed Lyon handed me the Gaia pendant. Backles was never directly affiliated with The Pleiades, but I performed it religiously for months, dangling the necklace first from one hand and then, when that got tired, the other.

The Pleiades had real staying power; at age twelve Lyon was still of the faith. She had forsaken the pendant and the more familiar rituals for a series of mystical practices, as Jews sometimes pursue kabbalah. One night she carefully ripped three flowery sheets into wide strips and asked me to swaddle her like a mummy in celebration of The Day of Hooray, which was like The Pleiades Christmas.

Tighter.

I think that's as tight as it can be.

Okay. Thank you.

She lay armless and inert, staring at the ceiling.

What if you have to go to the bathroom?

I'll go in here.

Okay.

All right. Good night, Deb.

Good night. Happy Hooray Day. Hooray!

Hooray.

In the middle of the night I was wakened by her yelling, which might have been expected; I mean, my God, how uncomfortable. I unwound the pee-soaked strips while she sobbed to the point of coughing.

I thought I was going to die.

Well, I never should have let you do it.

Don't say that!

But look at you, honey, you're freezing, you're upset and crying.

That's the ceremony! That's the end part of the ceremony!

Okay, well, great. Hooray.

Hooray! I'm okay!

In the fall of 2001 I met a man named Ed Borger. We all did actually, the four of us, once a week; he was our family counselor. This was the year that Lyon had acute allergies, a rageful year spent entirely in my care. The counseling was Tom's idea; I think he hoped this professional outsider would be stunned by our mess and blame Sarah. But Ed wasn't fazed; in fact, he suggested the dynamic had served each of us well. Something in the way he said this gave me the feeling that the dynamic was now moving on, perhaps down the block, where it would serve some other confused family. And we would be left dynamicless, four people alone with all-wrong feelings for each other.

The first few sessions were familiar to Lyon and me; we watched while Tom and Sarah slaughtered each other, then rose from the dead to love each other, and then became bored. Lyon rolled her eyes at me and even attempted to mouth, Let's get frozen yogurt after, okay? — which I ignored for Ed Borger's sake. Ed was, in my honest opinion, a wonderful man. I was paying my third of the $150 and wanted to be transformed by him.

In time, Lyon and I were encouraged to talk more. Lyon gave a gorgeously self-centered speech in which she enumerated her emotional needs:

I need peace and quiet and no fighting when I'm doing my homework and sleeping. I need a black JanSport backpack —

Hon, that's not really an emotional need —

I need Mommy to shut up and let me finish my list because who is she to say if it's an emotional need or not. I need to stay at Deb's house when I feel like it.

Here Ed gently pressed her.

Do you prefer living at Deborah's house?

Yeah, but my mom doesn't like it.

Sarah opened her mouth and then shut it.

Why do you think she doesn't like it?

Because, you know, Deb and my dad.

My left hand gripped my right. Tom looked at the floor.

What about Deb and your dad?

You know.

No, I don't. Do you feel comfortable saying what you are thinking?

They used to be married. That's why Deb's, like, my other mom.

Tom gasped, Sarah laughed, I spoke.

We were never married, we're just friends! We've always been friends.

Oh. But what about —

What?

Oh, I don't know. I thought . . . I don't know. Well, thanks for telling me, everyone. Now I feel dumb.

And we all rushed in at once to tell the child that she was not dumb, she was the opposite of dumb, she was insightful and sensitive and possibly even clairvoyant. Perhaps she was remembering something from a past lifetime? We laughed; maybe she knew something we didn't! Maybe that's why we were such good friends in this lifetime! Ed Borger observed us from a kind distance, clearly not buying any of it, but not judging, just watching the dynamic serve us another round, just one more round, please.

I was premenstrual on the day Ed Borger forced me to speak again. But I did not speak; instead I wept at various pitches and velocities, using my wail to describe a devastating unhappiness that surprised us all. After the session my three people hugged me, and within their tangle I felt safe. Lyon held my hand and Tom asked if I wanted to talk about my feelings. I looked at him, and his child, and for a fraction of a second I could see the spell that bound me, like a silvery spider thread catching the light. Cast upon me long ago at an age when I longed to be ensnared, it now spanned generations. Sarah rubbed my back with a chilly palm, the vision disappeared, and I felt certain I had nothing to say.

We had seen Ed for a whole month, nearly five sessions, and we all felt he had helped us a lot and we were ready to stop family counseling. Some of us (Sarah) had been ready to stop since before we started, but now we had consensus; Lyon's allergies seemed to be going away.

When Lyon's eyes and skin would become red and inflamed, Sarah was prone to saying things like, This is your way of seeking attention? Allergies? That's the best you can do? Ed had taught Lyon to say, Mom, I need you to take care of me, and he had taught Sarah to respond without yelling. They tried the technique in my living room; Lyon said her line perfectly, and Sarah had mastered the gentle tone but veered somewhat off course, whispering, Tell me how I can help my little girl, my big little girl, do you really want me to talk like this? Doesn't this make you feel like a baby?

Thus it may have been in self-defense that Lyon's aggravated pre-teen body suddenly replaced itself with an unaggravated, rather amazing woman's body the summer after her freshman year of high school. I thought this elegantly bubble-bottomed response was brilliant; I could not have said it better myself.

Ed had also suggested we work our way back to joint custody, so Lyon begrudgingly slept at home two nights a week. It was hard to know what to do with myself on these evenings. I wasn't used to sleeping alone, though I'd long since stopped having boyfriends. The first night I usually spent cleaning, but the second sent me into a spin. After a while I learned to clean more slowly, spreading it out over two fairly pleasant nights, which were always punctuated by a call from Lyon.

Mom is out with Juan and Dad is in the garage talking on his cell phone.

What are you doing?

I don't know, I might call Kevin and ask him to come over here and lick me.

Lyon.

What? I talked to him today.

No you did not.

Yeah, in seminar.

What happened?

He said —

He initiated? That's good.

I know.

Okay, go.

He said, I bet you've already read the whole book —

My Ántonia?

Yeah. And I said, No I haven't even finished last night's pages. And that's all.

That's good. He thinks you're smart.

I know. I'm going to masturbate thinking about him now.

Okay, you do that.

I'm kidding! Like I would tell you if I was going to.

By the time I ran into Ed Borger at Trader Joe's, Lyon was living at my house for only half the week, something Ed and I talked about with loaves of bread in our hands. He thought this was great progress. I said we owed it all to him. He said his bread always got moldy before he could finish the loaf. I said he should freeze the bread to prevent this problem. He said, But won't that ruin the bread? I said, Not if you're making toast with it. He said, You can just toast it frozen? And I said, Yep.

We put our groceries in our respective cars and guessed that we had about forty minutes before our perishables perished, enough time for a cup of tea.

Back when we were in family counseling, I used to daydream, What if Ed wanted to hear only what *I* thought, what if the rest of the family wasn't even allowed in the room, what if I could just talk and talk and talk, and what if when I was done Ed told me I was a genius and the rest of the bunch were loony-toons, and then what if Ed said he had always been attracted to me, and what if he took off my clothes and I took off his clothes and we held each other for more or less the rest of our lives? This thought was in the back of my mind while we sipped our tea. Mostly we talked about Lyon.

I think she's going to become a terrific woman one day.

She almost already is! She's grown a lot since you last saw her.

She's taller?

Yeah. And she's more developed.

Developed?

Yeah. Which seems to have calmed her allergies. Do you think that's possible? Medically speaking?

Well, anything's possible, medically speaking.

I feel the same way.

What do you mean?

That anything's possible.

Well, not anything. Pigs can't fly.

Yeah, but for some reason, sitting here with you, I feel like they can.

Can?

Fly.

Oh.

I'm sorry, am I being ridiculous?

No, no, you're not, no.

Ed Borger put his yogurt in my refrigerator and asked me to re-mind him to get it before he left. Lyon was at her parents' house, but her clothes were all over the bed. I picked them off and put them on the dresser. I turned out the light and we did not take off each other's clothes, but we took off our own clothes. Before we did anything, Ed asked for permission to cry and I said, Permission granted, and he settled his face between my breasts and moaned. When he was done, I noticed that his face wasn't wet.

That's because I cry dry tears.

Oh. Is that an actual term? Dry tears?

Well, I have a theory that men don't actually cry less than women, they just do it differently. Since we never saw our fathers cry, we are each forced to invent our own unique method.

My dad cried.

He did? Wet?

Yeah. All the time.

Is it possible that *his* father cried? And thus taught his son?

Well, maybe, but also my mom had a sixteen-year affair.

I went to the bathroom and washed my vagina in preparation. Before returning to the bedroom, I paused in the darkness of the hallway and beheld him kneeling on my big square bed, staring fiercely at a lamp, bringing his penis to an erect position by choking it with both hands. It was easy to remember him sitting in his chair in his office, observing, nodding, producing a hard-won chuckle. I decided that I wanted this. If you'll be my man forever, Ed Borger, I'll be your woman. He suddenly stopped his furious hand movements and turned his head directly toward me in the shadows — as if he had heard me, as if responding to my vow. I waved. But he wasn't looking at me, he was looking behind me, at Lyon.

Four excruciating interactions immediately followed this moment; the fifth was the drive to her parents' house. Lyon refused to sit beside me in the passenger's seat.

Why should I?

Because it makes me feel like a chauffeur when you sit back there.

But you are a chauffeur.

Lyon.

What? Aren't you basically a babysitter chauffeur? Isn't that what my parents pay you for?

You know they don't pay me.

Well, that's your problem, not mine.

Lyon, we're a family.

No, actually, you are not related to us, you are just a person who used to help us the way Ed used to help us. It's really perfect that you two should fuck. All the hired help should fuck each other. I am in favor of it. We're all in favor of it.

Please don't tell Sarah and Tom.

Duh.

Duh you won't, or duh you will?

Just duh.

But she didn't. She also didn't spend the night at my house again. She treated me like a friend of her parents, rushing past the three of us with her boyfriend, shouting, Bye y'all, with a wave. This change was buried among all the other changes, the learning to drive, the perpetual sarcasm, the feminism. Tom and Sarah assured me that she ignored them too, that we were all in the same boat, the one we came in on. But I knew, and the guilt was crushing. In moments I thought of calling Ed, as a professional. But would he be an objective outsider? He would not. The more I thought about this nonobjectivity, the more I wanted to call.

Dr. Borger.

Hi, Ed. It's Deb.

Deb, hi.

So we haven't talked in a while.

What's on your mind?

Well, you never called me back after that day.

I didn't think it was appropriate to pursue a relationship after what happened.

Lyon doesn't sleep at my house anymore, so it's not like she would even know.

Do you miss her?

Yeah, of course.

So this isn't really about me, is it?

Well, it is, in a way. You were involved.

Deb?

Yeah?

I hate to do this, but I need to call you back when I'm not in my office. Do you want me to call you back?

Do you want to?

If you want me to, I do.

But if I don't want you to, then you're totally fine with not calling?

I think it might be best if we let this go.

Inelegantly and without my consent, time passed. My relationship with Tom and Sarah became occasion-based; I was invited to Lyon's high school graduation, Tom's birthday, Thanksgiving, Christmas dinner. Lyon didn't come home from college for Christmas, but she sent the three of us UBC sweatshirts from the University of British Columbia at Okanagan. She went faster and farther than I had imagined possible; who goes to college in Canada? Under financial duress, she came back for summer vacation, lived at home, and got a job at a lesbian-owned and -operated organic-produce market. I shopped there more than was necessary, like an ex-boyfriend from high school, but I didn't ask if she missed me; I didn't try to get back together. I kept the conversation light.

Excited to see you have the Honeycrisps in.

Don't thank me; they're not my Honeycrisps.

Well, technically, they are. Isn't this place worker-owned?

Yeah, but you have to work here for more than a summer and, like, eat the manager's pussy or something. Do you want a bag?

I joined PFLAG (Parents and Friends of Lesbians and Gays). I bought books by and for lesbians and their supportive, surprised parents. When she went back to school I imagined her sitting in a dorm with her arm around a young woman's waist, perhaps a young butch woman. I had read about the butch/femme dynamic and was sure that Lyon would be the femme. I wondered if Tom and Sarah knew about Lyon's preference; my guess was they did not, because they were still quite self-involved. They probably had fewer dalliances, but a bitterness had replaced the mania; the past now looked almost carefree. In December, Tom called to invite me to Christmas dinner.

Lyon will be there. She's coming home.

Oh, great.

And she has a new boyfriend. You're going to flip out when you see him.

I quit PFLAG and moved through the next few days in weepy wonderment. I knew nothing about her. It was really over and I was really not her mother. I was really almost fifty. I really did not feel okay about any of this, and there was really nothing I could do. Somehow losing the lesbianism, the butch girlfriend, the need for tolerance, was worse than losing Lyon herself, years before. Or, more likely, I was still feeling the old loss, just in a new way.

I arrived late. Lyon wasn't even there; Tom and Sarah said she would show up by dessert. I talked to their other friends, some of whom I knew from our college days. I marveled at their nonchalant relations with Lyon. One man thought she was still in high school. Just as we sat down for dinner, the doorbell rang. Someone in a puffy down jacket stumbled in, unwrapping his scarf. It was Ed Borger. He waved and said, Hi, everyone. And then he said, Lyon's coming, she's finishing a phone call.

These words were lost on me because I was consumed with Ed's shirt. It was a particular kind of modern dress shirt, a reproduction of a dress shirt that would have been popular in the sixties but now had been modified to appeal to people who could not remember the sixties. Therein lay the problem, because Ed Borger *would* remember the sixties, he would remember being a teenager in the sixties, and he would avoid such a shirt because it would not seem retro to him, it would just remind him of a time before he had really gained social confidence. So someone else must have bought this shirt for him, a person who could not remember the sixties. My thoughts were interrupted by Lyon's entrance, her hand gently rubbing Ed's back as she said her hellos. Tom poured a glass of wine for Ed.

So how's the family-counseling business?

I can't complain, Tom.

We ate quietly, those of us who knew Ed and those of us who knew only that there was a funny feeling in the room.

I guess that's true, you really can't complain, can you?

We ate our yam casserole and our scalloped potatoes and our baked ham.

What are you saying, Tom?

Ed placed his hand over Lyon's; we all looked at Tom. Tom looked at Lyon; we all did. She was staring intently at Sarah, who slowly looked up from her plate and at her daughter. And then, casually, Lyon slipped her hand out from beneath Ed's and passed me the potatoes, though I had not asked for the potatoes. I took the dish and she did not release the dish and we held the dish together for a moment; it hovered over her parents' dinner table. My eyes ventured slowly from the dish to the front of her blouse, to her eyes. What did I fear I would find there? Meanness and gloating? Slyness? Shame? They were sparkling with the old love, the greatest love of my lifetime, and they were triumphant.

MATTHEW KLAM

■

Adina, Astrid, Chipewee, Jasmine

FROM *The New Yorker*

SATURDAY NIGHT Julia sat staring at a candle. It was after eight. She needed to eat.

She hadn't felt tired yet. She'd had a perfect pregnancy — no rashes, no fat feet, working full time, doing it all. A cartoonist couldn't have drawn a more adorable creature: rosy cheeks, pudgy nose, lime-green pregnancy pants drawn up over her stomach, white maternity smock.

Erica buzzed the front door with bags from the kebab place, and they set the coffee table and ate on the floor with their backs against two ottomans. Erica wore fish-net stockings and a cotton cardigan that let her cleavage fall out, and told Julia about the sex she was having with her outlaw boyfriend, Malcolm — who couldn't commit, said he needed to "live monastically," then showed up at her house every night so riddled with guilt that she ended up comforting him on the rug in her foyer as he ripped her clothes off.

Julia ate too fast, choking on hummus, and accidentally drank what was left of Erica's wine. It tasted like cough syrup. She finished her kebab and rubbed a food stain off her shirt. Erica stared across the table at Julia as though she were trying to unscrew her own head.

Julia was embarrassed. It was mid-April. She was due June 17. You were supposed to slip naturally into the new shape; you were supposed to love it. But she'd popped out hugely, and felt like a bear sipping tea. She was going to be a terrible mother.

After dinner, Malcolm arrived. He was tall and reddish, with a windburned face — he built houses for a living. He towered over them, touching them both, and invited Julia to join him and Erica at a party in the Palisades. Julia said she was too tired, and noticed him staring at her breasts and her belly, like a moron. When she kissed him good night, her face got hot. It was the wine, or hormones out of whack.

She got into bed but couldn't fall asleep. On TV, Brad Pitt was dressed in a black leather miniskirt, playing a warrior from ancient times who slept nude in animal skins. Lying there, she thought about Malcolm and his dog-like stare. She used her vibrator, in an attempt to wear herself out, and accidentally broke her water. But she was two months shy of her due date and whatever came out, this little puddle, meant nothing to her. She wondered instead whether she'd finally hit her G spot.

Sunday morning, she woke up with a warm physical pressure, almost like sadness, bearing down on her vagina. She was bleeding a little, but then it went away. By noon the pressure had shifted and was sitting in her pelvis, where her bowels were. She left a message for Kevin at his hotel in Hartford, then another, until he called back. She ate some chicken, and then walked a mile and a half down Wisconsin Avenue to her gym, swam for an hour, and walked home. At four that afternoon, she tried to nap, but her belly hurt. She gave up on napping and waited for Kevin to come home.

Kevin spent the weekend shooting video of people speaking at a journalism conference — a Nixon-era geezer, a dopey mountaineer whose only training before typing up his bestseller had been a job painting boats. Nobody stuck to the subject or laid out the fundamentals of writing Kevin needed for the video he had to put together. Famous people — Joyce Linden Fogg — whispered in a huge auditorium off the main lobby; Branson Kheils, a public-radio icon, rambled on about his first show in Minnesota (a pig slept in the yard behind the station) and brought down the house.

By Sunday afternoon, Kevin stood sagging under the weight of his twelve-pound camera; his overheating spotlight burned the side of his head as Dustin Christensen addressed the full session of two thousand to close the conference. Nothing about his latest project had been difficult, Christensen said, not the research or the writing. He'd infiltrated Afghani terrorists, slept beneath flying bullets. He'd used the proceeds from his blockbuster to build schools and roads in the mountains that once bred killers. Every word, every twitch transfixed the packed ballroom. It was the publicity tour that almost killed him, he said, and the Hollywood movie, and the luggage he'd lost on his way here. When the author finally took questions, Kevin slumped against the wall with the kind of exhausted relief you get from throwing up.

At last, back in his hotel room, Kevin wandered around in such a stupor that he packed too slowly and missed his plane. Waiting on standby at the airport, gazing at magazines at the newsstand as evening descended, he thought of all the things he'd never be, speeches he'd never give. He couldn't afford to buy a magazine because he was still waiting for the money from his last job, a heartwarming fundraising film he'd shot for a fancy private high school. He felt so rotten he almost phoned Julia, but their last conversation warded him off.

"Sorry," he'd said when he finally reached her during the lunch break.

"Oh, God, Kevin," she'd said.

"What's wrong?"

"I just dropped a piece of chicken down my bra."

"I only have a second."

"Now I'm all covered with slime and grease on me. It's disgusting."

"It's okay," he'd said, because she was alone, and apparently bleeding, and seemed to be having some kind of problem. "I'm sorry you don't feel well."

"I drank wine last night by mistake," she said. "She's probably dead."

"My session is starting."

"Somebody get this thing out of me. Cut it out of me now."

Kevin had been out of college for two years when he got his first real job, writing press releases for an American gas company. He'd been living in cheap countries as an experiment, traveling to avoid working, but ended up in Japan, where people worked so hard they dropped dead on the sidewalk. It made the expat thing a little pointless. Back home, he spent nine years doing video production at a PR agency before starting his own business.

Nobody in his family had ever made a living in an imaginative career, and Kevin had no great store of talent, but while at the agency he began quietly working on his own film, a documentary. He'd read about this kid in the paper, a five-foot-six-inch basketball phenom named Durrell, who'd been beaten and starved as a child, and now played at a nearby college. Kevin politely stalked Durrell and began making trips to his dorm room to tape these mind-blowing stories of life in the Montclair, New Jersey, projects. Durrell's mom was a "roller," and his dad had gone to jail for hitting someone with a sledgehammer. He had a stoic way of speaking that made him look, onscreen, like he was falling asleep. But so what. Kevin met the foster family, and filmed their evening meals, and flew to road games at his own expense, and shot hundreds of hours of footage — of coaches on leafy strolls, of Durrell playing Xbox and doing his raps. After almost three years, with no end in sight, he finally gained the trust of Durrell's twin sister, a single mother on welfare, who was killed sometime later in a random act of violence.

Durrell blew his knee out at the end of his junior year, and then flopped in a pro league in Europe, and stopped returning Kevin's calls. At about the same time, a film with an identical theme appeared in theaters, to huge acclaim, and Kevin sort of fell apart. Since then, he'd started a few other projects — documentaries, conceptual video art, screenplays, children's books — but had quit them all. Though he still dreamed of finishing the film, or at least editing a promo, or whatever you call it, or at least watching some of the footage, he felt that the time for his own dreams had ended, or would soon, because he'd be a father, and he'd have to stand aside for the next generation — while also remaining upright, embalmed, rotting, for eternity.

On the flight home, he sat in a broken seat by the toilet and stared out the window as the engine wobbled beneath the wing. If it fell off now, the plane would smash into the Jersey shore. Maybe, if he lived, he could make a documentary about that. He'd interview the survivors, teasing out his own story, then slowly turn the camera on himself to reveal the hideous burns all over his disfigured head! Or he could write some kind of magazine article about it, or a book, or novelize it, or try it as a feature-film script . . . It would be easier just to die.

*

At five, Julia thought she had to poop. She tried to call Kevin and took half a Midol. At seven, it came in waves; it bent her in half. I'm just wound up, she thought. I'm hung over. Because she was seven months pregnant, she got out the midwife's card and called, apologizing for bothering her on a Sunday evening. The midwife said, "If you go to the emergency room, they'll give you stuff to calm your cramps."

"The emergency room?"

"We can't do anything for you here." The pamphlet from the midwife's office described warm baths, lavender butter smeared on your forehead. What the hell was the point if at the first sign of anything they sent you to the hospital?

"All I eat is chicken. Do you think I have food poisoning?"

"It's possible."

"If I did, would it hurt the baby?" The woman didn't know. Jesus.

By the time Julia got downstairs, she was walking like her Grandma Gertie before Gertie had both hips replaced. She breathed heavily, leaning on a stack of magazines by the front door. She had a little trouble deciding on her next move and panicked and called 911. When a voice answered, she apologized and walked outside to her car. She felt like she was being whacked with a two-by-four.

Kevin landed at around seven and went straight to his office and dumped the footage onto his computer. The office was in a basement and his cell phone didn't ring down there; he ignored the regular phone, because the sequence of the sixty-eight speeches had to be tagged correctly.

At nine o'clock, he called home and to his relief got the machine. He left a message saying that he still had more work to do and that Julia should go to sleep without him. Please, God, he thought. And now he had to go find somewhere to eat. He hated eating alone. He just wanted five minutes with somebody other than Julia — who was grossly pregnant and uncomfortable and kept the fan turned on so high in the bedroom that he had to build a wall of pillows to keep from being blown onto the floor.

Times were hard, and bound to get harder. The sound of a key in the lock — anything triggered Julia's insomnia. She woke up if a bird flew past the window. Last week, a chunk of her hair fell out. She lost her wallet in the lining of her coat, and when she found it, she closed the bathroom door and cried. Her belly was immense and her boobs were veiny and her nipples were brown. She smelled different — like cooked custard. And she had an attitude now: "Stand back, here I come." She passed many sleepless nights eating nuts in bed, crunching with a squirrel's vigor. It altered their private business. Kevin loved sex, normally, anytime, anywhere. But now the sex was weird, because what exactly was going on down there? When he stared at that lump under the blanket, he felt self-conscious; he sensed an audience of skepticism and disapproval.

If he tried to talk to his sister or his mom about it, they got angry. If he said a word to his friends, the single guys acted horrified that a person could smell like custard, and the guys who had kids didn't care.

He and Julia got married three years ago, and right away they began trying. When nothing happened, he figured God was punishing him for something. They'd been together for almost a year before the wedding, and their early days had been filled, for him, with the excitement of loving her so much better than Roberta, his terrible last girlfriend, who'd slept on a horsehair mattress she inherited from her grandmother. Julia was by far the most beautiful woman Kevin had ever touched, and the most decent — passionate to the point of hysteria about a five-year plan for public charter schools. She was slight and wore the same T-shirt to bed every night and had a pretense of helplessness, which applied mainly to lifting the five-gallon water jug, but it made loving a skinny girl romantic, and he'd loved her in greater quantity than he'd ever loved anyone. He was in love; she was easy to love. He'd walk through the door every night and be, like, "I'm living with someone and I'm going to marry her."

She had a puffy little moonface, and Kevin loved to kiss the soft belly of each cheek, but within five minutes something always happened to ruin the moment. At first, he took the awkwardness between them for lack of experience, but that wasn't the problem. They just didn't like to talk to each other. She'd start a story in the middle, and if he asked a question she'd say "What? Huh?" as if she needed a hearing aid. Any time they spent alone together, whenever one of them asked the question "How are you?" it was like writing a thank-you note to a grandparent in a nursing home. By the time those moments ended, Kevin was a wreck. But then he'd been in relationships with good conversations, too. Understanding killed attraction just as quickly. Here at least the mystery kept things primitive and charged.

Their conversations improved with practice, but when he couldn't knock her up the awkwardness returned. At some point, he decided to shut up more, so she shut up more too, but that just made them strangers to each other. After a year, they found a clinic and she began making frequent trips to the doctor and they went ahead with it, not talking.

There was the Hawaiian porno tape he jerked off to at the clinic, the menstrual cycle on the refrigerator, the shots he gave her — big injections in her ass, little ones in her stomach. The pills she shoved in her pussy to make the lining more hospitable. The brave declarations they made as they faced the debate — donor egg versus flying to China.

Months passed, and it all became this tricky thing, like a blur in a photograph. She was blurring, smudging, not herself. Then there were the phone calls from the clinic — "Do it now" — the requisite screwing, the livestock feeling of it, the injunction against fiddling with himself, the creeping sensation that they were using up the last few drops he had, crawling toward the end.

She was ashamed. She starved herself on popcorn and soda and got too thin. He did everything he could to get away, staying late at work, eating dinner in a restaurant alone. A distance opened up between them. It was his failure, his weakness, but he couldn't tell anyone about it. He'd stopped loving Julia when he couldn't get her pregnant, but then, after two years of a humiliating and expensive $29,000 fertility process, they'd succeeded, and now that she was pregnant he wished she was dead.

There'd been a case on television of a man who'd killed his pregnant wife, spawning special news reports. Tooling around the Internet, Kevin had learned that one in five pregnant women who died was murdered. A quarter of men who killed their wives killed them when they were pregnant. Women were strangled, bludgeoned, choked, drowned, burned alive, shot on the way home from a birthing class. Why didn't the guys just leave? Now he knew. He couldn't imagine actually strangling anyone, but the existence of the trend lofted him up on a dizzy little puff of curiosity. Watching Julia's belly grow, seeing her change, altered his world like a snowfall quieting everything. And yet he was nuts. He felt like he'd sawed off the top of his head. Instead of wondering how to fix it, he gave himself a gift: despair without shame. Freedom from the necessary revulsion with himself. Like some miserable goth kid, his thoughts went straight to hell and made him stronger.

A paramedic took Julia up to the sixth floor in a wheelchair, and one nurse put a bracelet on her wrist while another drew five vials of her blood. She liked all the attention. She got the feeling that they'd seen cramps like these before, which reassured her. Another nurse entered with papers to sign, and a fourth asked concerned, insightful questions. Two of the nurses were blond and wore diamond engagement rings, and another was worn out and motherly. The prettiest one put Julia in stirrups.

As a teenager, she'd spent some time in a hospital for bulimia and suicidal behavior, and she'd always looked back on it as the regimen that put order in her life, helped her collect herself and recover. The friends she'd made there, bound to her by their secret shame, remained the most important ones she had to this day. Anyway, if she hadn't been locked up in that place, she'd be dead.

Tonight she lay in the maternity ward of a teaching hospital, and the young doctor on call, a third-year resident, stepped into the examining room a little bleary, feeling his way around the room, blinking at her as though he'd come from somewhere dark. One side of his face was wrinkled where it appeared he'd been sleeping on it.

"You're having some pain," he said, and gloved up. "You need to maintain your fluids." He sat on a stool, set a sealed plastic bag of metal instruments on top of her big bare stomach, and then began looking around, spinning on the stool. And then everyone had to laugh, because he was looking for the very bag that was right in front of him! He opened the bag and took out a speculum, which he stuck crookedly into her, accidentally cutting her. Her spasming innards rocketed into a worse state. She panicked. He twisted it around inside her.

"Yuh — you're in labor," he said loudly, "three centimeters," and his voice broke when he said it. "You're breech." He called for a sonogram and sent for the attending. When he withdrew the speculum, it had candy-apple-red blood on the end. There was blood on his glove, and he slid it off into the garbage as though it were covered with worms. He stared down at the floor and smiled apologetically, and the nurses rolled the sonogram machine into place and squirted gloop on Julia's belly.

The attending was a woman in her fifties with copper highlights in her hair. She held Julia's hand and spoke softly as she moved the sonogram thing around. She asked the young doctor what he saw on the screen. He studied the ghostly image. She turned to Julia and said, "Is there a possibility your water broke at some point in the last day or two?"

"My water?"

"Because there doesn't seem to be too much in there."

Julia remembered the stuff coming out the night before. "How much is missing?"

The attending wiggled the thing more. The contractions were seven minutes apart. Stopping them would be tricky, she said. Bringing the baby out now would be worse. More nurses came into the room. One asked if there was a family member Julia could call. She'd left messages for Kevin in three places. She gave them Erica's number.

They wheeled her into a room with a view of the plaza, and the attending put a clear bag of viscous-looking fluid called magnesium sulfate into the IV machine, assuring Julia that it was safe. "Some people don't love this drug," she explained. "But it helps the muscles to relax, to stop your contractions. We need to stop your contractions," she said, and left.

It hit her head first. Almost immediately, Julia went cross-eyed and half dead.

He called his buddy Ethan. He wanted to meet him at Schwann's, an old wood-paneled restaurant in Georgetown where Khrushchev had once sat with Nixon for a photo op, where the waiters were old men who wore smocks and kept their faces frozen while you ordered. Ethan understood what Kevin was going through; he was married, with three kids. But Ethan had a gigantic book contract that was killing him — he had to get some work done — so he told Kevin to stop by the house instead.

Ethan lived in this fucking mansion on P Street, a National Historic Landmark, according to the plate by the door. The doorknob was brass and the size of a grapefruit. Trips to Ethan's house left Kevin feeling worthless and desperate, although Ethan's family had enough problems: the older girl with two percent listening comprehension, the younger one shoplifting from stores on M Street, the three-year-old boy refusing to speak except in the broken English of the Guatemalan nanny. Ethan had written two decent books on politics and almost finished a third, and he had a good job talking on a cable news show. But he'd married Carrie, who was worth whatever the stock market did to the third of a billion dollars she'd inherited in 1990, and her wealth made it hard for him to keep his balls.

As Kevin came in, he could hear Ethan's girls screaming up the wide staircase, or maybe down in the ballroom they'd had painted like a jungle and filled with trampolines. If someone were being flayed alive it might have sounded the same way, that screaming, but Ethan just sighed and clucked his tongue, leading the way past fresh-cut flowers and oil paintings, until they entered the white-tiled kitchen with its endless counters, where a fat rottweiler looked up to see what they were doing. Kevin could hear Carrie, somewhere, calling Ethan's name.

In the refrigerator were sodas and open wine bottles, a tray of wilted vegetables from a caterer, and part of a cake. They stood smearing butter on pieces of focaccia, listening to the screams. When a lull hit, Ethan yawned. Over the weekend, he and Carrie had hosted three parties: one for Carrie's grandmother, one for a nine-year-old, and one for Eliot Spitzer.

"I'm not gonna make it," he said, meaning the deadline for his book.

"You'll make it." There was a bottle of scotch on the counter and they each had a shot. It tasted like gym socks soaked in gasoline. They had another. Soon the kitchen started to feel more like Schwann's.

"How was your thing in Hartford?"

"Fine."

"Julia okay? You ready? To become a father, a dad? You psyched?"

Kevin said yes.

"You're having a little girl."

"I know," Kevin said. "Here's to the greatest adventure a man can know."

"Aye, muchacho," Ethan said.

It sounded like furniture was being dragged across the floor upstairs. "Carrie!" Ethan yelled toward the dining room. "Honey, is everything okay?" They waited. "You'll be fine," he said to Kevin.

Carrie appeared in the back of the kitchen, having materialized from somewhere, like a ninja. She said hi to Kevin, but her lips were tight. "You're on for the rest of the night," she told Ethan, and filled a glass with water. "You haven't done a fucking thing all weekend." She walked out.

"Heh-heh," Ethan said. He walked to the foyer. "Don't leave."

"I should get going."

"I'm just gonna check on things."

"I'd better go."

Ethan called back. "Don't move."

"I'll see you later." Kevin let himself out as Ethan walked up the stairs.

An hour later, the young doctor threw the door open carrying a big yellow coffee mug with a smiley face on it and sort of skipped into the room as though he were kicking through rain puddles. "Doin' all right?" he asked, taking a drink from his mug. "How's the mag working out for ya?" He walked around, making notes on her chart. "Sometimes magnesium makes people irritable. It causes the heart to beat irregularly."

"Is this active labor?" She was shouting. "Is it stopping? Am I going to work tomorrow?" Her tongue tasted like aluminum.

"What do you mean by active labor?"

"My doctors told me to call if there was news. My midwife."

"We called them." He tapped her knees, her wrists, and her elbows, then her ankles and feet. No reflexes. The computer by Julia's head indicated that her contractions were getting stronger. "Let us know if you have any double vision," he said.

Julia said, "Yes, I do."

He made a note and turned the lights off and let the door bang shut.

On his way up Connecticut Avenue, Kevin stopped in Woodley Park, in front of the building where a woman named Cynthia lived. She was the ex-girlfriend of a guy named Artie, who'd made films for the Discovery Channel and had a shelf full of Emmys. She'd taken Artie's old job and brought Kevin in to help her with a two-hundred-page script she'd inherited on the birth of Islam. Together they'd cut it down to four and a half scintillating minutes, to be aired one day on the channel's website. Over the last three months, they'd met half a dozen times in a tiny editing suite, a cockpit with carpeted walls, and in that warm, hushed darkness they'd chatted and commiserated and drunk soda and confessed.

They'd discovered that they were both dying to move to New York City to jump-start their careers. They'd both pitched the same guy at Showtime, with the same result. Cynthia had been a dancer in her youth, and had debuted at the New York City Ballet at nineteen; two weeks later, she'd dislocated her hip — had to be lifted and hauled offstage. Kevin completely understood, because of his own unfulfilled promise. She couldn't explain to anybody how it made her feel, but Kevin knew that an awful, unfixable thing would never stay buried.

She was a tall, thin woman with broad shoulders and a skinny neck and a scrunched-up little mouse face. She had huge brown eyes, and this heavy bosom, and she'd lean over and put her boobs on the table between them in the editing suite and scream back at Kevin about their sketchy luck and stare into his eyes like a maniac. He liked that.

It was late. He probably should've called first. She was the only woman he could think of within eighty miles who was single and answered her phone after nine o'clock at night.

He didn't want to go home yet. It was spring, and a velvety breeze touched his arms, and tender little green buds hung softly under the streetlights. There was only now, and that made living exquisite. And anyway, he'd be dead someday and none of it would matter. Also, if he came in and woke Julia up, she'd lie there, devastated, for the next six hours, sighing her ass off, and would blame him, and he'd take the blame, and feel terrible.

The only light in the room came from the monitor by her head, hooked to her belly, a sickly orange glow. The only sound came from the baby's pounding rhythm, amplified through the machine like a little air compressor blasting away. *Choo-choo.* Julia turned her face to the wall when the pain came, and wrapped her hand around the rubber-coated railing on the bed, dug her nails into the rubber, squeezed her eyes shut, and opened her mouth wide, but there was no sound. Something flipped inside. During the gaps in the flipping, she let go. Her body had been built according to certain rules, but those rules had now been broken. If it got any worse, she would have to kill herself. She could crawl to the window and slide out. She dug into the rubber. When Kevin showed up, he would call everyone. She felt hopeless, lonely.

A soft, round, coffee-colored orb appeared near Julia's head. It was a face, powdery smooth, with trustworthy lines, and it spoke with an accent from somewhere — the Caribbean maybe — partly reading in a breezy rhythm, from notes, ". . . serious complications, of course, the risks in bringing a baby out of the womb prematurely are known . . . cerebral palsy, neurologic disorders, developmental delays."

There was white stuff caked around the edge of Julia's mouth. Her gums were bleeding and she moved her tongue to try to find out where.

"Higher risks of retardation, asthma, and congenital aortic deformities . . . It's not uncommon for preemies to undergo a number of surgeries."

Then it was quiet, thank God, and the woman asked if Julia had any questions. Ha, yeah. When Julia shook her head, it thudded, and fell into thudding rhythm with the *choo-choo* of the heart monitor, and the two of them sailed off on a glassy blue bay. The woman wrote something with what looked like a turkey thermometer. Julia turned her face to the wall when the pain came.

Scanning the face of the building for Cynthia's glowing windows, Kevin took a minute to think about what he'd say, then called from the street and told her how the man who ran publicity at the journalism conference had made him shoot the floral arrangements in the lobby, offering cinematic insights. "'Howzabout,'" Kevin said in a goofy voice, "'we drop that sunset over the Sheraton sign?'"

"You're kidding me!" Cynthia yelled. "Shut up!"

"I'm thinking about becoming a wedding videographer."

"Jesus, shut up!" she said.

"Hey, I have your lens," he said. "I didn't want to leave it in the office where somebody could swipe it. I'll drop it off on my way home."

He waited by his car on the corner, and a few minutes later Cynthia brought her dog, Jasper, downstairs. She wore a cute navy-blue miniskirt and a spangly T-shirt that said CIAO ROMA. They walked around the block and then back to the entrance to her building. In his mind, he was reporting these actions to someone. The dog, a white Yorkie with Milk Dud eyes, looked up at Kevin, and he took the leash from Cynthia's hand and ran his fingers over the dog's head.

Back in March, after a long night at the editing suite, Kevin had driven Cynthia home, but when he pulled up in front of her building she wouldn't get out. They'd been yakking all night. He hadn't had so much fun with anybody in five years. He'd wanted to do something. He shivered a little, and leaned over to say good night. She made an *oh* sound that caught in her throat, a garbage truck scared them, and they had a big laugh and she jumped out. Then, a few weeks later, they'd done the routine again, first talking exhaustively in the editing suite, getting that glow, then sitting in the car until he shivered. But there'd been no makeout session the second time either, and that was it.

Cynthia had been seeing a guy in New York, and as they stood at the door she told Kevin that, since the last time she saw him, she'd been floored by the realization that the guy was a drunk. "I'm not afraid to be alone," she said. "And I'm not afraid I'll never find love."

"Of course," Kevin said. "You're thirty-two years old."

"I don't need any fuckhead boyfriend. I do what I want. I go out almost every night."

"You're living your life."

"You know what I made for dinner tonight?"

"What?"

"An egg-white omelet. With scallions. You know when I ate it? Nine o'clock."

"I envy your freedom."

Her skirt had a big plastic zipper on the front, and sat loosely on her hips, and as she talked he noticed that the skirt had slid around and now the zipper was on the side. During her glory days she'd taught ballet to Madonna and dated a guy in the NBA. Kevin thought about those NBA hands on her. He reached forward to give the leash back, and as she took it from him he tipped his head toward hers but she turned away, smiling.

He tried to explain. "I wanted to touch you in the car that night."

"I always love talking to you," she said.

"Me too," he said.

She looked down. "Am I being too harsh?"

"What is this, ninth grade?" He took the lens out of his bag and handed it to her.

"You're a total freak," she said, smiling at him again and taking the lens. Then she got confused and stepped in and jangled him with a long soft hug, jamming herself against him.

He felt even more stupid now. "You sure you don't want to get one drink?"

"No, God, it's after eleven. I'm finished."

"Do you want to smoke a cigarette?"

"Don't give me all the power, Kevin. What do you think?"

"I think we should go upstairs."

"Right."

"Yeah."

"Don't look at me that way," she said. "I don't want to be the bad guy."

"You're just gonna go to sleep?"

"Go home to your pregnant wife."

Kevin stared at Cynthia. He had to hate her now. Maybe if he strangled somebody other than Julia he'd feel better. He blinked back tears and crumbled. "She ate three rotisserie chickens this week."

"That's good," Cynthia said sadly. "Fatten her up."

"She's fat enough. She looks like Tweedledee, with her preggo stretch pants pulled up to her armpits."

"That's cute."

"I'm gonna kill her in her sleep."

"What about the baby?"

"You think that would hurt the baby?"

"It might."

"See, that's the rub."

"It sounds like you don't like your wife."

"She has flaws."

"Well, God."

"Too many to name."

"Then she'll make an excellent mother."

It was almost midnight when Kevin got home. Julia's car was gone, the lights were on, and the front door was unlocked. What a fucking idiot. For a second he couldn't figure it out. But her book group met some Sundays and usually ran late. He wanted to slap her across the face with a brick.

He wanted her to go somewhere and never come back. He was so sick of this crap. If he left now . . . but that would be impossible. He had to find a way to get rid of her without getting rid of the baby. How could you do that?

He loved her, but he never wanted to see her again.

Kevin walked into the kitchen and without thinking began placing a stack of clean dishtowels into a drawer in color-coordinated piles.

Her face to the wall, her hand wrapped around the bedrail, she began to pant. Her eyes were fluttering behind her eyelids. Her cheeks puffed, her chin quivered. Then she gasped and her body stiffened. The nurse pushed her chair away from the bed and leaned over and placed her hand on Julia's forehead. The gesture startled Julia and big tears rolled down her face.

The young doctor stood at the foot of the bed. He clicked his penlight a few times and stared out the window at the plaza, at patients smoking cigarettes, trailing their IV poles. Against the weatherman's prediction, it had started to rain.

When the contraction ended, the nurse put Julia's bed down flat.

The young doctor said, "Heh-heh. I've just gotta, uh —" And he moved to his place between Julia's legs. An old goat from the obstetrics department strode in with military purpose and introduced himself to Julia. The young doctor very carefully inserted his fingers. "Please stop moving," he said. He thought he was feeling the skull, but then realized that it was still the hip. "Still three," he said.

"*Talk to her,*" the old goat barked.

"You're still three centimeters dilated."

The old goat bent over and stuck his hand into Julia as though reaching for car keys that had fallen down the drain, and then cleared some phlegm from his throat. "Show me three." The young doctor held his index fingers about three centimeters apart. The old goat said, "That's five," and pulled the young doctor's hands apart. "That's eight. Slide over. Get out of the way."

Kevin carried his luggage upstairs and got undressed, glancing out the window for Julia's car. He thought back to his one big breakup after college, a relationship that had ended fairly well after five years, and he pictured that late-afternoon goodbye — he and Lisa had packed up the car, the car they'd bought together, and sat on the steps and split up the pictures in the photo album, then stood and hugged. Then she'd said something he never forgot, "Hey, you were good to me," and he said that she'd been good to him, too, and she drove away. And even now, after all this time, he missed her so much it ached to think about that day. He still talked to her every once in a while, and it was so easy to talk, easier than it had ever been with Julia. After she left, he'd gone upstairs to the empty apartment where they'd both been crying for weeks and ordered Chinese food and turned on the TV and felt total relief. For a few months, he'd gone crazy, stayed out late, dated a cyclist named Jade, visited Cuba, and worked weekends. But he didn't establish anything with anyone, and he lived alone for a few years. There was the feeling of having been burned. By what, though? And now he had that feeling again, that lonely feeling, with Julia — he'd been burned by all of this, by his own hopes, and by his inability to do anything about the situation, to change the bad parts. Look at the mess, look at what he'd done. He was the only guy he knew who liked his wife and still tried to cheat on her every chance he got. That wasn't progress. It was nothing he'd recommend.

He felt, in the shower, as if he were washing off all the failures of the weekend. When he got out, she still wasn't home. The house was small and there was no other place for it, so one corner of the bedroom was being turned into a nursery. It had a stuffed penguin on the floor and a cardboard box of old baby clothes from his brother. The crib would be there in a month. Without unpacking his bag, Kevin got into bed and listened for Julia's car, but it had been a long day and he passed out.

The old goat hung his face at Julia and said, "We're getting a room ready. We're taking you in."

She felt herself going cold. The anesthesiologist pushed a painkilling narcotic into the IV and inserted the epidural. Nurses in masks flowed about her. They dropped the bedrail, slid her onto a gurney, and suddenly she lay there on the cold plate, chatty as hell, her euphoria ballooning.

"I'm not going to work tomorrow, that's for sure. I'm on maternity leave now, that's for sure."

People busied themselves around her. Finally the young doctor said, "That's right."

"I'm a mom now. I will be in a minute," she said. The young doctor grabbed her IV as they turned her. She caught his stare and held it and said, "I already love her so much."

Bin Laden got her. Kevin should've known. She'd been buried, and he looked everywhere and found her, at last, in Georgetown, in the middle of the street, probably dead and covered with pavement, except for her face, and he looked down and saw that cute little face of hers. Who'd done this? Bin Laden. He had to get her out. There were alarms going, ringing out loud, the police. They'd come from headquarters and were going door to door, banging on the houses along M Street. And you could hear the *boom-boom* of construction crews down on Thirty-fifth, trying to break up the street to save her, but they weren't here yet and he didn't know who else they had to save and he would just have to wait and it was awful, terrible — they were calling Kevin's name.

Then, in the fuzzy air between dreaming and consciousness, he heard Julia screaming his name, whapping on the door, and he stood dizzily and was moving downstairs in his underwear. From the other side of the door, she screamed for him. She didn't have her keys, she must have lost her keys. No wonder he'd had to marry her — she was so stupid.

But it was Erica, Julia's friend from the nutso ward, looking weird. Kevin said, "Julia's not here."

"You have to come to the hospital."

"What?"

"You're having a daughter."

"You what?"

"She's at the hospital." It went on like that for another ten seconds before he got it.

Julia said, "I was lying on the couch at seven o'clock tonight and I thought I had food poisoning."

"Uh-huh," the young doctor said. They were moving quickly, rolling her down the hall.

"I had the worst pain in my life and then it went away and five minutes later it came back. It never entered my mind I was in labor."

They stopped under the surgical lights inside the operating room. She could feel something cool, like ice water, across her belly.

"Can we wait a minute?" Julia asked. "He'll be here soon, I hope."

The young doctor pulled his mask down and looked at the clock.

"I have to tell you," Julia said. "You're a doctor, so you'll know."

"I'm in medical school. I graduate in June."

"They had this movie on TV with Brad Pitt." She started to cry.

"It's okay."

"I did something."

"All right."

"I wanted her out. I kept saying that, 'Get her out.'"

The young doctor waited another second. "You didn't mean it."

"I'm sorry."

"We're not machines," he said.

Erica pulled up to the hospital entrance and Kevin ran down the long corridor to the B-Wing elevator. Up on the sixth floor a nurse led him, shaking, into Labor and Delivery. It wasn't a heart attack so much as he'd strained the muscles that surrounded his heart. She gave him a paper suit, and he shook as though he were freezing to death, putting each stitch of his own clothes in a plastic bag that she took from him, leading him into the operating room, where he squinted into the light, smiling at everyone, grinning madly.

"Look who we found," the nurse said, squeezing his arm. "It's Dad."

Julia's feet were toward the door. There were a dozen people around her. By her head, one guy fiddled with knobs on a bank of machines that Kevin, in his sleepy state, mistook for a film-editing system. Her legs were strapped down by two black seat belts. She'd been shaved. The skin above her stomach, painted a strange brown, was coated in some kind of wax paper. From her hip bones to her chest, the whole of her torso had been pulled open, a gaping bloody maw, pooling and flooding, stretched. A single band of gauze was tied, on one end, to a hook on the wall and on the other end to a small metal plate stuck in her skin that yanked her open, like something a sailor would rig up to hold a hatch in place. Naked of flesh, brimming with blood, her parts gushing, the pieces of her torso jiggled like gelatin. It looked like a torpedo had crashed through the roof and torn her in half.

Something like adrenaline moved him to the stool beside her head, where he sat behind a sheet that had been raised to hide the surgery from her, and took her hand and kissed it, and kissed her face.

"I feel so bad," he said, strangling off tears.

"Don't worry," she said. "Everything is okay." She was gone, stoned, and so pale beneath her blueberry bonnet.

"Did you see anything?" she asked hopefully.

Kevin leaned over her disembodied head. He stroked her cheek. "Nothing. You're fine." He tried not to fall apart. His own stomach swam.

They had a little laugh then, in a bubbly, forced way, about the timing of it, how he would've been in Hartford if it had happened a night earlier. And laughed about the name they hadn't picked yet — Adina, Astrid, Chipewee, Jasmine. The people on the other side of the sheet clinked metal tools and mumbled and moved with urgent, clipped streams of nonsense. The old goat grunted epithets. The group fell into a rhythm.

Julia stopped midsentence, wincing, and Kevin lifted a bean-shaped plastic trough to her lips and she vomited into it. He glanced over the curtain and went a little cross-eyed at the sight of her. It was too much.

Two nurses placed their little bloody sponges on a tray and counted them in unison like children singing a nursery rhyme: *one, two, three,* touching each one, *four, five, six,* to twenty-five. Then they did it again, and then again.

When the baby came, screaming, Julia and Kevin stared at each other and froze, smiling dumbly. Finally the old goat said, "Dad, you can look," and Kevin glanced over the sheet and saw the young doctor holding the baby girl in his gloved hands. She was entirely fish-like and more purple than Kevin had feared, her tiny private parts swollen, her eyes sealed shut, and they wiped her face off as she tried to grab and hug the air in front of her. The doctor held the soft part of his pinkie to the roof of her mouth as the nurse rinsed her face. Then they whisked her away. Kevin kissed Julia and cried.

Without fanfare, Kevin was led to the baby, one room over, curled in a plastic tray under a heat lamp, writhing and screeching dryly and kicking her legs in the air. He examined her ears and lips and mottled purple skin. Oh, God, he thought as she screamed. Now there are two of them.

A tall, angular, dark-haired nurse strolled over, using the new familiar "Dad," and lifted the baby's foot. She needed blood and pricked it, and the baby screamed in a different way, and screamed and screamed, as the nurse calmly worked to bring blood to the glass tube, squeezing the little foot like a lemon, one drop, then another, bending the toes back against the shin, the little earthworm leg held up in the air. It appeared that, in her exuberance, the nurse had pinched off the blood flow to the foot by holding it this way, and Kevin felt sweat run down his back as the white-hot rage of a thousand burning suns stoked his belly. He imagined himself kicking her, like Bruce Lee, in the head until she finally released the foot. Because the baby had been in the breech position, her feet sprang up around her ears, and when the nurse pulled them down again they sprang back up, and the nurse laughed as the baby screamed. She went to the other heel for blood, and then to a finger. In the end the baby was screaming so hard no sound came out.

Kevin sighed, covered in sweat, and smiled weakly at the nurse, who placed a tiny washcloth in his hand and suggested that he wash his baby. He put a hand on her chest and felt her soft kitten belly, her ribs like pasta. She looked a little like George Costanza.

It was sometime after three in the morning on the fourteenth of April. Everything about this night reminded Kevin of powerful psychedelic drugs: his endless need to burn energy, his ultra-aware calmness, the sense of solace he found in his own oblivion, the way he moved among normal people, a changed human, unseen, and the feeling that he'd held back from learning all this until now. A torrent of new insights refused to recede. He checked in on Julia, then went back to the baby. He patrolled the sixth floor. He'd shifted his consciousness into a cosmic framework that no one on earth had experienced before. The lights were down in the neonatal ICU. The baby had two IVs and five wires connected to her, four on her chest, one on her ankle. The monitors glared above her. One was heart rate, one was respiration, one was oxygen level in the blood. He watched the beats. He watched and watched. He had nothing else in the world to do, and felt more peaceful and alert than he could ever remember. Beside him in the dark room, a mother sat bleakly rocking in front of her glass case. Inside the case was a very tiny baby with a thin tube taped to its face, staring into space, dwarfed by its diapers, with a sock on its head and huge, scary bug-out eyes. When he looked back, he realized that his baby was no bigger.

He watched his daughter's chest rising, a little hamster movement. He noticed that the tape holding the IV to the back of her ridiculous little hand was bloody. She slept peacefully, and her face shifted, and as it did she looked a little like his grandfather, then Jack Welch, and then Charlie Brown, snoozing by the window on a rainy afternoon.

He went back and sat at Julia's side. The lights were off there too. He checked her chest, rising and falling, watched her breathe. She also wore a diaper. The temperature in the hospital was frigid. On her hand he noticed a bloody piece of tape holding her IV in place and his heart ached for her and his throat burned. It came over him in a rush, in a moment, and he got rid of it just as quickly. She'd gone through it alone, and now she needed everything; she needed rest, she had to sleep. When she woke up, he'd be in this chair with his two eyes open. A new motor inside him was running on high.

LEE KLEIN

■

All Aboard the Bloated Boat: Arguments in Favor of Barry Bonds

FROM *Barrelhouse*

ON JULY 6, 2005, Girlfriend and I drove to Fairfield, Iowa, home of the Maharishi University of Management (www.mum.edu), a business and spirituality school led by His Holiness Maharishi Mahesh Yogi. A distinctly Vedic-flavored midwestern town, Fairfield is famous for rumors of rampant levitation among its citizenry — a significant thematic fact, considering that this essay's final sentences offer some thoughts about transcendence in a freaked-out world. Please realize the following isn't about rampantly levitating New Age freaks in Fairfield, Iowa, however; it's more about the ocean of corn (and maybe an iceberg lurking somewhere in it?) we saw when we drove to Fairfield two days ago. You know the old saying about how the corn's knee high by the Fourth of July? Well, as we drove through southeast Iowa to see the levitators of Fairfield, we passed not much knee-high corn, a whole lot of the eye-high stuff, and a handful of cornstalks so impressive you wanted to uproot one, take it home, and hang a basketball hoop from it.

The sight of sky-high cornstalks made Girlfriend say: "No wonder nine-year-olds menstruate these days."

To which I replied: "Huh?"

"All the hormones in food," she said, "they hit puberty when they're like *nine*."

This exchange inspired what I thought might be the first line of an essay I'd been gearing up to write for months: "If Barry Bonds were a vegetable, he'd be the biggest, reddest, juiciest tomato that ever made your daughter bleed before her time."

Bonds

Much is made of steroid use by home-run hitters. People say their records are tainted. People say these guys are terrible role models. People say they're cheaters. And yet, in ever-earnest Iowa, the corn is sky high two days after a birthday celebration for a country in which televisions are now how many inches wide? XXXL is not so uncommon a size. Instead of Mustang, Pinto, Bug, or Beetle, today's enormous cars are called Sequoia, Tundra, Rainier, and Yukon (not to mention the environmentally evocative Avalanche). Our armed forces' capabilities to kill, often while miles out of retaliation's reach, seem downright Atarian, if not PlayStation2-ian. Our meal portions are famously super-sized, occasionally complemented with vegetables that make children hit puberty before they can spell "menstruate." And who best personifies all this?

Barry Bonds, of course. He who grew up around the professional game. Whose father (Bobby) and godfather (Willie Mays) are baseball legends. Who worked hard. Who excelled at every level he played. Who, at age thirty-seven, hit seventy-three homers in one year and seemed on track to shatter Henry Aaron's career home-run record. Except he was on steroids, supposedly. You know all this. No need to waste words. But the thing to think about when you think about the effect steroids may have had on Barry Bonds, I think, is that, from Little League to last year's season, he's always been one of the best, if not *the* best.

Imagine you, like me, know what it's like to be one of the best Little Leaguers. Imagine you know what it's like to take the mound and win a high school state championship. Imagine you know what it's like to strike out fourteen in a twenty-one-out college game against the number-ten-ranked Division III team in the country. Imagine you know what it's like to dominate. Imagine you excelled at pitching for thirteen years but didn't take your game to the next level, didn't spend your spare time lifting and running and throwing weighted balls to increase your heater's speed seven measly miles per hour so it'd hit

90 on the radar gun. When you threw a slider at a righty's head, the batter bailed in fear, called out on strikes as the ball cut across the zone. When you threw a curve, it looped so high and dropped so quickly field umps often said "wow" as they tipped the pointy brims of their tiny black caps. When you threw a forkball, it tumbled and fell without much rotation, sometimes skidding unpredictably like a knuckleball. But your fastball, your 83-mile-per-hour heater, college kids caught up with it. It was more than fast enough in high school. But not in college, not even in Division III.

Faced with college-level competition, you didn't work harder on and off the field. You definitely didn't live in the weight room. You, like everyone you've ever played with, didn't do what Barry Bonds did. Instead, *just like everyone you've ever played with,* your interest switched to something else. In my case, guitar. Barry Bonds, meanwhile, committed himself to transforming his natural baseball talent into something almost scary. And it was this drive to be baseball's best — not just of his era, but of all time — that may have compelled him to take a legal substance, widely used by power hitters and pitchers alike, on which he began to compete more with history than with contemporaries who once walked him 232 times in one season. He was that good.

And being that good made people who could never play baseball well in Little League, let alone the high school, college, or professional levels — let alone drunken games of Wiffle Ball — question an ability that seemed to raise the bar high over the head of even the greatest hitters of old. Forget that the Babe hit in a stadium known as "the House that Ruth Built," famous for its short porch in right over which he hit many a home run. Babe Ruth lived on hot dogs and beer, not steroids, though, so it's okay, or so people say. Having a stadium built to your advantage is not cheating.

Further, how many of Bonds's home runs just barely cleared the fence? Mostly they were towering shots into the water, over the bleachers in right. Home runs anywhere. And how many homers would he have had if pitchers actually pitched to him? Instead, they never came close to throwing him strikes, so intimidated were they by his stroke, which was not built on steroids alone: Bonds worked out one winter with David Eckstein, because Barry admired the pesky in-fielder's bat speed . . .

Enough Theory, Let's Practice

Try this at home: (1) sniff out the cell-phone number of your neigh-borhood's performance-enhancing drug dealer, (2) shoot some ste-roids into your limp white office-worker limbs, (3) go stand in the bat-ter's box as some lanky twenty-five-year-old Dominican, Venezuelan, or Texan, out of his mind on amphetamines, cranks 95 mph heaters high and tight, and (4) try touching one of these pitches. C'mon, let's see you get some wood on an 87 mph changeup. Let's see your ste-roid-addled butt play in front of tens of thousands of people every day, every summer, for a dozen years while wearing clingy pinstriped pants completed with gay little elastic stirrups.

Before you find that cell-phone number, imagine for a second all the work it'd take to go from watching your fantasy baseball stat tracker and popping your steroids to hitting a ball into the water over the right-field bleachers and trotting around the bases just once in real life. (Bonds currently has 703 home runs.) Imagine all the work it'd take just to hit one out. Imagine going back in time to when you were six. Imagine hanging all day with Willie Mays (often considered the best of the best) and Bobby Bonds (not to mention your dad's teammates: Willie McCovey and Don Baylor), these guys giving you hitting tips long before you knew how to spell the word "cheating." Imagine every pitch you crushed from age seven onward. Imagine all the time in the weight room. All the time running. All the time studying pitchers. All the time denying indulgences because it's baseball season. Imagine all the flights around the country. Imagine all the home runs. All the cheers. Imag-ine all this happening before you decide to take some hormonal sup-plement to make it easier to work out harder, to compensate for the natural aging process. Imagine the confidence you'd have, knowing how well you're working out these days thanks to the juice. Imagine the swagger. Imagine standing in the batter's box, your arm (usually ex-posed to the bean balls scared pitchers throw in self-defense) now cov-ered in gladiator-like armor. Just imagine what it'd be like to play the

game for two decades before you ever took any sort of hormonal en-
hancement . . .

Now imagine everyone turning on you. Writing off all those years
of work that enhanced your natural talent. Writing you off because
you took a drug late in your career that helped you work harder and
perform better. A drug the pitchers took too. Imagine they make you
the poster boy for steroids, citing the obvious symptom of the long
ball, while half of everyone grousing is on antidepressant pills. While
a steroid-addled Rafael Palmiero cashes in on his five hundred home
runs by appearing in ads for Viagra ($4,000 of which he donated to
George W.'s reelection campaign, by the way). While you spurn the
posturing required to win endorsements. No different from Ted Williams, controversy has always fueled your performance. You thrive
when it's you against the world, and so you bark at the media, talk
trash, and antagonize your teammates, just so it'll spur you on to win.
You fight with everyone to improve your game. Everything you do,
you do to make your game better.

And that's your fatal flaw. All those years of work, all those batting
tips from Mays, Stargell, Parker, etc., the seven MVPs, the eight Gold
Gloves, the thirteen All-Star games, the thirteen consecutive years
hitting thirty or more homers, the single-season on-base percentage record of .609 (!), being the all-time leader in walks (holding
the single-season record for walks with 232 [my god!], as well as
the record for intentional walks with 120), not to mention hitting
seventy-three homers in a season and being one of only three human
beings ever to hit more than 700 homers in their careers, all these records and awards and years of commitment to the game mean absolutely freakin' nothing because you, like everyone else in the league
at the time, it seemed, took what was available to make yourself
better. And since you were already better than everyone, it made
you better than anyone *ever*, and that didn't sit well with some people
who envied what you could do. The drive that got you where you are
destroyed your reputation. Similar ambition has caused the fall of
empires.

Sky High

But, hey, it's not like you're Dock Ellis, who in the early seventies threw a no-hitter on acid, who also took a handful of uppers every time he hit the mound, like so many others. You weren't tripping out there. You were working. In fact, you were a lot like this little black boy from the Pacific Northwest who loved his guitar so much he slept with it, who played and played, who spent most of his time in the air force playing guitar, who traveled all around the South playing guitar, who played rhythm guitar for the Isley Brothers and Little Richard, who played in New York in the mid-sixties under the name Jimmy James, until certain performance-enhancing drugs entered the scene and all that talent and all that work met all those drugs, transforming Jimmy James into the most exciting guitar player Brian Jones of the Stones had ever heard, or so he said when he introduced the relatively unknown Jimi at the Monterey Pop Festival in 1967. Ever hear the rumor that Hendrix sliced his forehead with a razor blade, pressed tabs of acid to the slit, then tied it down with a headscarf so the hallucinogen seeped directly into his brain as he played? Ever hear Jimi's rhythm playing on "Wait Till Tomorrow"? Ever hear the bombs dropping toward the end of "Machine Gun" on the *Band of Gypsys* album?

The comparison between Bonds and Jimi is clear: natural talent + obsessive work/play + performance-enhancing drugs = godlike greatness.

In both cases, it wasn't just the acid or the steroids that created the legend. The equation is much more complicated than just simple addition involving drugs. Mind-blowing performance was founded on sleeping with baseball bats and guitars, years of obsessive practice, tons of natural talent, and then (and only then), the drugs.

Think of the Beatles before *Rubber Soul*. Myth has it that Dylan intervened, performing two of the most important miracles in the history of rock: (1) "Why are you guys singing that 'love me do' crap," he supposedly said, "you're too good for that," and (2) he introduced the mop-headed musicians to weed. What came next? "Norwegian Wood" on *Rubber Soul*. And after that? *Revolver*, which (like Bonds and Jimi) some call the greatest. Which reminds me of Bill Hicks's standup routine about "the war on drugs": how all great music was played by people on drugs, so if you're against drugs, the first thing you should do is take all those great albums by the Beatles and the Stones and burn them, because they were all made while everyone involved was "real high on drugs."

Like Bonds, I played baseball. And like Jimi and the Beatles and the Stones, years ago I played a lot of music while "real high on drugs." But the drugs didn't transform what natural talent I had into something special. Most likely, steroids wouldn't have helped my pitching much either.

So where does that leave us?

Bombs

Right after I typed that question, I got an IM from a friend in London:

FRIEND: p.s. i'm alive
ME: huh
FRIEND: seen the news?
ME: you won the olympics bid!
FRIEND: are you joking?
FRIEND: did you just wake up?
ME: i just checked nyt.com
ME: damn
FRIEND: right
FRIEND: six bombs
FRIEND: and a scare in my street
ME: damn
FRIEND: just got back in the house
FRIEND: it ain't 3000 people, but we're scared
FRIEND: they think about 50 or so dead
FRIEND: about a 1000 injured
FRIEND: some critically
FRIEND: we've been waiting for ages and now it's here
ME: i'm reading this now — the tube — damn
FRIEND: yeah

Tragedy so weirdly appeared when I was paused after that Hendrix/ Beatles-on-drugs rant, trying to figure out how to steer the argument toward the bigger picture. And, lo, an eerie segue appeared to provide the following simple idea: who cares if some idiot kid is influenced to take steroids to make his fastball hit the 90s when this idiot kid lives in a world where idiots try to enhance their ideological performance with explosives, whether it be the bad guy's makeshift sack of dynamite on a double-decker bus or the good guy's million-dollar missiles jettisoned from miles away as though playing some "graphically rich" evolution of Atari's Defender. (Make no mention of the good guy's weapons of mass destruction, set to destroy all life on the planet how many hundreds of times over was it again?)

I swear there's a connection here. I swear there's something that makes steroid use defendable as an evil so lesser it's comparatively angelic. I swear Barry Bonds is a scapegoat for larger troubles. Compare with any sort of warfare the significance of Barry Bonds juicing himself — like Robert Johnson selling his soul to the devil so he can play guitar better than anyone's ever done before — so baseball fans around the country can come away from a game saying those inflated ticket prices were worth it to see Bonds hit a five-hundred-foot moon shot. Compare steroid use with "shock and awe" in Afghanistan and Iraq, with Al Qaeda's actions in New York, Washington, Madrid, and now London. Imagine you've been orphaned by an American missile. Imagine you've consequently developed a hatred for the United States, a hatred you sleep with every night beside you in bed. You work at that hatred, plan to unleash that hatred, and then there's an opportunity to get your filled-with-hatred hands on something abstractly analogous to performance-enhancing drugs: instead of Barry Bonds with steroids and a mighty baseball bat in his hands, imagine you're some anonymous terrorist with uranium and a mighty hatred of America in your heart. The wonder of the bombings in London and Madrid is that both have been surprisingly rinky-dink compared to the expectation of an atomic blast.

The inevitability of a devastating urban strike has nothing directly to do with Barry Bonds's steroid-addled assault on the home-run record. But tainted homers, I think, are a sliver of something more invasive, if only in that we focus on overinflated home-run records because the scandal distracts from the overinflation of American bodies, the overinflation of houses, the overinflation of cars, the overinflation of our armed forces' capabilities, the overinflation of patriotic self-importance, the overinflation of self-righteous nationalistic cluelessness, the overinflation of a sort of laziness that makes you think you can get results without any effort (that makes people think baseball players simply stand at the plate on steroids and hit homers without the physical memory of two dozen years of effort and experience having anything at all to do with how far the ball soars), and finally, of course, we focus on overinflated home-run hitters instead of the overinflation of performance-enhanced produce that makes our daughters' bodies mature way before their prime.

But what about their minds?

Here's where I offer some final thoughts about transcendence in a freaked-out world, a world in which joys as simple as the home run, the corncob, and the tomato are tainted. Why do we question the long ball more than international difficulties caused by an out-of-control addiction to oil that makes us a sedentary society that drives to fast-food chains and then wants pharmaceutical companies to offer obesity pills that don't make us crap our pants? Why do we holler about some naturally gifted, hard-working athlete's semi-unnatural ability to hit a baseball hundreds of feet over a fence when a simple foot would do? How might one transcend the hypocrisy of booing Bonds when his homers are no more bloated than most everything else? Maybe by driving to weird places like Fairfield, Iowa, where no Al Qaeda member would ever think to strike, where the drug of choice is surely crystal meth (or Maharishi mind warp), where a hot-air balloon hung over town as we walked around the gazebo on which leaned a lonely saxophonist who sent overly enlightened licks into the summer air, where the Thai food was really freakin' remarkably good.

What I mean to say is that, like in Fairfield, Iowa — where so many fliers for transcendental-meditation sessions hang around the traditional midwestern town square — maybe the only way to transcend the hypocrisy is to expect your home-run hitters to take performance-enhancing drugs, sort of like tribal shamans reflecting the current state of the world. If everything's naturalness can be questioned, please don't deride one man's ability for doing something as pleasurable and benign as hitting dingers — unless you're consciously singling out Bonds & Friends because you believe sports are an alternate reality where steroids stand in for everything in the world that's wrong that you'd like changed but don't have a clue where to start. But if you see steroids in baseball as part of a whole in which even the tomatoes are juiced, maybe it's better if puberty begins when kids are no older than ten. Maybe a head start on the maturation process will make it easier to realize that steroids are not even the tip of that icy impediment up ahead of our bloated American boat.

NAM LE

Love and Honor and Pity and Pride
and Compassion and Sacrifice

FROM *Zoetrope: All-Story*

MY FATHER ARRIVED on a rainy morning. I was dreaming about a
poem, the dull *thluck thluck* of a typewriter's keys punching out the
letters. It was a good poem — perhaps the best I'd ever written. When
I woke up, he was standing outside my bedroom door, smiling ambig-
uously. He wore black trousers and a wet, wrinkled parachute jacket
that looked like it had just been pulled out of a washing machine.
Framed by the bedroom doorway, he appeared even smaller, gaunter
than I remembered. Still groggy with dream, I lifted my face toward
the alarm clock.

"What time is it?"

"Hello, son," he said in Vietnamese. "I knocked for a long time.
Then the door just opened."

The fields are glass, I thought. Then tum-ti-ti, a dactyl, end line, then
the words "excuse" and "alloy" in the line after. *Come on,* I thought.

"It's raining heavily," he said.

I frowned. The clock read 11:44. "I thought you weren't coming until this afternoon." It felt strange, after all this time, to be speaking
Vietnamese again.

"They changed my flight in Los Angeles."

"Why didn't you ring?"

"I tried," he said equably. "No answer."

I twisted over the side of the bed and cracked open the window. The
sound of rain filled the room — rain fell on the streets, on the roofs,

on the tin shed across the parking lot like the drumming of a thousand fingertips. Everything smelled of wet leaves.

"I turn the ringer off when I sleep," I said. "Sorry."

He continued smiling at me, significantly, as if waiting for an announcement.

"I was dreaming."

He used to wake me, when I was young, by standing over me and smacking my cheeks lightly. I hated it — the wetness, the sourness of his hands.

"Come on," he said, picking up a large Adidas duffel and a rolled bundle that looked like a sleeping bag. "A day lived, a sea of knowledge earned." He loved speaking in Vietnamese proverbs. I had long since learned to ignore it.

I threw on a T-shirt and stretched my neck in front of the lone window. Through the rain, the sky was as gray and sharp as graphite. *The fields are glass* . . . Like a shape in smoke, the poem blurred, then dissolved into this new, cold, strange reality: a windblown, rain-strafed parking lot; a dark room almost entirely taken up by my bed; the small body of my father dripping water onto hardwood floors.

I went to him, my legs goose-pimpled underneath my pajamas. He watched with pleasant indifference as my hand reached for his, shook it, then relieved his other hand of the bags. "You must be exhausted," I said.

He had flown from Sydney, Australia. Thirty-three hours all told — transiting in Auckland, Los Angeles, and Denver — before touching down in Iowa. I hadn't seen him in three years.

"You'll sleep in my room."

"Very fancy," he said, as he led me through my own apartment. "You even have a piano." He gave me an almost rueful smile. "I knew you'd never really quit." Something moved behind his face, and I found myself back on a heightened stool with my fingers chasing the metronome, ahead and behind, trying to shut out the tutor's repeated sighing, his heavy brass ruler. I realized I was massaging my knuckles. My father patted the futon in my living room. "I'll sleep here."

"You'll sleep in my room, Ba." I watched him warily as he surveyed our surroundings, messy with books, papers, dirty plates, teacups, clothes — I'd intended to tidy up before going to the airport. "I work in this room anyway, and I work at night." As he moved into the kitchen, I snatched the three-quarters-full bottle of Johnnie Walker from the second shelf of my bookcase and stashed it under the desk. I looked around. The desktop was gritty with cigarette ash. I threw some magazines over the roughest spots, then flipped one of them over because its cover bore a picture of Chairman Mao. I quickly gathered up the cigarette packs and sleeping pills and incense burners and dumped them all on a high shelf, behind my Kafka Vintage Classics.

At the kitchen swing door I remembered the photo of Linda beside the printer. Her glamour shot, I called it: hair windswept and eyes squinty, smiling at something out of the frame. One of her ex-boyfriends had taken it at Lake MacBride. She looked happy. I snatched it and turned it face-down, covering it with scrap paper.

As I walked into the kitchen, I thought for a moment that I had left the fire escape open. Rainwater gushed along gutters, down through the pipes. Then I saw my father at the sink, sleeves rolled up, sponge in hand, washing the month-old, crusted mound of dishes. The smell was awful. "Ba," I said, frowning, "you don't need to do that."

His hands, hard and leathery, moved deftly in the sink.

"Ba," I said, halfheartedly.

"I'm almost finished." He looked up and smiled. "Have you eaten? Do you want me to make some lunch?"

"*Hoi,*" I said, suddenly irritated. "You're exhausted. I'll go out and get us something."

I went back through the living room into my bedroom, picking up clothes and rubbish as I went.

"You don't have to worry about me," he called out. "You just do what you always do."

The truth was, he'd come at the worst possible time. I was in my last year at the Iowa Writers' Workshop; it was late November, and my final story for the semester was due in three days. I had a backlog of papers to grade and a heap of fellowship and job applications to draft and submit. It was no wonder I was drinking so much.

I'd told Linda only the previous night that he was coming. We were at her place. Her body was slippery with sweat and hard to hold. Her body smelled of her clothes. She turned me over, my face kissing the bedsheets, and then she was chopping my back with the edges of her hands. *Higher. Out a bit more.* She had trouble keeping a steady rhythm. "Softer," I told her. Moments later, I started laughing.

"What?"

The sheets were damp beneath my pressed face.

"What?"

"*Softer,*" I said, "not *slower.*"

She slapped my back with the meat of her palms, hard — once, twice. I couldn't stop laughing. I squirmed over and caught her by the wrists. Hunched forward, she was blushing and beautiful. Her hair fell over her face; beneath its ash-blond hem all I could see were her open lips. She pressed down, into me, her shoulders kinking the long, lean curve from the back of her neck to the small of her back. "Stop it!" her lips said. She wrested her hands free. Fingers beneath my waistband, violent, the scratch of her nails down my thighs, knees, ankles. I pointed my foot like a ballet dancer.

Afterward, I told her my father didn't know about her. She said nothing. "We just don't talk about that kind of stuff," I explained. She looked like an actress who looked like my girlfriend. Staring at her face made me tired. I'd begun to feel this way more often around her. "He's only here for three days." Somewhere out of sight, a group of college boys hooted and yelled.

"I thought you didn't talk to him at all."

"He's my father."

"What's he want?"

I rolled toward her, onto my elbow. I tried to remember how much I'd told her about him. We were lying on the bed, the wind loud in the room — I remember that — and we were both tipsy. Ours could have been any two voices in the darkness. "It's only three days," I said.

The look on her face was strange, shut down. She considered me for a long time. Then she got up and pulled on her clothes. "Just make sure you get your story done," she said.

I drank before I came here too. I drank when I was a student at university, and then when I was a lawyer — in my previous life, as they say. There was a subterranean bar in a hotel next to my work, and

every night I would wander down and slump on a barstool and pretend I didn't want the bartender to make small talk with me. He was
only a bit older than I, and I came to envy his ease, his confidence that
any given situation was only temporary. I left exorbitant tips. After a
while, I was treated to battered shrimps and shepherd's pies on the
house. My parents had already split by then: my father moving to Sydney, my mother into a government flat.

That's all I have ever done, traffic in words. Sometimes I still think
about word counts, the way a general must think about casualties. I
had been in Iowa more than a year — days passed in weeks, then
months, more than a year of days — and I had written only four and a
half stories. About seventeen thousand words. When I was working at
the law firm, I would have written that many words in a couple of
weeks. And they would have been useful to someone.

Deadlines came, exhausting, and I forced myself up to meet them.
Then, in the great spans of time between, I fell back to my vacant
screen and my slowly sludging mind. I tried everything — writing in
longhand, writing in my bed, in my bathtub. As this last deadline approached, I remembered a friend claiming he'd broken his writer's
block by switching to a typewriter. You're free to write, he told me,
once you know you can't delete what you've written. I bought a Smith
Corona electric at an antique shop. It buzzed like a tropical aquarium
when I plugged it in. It looked good on my desk. For inspiration, I
read absurdly formal Victorian poetry and drank scotch neat. How
hard could it be? Things happened in this world all the time. All I had
to do was record them. In the sky, two swarms of swallows converged,
pulled apart, interwove again like veils drifting at crosscurrents. In
line at the supermarket, a black woman leaned forward and kissed the
handle of her shopping cart, her skin dark and glossy like the polished wood of a piano.

The week prior to my father's arrival, a friend harassed me for my
persistent defeatism.

"Writer's block?" Under the streetlights, vapors of bourbon puffed
out of his mouth. "How can you have writer's block? Just write a story
about Vietnam."

We had just come from a party following a reading by the workshop's most recent success, a Chinese woman trying to immigrate to

America who had written a book of short stories about Chinese characters in stages of migration to America. The stories were subtle and good. The gossip was that she'd been offered a substantial six-figure contract for a two-book deal. It was meant to be an unspoken rule that such things were left unspoken. Of course, it was all anyone talked about.

"It's hot," a writing instructor told me at a bar. "Ethnic literature's hot. And important too."

A couple of visiting literary agents took a similar view. "There's a lot of polished writing around," one of them said. "You have to ask yourself, what makes me stand out?" She tag-teamed to her colleague, who answered slowly, as though intoning a mantra: "Your *background* and *life experience*."

Other friends were more forthright. "I'm sick of ethnic lit," one said. "It's full of descriptions of exotic food." Or: "You can't tell if the language is spare because the author intended it that way, or because he didn't have the vocab."

I was told about a friend of a friend, a Harvard graduate from Washington, D.C., who had posed in traditional Nigerian garb for his book-jacket photo. I pictured myself standing in a rice paddy, wearing a conical straw hat. Then I pictured my father in the same field, wearing his threadbare fatigues, young and hard-eyed.

"It's a license to bore," my friend said. We were drunk and wheeling our bikes because both of us, separately, had punctured our tires on the way to the party.

"The characters are always flat, generic. As long as a Chinese writer writes about *Chinese* people, or a Peruvian writer about *Peruvians,* or a Russian writer about *Russians* . . . ," he said, as though reciting children's doggerel, then stopped, losing his train of thought. His mouth turned up into a doubtful grin. I could tell he was angry about something.

"Look," I said, pointing at a floodlit porch ahead of us. "Those guys have guns."

"As long as there's an interesting image or metaphor once in every *this* much text" — he held out his thumb and forefinger to indicate half a page, his bike wobbling all over the sidewalk. I nodded to him, and then I nodded to one of the guys on the porch, who nodded back.

The other guy waved us through with his faux-wood air rifle. A car with its headlights on was idling in the driveway, and girls' voices emerged from inside, squealing, "Don't shoot! Don't shoot!"

"Faulkner, you know," my friend said over the squeals, "he said we should write about the old verities. Love and honor and pity and pride and compassion and sacrifice." A sudden sharp crack behind us, like the striking of a giant typewriter hammer, followed by some muffled shrieks. "I know I'm a bad person for saying this," my friend said, "but that's why I respect your writing, Nam. Because you could just write about Vietnamese boat people all the time. Like in your third story."

He must have thought my head was bowed in modesty, but in fact I was figuring out whether I'd just been shot in the back of the thigh. I'd felt a distinct sting. The pellet might have ricocheted off something.

"You could *totally* exploit the Vietnamese thing. But *instead* you choose to write about lesbian vampires and Colombian assassins and Hiroshima orphans — and New York painters with hemorrhoids."

For a dream-like moment I was taken aback. Catalogued like that, under the bourbon stink of his breath, my stories sank into unflattering relief. My leg was still stinging. I imagined sticking my hand down the back of my jeans, bringing it to my face under a streetlight, and finding it gory, blood-spattered. I imagined turning around, advancing wordlessly up the porch steps, and drop-kicking the two kids. I would tell my story into a microphone from a hospital bed. I would compose my story in a county cell. I would kill one of them, maybe accidentally, and never talk about it, ever, to anyone. There was no hole in my jeans.

"I'm probably a bad person," my friend said, stumbling beside his bike a few steps in front of me.

If you ask me why I came to Iowa, I would say that Iowa is beautiful in the way that any place is beautiful: if you treat it as the answer to a question you're asking yourself every day, just by being there.

That afternoon, as I was leaving the apartment for Linda's, my father called out my name from the bedroom.

I stopped outside the closed door. He was meant to be napping.

"Where are you going?" his voice said.

"For a walk," I replied.

"I'll walk with you."

It always struck me how everything seemed larger in scale on Summit Street: the double-storied houses, their smooth lawns sloping down to the sidewalks like golf greens; elm trees with high, thick branches — the sort of branches from which I imagined fathers suspending long-roped swings for daughters in white dresses. The leaves, once golden and red, were turning dark orange, brown. The rain had stopped. I don't know why, but we walked in the middle of the road, dark asphalt gleaming beneath slick, pasted leaves, like the back of a whale.

I asked him, "What do you want to do while you're here?"

His face was pale and fixed in a smile. "Don't worry about me," he said. "I can just meditate. Or read."

"There's a coffee shop downtown," I said. "And a Japanese restaurant." It sounded pathetic.

He kept smiling, looking at the ground moving in front of his feet.

"I have to write," I said.

"You write."

I realized I could no longer read his smile. He had perfected it during his absence. It was a setting of the lips, sly, almost imperceptible, which I would probably associate with senility but for the keen awareness of his eyes.

"There's an art museum across the river," I said.

"Ah, take me there."

"The museum?"

"No," he said, looking sideways at me. "The river."

We turned back to Burlington Street and walked down the hill to the river. He stopped in the middle of the bridge. The water below looked cold and black, slowing in sections as it succumbed to the temperature. Behind us, six lanes of cars skidded back and forth across the skin of the road, the sound like the shredding of wind.

"Have you heard from your mother?" He stood upright before the railing, his head strangely small above the puffy down jacket I had lent him.

"Every now and then."

He lapsed into formal Vietnamese: "How is the mother of Nam?"

"She is good," I said, loudly — too loudly — trying to make myself heard over the groans and clanks of a passing truck.

He was nodding. Behind him, the east bank of the river glowed wanly in the afternoon light. "Come on," I said. We crossed the bridge and walked to a nearby Dairy Queen. When I came out, two coffees in my hands, my father had gone down to the river's edge. Next to him, a bundled-up, bearded figure stooped over a burning gasoline drum. Never had I seen anything like it in Iowa City.

"This is my son," my father said, once I had scrambled down the wet bank. "The writer." He took a hot paper cup from my hand. "Would you like some coffee?"

"Thank you, no." The man stood still, watching his knotted hands, palms glowing orange above the rim of the drum. His voice was soft, his clothes heavy with his life. I smelled animals in him, and fuel, and rain.

"I read his story," my father went on in his lilting English, "about Vietnamese boat people." He gazed at the man, straight into his blank, rheumy eyes, then said, as though delivering a punch line, "*We* are Vietnamese boat people."

We stood there for a long time, the three of us, watching the flames. When I lifted my eyes it was dark.

"Do you have any money on you?" my father asked me in Vietnamese.

"Welcome to America," the man said through his beard. He didn't look up as I closed his fist around the damp bills.

My father was drawn to weakness, even as he tolerated none in me. He was a soldier, he said once, as if that explained everything. With me, he was all proverbs and regulations. No personal phone calls. No female friends. No extracurricular reading. When I was in primary school, he made me draw up a daily ten-hour study timetable for the summer holidays, and punished me when I deviated from it. He knew how to cane me twenty times and leave only one black-red welt, like a brand mark across my buttocks. Afterward, as he rubbed Tiger Balm on the wound, I would cry in anger at myself for crying. Once, when my mother let slip that durian fruit made me vomit, he forced me to eat it in front of guests. *Doi an muoi cung ngon:* hunger finds no fault with food. I learned to hate him with a straight face.

When I was fourteen, I discovered that he had been involved in a massacre. Later, I would come across photos and transcripts and books; but there, at a family friend's party in suburban Melbourne, and then, it was just another story in a circle of drunken men. They sat cross-legged on newspapers around a large blue tarpaulin, getting smashed on cheap beer. It was that time of night when things started to break up against other things. Red faces, raised voices, spilled drinks. We arrived late and the men shuffled around, making room for my father.

"Thanh! Fuck your mother! What took you so long — scared, no? Sit down, sit down —"

"Give him five bottles." The speaker swung around ferociously. "We'll let you off, everyone here's had eight, nine already."

For the first time, my father let me stay. I sat on the perimeter of the circle, watching in fascination. A thicket of Vietnamese voices, cursing, toasting, braying about their children, making fun of one man who kept stuttering, "It has the power of f-f-five hundred horses!" Through it all my father laughed good-naturedly, his face so red with drink he looked sunburned. Bowl and chopsticks in his hands, he appeared somewhat childish sitting between two men trading war stories. I watched him as he picked sparingly at the enormous spread of dishes in the middle of the circle. The food was known as *do an nho:* alcohol food. Massive fatty oysters dipped in salt-pepper-lemon paste. Boiled sea snails, large grilled crab legs. Southern-style bitter shredded chicken salad with brown, spotty rice crackers. Someone called out my father's name; he had set his chopsticks down and was speaking in a low voice:

"Heavens, the gunships came first, rockets and M-6os. You remember that sound, no? Like you were deaf. We were hiding in the bunker underneath the temple, my mother and four sisters and Mrs. Tran, the baker, and some other people. You couldn't hear anything. Then the gunfire stopped and Mrs. Tran told my mother we had to go up to the street. If we stayed there, the Americans would think we were Vietcong. 'I'm not going anywhere,' my mother said. 'They have grenades,' Mrs. Tran said. I was scared and excited. I had never seen an American before."

It took me a while to reconcile my father with the story he was telling. He caught my eye and held it a moment, as though he and I were sharing a secret. He was drunk.

"So we went up. Everywhere there was dust and smoke, and all you could hear was the sound of helicopters and M-16s. Houses on fire. Then, through the smoke, I saw an American. I almost laughed. He wore his uniform so untidily — it was too big for him — and he had a beaded necklace and a baseball cap. He held an M-16 over his shoulder like a spade. Heavens, he looked nothing like the Vietcong, with their shirts tucked in and buttoned to their chins even after crawling through mud tunnels all day."

He picked up his chopsticks and reached for the *tiet canh* — a specialty — mincemeat soaked in fresh congealed duck blood. Some of the other men were listening now, smiling knowingly. I saw his teeth, stained red, as he chewed through the rest of his words: "They made us walk to the east side of the village. There were about ten of them, about fifty of us. Mrs. Tran was saying, 'No VC no VC.' They couldn't hear her over the sound of machine guns and the M-79 grenade launchers. Remember those? Only I heard her. I saw pieces of animals all over the paddy fields, a water buffalo with its side missing — like it was scooped out by a spoon. Then, through the smoke, I saw Grandpa Long bowing to a GI in the traditional greeting. I wanted to call out to him. His wife and daughter and granddaughters, My and Kim, stood shyly behind him. The GI stepped forward, hit the top of his head with the rifle butt, and then twirled the gun around and slid the bayonet into his neck. No one said anything. My mother tried to cover my eyes, but I saw him switch the fire selector on his gun from automatic to single-shot before he shot Grandma Long. Then he and a friend pulled the daughter into a shack, the two little girls dragged along, clinging to her legs.

"They stopped us at the drainage ditch, near the bridge. There were bodies on the road, a baby with only the bottom half of its head, a monk, his robe turned pink. I saw two bodies with the ace of spades carved into their chests. I didn't understand it. My sisters didn't even cry. People were now shouting, 'No VC no VC,' but the Americans just frowned and spat and laughed. One of them said something, then some of them started pushing us into the ditch. It was half full of muddy water. My mother jumped in and lifted my sisters down, one by one. I remember looking up and seeing helicopters everywhere, some bigger than others, some higher up. They made us kneel in the water. They set up their guns on tripods. They made us stand up again. One of the Americans, a boy with a fat face, was crying and moaning softly as he reloaded his magazine. No VC no VC. They didn't look at us. They made us turn around and kneel down in the water again. Then they started shooting, and I felt my mother's body jumping on top of mine; it kept jumping for a long time, and then everywhere was the sound of helicopters, louder and louder like they were all coming down to land, and everything was dark and wet and warm and sweet."

The circle had gone quiet. My mother came out from the kitchen, squatted behind my father, and looped her arms around his neck. This was a minor breach of the rules. "Heavens," she said, "don't you men have anything better to talk about?"

After a short silence, someone snorted, saying loudly, "You win, Thanh. You really *did* have it bad!" and then everyone, including my father, burst out laughing. I joined in unsurely. They clinked glasses and made toasts using words I didn't understand.

Maybe he didn't tell it exactly that way. Maybe I'm filling in the gaps. But you're not under oath when writing a eulogy, and this is close enough. My father grew up in the province of Quang Ngai, in the village of Son My, in the hamlet of Tu Cung, later known to the Americans as My Lai. He was fourteen years old.

Late that night, I plugged in the Smith Corona. It hummed with promise. I grabbed the bottle of scotch from under the desk and poured myself a double. Fuck it, I thought. I had two and a half days left. I would write the ethnic story of my Vietnamese father. It was a good story. It was a fucking *great* story.

I fed in a sheet of blank paper. At the top of the page, I typed

"ETHNIC STORY" in capital letters. I pushed the carriage return and scrolled down to the next line. The sound of helicopters in a dark sky. The keys hammered the page.

I woke up late the next day. At the coffee shop, I sat with my typed pages and watched people come and go. They laughed and sat and sipped and talked and, listening to them, I was reminded again that I was in a small town in a foreign country.

I thought of my father in my dusky bedroom. He had kept the door closed as I left. I thought of how he had looked when I last checked on him: his body lost in the blankets and his head so small among my pillows. His skin glassy in the blue glow of dawn. He was here, now, with me, and already making the rest of my life seem unreal.

I read over what I had typed, thinking of him at that age, connecting him with who he would become. At a nearby table, a guy held out one of his iPod earbuds and beckoned his date to come around and sit beside him. The door opened and a cold wind blew in. I tried to concentrate.

"Hey." It was Linda, wearing a large orange hiking jacket and bringing with her the crisp, bracing scent of all the places she had been. Her face was unmaking a smile. "What are you doing here?"

"Working on my story."

"Is your dad here?"

"No."

Her friends were waiting by the counter. She nodded to them, holding up a finger, then came behind me, resting her hands on my shoulders. "Is this it?" She leaned over me, her hair grazing my face, cold and silken against my cheek. She picked up a couple of pages and read them soundlessly, as though praying. "I don't get it," she said, returning them to the table. "What are you doing?"

"What do you mean?"

"You never told me any of this."

I shrugged.

"Did he tell you this? Now he's talking to you?"

"Not really," I said.

"Not really?"

I turned around to face her. Her eyes reflected no light.

"You know what I think?" She looked back down at the pages. "I think you're making excuses for him."

"Excuses?"

"You're romanticizing his past," she went on quietly, "to make sense of the things you said he did to you."

"It's a story," I said. "What things did I say?"

"You said he abused you."

It was too much, these words, and what connected to them. I looked at her serious, beautifully lined face, her light-trapping eyes, and already I felt them taxing me. "I never said that."

She took a half step back. "Just tell me this," she said, her voice flattening. "You've never introduced him to any of your exes, right?" The question was tight on her face.

I didn't say anything, and after a while she nodded, biting one corner of her upper lip. I knew that gesture. I knew, even then, that I was supposed to stand up, pull her orange-jacketed body toward mine, speak words into her ear; but all I could do was think about my father and his excuses. Those tattered bodies on top of him. The ten hours he waited, mud filling his lungs, until nightfall. I felt myself falling back into old habits.

She stepped forward and kissed the top of my head. It was one of her rules: not to walk away from an argument without some sign of affection. I didn't look at her. My mother liked to tell the story of how, when our family first arrived in Australia, we lived in a hostel on an outer-suburb street where the locals, whenever they met or parted, hugged and kissed each other warmly; how my father — baffled, charmed — had named it "the street of lovers."

I turned to the window. It was dark now, the evening settling thick and deep. A man and woman sat across from each other at a high table. The woman leaned forward, smiling, her breasts squat on the wood, elbows forward, her hands mere inches away from the man's shirt front. Throughout their conversation her teeth glinted. Behind them, a mother sat with her son. "I'm not playing," she murmured, flipping through her magazine.

"L," said the boy.

"I said I'm not playing."

Here is what I believe: we forgive any sacrifice by our parents so long as it is not made in our name. To my father there was no other name, only mine, and he had named me after the homeland he had given up. His sacrifice was complete and compelled him to everything that happened. To all that, I was inadequate.

At sixteen I left home. There was a girl, and heroin, and the possibility of greater loss than I had imagined possible. She embodied everything prohibited by my father and plainly worthwhile. Of course he was right about her: she taught me hurt — and promise. We were two animals in the dark, hacking at each other, and never since have I felt that way — that sense of consecration. When my father found out my mother was supporting me, he gave her an ultimatum. She moved into a family friend's textile factory and learned to use an overlock machine and continued sending money.

"Of course I want to live with him," she told me when I visited her, months later. "But I want you to come home too."

"Ba doesn't want that."

"You're his son," she said simply. "He wants you with him."

I laundered my school uniform and asked a friend to cut my hair and waited for school hours to finish before catching the train home. My father excused himself upon seeing me. When he returned to the living room, he had changed his shirt and there was water in his hair. I felt sick and fully awake — as if all the previous months had been a single sleep and now my face was wet again, burning cold. The room smelled of peppermint. He asked me if I was well, and I told him I was, and then he asked me if my female friend was well, and at that moment I realized he was speaking to me not as a father — not as he would to his only son — but as he would speak to a friend, to anyone, and it undid me. I had learned what it was to attenuate my blood, but that was nothing compared to this. I forced myself to look at him and I asked him to bring Ma back home.

"And Child?"

"Child will not take any more money from Ma."

"Come home," he said, finally. His voice was strangled, half swallowed.

Even then, my emotions operated like a system of levers and pulleys; just seeing him had set them irreversibly in motion. "No," I said. The word shot out of me.

"Come home, and Ma will come home, and Ba promises Child to never speak of any of this again." He looked away, smiling heavily, and took out a handkerchief. His forehead was moist with sweat. He had been buried alive in the warm, wet clinch of his family, crushed by their lives. I wanted to know how he climbed out of that pit. I wanted to know how there could ever be any correspondence between us. I wanted to know all this, but an internal momentum moved me, farther from him as time went on.

"The world is hard," he said. For a moment I was uncertain whether he was speaking in proverbs. He looked at me, his face a gleaming mask. "Just say yes, and we can forget everything. That's all. Just say it: yes."

But I didn't say it. Not that day, nor the next, nor any day for almost a year. When I did, though, rehabilitated and fixed in new privacies, he was true to his word and never spoke of the matter. In fact, after I came back home he never spoke of anything much at all, and it was under this learned silence that the three of us — my father, my mother, and I — were conducted irreparably into our separate lives.

The apartment smelled of fried garlic and sesame oil when I returned. My father was sitting on the living room floor, on the special mattress he had brought over with him. It was made of white foam. He told me it was for his back. "I made some stir-fry."

"Thanks."

"I read your story this morning," he said, "while you were still sleeping." Something in my stomach flipped over. I hadn't thought to hide the pages. "There are mistakes in it."

"You read it?"

"There were mistakes in your last story too."

I tried to recall those sections where I'd been sloppy with research. Maybe the scene in Rach Gia, before they reached the refugee boat. I

came out of the kitchen with a full plate of rice, marinated tofu, cashews, and chickpeas. "They're *stories*," I said casually. "Fiction."

He paused for a moment, then said, "Okay, son."

My diet had consisted of chips and noodles and pizzas for so long,
I'd forgotten how much I missed home cooking. As I ate, he stretched
on his white mat.

"How's your back?"

"I had a CAT scan," he said. "There's nerve fluid leaking between
my vertebrae." He smiled his long-suffering smile, right leg twisted
across his left hip. "I brought the scans to show you."

"Does it hurt, Ba?"

"It hurts." He chuckled briefly, as though the whole matter were a
joke. "But what can I do? I can only accept it."

"Can't they operate?"

I felt myself losing interest. I was a bad son. Since he'd separated
from my mother, he'd brought up his back pains so often — always
couched in Buddhist tenets of suffering and acceptance — that the
cold, hard part of me suspected he was exaggerating, to solicit and
then gently rebuke my concern. He did this. He'd forced me to take
karate lessons until I was sixteen; then, during one of our final arguments, he came at me and I found myself in fighting stance. He had
smiled at my horror. "That's right," he'd said. We were locked in all
the intricate ways of guilt. It took all the time we had to realize that
everything we faced, we faced for the other as well.

"I want to talk with you," I said.

"You grow old, your body breaks down," he said.

"No, I mean for the story."

"Talk?"

"Yes."

"About what?" He seemed amused.

"About my mistakes," I said.

If you ask me why I came to Iowa, I would say that I was a lawyer and
I was no lawyer. Every twenty-four hours I woke up at the smoggiest
time of morning and commuted — bus, tram, elevator, often without
saying a single word, wearing clothes that chafed against me and

holding a flat white in a white cup — to my windowless office in the tallest, most glass-covered building in Melbourne. Time was broken down into six-minute units, friends allotted eight-unit lunch breaks. I hated what I was doing, and I hated that I was good at it. Mostly I hated knowing it was my job that gave my father pride and happiness. When I told him I was quitting and going to Iowa to be a writer, he said, *Trau buoc ghet trau an.* The captive buffalo hates the free buffalo. But by that time, he had no more control over my life. I was twenty-five years old.

The thing is not to write what no one else could have written, but to write what only you could have written. I recently found this fragment in one of my old notebooks. The person who wrote that couldn't have known what would happen: how time can hold itself against you, how a voice hollows, how words you once loved can wither on the page.

"Why do you want to write this story?" my father asked me.

"It's a good story."

"But there are so many things you could write about."

"This is important, Ba. It's important that people know."

"You want their pity."

I didn't know whether it was a question. I was offended. "I want them to remember," I said.

He was silent for a long time. Then he said, "Only you'll remember. I'll remember. They will read and clap their hands and forget." For once, he was not smiling. "Sometimes it's better to forget, no?"

"I'll write it anyway," I said. It came back to me — how I had felt at the typewriter the night before. A thought leapt into my mind: "If I write a true story," I told my father, "I'll have a better chance of selling it."

He looked at me a while, searchingly, as though seeing something for the first time. Then he said, in a considered voice, "I'll tell you. But believe me, it's not something you'll be able to write."

"I'll write it anyway," I repeated.

Then he did something unexpected. His face opened up and he began to laugh, without self-pity or slyness, laughing in full-bodied breaths. I was shocked. I hadn't heard him laugh like this for a long time. Without fully knowing why, I started laughing too. His throat was humming in Vietnamese, "Yes . . . yes . . . yes," his eyes shining, smiling. "All right. All right. But tomorrow."

"But —"

"I need to think," he said. He shook his head, then said under his breath, "My son a writer. *Co thuc moi vuc duoc dao.*" Fine words will butter no parsnips.

"*Mot nguoi lam quan, ca ho duoc nho,*" I retorted, then translated: "A scholar is a blessing for all his relatives." He looked at me in surprise before laughing again and nodding vigorously. I'd been saving that one up for years.

Afternoon. We sat across from each other at the dining room table. I asked questions and took notes on a yellow legal pad; he talked. He talked about his childhood, his family. He talked about My Lai. At this point, he stopped.

"You won't offer your father some of that?"

"What?"

"Heavens, you think you can hide liquor of that quality?"

The afternoon light came through the window and held his body in a silver square, slowly sinking toward his feet, dimming, as he talked. I refilled our glasses. He talked above the peak-hour traffic on the streets, its rinse of noise; he talked deep into evening. When the phone rang the second time I unplugged the jack. He told me how he had been conscripted into the South Vietnamese Army.

"After what the Americans did? How did you fight on their side?"

"I had nothing but hate in me," he said, "but I had enough for everyone." He paused on the word "hate" like a father saying it before his infant child for the first time, trying the child's knowledge, testing what was inherent in the word and what learned.

He told me about the war. He told me about meeting my mother. The wedding. Then the fall of Saigon. 1975. He told me about his imprisonment in reeducation camp, the forced confessions, the indoctrinations, the starvations. The daily labor that ruined his back. The casual killings. He told me about the tiger-cage cells and connex boxes, the different names for different forms of torture: the honda, the airplane, the auto. "They tie you by your thumbs, one arm over the shoulder, the other pulled around the front of the body. Or they stretch out your legs and tie your middle fingers to your big toes —"

He showed me. A skinny old man in tantra-like poses, he looked faintly preposterous. During the auto he flinched, then, immediately grinning, asked me to help him to his foam mattress. I waited impatiently for him to stretch it out. He asked me again to help. *Here, push here. A little softer.* Then he went on talking, sometimes in a low voice, sometimes smiling. Other times he would blink — furiously, perplexedly. In spite of his Buddhist protestations, I imagined him locked in rage, turned around and forced every day to rewitness these atrocities of his past, helpless to act. But that was only my imagination. I had nothing to prove that he was not empty of all that now.

He told me how, upon his release after three years' incarceration, he organized our family's escape from Vietnam. This was 1979. He was twenty-five years old then, and my father.

When he finally fell asleep, his face warm from the scotch, I watched him from the bedroom doorway. I was drunk. For a moment, watching him, I felt like I had drifted into dream too. For a moment I became my father, watching his sleeping son, reminded of what — for his son's sake — he had tried, unceasingly, to forget. A past larger than complaint, more perilous than memory. I shook myself conscious and went to my desk. I read my notes through once, carefully, all forty-five pages. I reread the draft of my story from two nights before. Then I put them both aside and started typing, never looking at them again.

Dawn came so gradually, I didn't notice — until the beeping of a garbage truck — that outside the air was metallic blue and the ground was white. The top of the tin shed was white. The first snow had fallen.

He wasn't in the apartment when I woke up. There was a note on the coffee table: *I am going for a walk. I have taken your story to read.* I sat outside, on the fire escape, with a tumbler of scotch, waiting for him. Against the cold, I drank my whiskey, letting it flow like a filament of warmth through my body. I had slept for only three hours and was too tired to feel anything but peace. The red geraniums on the landing of

the opposite building were frosted over. I spied through my neighbors' windows and saw exactly nothing.

He would read it, with his book-learned English, and he would
recognize himself in a new way. He would recognize me. He would
see how powerful was his experience, how valuable his suffering —
how I had made it speak for more than itself. He would be pleased
with me.

I finished the scotch. It was eleven-thirty and the sky was dark
and gray-smeared. My story was due at midday. I put my gloves on,
treaded carefully down the fire escape, and untangled my bike from
the rack. He would be pleased with me. I rode around the block, up
and down Summit Street, looking for a sign of my puffy jacket. The
streets were empty. Most of the snow had melted, but an icy film covered the roads and I rode slowly. Eyes stinging and breath fogging
in front of my mouth, I coasted toward downtown, across the College Green, the grass frozen so stiff it snapped beneath my bicycle
wheels. Lights glowed dimly from behind the curtained windows of
houses. On Washington Street, a sudden gust of wind ravaged the
elm branches and unfastened their leaves, floating them down thick
and slow and soundless.

I was halfway across the bridge when I saw him. I stopped. He was
on the riverbank. I couldn't make out the face, but it was he, short and
small-headed in my bloated jacket. He stood with the tramp, both of
them staring into the blazing gasoline drum. The smoke was thick,
particulate. For a second I stopped breathing. I knew with sick cer-
tainty what he had done. The ashes, given body by the wind, floated
away from me down the river. He patted the man on the shoulder,
reached into his back pocket, and slipped some money into those
large, newly mittened hands. He started up the bank then, and saw
me. I was so full of wanting I thought it would flood my heart. His
hands were empty.

If I had known then what I knew later, I wouldn't have said the
things I did. I wouldn't have told him he didn't understand; for clearly,
he did. I wouldn't have told him that what he had done was unforgiv-
able. That I wished he had never come, or that he was no father to me.
But I hadn't known, and, as I waited, feeling the wind change, all I

saw was a man coming toward me in a ridiculously oversized jacket, rubbing his black-sooted hands, stepping through the smoke with its flecks and flame-tinged eddies, who had destroyed himself, yet again, in my name. The river was behind him. The wind was full of acid. In the slow float of light I looked away, down at the river. On the brink of freezing, it gleamed in large, bulging blisters. The water, where it still moved, was black and braided. And it occurred to me then how it took hours, sometimes days, for the surface of a river to freeze over — to hold in its skin a perfect and crystalline world — and how that world could be shattered by a small stone dropped like a single syllable.

JEN MARLOWE, AISHA BAIN,
AND ADAM SHAPIRO

∎

Darfur Diaries

FROM *Darfur Diaries: Stories of Survival*

From the Introduction by Aisha Bain

FALL 2003: I had started a master's program in International Peace
and Conflict Resolution and was interning at a small NGO (non-
governmental organization) called the Center for the Prevention of
Genocide. Within two days the director had dropped a folder on my
desk with the word "Darfur" handwritten in black marker on the tab.
"We're getting some strange reports coming out of the region. Figure
out what's going on."

Right, I thought. First things first — where's Darfur?

After reading the file and doing some preliminary research, I discovered that refugees had begun spilling into Chad in February 2003
— the first the world learned of a crisis in the neighboring western
state of Sudan. Yet I hadn't heard anything about any refugees or any
problems along the Chad-Sudan border. All the focus on Sudan had
been on the long-awaited north-south agreement to end Africa's lon-
gest-running civil war. Many world powers were hungrily anticipating
an agreement, waiting for safe and full access to the country's oil re-
serves that lay in the middle of the battleground for the past few decades. It seemed like nothing could interfere with such a high-stakes
process, not even thousands of refugees marooned on the Chadian
border in the Sahara Desert.

The Center's file also held reports of attacks, killings, and razed villages, but nothing had been confirmed. My research continued to
uncover more alarming information: the government of Sudan had

closed all the borders of Darfur (it was uncertain exactly when), expelled the international presence from the entire region, and instituted a media blackout. I contacted Médecins Sans Frontières (Doctors Without Borders) and learned that its staff had been made to leave the country, and a few doctors tried to remain behind to help. They had received some terrifying reports — bombings, militia attacks, people internally displaced — but asked that we keep everything confidential for the safety of the doctors. I began calling other organizations and found a Christian group that had been operating in the area which gave similar reports before its staff had to flee. I began to track down Sudanese people in Washington, D.C., trying to find some way to contact people in Darfur and get firsthand reports.

Then we got an unexpected visit. Dr. Tigani Sissi, a Darfurian who had worked as a local governor in his home district, had fled Sudan, fearing for his life. He continued to get horrifying reports from his people on the ground and was trying to obtain support from the international community. From exile in England, Dr. Sissi had traveled to the United States, certain that once people were made aware of what was happening, they would help his people.

He and his three Darfurian colleagues described what was happening on the ground. Arab militias, called the Janjaweed, were razing villages all over Darfur. Attacks included aerial bombings, villages being burned to the ground, the killing of civilians, people fleeing, government soldiers involved — he painted a picture of total chaos.

"The government?" I asked. "The Sudanese government is involved?"

"Yes," Dr. Sissi assured me. Not only had civilians reported seeing government soldiers and vehicles, but there was no way that the militias would have had access to the planes needed to carry out such a massive bombing campaign, he said.

He explained that when President Omar Bashir came to power in a coup in 1989, he struck an alliance with certain tribal groups and the military to promote an Islamic agenda. While this consolidated support for the government among some people in Sudan, the government remained unpopular with a majority of the population.

Darfur, an impoverished area with little development or infrastructure, was one of the regions that opposed the government. Having fought lengthy wars in other parts of the country to gain control, the ruling party had turned its attention to Darfur. Its plan was to remove opposing populations by exploiting the region's tense tribal relations. Its support for Arab nomads in a growing conflict with settled farming populations began with the Arab–Fur war of the late 1980s but grew into an all-out war after an attack on Fasher by the Sudan Liberation Army (SLA) in April 2003.

I took out a map. "Where exactly is this happening?"

Dr. Sissi pointed to his region, in the central-westernmost part of Darfur. "This is where I am from. This area is devastated," he declared.

"Where else?" I asked.

"We have reports coming from the north and south of Darfur as well. It is happening all over."

"Do you have names, places, villages, numbers of people — any facts I can use?"

"You can talk to all of my people on the ground."

I soon established an intricate reporting network. I was talking to civilians, rebel fighters, family members, anyone I could get hold of. I talked to a doctor in Darfur who said that his hospital was overflowing with burn victims, gunshot victims, rape victims, people who had been left for dead.

We sent press releases to the local, national, international, and United Nations newswires. We sent press releases to all the local media. We began calling all of our contacts in the U.S. House, the Senate, the State Department, various embassies, and human rights organizations.

I hunted down the *New York Times,* the *Washington Post,* NBC, ABC, CNN, the *Herald* — their foreign desks, their correspondents in Africa, the list went on and on. I left messages, kept calling back, and gave them all the information I was receiving. I offered them all the contacts I had — the reporters could talk to people in Darfur themselves. I urged them to go to Chad and see the refugees, or go to Darfur, and told them I had contacts who would help them and take them around the region.

"Thank you so much for the information. We'll be in touch," I was told.

"We're unable to cover this at this time," they said.

"We'll have to look into this, and we'll get back to you," they responded.

"I'll connect you to our news desk. Just go ahead and leave a message there," they said nicely.

"We've got no one heading to that region at the moment," they apologized.

"We just did a story on Uganda," they told me.

"Well, if it's not already in the news, it must not be a big enough story," they said.

A friend at my university, Adam Shapiro, was also interested in the region and had begun reading the releases put out by human rights groups. I filled him in on what I knew. He did some of his own research, and a few days later he came back and said, "Aisha, I want to go."

Adam, a filmmaker, had done his first documentary in Baghdad the summer before. I told him it was a total mess inside Darfur: the borders closed, the fighting intense, and there was a media blackout.

He looked at me and nodded and matter-of-factly said, "Aisha, there's always a way in."

I knew that people had been crossing the border with Chad frequently since the conflict started. I smiled, excitement filling my voice. "You are absolutely right! I will help. I've been talking to people all over, in Chad and in Sudan. I've got contacts with rebels and people who will help you get in, places to stay. I'll help you any way I can."

"You wanna come?" he asked, ever so casually.

We smiled at each other, and it all made perfect sense: we were going to shoot a documentary in Darfur.

Aisha and Adam were joined by another friend, Jen Marlowe, who had been doing nonprofit work in Palestine and Israel. Adam, Aisha, and Jen made their way to eastern Chad with the help of UN Refugee Agency (UNHCR) puddle jumpers — small planes that can land on water — and in Chad they spent time talking to refugees in several camps. In a border town between Chad and Sudan they made contact with the SLA, the larger of the two rebel groups resisting the Sudanese government, hoping that the rebels would take them across the border into Darfur so they could see for themselves what the refugees in Chad had been describing. The next morning, a pickup truck emerged from the desert near the UNHCR compound where they were staying.

"Adam," Jen called to her colleague as two men in white turbans, djellabas, and Ray-Ban sunglasses climbed out of the truck. "I think our ride is here."

Fifteen minutes later, Adam, Aisha, and Jen were sitting in the back of the truck, being driven across the border into Darfur.

From Chapter 4: Destruction of Darfur

(The narrator is Jen Marlowe)

I was leaning against Adam, trying to warm my face in the sun. He tapped me and pointed. We were driving past a pile of charred stones. I sat up and looked around. We passed another group of burnt stones, built as a tight circular wall. There were more up ahead. It took me a moment to register that we were passing our first signs of life in Darfur, or what used to be life: round stone and mud-brick enclosures with charred conical thatched roofs, or no roofs at all; piles of rubble and stone; smashed or charred pots made of clay and mud.

"Furawiya." The young man sitting next to Aisha pointed, identifying the remains of the village.

The truck rumbled up to a makeshift checkpoint. Two young men with old guns stared for a long moment and then smiled, exchanging repetitive greetings of *"al-hamdulillah"* with our escorts. We were waved through. The truck stopped after a few more yards. We dismounted and silently took our equipment from the back of the truck. The rebels drove off with an unspoken agreement to come back to get us shortly.

We walked toward the nearest destroyed home to take a closer look. The sun was bright and the air was getting hot. It was quiet, eerie. A thin, tall man approached us. His head was wrapped tightly in a white turban, and his face was obscured by the covering. Only his eyes were revealed. They were intensely serious and somewhat jarring in a man so thin. His name was Musa.

Was he from Furawiya?

He was.

Would he mind taking us around and explaining what had happened to this ghost town that was once a village?

He agreed.

He slowly showed us around the village. The destruction was remarkably thorough and systematic. We passed piles of stones that used to be people's homes. Everything inside — clay pots, tea kettles — was charred or smashed. Sheets of twisted aluminum siding were lying on top of a heap of charred wood — former market stalls. Musa took us to the remains of one particular stall. It was his, he explained, and went on to describe how armed men on horseback had stormed the village and smashed everything.

Perhaps most disconcerting was the emptiness. Adam, Aisha, and I had been to other scenes of large-scale devastation. In all those places, people seemed to spring up out of the remnants the way weeds stubbornly grow out of cracks in the sidewalk. In Jenin, for example, days after the refugee camp had been flattened, Palestinians had created makeshift tents with poles and blankets on top of the rubble of what used to be their homes. New structures had been built inside, on top of, and around the destruction in Afghanistan. I had even seen a little boy flying a kite while perched atop a hill of rubble of what used to be the Kabul Hotel.

But here it was different. It was almost entirely depopulated. Besides Musa and the young men at the checkpoint, there were no people in the village. Even the birds had left. The only sound was the wind and the hard sand crunching beneath our feet.

Musa wove through the rubble and led us to the school. Desks were smashed and broken. The floor was ankle-deep in strewn paper. It was apparent that a school day had been brutally interrupted. There was still writing on the chalkboard.

"Who did this?"

"Janjaweed."

We exited the school and walked without speaking across a wadi. Musa silently pointed out a large crater. We peered over the edge. Remnants of a projectile were scattered inside.

"From Antonovs," he said quietly. "Government planes."

He led us to another missile, three feet long. It lay unexploded.

"Also from Antonov," he said.

Aisha took a photograph of the Russian lettering on the side of the ordnance. Russia was Sudan's largest arms supplier. Antonovs were Russian-made bombers. It wasn't only Russia, however, who was engaged in a lucrative business with Sudan. China was the largest investor in Sudan's oil industry. No wonder the UN had been so lacking in political resolve regarding Darfur. China and Russia hold two of the five permanent seats in the fifteen-seat UN Security Council. I wondered some more about my own government's response. The U.S. Congress had named the situation "genocide" several months before. But nothing had been done since.

Musa described the bombing campaigns to us. Enormous missiles were rolled out of low-flying government planes, striking populated areas with little or no accuracy or control. The villagers fled, Musa told us, and just kept going.

Musa showed us his own home, scorched to the ground.

"Where is your family? Where are the rest of the people?"

"In Kariare." Kariare, we learned, was the name Darfurians used for the refugee camp near Bahai, Chad, which the UN labeled Oure Cassoni. "No one is left now . . . They are all killed or had to run."

The SLA truck returned to get us. It was time to move on.

We rode for the rest of the morning over rocks, under trees, and on terrain that I don't think Toyota engineers had in mind when building their pickups. Jutting out of the rocks and sand were scattered lone trees. The driver seemed to enjoy guiding the truck under them, no matter how low-leaning or sharp their branches. In the early afternoon, the truck stopped.

"Shegeg Karo," the same young man told Aisha. "A market village." We climbed down, stretched our legs, and looked around. Shegeg Karo now seemed to be a makeshift SLA command center. There was a small cache of weapons and one young man with a Thuraya satellite phone who identified himself as the commander. Fadi jumped off the top of the cab eagerly and began to inspect the arsenal. Everything looked archaic. I compared the rusty weapons lying on the ground in front of me to the enormous unexploded missile we had just seen in Furawiya.

We were talking to the commander when we noticed a young man shyly hovering near us. He seemed to be waiting for a good moment to approach. Aisha smiled widely, giving him confidence. He stepped up and greeted us in English.

"Hello. Where are you from?"

He was of medium height and build, with deep brown skin, warm friendly eyes, a wispy mustache with a bit of peach fuzz on the sides, and two small vertical markings at the corners of his eyes. His name, he told us, was Dero. The name was familiar.

"Dero . . . Dero . . . Do you know the photographers Jehad and Ben who were just inside Darfur?" Aisha asked.

Dero's face lit up. "Yes, they are my good friends! I traveled with them for two weeks. I translated for them. I helped them in everything!"

"They told me about you. I wanted to contact you, but they said you didn't have a sat phone. They didn't even know the name of the village where we could find you," Aisha explained.

Dero shrugged. He didn't seem to find the coincidence as amazing as we did. "I am from here, from Shegeg Karo. It is easy to find me."

We told Dero about our project.

"Do you want me to come with you? I can translate, help in whatever you need."

"We would love to have you come with us, if you're able," Aisha answered for all of us.

"I am available. There is no work, so I have nothing to prevent me."

Dero led us down a small hill into the market and sat us down in a stall.

"Wait here for me. I'll be right back."

Dero returned minutes later with slightly chilled Pepsis. We had no idea how he had been able to procure them or keep them cool.

As we sipped, Dero told us a bit about himself. Having taken two English courses years ago in Libya, he was now translating for the handful of journalists and photographers trickling into the rebel-held area of northern Darfur. He haltingly mentioned that his brother had been killed, but changed the subject almost immediately.

"Come, you can meet some people." We followed Dero through the market and the wadi, collecting more than a few stares on the way. The sand was filled with dried goat and ibex droppings. Dero led us up a small hill to a conical thatched straw roof supported by thin wooden beams. Sitting inside was a wizened old man with a white beard and a wooden walking stick. From his hut we could see for miles around.

"The sheikh of Shegeg Karo," Dero told us. "He is very old. He knows everything about this area. You can ask him many questions."

The sheikh seemed pleased to see us and happy to talk. "My name is Ali," he said as he invited us to sit.

Aisha snapped a photograph of the stately old man, the last on her roll of film. She tried to muffle the sound of the automatic rewind as the sheikh launched into his history.

"The story of my home goes back a long time. Thirteen of my grandfathers were the leaders of this region. I am eighty-six years old. I know everything about the history. Whatever nation comes to my country, I remember. Whatever events happen in Sudan, I know about it."

The sheikh paused, his eyes gleaming as Dero tried to translate. It was obvious that we weren't getting each and every word. No matter, we thought. We would get the footage translated fully after we arrived home. The sheikh pointed to a mountain in the distance.

"My ancestor came to settle here when he saw this mountain, in the eleventh century. After that the Turks came. Hussein came. After Hussein came Sultan Ali-Dinar, in the time of the Mahdi."

The Mahdi was considered a national hero because he had defeated General Gordon, whom the British had sent in 1885 to conquer him. The Mahdi died shortly thereafter, however, and was unable to prevent the eventual colonization of the country.

"After that the English came. Under the British, there was no country called Sudan, but, *insha'allah*, we became Sudan. After the English left, we were still okay, but at Bashir's time they came and separated Arab people and black people. Bashir took the light-skinned people, and he threw us away." The sheikh tapped his walking stick on the ground for emphasis. "Omar never liked black-skinned people."

I wondered about his assessment that everything was fine from Sudan's 1956 independence until Bashir's time. Bashir's military coup was not until 1989; oppression and violence in both Darfur and southern Sudan began long before that. The Bashir government took the brutality to a new level, perhaps, but power had been in the hands of a few elite tribes from the north since 1956. Regimes changed frequently, but always among the same privileged groups.

The sheikh began to tell us about the attacks his people had endured at the hands of the government and the Janjaweed, giving details that were becoming all too familiar.

"The government came first, shooting and bombing. The people ran away to the mountains to hide. The Janjaweed came after to finish. There has been nobody to protect us but Allah."

He spoke with great affection about the camels, goats, cows, and sheep the villagers used to own. "We rely totally on the animals."

He then described how the animals were taken by the Janjaweed, houses looted and burned, and how, on top of everything else, nature also seemed to be conspiring against them.

"The rains were short this season . . . and now the place has become like the desert. We are starving. We are just waiting for people from the international community to come and bring food. Only they and Allah can help us. The organizations tried to send food to us, but the government forced them to turn back. Since the government stopped everything, the people have to eat burrs."

The sheikh pointed to the burrs on the ground, which had been sticking to our socks, pants, hiking boots.

"Now mothers are suffering from hunger and don't have milk to feed their children. In the past, we were not hungry." He picked up a burr and rolled it between his fingers thoughtfully. "In Darfur, we were raised on milk." Dero explained that this meant that in the past, life in Darfur had been bountiful and the people were well fed.

The sheikh's hands were marvelous. Pointing, fluttering, gesturing, they illustrated every sentence.

"When I was young, the life was good. We were in our places. Arab people don't have land; they live on their camels as nomads. Arabs have been against the black people for a long time. In the past they were afraid of us, but now the government is helping them, so they come to attack us. Before, this was impossible."

The sheikh was impatient and interrupted as Dero tried to accurately summarize his previous statement.

"The people who fled from here are now in Kariare camp in Chad.

But I am strong. If there is peace or not, we will stay here. If they come to bomb us again, we will die here. We will never leave this area. We will defend ourselves." His hands fluttered with long, delicate fingers to accent his point. "We will die here. *Insha'allah*."

Why was it so important for him to be here until he died? The sheikh referred again to the thirteen generations of his family that had been leaders of the area.

"They are all buried on top of the mountain." He waved into the distance with his walking stick. "My ancestors' graves are still there."

"Can we go and see them?" we asked.

"No problem. This young man will take you." He tapped Dero lightly with his walking stick. "He knows where it is."

"Will you come with us?" Adam asked, but the sheikh smiled and shook his head.

"I can't climb because I have bad knees. I've had this condition for a long time, but no medicine."

"Your walking stick," Adam said, pointing to it. "Does it have any special meaning?"

We wanted our documentary to show the culture and heritage of Darfur as a backdrop to the current tragedies. Perhaps people's personal items held cultural significance.

The old man laughed, deep and hearty. "My stick? The only special thing about it is, it helps me to walk!"

We thanked the sheikh and left him sitting in his hut, perched on a stool with his walking stick, presiding over a village that barely existed. Somehow he maintained a sense of dignity and purpose.

Dero brought us to an unscathed home on the outskirts of the village. A group of small children were standing outside the hut. They were very thin, covered in dust, and wearing rags with gaping holes. Several of them had yellowing hair. They stared at us in silence. We approached them, expecting them to be curious about us, wanting to play, as the children in Iridimi had. These children, however, retreated from us in fear. Only one little boy and his younger sister, bolder than the others, held their ground, staring at us. We knelt down and smiled. There was no return smile.

"*Salaam, habibi,*" Adam attempted to greet them in Arabic. The little girl started to cry, and her brother dragged her by the hand back to where the other children had regrouped, watching us from a safer distance.

I tried to understand the difference in reaction. While the kids in the refugee camp at least had access to humanitarian aid, these children still faced an extremely precarious existence. The children in Iridimi had also met, or at least caught glimpses of, aid workers from all over the world. We were probably the only foreigners the kids here had ever seen.

Dero took us inside the hut and introduced us to a woman named Hassaniya. She was wearing a blue shawl and cradled a three-year-old boy in her lap. The little boy was wearing only a dirty brown T-shirt. His head lolled about on his mother's lap. It was immediately evident that there was something wrong with him.

"What's the little boy's name?" Adam inquired.

"Tugud," Dero told us.

Flies were settling around. We were sweating. Tugud's six-year-old brother sat nearby, eyeing us silently, protectively.

"What is . . . what happened . . . what happened to the child?" There was no easy way for Adam to ask.

"His body is hot. It started like a fever sickness," his mother explained. "From the injury. When the missile was thrown, I was carrying him on my back. I was at the well watering my cows."

"Were you able to take him to a doctor?" Aisha asked.

"We didn't find any treatment for him. We couldn't get him to a hospital. The wound still bleeds. He has a problem with his neck. It cannot stay upright. It drops this way and that way."

Hassaniya lifted the boy to a sitting position and demonstrated to us the instability of the little one's neck.

"He cries a lot and he doesn't sleep at night."

The boy struggled to look around as flies circled his face, feasting on his eyes and his drool. He was unable to brush them away.

"How old is he now?" Adam asked.

"Four years old," his mother replied.

"And can he speak?"

"No, he doesn't talk. Also, he doesn't walk. He cannot sit. He used to walk, crawl, and could hold water and stayed in the shadows of the tree, but he cannot move now. The injury is down his neck, here."

Hassaniya propped Tugud higher on her lap and tried to gently lift the boy's head, to give us a better look at the deep puncture wound just under his chin. It had scarred horribly. Tugud began to cry.

"That's okay," Aisha said.

We didn't want Hassaniya to maneuver her son for our sake. We were concerned that she thought we could provide medical help.

"Was she hurt in the bombing?" Adam asked Dero to ask Hassaniya.

"No, I wasn't hit. We were carrying this baby, and my clothes were punctured, but, *insha'allah,* I wasn't injured."

Adam made clucking noises to see if the child would respond. He didn't.

"I want to tell Doctors Without Borders about this kid. Maybe they could send someone out here," Aisha said. "If any NGO might be willing to take the risk, it would be them."

"No help ever comes to this part," Dero answered simply.

When we exited the hut, the other children were sitting on a woven mat under the shade of a tree. They seemed a little less afraid of us. When Hassaniya invited us to sit on the mat with them, they didn't run away or burst into tears. They merely scooted to one side of the mat and continued to stare at us. Hassaniya brought us a tin bowl of flavored water. We were being treated as honored guests. Water was extremely scarce, and whatever means she had used to flavor the water must have been in short supply. Adam, Aisha, and I weren't sure what to do. We didn't want to drink the water, both because of its scarcity and because it was untreated, yet we didn't want to offend our host or waste the water. When Hassaniya went back into the hut, Aisha offered the bowl to the oldest child sitting on the mat opposite us, a girl of about eight. She took it shyly and passed it on to a younger child. Once all the kids had drunk, the smallest ones needing her help, she drank her share as well. The empty metal bowl was placed carefully in the center of the mat.

We returned to the SLA truck. Fadi was washing his feet with water from a jerry can. We asked if we could interview him. He nodded, neatly rewrapped his green turban around his head, and followed us to a shady area so that the blazing afternoon sun wouldn't make him look washed out on camera. The view behind him was spectacular — yellow rolling hills with patches of light green and clumps of bushes and trees.

"Why did you come to Darfur from N'Djamena?" Adam asked.

"To be in the movement. The Sudan Liberation Army. I've been a soldier for two years. I came here from N'Djamena because of injustice. I want human rights only. I want to liberate Sudan." Fadi muttered his words almost inaudibly. We hoped the microphone was picking up his voice.

"Liberation for whom?" Adam pressed.

"All people. Zaghawa, Fur, and many people . . ."

Fadi described, mumbling in incomplete sentences, some of the atrocities he had witnessed in the past two years.

We wanted to know whether teenage boys like him were forced to join the rebel movement. We wanted to know if children were being armed.

"I shot a gun once, during the training," Fadi told us.

"Have you fought the Janjaweed?" Aisha asked.

"No."

"The Sudanese government?"

Again he shook his head.

"How do the older guys from the SLA treat you?" Adam asked.

"They are good," Fadi answered.

"If you wanted to return to N'Djamena, could you?" Aisha asked.

"Yes."

I told Adam to ask Fadi if there had been a time when he was frightened.

"No," Fadi said emphatically. "I was never afraid." How many fifteen-year-old boys would want to ever admit feeling fear?

He told us more about his family, whom he had left in N'Djamena. "What matters most to me are my parents and my brother and sister. I'm the oldest."

We asked if he wanted to film a message for us to take back to his family when we returned to the capital.

He smiled broadly. "Yes! Tell them hello, how are they doing? How are they living their life? My father, he is sick, and I want him to recover from his illness."

"And to your brother and sister?" Adam asked.

Fadi thought for a moment and then delivered his message:

"Their future is to continue to study, to be educated, and to be a teacher or director, minister, and president too."

"Do you have anything to say to kids in America, the same age as you?"

"Yeah. Students, go to school. Study." Fadi flashed a big grin. "Greetings from Sudan Liberation Army."

He wrote down his parents' names and phone number in Aisha's notebook. Dero had disappeared while we interviewed Fadi, but without much warning, we were told it was time to continue driving. Everyone climbed into the truck again. Just as we were about to pull away, Dero ran up carrying a tarp with his possessions tied inside, and he jumped onto the truck. And then there were eighteen.

DAVID J. MORRIS

◼

The Big Suck: Notes from the Jarhead Underground

FROM *The Virginia Quarterly Review*

1

*There are places even in Fallujah where the streetsong drops away to noth-
ing, shaded alleys devoid of sound: you step inside them and for a moment
it seems like nothing outside could ever get to you. Keep your steps right and
you could let the patrol you are with get just far enough ahead to leave you
out of earshot and with nothing but your thoughts, and for a brief time you
could begin again to feel human, like something approaching whole. But
the war never leaves you. It is always here, stalking you like a shadow. The
war, it seems, has always been here and it colors and obscures everything,
even the country itself. In the quiet times, in the middle of long hot patrols,
you can't help wondering what this place was before it became the dark
muse of the American military. What chatter filled its cafés? How did they
name their winds? Did they love the desert as you do now? You close your
eyes but smell only the familiar Third World stench of burning trash and
hot diesel fumes mixed with Fallujan streetfunk, dudesweat, sheepshit.*

On the wall of the quarters I shared with a Marine lieutenant in
Ramadi there was a large metal wipeboard and every morning before
I went out into the city on patrol I would study it. The lieutenant had
inherited it from the previous occupant and covering its every square
inch was the collected wisdom of the Occupation, written in a frag-
mented, aphoristic style. The wipeboard was a marvel, a palimpsest
containing at once several generations of tactical conceits and proph-
ecies, a snapshot of the ever-evolving American mission in Iraq, a cat-

alogue of items to unlearn, notes from the lieutenant underground, a prayer to the muse of history.

Here are a few of my favorites:

YOU HAVE FIREPOWER. FIREPOWER ALONE WILL NOT WIN.

THE BEST SHOT IS THE SHOT YOU NEVER HAVE TO TAKE.

THE MARINE CORPS IS A GOVERNMENT BUREAUCRACY. YOU WILL BE JUDGED BY LAWYERS WHO HAVE NEVER SEEN A FIREFIGHT.

Floating above all these admonitions in scrupulously drawn letters and seeming to preside over everything else scrawled on the board, someone had written simply: THINK.

It was mid-2006 now and a lot of the truisms on the board either were outdated or had been reversed by events. Lessons had been learned, some too late. But to spend time in Iraq is to acquire a visceral understanding of the flexibility of information and the power of place over knowledge. What is true in Ramadi is not necessarily true in Iskandariyah. What is true in Baghdad is almost never true in Basra. In Iraq, information is tribal, like the people who live there. It keeps its own company. Things seem absolutely true only in Washington. The closer you get to the killing, the harder it is to know anything for sure. Even the journalists I talked to spoke of the war as beginning to dissolve as a story. It had all gotten so weird, so disparate, that none of the familiar narratives felt convincing anymore. Such was the mistrust of the official line, so heavy was the spin, that with any new piece of information you learned to do a kind of mental arithmetic whereby you divided the information given by the speaker's rank, multiplied by his or her time in-country, and subtracted based on the number of miles the speaker was distant from the fighting.

The most useful information invariably came in the form of the anecdote, the casual aside that over time became the platoon mantra, the anonymous epigraph written on the latrine wall (TUPAC IS IN RAMADI), the accidental remark that encapsulated an entire operation, the eavesdropped epithet that is recalled months later and thousands of miles away and only in dreams. By the time I arrived, Iraq had entered the realm of found art.

I told the lieutenant that he ought to send the wipeboard to the Marine Corps Historical Center after his tour was over. There was a lot of great stuff on that board, I told him. He just shrugged and stomped off to the company operations center, a couple of doors down. Later, I thought about all the aphorisms written on the board. In theory, each lesson represented a life. In order to know that driving on dirt roads in Ramadi was dangerous, you had to have an IED (improvised explosive device) go off in your face. Before you started draping camouflage netting over the gunner's turret atop a Humvee, you had to lose a gunner to a sniper. In order to learn the lesson, you had to lose somebody.

To hear the Marines describe it, Ramadi is the Chernobyl of the insurgency, a place where the basic proteins of guerrilla warfare have been irradiated by technology and radical Islam, producing seemingly endless cells of wide-eyed gunslingers, bomb gurus, and aspiring martyrs. Globalization wrought with guns and God. A place devoid of mercy, a place where any talk of winning hearts and minds would be met with a laugh, both sides seeming to have decided, *This is where the killing will never stop, so give it your best shot.*

The state of the war in Iraq has been grim for a long time, but the news coming out of Ramadi has always been darker and weirder than just about anywhere else. Even now, when I try to recall what the city looks like, what comes to me is nothing more than a pocked stretch of boulevard surrounded on both sides by heaps of rubbled concrete, iron palings, trash. Swirls of dust playing over the blacktop. The smell of cordite. Everything still but a grizzled dog patrolling the ruins. It can be like this — high noon, not a soul around, no threat imminent — but you can feel the sheer sinister energy of the joint. As if even the streets want you dead. Driving through downtown Ramadi for the first time gave me an unshakable vision of mystery and death. Just staring at the rubble set my heart pounding with the knowledge of the lives lost per yard.

This is not what the Marine Corps expected from Ramadi. After the quixotic invasion in 2003, the Marines had returned to Iraq the following spring with high hopes, full of the infectious zeal for the field that has always made them so alluring to outsiders. They were America's most experienced antiguerrilla force, and the general consensus among the class of observers and analysts who report on the U.S. military was that the Marines would bring some much-needed expertise to the increasingly restive nation. Numerous experts named the Corps' 1940 *Small Wars Manual* as the definitive document on counterinsurgency and talked about the Corps in such gauzy, superlative terms that it seemed a fait accompli. As the officers liked to remind the press, not a single marine had been killed by hostile action after Baghdad fell. Their confidence was so high that prior to the deployment a few Marine generals began making disparaging comments about the U.S. Army's postinvasion handling of the situation in Iraq. Army troops were too heavy-handed, they said, too enamored of their tanks and armored vehicles, too "kinetic," too brusque with the locals. It was like crushing a walnut with a sledgehammer. It was no wonder that the Iraqis had responded by planting homemade bombs in the streets, they said. You had to listen to the locals. You had to spend time with regional leaders. You had to rely on what Marine leaders referred to as "the velvet glove" approach.

As with everything in Iraq and Al Anbar, the Marines' plan changed on March 31, 2004. All that the war was to become, all the searing images, all the familiar narratives of quagmire were first written then. On that day, four American contractors were ambushed in Fallujah and their mutilated bodies hung from a pedestrian bridge that spanned the Euphrates. Soon after, the word came down from on high (some sources indicate the call emanated from the White House itself) that the locals were to be punished for this depredation, and four Marine battalions were ordered to seize the city. The Marines were closing the noose when the media coverage of the offensive got to be so bad that the generals in Baghdad called the whole thing off and ordered the Marines to begin withdrawing.

Control of Fallujah was eventually turned over to a local Iraqi militia known as the Fallujah Brigade. This move seemed to fit hand-in-glove with the more nuanced Marine approach, the idea being to let the locals do their own policing. However, almost immediately after the Fallujah Brigade stood up, reports began to emerge that the force was little more than a conglomeration of the very gunmen and criminals that the Marines had been trying to kill in the first place. This awkward state of affairs continued throughout the summer of 2004.

And while the city was increasingly viewed by Marine officers as the hotbed of the insurgency in western Iraq, the word from Washington was clear: keep Iraq out of the headlines until after the presidential election. Privately, many Marine officers complained bitterly about the situation and argued that Washington had robbed them of a victory.

After the election, a second, this-time-we-mean-it offensive was authorized. The November battle of Fallujah, which senior Marine commanders repeatedly portrayed as a long-awaited coup de grâce to the insurgency, was the most intense American engagement since the Vietnam battle of Hue City and quickly earned a place in the pantheon of Marine Corps battles, alongside Guadalcanal, Iwo Jima, and the Chosin Reservoir — but while the Marines certainly killed a lot of insurgents and restored order to the city, thus far the battle has not proven to be the decisive engagement that commanders had hoped for. Worse still, according to some Iraqis I spoke to, the locals never looked at the Marine Corps in the same way after that. The entire sequence of events had had the ultimate effect of alienating and radicalizing large portions of the local population.

In April 2004, while the world's attention was focused on the debacle in Fallujah, an entire squad from Second Battalion, Fourth Marines was ambushed and wiped out by a cell of one hundred local insurgents. Up to this point, the Marines had never lost a firefight in Iraq, and no one had any immediate explanations for it. People familiar with the attack speak of how it seemed to materialize out of nowhere, and everybody who heard the story got in sudden, intimate touch with the terms of their own mortality. This attack, as utterly unexpected as it was, seemed to fit into a larger picture of an insurgency growing steadily in expertise. A threshold had been passed. The insurgency, which before had appeared a decidedly amateur affair, seemed to be finding its legs, tapping into preexisting bodies of tactical knowledge, watching the Americans, learning their habits.

Two months later a four-man Marine sniper team was discovered and executed on a rooftop near downtown Ramadi. Video footage of the executions was running on several local Arab television networks before the Marines could even mount a patrol to investigate. The event sent shock waves through the ranks. In the Marine Corps, snipers are venerated figures, the embodiment of the exalted marksman, and the idea that a sniper team could have been so crudely dispatched seemed an affront to the very cosmology of the Marine Corps, which, despite all the advancements of modern technology, has held fast to the belief that the battlefield's final arbiter is the well-trained man with a rifle. And while this engagement was far from decisive, it was definitive in its own way and helped to create the impression of an elite corps — one that had prided itself on its handling of insurgencies past — that was struggling to get its footing in a troubled province. The situation was so unsettling that Marine commanders eventually ordered the nominally civilian Naval Criminal Investigative Service (NCIS) to launch a formal inquiry into the matter. The logic seemed to be that Marine snipers don't get killed that way. Local fighters with a week's training in the desert didn't just roll up on a sniper hide and whack everyone. It had to be an inside job.

Among many Marines operating in the Ramadi area there is an intense desire for a Fallujah-style offensive to clear the decks. The arguments here are chilling in their resemblance to paradigms deployed during Vietnam and their seeming faith in the redemptive power of violence. As one gunnery sergeant in Habbaniyah told me, "Fuck, just *once* I would like to go toe to toe with these motherfuckers. Leave the jets and the .50 cals behind and have a small-arms fight. Just M-16s and AKs, man to man." Another marine, a second lieutenant whom I knew well and who was otherwise an unusually calm and circumspect officer, explained, "An IED goes off and kills one of your guys and you see one dude standing by the side of the road talking on a cell phone — no one else is around and you can't even arrest him. I wish we could do what we did in Fallujah in 2004. It's so much easier when you can just shoot anybody."

By the time I arrived in Ramadi, it had already gained a reputation as a place that was bankable for a good, bloody story for journalists looking for a bit of the "bang-bang." Many reporters were expecting, perhaps even hoping for, a Fallujah-style assault on the town, but the American high command, not wanting to repeat the mistakes of 2004 and not wanting to be seen as usurping the power of the fledgling Iraqi government, never allowed a full-scale offensive in Ramadi. Accordingly, the insurgency in the city has continued to grow in both scale and sophistication, such that Ramadi has come to be viewed as a sort of graduate school of the insurgency.

Marines and soldiers stationed in the city spoke of the place with a sort of detached awe because of the baroque madness that had taken root there. The month before my visit, marines had killed a group of insurgents who were using water-cooled saws to slice open an entire city block to plant an enormous roadside bomb. Local fighters had staged sham funeral processions that marines were obligated to observe. When the lines of mourners drew near Marine positions, they would all reach into the coffin and pull out RPGs (rocket-propelled grenades) and AK-47s. Insurgents in Ramadi had been known to fly kites to help adjust their mortar fire and to release pigeons to signal the approach of U.S. troops. One marine, with a heavy-weapons company whose job it was to conduct raids around the city, told me that the guys in his unit had become amateur ornithologists, learning to spot with binoculars any birds that weren't indigenous to Ramadi.

The tactical permutations were endless, and in some cosmic convergence of reality crashing head-on with the local grunt imagination, the Marine rumor mill began to seem like a legitimate source of intelligence: the *mujahideen* were all on speed; the *muj* were using remote-controlled cars as suicide vehicles; the *muj* had stolen an American tank and were waiting for just the right moment to use it; one of the *muj* snipers is a turncoat U.S. marine; the *muj* had trained local dogs to act as scouts. (Most of the marines I knew bit on this last one and were inclined to shoot a dog as soon as look at one, and for some it was just one more drop in the karma bucket: the locals hate you; Allah hates you; hell, even the fucking *dogs* want you dead.) The official chain of command seemed at times to struggle to keep pace with the street mojo.

Among the marines, who had been stationed in Ramadi longer than any Army unit and saw themselves as the keepers of the city, the months of sustained combat began to have a corrosive effect on their basic humanity. There were daily situations on the streets of Ramadi that would have overwhelmed anything covered in a Law of War seminar at the Army War College. The way the marines saw it, the standard-issue moral equipment simply wasn't working, and they fashioned their own with what they found in the streets. As one Marine master sergeant put it, "Over here, you have to change your definition of what an innocent bystander is."

Yet it was immediately clear to anyone who spent time with marines in Ramadi that they relished their special status as the caretakers of the war's premier hell, the Big Suck, the Deep End, ground zero, the heartland of the insurgency, where the World's Worst come to die at the hands of the World's Best. Month after month, it never let up, and they absorbed the war's worst casualties with a kind of high stoicism that was both inspiring and chilling. In some companies a refracted sense of the value of human life took hold, an unspoken understanding that casualties weren't something to get too worked up about. Many echoed the old line from Stanley Kubrick's *Full Metal Jacket:* "Marines die. That's what we're here for." The important thing, really, was to give as much as you got.

Some Army officers I spoke with were appalled at the Marine mentality. One such officer remarked, "With an attitude like that, no wonder they take so many casualties." When the story of the alleged atrocities at Haditha broke, some soldiers were more than willing to believe that the Marines had murdered those civilians and possibly more. One Army armor officer who had served with the Marines before the war chalked all this up to the "Tarawa mentality," in reference to the World War II battle where 990 marines died seizing a Pacific atoll of questionable strategic value. At one point during an Army–Marine coordination meeting, an Army officer who had just come down from the Tal Afar region complained about the danger of driving a Marine-controlled route because of the number of roadside bombs. His complaint was immediately dismissed. "Unless there are people melting inside of Humvees," he was told, "then it's not a real problem."

Welcome to Ramadi.

When I first checked in at Hurricane Point, the major Marine base near the city, I met Captain Max Barela, a company commander who had a reputation within the battalion for being somewhat of a maverick, having developed his own unique style of dealing with insurgents in his sector (one reporter had credited him with inventing "the anti-Fallujah strategy," one of courting the local sheikhs and instructing his marines to strictly limit their fire into the city). He was a cagey guy, clearly skeptical of the press — or, for that matter, any outsider — and he had a talent (as the battalion executive officer put it) for "fucking with reporters." When I first met him, he was telling the battalion commander about how one of his lieutenants had pulled a photographer from the *Chicago Tribune* out of the field, confiscated his camera, and told him in no uncertain terms that he was not to photograph wounded marines. It was a tense scene: the photographer was from Great Britain but should have known better; he was clearly shaken and asked sheepishly if he was going to be sent back to Baghdad. Barela was visibly proud of his lieutenant's handling of the situation.

In a way, I couldn't help but identify with Barela. He was clearly playing a different game than most of the officers I'd met and had an elemental understanding of what was at stake for the locals, which escaped most marines. He had an enigmatic air about him, a way of testing you before he allowed you to get close, before he really started talking to you. If he thought you were anything less than 100 percent serious about learning Ramadi, or if you flinched in the face of confrontation, he would completely ignore you. He knew that there was something extraordinary going on in his sector, and he wasn't giving out tickets to just anyone. When I introduced myself and inquired about embedding with his company, he looked me up and down and, in a pronouncement that later seemed to me to be a sort of litmus test, a rite of passage to see if I had the balls to roll with him and his boys, said, "If you don't do exactly what I tell you, you'll be fucking dead in a week."

Before I could formulate a response, he stepped out of the CO's office and, with some marines in trace, got into a Humvee and drove back to his company patrol base in the city.

2

Maybe it's all the hip-hop the grunts listen to, all that pent-up urban rage echoing in your brain as you roll down the streets, but look around, it's Jay-Z, dead-on: swaggering, thuggish rhythms that seem to embrace these streets, defying all religion and geography. At times like this, you can almost feel the hate seeping through the bulletproof glass, the antipathy pressing in through osmosis. You might find a moment of grace, turn a corner, blink, catch sight of the cutest little girl; she's out watching her brothers play soccer in the rubble, twirling in the kind of sundress you could have sworn didn't exist in the Arab world. But blink again and you can feel the streets rising up to kill you, the battle that gripped the city for weeks, the bang, the flash, the blur, sweat pouring down your back as you squeeze yourself into the space beneath a window, praying to join with the concrete.

In western Ramadi, just south of the highway that bisects the town, there's an observation post, manned by marines from Captain Barela's company, called OP VA, because the main building comprising the observation post had been the local veterans administration office before the war. The post was larger than most Marine OPs and much better built, having been reinforced with thousands of sandbags and ringed by a series of eight-foot-high dirt-filled barriers. It sat overlooking Highway 10, the artery that connected the town to Damascus in the west and to Baghdad in the east, and was manned by forty marines.

Sometime in the early morning of April 17, 2006, local Al Qaeda–affiliated insurgents attacked it in a style that had never been seen before in Iraq but that clearly harked back to the 1983 Hezbollah attack on the Marine barracks in Beirut — an assault that had precipitated the U.S. withdrawal from Lebanon and was later cited by Osama bin Laden as one of the primary examples of American impotence. This assault began when a yellow dump truck filled with an estimated one thousand pounds of plastic explosives crashed into the earthen barrier surrounding the Marine position and detonated. Dozens of explosive-laden suicide vehicles had been staged along the highway, waiting for the inevitable American reaction forces that would be dispatched to reinforce the post. The force of the blast at OP VA was so great that everyone who heard the explosion assumed that all the men who were there had been killed instantly. I was told by several marines who were in western Ramadi at the time, "There was no way anyone could have survived that blast." They inevitably paused for dramatic effect. "No *fucking* way."

In quick order, teams of insurgents with RPGs and machine guns moved in on the American post, engulfing the building in a hail of fire. For a period of time that no one can pinpoint exactly — time becomes a staggeringly malleable commodity in combat — there was no return fire, and the absence of any radio traffic from the marines there led many to conclude that the position had been lost. What no one in authority knew at the time was that almost every man at OP VA had been knocked unconscious by the raw concussive force of the dump truck explosion. Survivors spoke later of waking up to a desolate, last-man-on-earth feeling that gripped them as they looked around and saw dozens of their comrades lying immobile and presumably dead. Many veterans of the battle whom I spoke with claim to have no memory of the blast whatever and simply recall waking up to the gut-clenching *whoosh!* sound of RPGs as they hit the sides of the building. Visibility inside the OP was down to two feet. Most of the men made their way around by touch.

One by one, the marines at OP VA stirred from their involuntary slumbers and took up positions around the building. The outgoing fire, which had at first been a goose egg, then a trickle, within an hour had turned into a hailstorm, and it wasn't long before the marines had suppressed the various teams of insurgents who had besieged the compound.

As the battle turned, Marine noncoms began taking a head count, trying to get a sense of the casualties they were looking at, and were flabbergasted to discover that no one had been killed or seriously wounded. It was beyond miraculous. The barrier system, created with an ample standoff range, had saved them. Like most firefights in Iraq, the battle for OP VA ended with an ever-increasing volume of fire coming from the American position, followed by the insurgents' fading back to their urban hideouts. In terms of ground held, nothing had changed in Ramadi.

Still, no one who was there and who repeated the story of the attack had outlived the mystery of his own survival or found a way to express his dark fascination, bordering on nostalgia, with it. Each acknowledged the sheer horror of it and the fact that, had the attack enjoyed even slightly better luck or a few more elements in its favor, it would have proven disastrous for the marines. At times in the retelling, the story seemed to possess these men, and they struggled with the impossibility of conveying the intensity of the experience to others who had not been there. It was, as with so many things in Iraq, lost to the

vapors and the shadows beyond human knowledge, and yet was ines-
capably central to the experience itself.

Sometime after my first encounter with Captain Barela, I met a second lieutenant in his company, who was from Alabama. He was so
young and good-looking and so new to the Corps that most of the
guys in the company, including Barela, looked right past him. It was
an exquisite form of cruelty to be so subtly snubbed day after day, but
he didn't seem to mind, or maybe he just didn't notice. I could see
how it happened. He was soft-spoken, had the eyelashes of a dreamer,
and I think the other marines took his gentle good looks as a sign of
weakness.

One night before we headed out on a patrol, he asked if I'd seen the
big crater out at the edge of the compound. I hadn't. Well, when we
get out there, remind me and I'll show you, he said. Later, we made
our way out of the massive, vaguely Egyptianate building and stood in
the open yard of the perimeter as he toed the dirt with his boot. I
could tell he was getting ready to lay something on me and that he
was trying to summon the drama he would need to get it right. Still,
true to what I took to be his gentle nature, he spoke simply and without the bluster that I'd seen in other marines. He told me about April
17 and how all he could remember was waking up behind a machine
gun, pouring fire into the highway to the north, RPGs rushing by his
head.

"This is all that's left," he said, looking into the dusty, ten-foot-deep
crater. Yet this crater, this meager defile, was far from the only remaining evidence of the battle. We walked back inside and he down-
loaded a video celebrating the April 17 attack, produced by an Al
Qaeda–affiliated cell and burned to CDs that sold by the thousands in
Baghdad. As the video streamed, I had the vague realization that I
was watching the birth of a new form of ordnance, a weaponized
movie, made by a new kind of soldier, the guerrilla auteur.

It began with an ornate title sequence, the name of the dump truck
driver slung across the top of the frame in a looping, golden scrawl.
This was clearly a film with religious aspirations, everything done up
in gaudy tones and accompanied by overdriven Arabic orchestral music. Then an earnest-looking young man read his will beneath a tree,

birds singing in the background. Then a montage: the young man behind the wheel of a truck, the scene set to triumphant Arabic music; the young man singing along, smiling brightly; the young man addressing and swearing his allegiance to someone off camera; the young man hugging his comrades, on his face a look of rapture. We were looking at a martyr in the making.

Then the image quality changed, everything becoming jostled, and we were back in the world of amateur Internet video. There was the blocky veterans administration building, the long brown row of earthen barriers that surrounded it. The yellow dump truck appeared in the lower left corner of the screen and moved toward the center of the frame. The flash was for a moment as bright as the sun, and it washed out the entire frame. The light dropped and there was the heavy spray of dirt and marl as the explosion rebounded off the barrier wall, the terrain suddenly airborne. Then, through the dust and smoke, the hammering of many guns, the whistle of the air being split, the echo and pop of gunfire as rounds arced away and hit and skipped off the walls of the building, the architecture enshrouded in dust as round after round made impact with the concrete.

At first, no gunfire emerged from the veterans administration building. Then, after several minutes of punishment, as the concrete soaked up gales of lead, the building seemed to awaken and muzzle flashes could be seen winking on the roof. Rounds began to zip and zing by the camera, and then we became aware of the presence of the cameraman, who was now mobile, the picture suddenly blurred by movement, and the narrative devolved into a fog of brown shapes and occasional snatches of Arabic dialogue. With that the file ended.

I looked around awkwardly at the now deserted company operations center, where we had been sitting for the past hour, not realizing the gravity of what had just happened. Only later did I begin to understand. In some small way, the lieutenant had been trying to guarantee himself a piece of remembrance, to ensure that if he was killed by a sniper shot to the cranium, or by a rigged 105 round buried in some roadside trash, or by a taxi packed with Soviet-era plastic explosives and driven into a convoy, that this video might not be the only version of history, that somebody might have recorded the crucial details of his last days.

The lieutenant showed me a picture of his wife. She was blond and beautiful in a very American kind of way, and her face carried on it the promise of the country, the allure of shelter, the hope of being whole again. The tenderness of women is conspicuously absent from the grunt universe, and unless you got off on enemy contact, it was all death and no sex over there. The smiling visage of the lieutenant's wife was irreconcilable with those pixilated images of death. I had to force myself to remember that there are lovers and killers in all of us.

It was then that the lieutenant told me with some mirth how the marines had searched extensively for the remains of the driver, as they always did after these sorts of attacks. So intense was the blast that nobody could find a single scrap of flesh. The young man, so exhilarated in the video about his impending martyrdom, had, it seemed for a while, passed straight into the ether. Then, some days later, a marine loping around on the far side of the compound looked down, and there it was: the driver's disembodied and blackened penis. The lieutenant laughed about how the "*muj* cock" had probably never been used (most rural Iraqi men are virgins until marriage), and now it just lay there curled up on the ground, dozing like a little seahorse.

In December 2005, after the Marines retook Fallujah, they established a ring of heavily fortified observation posts looking into the city. The men would sit in these for days, scouring the streets with binoculars, memorizing every stretch and corner of streetscape. For weeks on end, there was nothing but the blank routine of radio checks and the lieutenant making his rounds.

None of the observation posts had electricity or air conditioning or any form of diversion, and the heat and monotony bore down on the men. It didn't take long for the worst kind of boredom to set in, a deep-seated, aggressive ennui that scorched everything, the kind that can make a man's deepest convictions seem like pure folly, his family a fading photograph. The kind of boredom that could make a man do things and want things that were clearly irrational. A reservist from Brooklyn told me that marines there started *hoping* that they would get attacked just to break up the monotony. *Please, Lord, anything, just make the time go faster. And not just any old pussy potshot from a local shopkeeper who's been paid by the* muj.

The marines knew they could handle anything the *muj* could throw at them. The posts they manned had been constructed with memories of nightmare attacks built into the placement and composition of every sandbag. The post itself, a small ziggurat made out of sandbags and lumber, was mazed in concrete barriers that made a car bomb an exercise in futility. The post was a feat of military engineering designed to preserve the lives of the guys who manned it.

The attack never came.

Eventually, however, and for reasons that no one can seem to recall, one marine snapped. A couple of the guys started arguing about something, and out of nowhere one of them just leaned over, picked up his M-16, and jammed it into his buddy's chest. Now came a moment of unparalleled intimacy. *Is he gonna do it? Does he have the balls? Naw, I don't think so. He ain't got the balls.*

He was right.

The marine dropped his weapon dejectedly, saying nothing, while the other guys looked on in amazement. He stripped off all his gear, took off his flak vest, his helmet, and his CamelBak, and started walking down from the observation post and stomped away from the city and into the desert. His buddies stood there dumbfounded. What the fuck were they supposed to do? They had an observation post to man. It was their company's primary mission. They figured he would eventually walk his anger off and come to his senses. They would all be laughing about this over an MRE in an hour.

But that moment never came. After about an hour or so, the marines in the post decided that they had to let higher headquarters know what was up. This was some major league shit. When the battalion commander found out, he ordered every available body from the thousand-man battalion out to search for him. He requested a company of tanks from a nearby base and some air cover for his marines on the ground. There was a small air-ground task force out looking for this one wayward marine, and the colonel knew it was only a matter of time before the high command would start wondering what the fuck was going on north of Fallujah. The precedents for this sort of thing were bad: in 2005, a Lebanese-American marine had gone

AWOL and eventually turned up at a relative's house in Beirut. The whole affair had played out in the press, which, of course, amounted to incredible embarrassment for the Corps.

In the end, the errant marine was found, fetal and shivering in a ditch. No one I spoke to had any idea what had happened to him after that.

3

Think about the town and the battle that possessed it for a time. The thousands of bullets that wandered the streets day and night, looking for a home in a human body. Stick your finger into one of a million bullet holes made by a Spectre gunship, crane your head down an alley to see a half-dozen houses Swiss-cheesed by gunfire. Blast holes exactly large enough to fit a squad through. Freeze this image. Behold it, strain for its patterns, learn its lessons, imagine the ironstorm that came, then passed on, looking for other cities to ruin. If these streets cannot tell you what war is, then nothing can.

One day I went out on an Iraqi Army patrol in a lush, jungly area across the Euphrates from Fallujah — twenty nervous Iraqi troops, some wearing masks so that the locals couldn't identify them, and three Americans, all walking in a line through dry rice paddies, waiting for somebody to open up on us. The major in charge of the U.S. advisory team I was living with had insisted that I carry a rifle. It was just too hot around here, he'd said. I'd feigned my grudging assent, but inside I felt a stab of elation. I'd done a tour in the Marine Corps in the nineties, but I didn't lose my combat cherry. So I couldn't help it: in defiance of my better judgment and everything that I knew about the laws of war and the rights of journalists in wartime, the gun felt good in my hands. Cold, hard, precisely made, and with an impressive array of angular attachments.

Practically speaking, the team was ridiculously undermanned, and if I intended to go out on this sort of patrol, I needed to be able to protect myself. Still, I could feel the folkloric prickle at the base of my neck; I was no longer a journalist there to observe the scene. I had crossed over, embraced the Hemingway disease. There was no turning back, no use denying it: I had stepped past that imperceptible but morally binding threshold and emerged a darker, fatally enabled man. I was a combatant, a shooter, and I wondered how I would explain this to myself if I ended up having to shoot somebody.

Some of the grunts thought it was pretty Tarzan of me. To them I was just a different kind of combat person. A guy approximately as mental and locked in as they were. The way I saw it, we all had our reasons for being over there, some personal, some financial, some physiochemical, some political, but if you were over there and you weren't an Iraqi, then you were a volunteer. Call it a morbid curiosity or a disturbing disregard for human life, if you like, but all of us were, at some point in time and on some level and in varying degrees, possessed by The Question: What is killing like?

During my first few patrols, I'd started to have visions of myself captured in the field of a sniper's scope, imagining the final casual gestures of my life. I saw myself scratching my cheek and tilting my helmet back to wipe my brow, then the final moment, the strength passing out of my legs as I crumpled to the earth, my face unaltered except for the perfect hole over my left eye. The fact that I had worked at the Marines' scout sniper school at Camp Pendleton during my last year in the Corps was the icing on the cake. Mine was to be a supremely ironic death. It was the worst possible line of thinking to have while on a patrol. I would find certain body parts growing hypersensitive, then tingling, and I'd think: That's where the round will hit, I know it.

We made our way through a string of farms bounded by ancient palm trees. I weaved through paddies, trying to put my feet down in the most improbable places in order to make myself a harder target for the snipers. Booby traps were the real problem in this sector, but somehow the idea of a sniper giving it to me seemed more offensive than stepping on a booby trap. To my way of thinking, a booby trap seemed somewhat inevitable, pointless to worry about, but I hated the idea of some two-bit triggerman tracking me, observing me through an old Soviet scope before picking me off. I think it's the voyeurism of sniping that bothers me most, the idea of being watched, appraised, judged, and then dispatched. It seems to me the most intimate way to die save strangling, and unless the shot is flawless, it includes a moment of regret — worse still, recognition, a final frozen moment bonding the shooter and the shot.

*

Common wisdom holds that 140,000 generally churchgoing Americans in Iraq are locked in mortal combat with some of the world's most serious monotheists. To me, a new, less orthodox faith seems to have arisen, something far more personal and circumstantial. You could see it every time you watched a grunt throw away a box of Charms candies that came in the field rations (bad luck) or toss rounds that had been dropped (no matter how much you cleaned them, bullets that had been dropped always jammed). Like so many others, I had been inclined to believe in the bromide "There are no atheists in foxholes," but based on my admittedly less than systematic observations, there were at least as many blessed lance corporals, lucky ladybugs, stuffed giraffes, coins, and saved M-16 rounds as there were rosary beads. The marines I lived with seemed to have moved on from the Twenty-third Psalm and were now deep into *One Hundred Years of Solitude*.

One afternoon I was watching TV at an Iraqi house that some Marine advisers had commandeered. It was a lazy afternoon, not much going on in-sector. We were all sitting around watching *The Breakfast Club* on a wide-screen. On the floor in front of us a lieutenant was cleaning a .50-caliber machine gun with what looked like Victorian surgical instruments. As Molly Ringwald declaimed her particular strain of late-eighties suburban anomie, the lieutenant's hands flashed over the weapon in practiced, weirdly maternal gestures. A microwave oven buzzed in the background. The echoes of domesticity were unignorable: we were like a deranged, unexplainably well-armed family. An artillery forward observer who was new to the team said, "Man, we haven't gotten IED'd in a while." The team's executive officer, a high-strung captain who'd been a logistics officer back in the States, stomped into the living room and yelled, "God *damn* it, dude, I *know* you didn't just say that." He craned over melodramatically to some plywood shelves near the corporal's head and knocked on one of them. Guys were always doing this sort of thing. Whenever somebody started talking about how much time they had left or the fact that recently they'd had a run of good luck, eyes began to search frantically for a horizontal surface to knock on.

A couple of weeks later I read in the *New York Times* that one of the team's Humvees had struck an enormous IED, killing two marines.

After I returned to the States, I received an e-mail from the team leader saying that the *Times* report had been in error, but this welcome correction failed to fully erase the causal chain that had haunted my mind before that. A corporal had given voice to an idle observation about not having been IED'd in a while and some of his comrades had been killed. And, even now, this is the memory trace, the psychological residue that remains: in Iraq, thinking the wrong thoughts can kill you.

The trick was to focus your mind, to yoke your paranoia to your technical knowledge. One master sergeant I met in Al Qa'im told me that sometimes he could sense *muj* attacks before they came. I was skeptical until the day I saw him do it. We were in a convoy of six Humvees doing a standard security patrol when he picked up a radio handset and said, "We're gonna get hit today, I can feel it." When a small plume of dust arched in the sky ahead of us — the shock wave from the IED hitting us a few seconds later — he just shook his head. He didn't consider himself prescient or anything; the skill was something he'd developed over time in the field, the ability to interpolate among thousands of seemingly arbitrary microevents and anticipate the narrative, to see the dance in the data. Scientists who study this sort of phenomenon refer to it as apophenia — a handy piece of nomenclature, to be sure, but to my haunted mind the master sergeant was nothing less than a wizard, and I tried to stay as close to him as I could.

During halts on patrol, I talked with the team's medic. He was a healer, a professional reliever of pain, and perhaps because empathy was central to the job description, he seemed to let himself feel a little more than most of the men. He'd been in Fallujah during the Big Push in 2004, and he told me that he'd kept a casualty log during that time, recording the particulars of all the wounds he'd treated. A Fallujan book of the near-dead. He had clearly tried to get some standoff distance from it, but I could tell he cared deeply about the men he treated, probably more deeply than he knew. There were doctors in Iraq who had seen more gore than this guy, but they almost never knew the patients they treated. This young medical corpsman, twenty-two with three years in the service, enjoyed no such luxury.

He'd lived and trained with all of his patients for months, in some cases years.

"When you're stabilizing a patient, there's no time to think, you're just reacting. You don't think to remember anything. I started writing it all down so that I would force myself to remember." As he talked, visions of the log scrolled through my head: gunshot wound to the pelvis, laceration of the neck, shrapnel to the face (after fights like Fallujah, the grunts would often return with dozens of small shrapnel-caused welts to the face, so that they looked as if they had chickenpox), blowout wound of the gluteus, traumatic amputation of the forearm. It seemed like a particularly deranged form of accounting, but I understood the motive. In Iraq you hear stories so brand new, so off-the-charts weird and confounding and heart-rending, so *unbelievable,* that all you can do is stand there and say, "Wow." I always made a point of taking notes, looking engaged, even when the story had drifted off into a cul-de-sac or the teller was waiting for the force of the memory to hit him again. I wanted them to know that someone was listening, that somebody was there to write it down, to ensure that it was remembered, if imperfectly. For this medic, his logbook filled the same need — a catalogue of woe, a portable place to store all the pain he had seen. He had become a sort of self-designated re-memberer.

He kept talking, and I started to worry that we were going to be left behind by the rest of the patrol, but he needed me to hear his story. "It was the damnedest thing," he said. "In three tours over here, I've only had two guys die on me, but both of 'em were real heartbreakers. One guy was from Columbine. He'd survived the big shootout by hiding under a desk in the library. He joined the Corps straight after that. Didn't even go to his own graduation. He'd made it through the invasion of '03 and then the push through Fallujah. He'd done it. Been through the worst of the worst. And then the word came down that we had to back-clear some buildings in a sector vacated by a Marine unit from Hawaii that was rotating home. He walked into an old schoolhouse where there were some *muj* holdouts. He took a sniper round just under his helmet."

He paused a moment to think about it. "I worked on another guy who'd been bugging the first sergeant all that day to let him call home on one of the battalion's satellite phones because his son was supposed to be born soon. Later, when we got home, I spoke with his wife and we compared notes. I figured out that he'd been killed the same hour that his son was born. That was some dirty math."

His eyes stayed fixed on a far point on the horizon, as if he were looking for a new way out, a new ending to the story, this tale he might've told a thousand times, this tale he knew better now than the story of how his own parents met, and all I could do was give back my amazement.

"Wow," I said.

Toward the end of my tour, I met a kid in Third Battalion, Eighth Marines, a real hard case. He'd come from a bad family in southern Ohio, and the Corps was probably the best home he'd ever had. I'd met so many guys like him, for whom the Corps served a role not unlike the French Foreign Legion — a place to start over, a place to forget. His arms were all inked up. On one he had "1775" — the year the Corps was founded — in a huge spiraling script. On the other were the letters OTAN. I asked him what the letters stood for, and he said that he couldn't say, that he'd gotten that one just for himself, a secret he'd take with him to the grave. (At first I thought he was playing me, but later I talked to his platoon sergeant, a grizzled former sniper and no bullshit artist, and he confirmed it, said he'd sent him out behind the barracks at Camp Lejeune to dig foxholes until he told. He shoveled for an entire weekend, but he never gave it up.)

The kid and I used to find each other out on a veranda at the battalion command post in Ramadi. We'd sit and look toward the Euphrates, watch the sunset, and trade French cigarettes. Three-Eight had seen some of the worst fighting and had taken its share of casualties. At times like these, between engagements, it wasn't uncommon to see marines breaking down and sometimes crying, and because I was viewed by many as a sympathetic outsider, someone who would never reveal their secrets to their buddies, I'd had a few guys break down on me. Not this kid. I never once saw his face crack, and I began to see that in its own way this toughness, this stoicism polished to a high sheen by the unspeakable privations of grunt life, was a magnificent thing. There was a rough beauty to him, a beauty made for just this kind of place, and I wondered if the hardness developed over the years hadn't become something more than a mask for him. It was his gift, a talent that held him together, kept him whole through cold rainy nights on post, through the dust storms of spring, through the pitiless heat of summer.

Later he showed me another tat he had, on the inside of one of his biceps. It was a stylized version of a forties pinup girl, bent at the waist with a hand held coyly up to her mouth. He said she was the only girl he'd ever been faithful to. As we talked, it came out that earlier in the morning he'd mouthed off to the battalion commander and gotten himself in trouble again. He shrugged and added, by way of closure, a catch phrase I'd heard many times before: "The Corps is just like any other woman . . . a bitch."

Before I headed back to Baghdad, I saw him standing in the middle of a wide landing zone near some other marines waiting for a chopper. It was a windy day, dust storms cooking on the horizon, and it was looking like all flights were going to be grounded. He stood there alone, keeping his distance from a line of guys hoping to get picked up and flown out. As I watched, he bent his head skyward and began bellowing something with a practiced familiarity that made me think it was his own personal inside joke. He had his back to me, but I heard him distinctly.

"Allah has no balls, you hear me? No balls!"

Safely back home now, I have trouble explaining why I went to Iraq, let alone why I've been there twice. I'm worse yet at explaining why, in all likelihood, I'll go back. There's really no conventional logic that can do that sort of heavy lifting. When I first went over in the spring of 2004, I had some vague notions about trying to come to grips with the essence of war and about studying modern insurgency. But that was mostly a cover, a head-fake for myself as much as anyone else, something I'd cooked up in order to get my ass over there.

In reality, I think I just couldn't bear the thought of missing out. In the nineties, I'd served with guys who had the most stupendous stories. Stories that made you feel like you'd aged about ten years after the first listen. One old sniper in my company filled my head with apocrypha about being in Beirut in the eighties and having had Yasir

Arafat glassed cold, center mass in his scope. He'd started his preshot breathing drill (breathe, relax, aim, squeeze, surprise), inhabited the whole process, saw him dead, dusted, but didn't take the shot. Did it just to prove that he could go to the edge and not let the dime drop. I think now, looking back, that it was me in the crosshairs. I was the one who took the round.

In the most self-serving sort of way, I went to Iraq because I wanted my own stories to tell, and any war correspondent who is being honest with you will tell you the same. It's a variation of another apocryphal story: a reporter was supposed to have asked Willie Sutton, the infamous criminal, why he robbed banks, to which Sutton replied, "Because that's where the money is." I went to Iraq because that's where the stories are. It's the Hemingway disease, and everyone there has it. Most of the reporters working in Iraq wouldn't know Nick Adams from Samuel Adams, but they know the mythology. They know it better than they know the *AP Stylebook. Get your war on. Catch some of the bang-bang. Another dispatch from the Newest Suburb of Hell.* Any newsman worth his salt knows the market value of combat, captured on film or on the page. But once you've seen it for yourself, you realize how impossible it is to capture, and the more you try to tell the truth, the more it seems to vanish in the smoke. So instead you tell stories.

This one is mine. We were all strapped into a Sea Stallion over Fallujah, thirty of us, when the sky outside the crew chief's hatch went suddenly orange. It was beautiful, so beautiful, until I realized what it was: incoming. We were being lit up. The chopper started swinging horribly, as if on the end of a colossal yo-yo, and the crew chief opened up with his .50 cal. You could hear the incoming and outgoing even over the sound of the rotor blades, and I wondered how long it could go on.

This was the moment I'd been waiting for forever, and now that it had arrived, I realized that I had no idea what to do. It was no use ducking; the chopper was unarmored; there was no cover to be had. I felt my ass getting all buzzy waiting for the shot that would claim me from below. The guy next to me started squeezing and pulling at my arm, looking for some form of comfort as the fire kept coming in. He looked around the cabin hurriedly. I remember thinking, At least I'm not losing it like *this* dude.

It wasn't long after we touched down, the helicopter safely on the tarmac, the smell of burning jet fuel filling my nostrils, that one of the guys started in on the *Black Hawk Down* jokes. I looked over to see who was cracking wise. It was the guy who'd grabbed me, a young civilian contractor. I kept watching him, but he wouldn't meet my gaze. He was laughing and looking past me into the deep distance. I could see something happening in his eyes: the story belonged to all of us, but he was inside now, doing the work, making it his own.

Sometimes you could do that, shoulder it on your own, but sometimes you needed to find somebody with a story that would help explain what you were seeing, someone to take a little of the pressure off. Everybody in Iraq gets a little spooky and mystical at times, so you didn't have to look hard. At a patrol base north of Fallujah, I met a black platoon sergeant who liked to read the Bible every day while listening to Metallica. His father was a prominent pastor in Chicago, and he dropped Bible verses like most guys dropped hip-hop lyrics. He had the most soothing voice I'd ever heard, the kind of voice that doesn't happen naturally but only comes from growing up in a certain kind of church and being in a certain kind of choir your entire life. I would sit next to his cot and listen to him talk for hours. He told me that while Jews and Arabs were both descendants of Abraham, the Arabs had descended from the house of Shem and were a quarrelsome people, had always been quick to complain, quick to point their fingers in accusation. What he saw in Iraq was merely the embodiment of a script written millennia before. It was a simple story. It was elegant and illogical, but it was his story, and it kept him whole for all the months he'd been there. It got him through the firefights, through first Fallujah, through to the Freedom Bird.

Sometimes over there, when I was tired and my mind started drifting, I would find myself on the same tracks as that platoon sergeant, on the same tracks but headed the other direction. Sometimes I found myself thinking that, in its own way, Iraq is a miracle, a miracle of destruction, and that in a disaster of such magnitude there must be some order beneath the chaos, some evidence of God's handiwork, for surely such a maelstrom could not have been created by man alone. Surely there is a divine energy being worked out in this land, so great is the devastation, so profound is the suffering.

Or maybe this is just the story I'm telling.

■

Stuyvesant High School Commencement Speech

THANK YOU graduating seniors, faculty, parents, SAT tutors, college placement coaches, jealous siblings, grandparents who have no idea who I am because they fall asleep during Leno, and people who wandered in accidentally because they have season tickets to Lincoln Center.

Before I begin, I'd like to thank you for inviting me here today. Over the years, I've been asked to give commencement speeches at many prestigious institutions. Just last year I was offered fifty thousand dollars to speak at a graduation, but I said, "You go to hell, Bronx Science." Then they said "Sixty thousand," and I took it, but I never showed up. Man, those guys are idiots.

I am truly honored to be here today. Of course, when I first got the call, no one mentioned that I had to show up at 8:45 in the morning and wear a dress. By the way, I'm wearing a ceremonial robe decorated in the colors of my alma mater, Harvard University. I chose to wear it because it's the fastest way to let everyone know I'm a pompous, self-important jackass. And, by the way, if you're curious, under this thing I'm "going commando."

I'm especially honored because I've been told that it was the students who wanted me to be here today. It's very flattering to know that I was up there with your other first choices, skateboarder Tony Hawk and Bow Wow. So, I thank you for your graciousness, your good taste, and your ability to stay up until 1:30 in the morning without flunking out of school.

This is a sentimental occasion for me, because I remember my own high school graduation so well. Just like you, I sat in a large auditorium daydreaming about experiences yet to come: college, my first job, puberty. Yes, I'm even reminded of something my dad said to me at my graduation. He put his hand on my shoulder, looked me right in the eye, and said, "I'm not your father." Then he wrapped me in his strong Samoan arms and said, "Don't ever call me."

Yes, graduation is a day you will never forget, and many of you have been signing notes in each other's yearbooks that you will read years from now, things like "Best friends forever" or "Keep in touch." And that's fine, but some of you might want to do what I did. I wrote incredibly specific, untrue memories just to confuse my friends when they took out their yearbooks twenty years later. Things like "I'll never forget the time you stole those mothballs, you shoe-sniffing Wildman" or "Keep head-butting alligators, Señor Cinnamon Shorts!" Trust me, when they read that stuff years later, they'll call you, crying and shouting, "What does it mean!?"

You should cherish this day, because this morning is one of the most important experiences of your life. Then, afterward, it's off to brunch with your parents. It starts off well, but halfway through they mention dinner plans with your grandparents and Aunt Rose, who hasn't seen you in ages. "But I made plans," you say. "I'm going out with Kirsten and Dylan. There's a party at Galapagos, and J.R.'s rented the VIP room." "But Aunt Rose came all the way from Garden City," they say, "and who's this J.R.?" Suddenly you jump up from the table. "Oh, my God, I can't believe this! It's Jason Rubinstein. I told you this like *twenty times*. You never listen. You *never listen!*" Yes, you'll cherish this day forever.

Because this ceremony is so important, I've thoroughly prepared and researched your school. According to Wikipedia, which I desperately accessed on my BlackBerry five minutes ago, this institution was named after Peter Stuyvesant, head of the Dutch West India Company. This explains, by the way, why your teachers are still paid in grain and bags of salt.

Stuyvesant, as you know, is not your typical high school. In 1950 students at Stuyvesant tried to build a particle accelerator. By way of comparison, that's the same year my public high school discovered fire.

In 1969, girls were admitted to Stuyvesant for the first time. This started a new trend among the boys called "showering." Today Stuyvesant has a remarkably diverse and varied student body, ranging from math geeks to science nerds. Yes, you're a glorious, beautiful rainbow of brainiacs. And that can be very intimidating. Let's face it: most of you are smarter than me.

It's a proven fact that as you get older, your brain shrinks and you get dumber. This is why you have to explain to your parents what a TiVo is, and they have to explain to your grandparents what a cat is. Even I've gotten a lot dumber. I graduated from Harvard twenty years ago, and I'm currently reading at the sixth-grade level. If anyone here spoils the ending of *Charlotte's Web*, I am so going to freak.

So what can I tell you this morning? What advice can I give you? Well, I'll tell you what I *won't* do. I won't spout a lot of meaningless clichés. You know the ones — the trite phrases that pollute most commencement speeches: "Reach for the stars," "Follow your dream," "Keep your eyes on the prize." No, you guys are too smart for clichés, so I'm going to give you real, concrete advice that will get you through the next four years of college.

1. Most of you are going to competitive schools, so psych out the competition right away. It's simple. Show up at freshman orientation with a copy of Steven Hawking's *Brief History of Time* and a black marker. Sit in the dining hall and start crossing out whole paragraphs of the book while yelling, "Wrong, idiot, try again."

2. Rip out a picture in a magazine of a hot guy or girl and frame it. Tell people it's your boyfriend or girlfriend, who goes to Ohio Wesleyan, and that your relationship is purely physical. When people ask you why she looks suspiciously like Jessica Alba, throw a hot drink in their face and run away.

3. Be warned: everyone has a weird roommate. If you don't have a weird roommate, that means *you're* the weird roommate.

4. If you want to get out of a test, don't say you have a family emer-

gency. Everyone says that, and it never works. Say you have diarrhea. No one ever says they have diarrhea unless they do.

5. Some of you guys will be tempted to grow a goatee. Do not grow a goatee. A goatee is just a beard with low self-esteem. On the same note, some of you girls will be tempted to get a lower-back tattoo. I just want to say: that's totally awesome.

6. People will tell you that your future depends on what major you choose. This is not true. Einstein majored in hotel management. Dick Cheney majored in modern dance, and Britney Spears wrote a thesis on socialist labor relations in post-glasnost Poland.

Okay, those were silly and a complete waste of time. But believe it or not, I actually do have some real advice for you.

I don't want to freak you out, but twenty-five years ago I could have been any one of you. I went to a public high school and I was a bright, ambitious, hard-working kid who wanted more than anything to go to a good college. The only problem is that I was much more interested in succeeding than in really learning. When you're a smart kid in a competitive school it's an easy trap to fall into. So I did a lot of things in high school not because I enjoyed them but because I thought they'd look good on an application. I was on the debate team — hated it. I ran track — I was terrible, and I got so bored running the two-mile that I tried to talk with my opponents during the race. I joined the school government, banged a gavel, and said things like "Motion denied," even though I had no idea what I was doing. And of course, like many of you, I worried obsessively about my GPA and my SAT scores.

And, of course, it worked. I got into the college of my choice, and to this day I'm proud of the work I did in high school. But old habits die hard, and once I got to college, I had every intention of joylessly grinding away again. I was going to turn college into just another step on the road to being successful, whatever that meant. I told people my plan was to go to graduate school in law or government, just because I thought that's what smart people were supposed to do.

And then something weird happened. My roommate (by the way, *he* was the weird roommate) was going to an orientation meeting at the *Harvard Lampoon,* the school humor magazine, and I decided, for some reason, to tag along. I wrote one piece, then another, then another, and before long I was running the place. The only difference was, I was joyously happy. I was succeeding at something because I loved the process, not because I was trying to get anywhere. I had found the thing I wanted to do for the rest of my life, and I honestly didn't care where it took me or what it paid.

So when I graduated from college in 1985, I told my parents, "Thanks for the amazing Ivy League education. Now I want to be a comedian." Later, in the emergency room, after they woke up, they said they were fine with my decision, and I was on my way. I've had a lot of highs, I've had my share of lows, but if I hadn't allowed myself to experiment and risk doing something without a clear career payoff, I would have missed out on so much.

I never would have written for *Saturday Night Live.* I wouldn't have performed onstage in Chicago in a diaper in 1988. I never would have spent hours crafting the Homer Simpson line "The bee bit my bottom and now my bottom is big." I never would have jumped out a window in the *South Park* movie. I never would have danced with the Masturbating Bear or been pooped on by Triumph the Insult Comic Dog. I never would have swum naked in Arctic waters with the Finnish Ministry of Defense.

Yes, it's been a wasted life. But I honestly believe that I found the best use for Conan O'Brien. Don't get me wrong — I've worked extremely hard at being an ass. And, yes, I've made some sweet, sweet coin. But what I'm asking you to consider is that the next four years don't have to be just a steppingstone. You're very bright, impressive young people, but for the last four years your GPA has been calculated to two decimal points and you've pushed yourself very hard. Many of you have succeeded because you have stuck to a very rigid, linear path. And that's fine. All I'm asking you to do in college is to take a moment every now and then to breathe and look around you. If something intrigues you, take a small chance. You might just find an entire life you weren't planning on. It could be biophysics. Medicine. Puppetry. Ultimate fighting. Beekeeping. Government. Or doing whatever it is Ryan Seacrest does.

The point is, at this moment many of you have ideas of what you want to do with your lives, but for many of you those ideas will change. And that's because you think you know who you are right now, but you don't. Trust me. When I look back at eighteen-year-old Conan, it's a ridiculous sight. Six feet four, of pale skin and bone. Scared of girls. Squeaky voice. Wait, I'm sorry, that's forty-three-year-old Conan. But life and the choices I've made have changed me in a thousand ways. And none of it would have happened if I had rigidly "kept my eye on the prize" or decided, with great determination, to "follow my dream." I didn't have the slightest idea what my dream was when I was eighteen. It had to find me.

So enjoy the next phase of your life. And make sure you enjoy today as well. You've all achieved something pretty remarkable today, and you should be infinitely proud. And, before I go, let me leave you with one last message. Tonight many of you will party, and it could get pretty rockin.' All I ask is that you remember to stop for a moment, take out your cell phone, and invite me along. My home number is . . . Seriously, I have no plans.

Thank you, and congratulations.

■

Humpies

FROM *Agni Online*

GO-BOY ASKED a girl to marry him. He had just told me this when his dad freaked out.

It was five in the morning. We were in Go-Boy's room and I was sitting on his dresser, sideways. My feet dangled over a missing patch of fake wood grain, torn back like a bed sheet, exposing particleboard. I was telling him we needed to get to work because we were late, but he wasn't hearing anything. Go was on his bed. His eyes were wound up like yo-yos ready to drop.

He was telling me about this girl, that he was showing her how to use his boat the night before. He told her the throttle gets stuck sometimes. Then they drove out to the mouth of the river. He told me he shut the engine down and explained that the fuel pump doesn't always work right and that you have to pump it by hand. She hopped in the driver's seat. It just felt right, he said. Right then. Before she started the motor. So he asked her.

I was sitting on that dresser as he told me all of this, not believing my ears. Go-Boy was really excited, and I wondered if he'd ever had a girlfriend at all. Then we heard his dad in the living room. He was screaming so loud it sounded like someone was cutting metal out there. Go-Boy almost didn't even react, though, like it wasn't weird, and that's when I wanted to leave. But he got up and I followed him down the hall, walking on the little floor rugs with knotted-string tassels into the living room.

Go-Boy had been telling me how this girl said no. He was bummed at first. She didn't even think he was serious, but he was. They were floating out there in the water in a small aluminum fishing boat, around midnight. Daylight was about to drop behind the north end of the ocean, adding that eeriness of a sunset that nobody would see. It was probably graveyard quiet, the occasional slurping sound of a wave hitting the boat. Then she said she didn't know him very well. She said she was only nineteen, and they had just started dating. But Go said it felt right, that's why he asked her.

And then we heard that cutting-metal scream, and I followed him into the living room. Then we saw his dad put Go's three-year-old brother in a coma.

That was the day the humpies came — early that morning, before I went to Go's place. There were thousands of them. Even more. They were in the river, jumping and splashing like it was raining size-nineteen Chuck Taylors. I was at the shore, sitting in my flatboat, waiting for Go. We were supposed to work, to motor upriver to the fish tower. But the tide went out that morning, and my boat wasn't back-anchored, so it got beached. I tried pushing it alone, but the damn thing was heavy.

Down the shoreline, old guys were standing around in rubber boots, drinking coffee from silver cups and talking and watching these fish jump. They walked along the mossy gravel shore, along with the seagulls and the random fish guts, where the water had been a couple feet deep not too long ago.

"Lots," some guy said to me, smiling, dropping waders and buckets into his boat.

I just nodded, because this shit meant headaches for us up at the tower. It was tough enough counting these salmon from twenty-five feet in the air. It was tougher to know which kind was which. And now it would be a nightmare. It was like babysitting the entire river, keeping tabs on which ones swam upstream and which ones swam down.

This guy asked if I needed help with my boat, but I said no.

"It's like '94," he said, firing up his motor and grinding away.

That's when I gave in and headed for Go's house. I normally wouldn't have gone there. His sister, Kiana, had just chewed my ass a few days earlier, and her boyfriend was threatening to kick my face in.

But I thought at five in the morning nobody would be awake. I'd nudge Go and we'd be on our way.

We didn't work that day. We didn't radio the tower to let them know what was happening. We didn't call our bosses at IRA or Fish and Game. We didn't do anything. I left Go's place and went home and back to sleep.

When a cop showed up at our house later that morning, Mom was red in the face. She probably knew the guy from when she grew up here. I was lying in bed, studio headphones blocking out all noise except the music in my ears. She came into the room, said something, but I couldn't hear.

"Why are the cops asking for you?"

Her black hair was pulled back and messy, and she had a wad of gauze bundled around her infected thumb — the thumb she sliced open while trying to remember how to cut fish with an ulu. I wasn't sure if she was embarrassed that the cops were looking for her son, or if she was embarrassed to be caught looking so disassembled.

"I don't want this shit to be following you up here," she said, already mad before anything even happened. "I'm not gonna put up with another thug living under my roof."

I walked past her and out the back door to tell these cops that I didn't know anything about Go's dad and brother. Mom was so out of whack it was unbelievable. Up here, near the Arctic Circle, where everybody knew everybody, she wasn't concerned about her son ending up dead. She was concerned about her son looking like a thug — getting that reputation. Everybody already knew her oldest son was in prison back in California because of some gang stuff. What did that say about the mother? What would it say if the second son turned out the same way? But I didn't give a fuck, because Pop wouldn't sell me out like that to save himself. If Pop were up here with us, he would stand up to the cops. Say, "Yeah, my son's here. There something I can help you with?"

I first knocked on Go-Boy's bedroom window. The boat was beached and Go was a half hour late. I knocked a second time and he parted the curtains and waved me in. The front door was open. I left my shoes in the entryway and walked through the living room into the hall. A kitchen light was on, even though the sun was pretty bright that early. Cheap plastic sports cups were everywhere in the living and dining room — mostly basketball cups with a picture of the player and his signature. Dream Team, from way back, with Michael and Magic. Some football. Barry Sanders. A few commemorative baseball cups.

Go-Boy's bedroom smelled like coffee. There were a couple mugs half full on his nightstand. One was steaming. He had a notebook and it looked like he was writing a letter. In about five minutes he would tell me about that girl he asked to marry him, the girl that said no. But right then his yo-yo eyes glanced up at me, quick, barely acknowledging I was in the room. Those eyes didn't know what time it was. Those eyes hadn't slept.

Before this I hadn't talked to Go for a few days, not since his sister bitched me out at the potluck. She had grabbed my arm like she was planning to pull me aside, out of my seat, but instead she just squeezed and said all sorts of stuff about me spreading rumors and talking bad about her. Go-Boy was sitting next to me. He heard it all. She said she was drunk when she slept with me at that party, and it was a mistake, and I shouldn't be telling people we were dating when she had a boyfriend. But she was just making a big deal out of something dumb. Seventeen-year-old drama.

When I hopped up on Go's dresser, waiting for him to stop scribbling on his legal pad, I squeezed my fist open and closed, still feeling that sensation of Kiana's little fingers wrapped around my forearm, her nails digging into my long-sleeve shirt. There wasn't a bruise or anything. It was a memory.

"We gotta work, man."

He glanced up like he was surprised I was there. But right away he turned back to the pad, scribbling a list of things with his left-handed grip and his elbow high.

I said, "Damn, dude, you don't look good."

"Yeah?"

"Yeah," I said. "Maybe you're sick."

There had to be millions of those fish. Those humpies. When they jumped you could see their fleshy bellies, silver and black fading down to that pink. When I waited for Go that morning, I sat in my boat and tried to count every one I could see and hear. But that was dumb, like counting waves.

I thought about these things swimming in from the Bering Sea — a school of a million darting this way and that, covering thousands of miles. Every single one of them, down to the last one, could change the direction of the whole group. At least that's how I imagined it. Fish are so nervous all the time. With their unblinking eyes peeled on both sides, any little movement by one freaks them all out. It's a miracle they can end up at a single destination. It's a miracle they don't get so sidetracked that they never find a river to swim up and spawn in. It's a miracle they ain't all extinct.

"Why are they asking you about that?" Mom said after that cop had left. She was interested in me for real now. Word had spread throughout the day that Go's three-year-old brother, Sean, was in a coma. A church group was getting together to pray about it at six o'clock. Mom had cooked meatloaf in an aluminum bread pan for Go and Kiana and their dad. Nobody knew anything happened the way me and Go-Boy did, though, and he must not be talking.

"Do you know something?" she asked.

I shrugged and turned away.

"There are a few different stories circulating around town," she said. "If you know something —"

"Nah, Mom. I don't know anything."

"I heard Sean had been staying up past midnight," she said. "And that he walks in his sleep when he's real tired." Mom had removed the bandage from her thumb and was wiping down the counters. These kinds of events, like big news and rumors, made her a marathon cleaner. "They medevaced him to Anchorage. He's in a coma."

I said, "I haven't talked to Go-Boy either."

She told me nobody had talked to Go, that they couldn't find him. She told me Kiana discovered Sean lying on the living room floor. Their dad was in his bedroom, passed out. His story was that Sean must've sleepwalked, fallen, knocked his head.

Go-Boy wasn't home, or at work, or anywhere.

*

After me and Go saw his old man put the little kid in a coma, neither of us moved. His dad stumbled out of the living room, not even noticing that we were right there, seeing it all. And that's when I left. That's the way I left. Go-Boy frozen there. His dad swaying into the kitchen.

They lived in a HUD home on the northeast side of the village, a place called Happy Valley. It looked like a clean version of an Indian reservation, or at least compared to those I had seen. Rows of redundant houses. Yards and streets bare of trees or grass. Crooked telephone poles tying everyone together. Behind it was the dried-up marsh that went a mile in both directions till it ran into the hills. I headed for Grandpa's house, where me and Mom stayed, over on the west side where the river opened to Norton Sound, to the Bering Sea.

I walked the long way home, down the gravel roads, zigzagging around muddy truck-sized puddles. To my right was the cemetery, full of fireweed with white crosses poking above the brush, looking like a picket fence gone wrong. Behind that was the dark gravel runway for the airport. Next to one of the sheds a forklift spun around, stopped next to a plane, and raised a plywood box they were throwing cargo into.

Or maybe the forklift wasn't running that morning. Maybe it was just parked.

When Kiana called that night, I told Mom I didn't want to talk to her.

The cop had been back again around suppertime. He took me out to his truck and sat me in the front seat. Some older kids I recognized from playing ball at open gym were walking past, and it made me feel immature to be in that patrol car, to be restrained. The cop started the motor and spun the temperature dial over to red for some heat. He asked me the same questions and stroked his mustache. Was I at Go's place that morning? Had I seen anything happen to Sean? Had I seen Go-Boy since?

Out the window, I could see the mouth of the river where Go and that girl floated just before he asked her to marry him. It was the same place all those humpies were racing through to get upriver, to lay their eggs, to spawn and make more fish.

This cop told me the seriousness of witnessing a crime. And then, when I still wouldn't say shit, he told me neighbors saw me leaving

Go-Boy's house early that morning. But I was cool. I said that I had been there but that nothing weird happened. Nobody was awake. Go-Boy was sick and didn't want to work, so I put my shoes on and walked home.

Even if I would tell somebody, I hadn't yet decided what I would say or who I would say it to. Truth is, I was waiting for Go to pop up, to talk to him, let him deal with it.

The cop was quiet a moment. I asked him if I could go right then, but he didn't respond. He waited a little longer, then said, "Why didn't you head to work after you left?" But that was easy. I said my boat was high and dry. Then I opened the truck door and went back in the house.

Mom told me I had to tell her what was going on, why the police were still bugging me. She had this newfound sense of dominance since we moved here. Because she ditched Pop, she was now redis-covering her power. I was just a small detail in that plan.

I grabbed a Pepsi from the fridge, and she was on my every move, checking right down the list: Did I steal something? Was I doing drugs? Did I get in a fight? Did I tag a building? Sure I had. But not since California.

"Nothing," I said. I told her that the police were trying to find Go, which wasn't a total lie. They had people out in boats and trucks, look-ing for him everywhere. All his uncles had dropped everything and formed a search-and-rescue team. He had only been gone since that morning, but considering what happened to his brother, everyone was worried. He wasn't at home or at the fish tower or at the gym or anywhere.

And I wouldn't tell Mom the truth. Seeing what I had gave me too much responsibility. Talking about it would make it worse. I just wanted to forget the whole thing.

After Go's dad freaked out I went home, but I didn't really sleep. I lay in bed, listened to headphones. I put a tape that used to be my brother's in the stereo. It was a blank, recorded for him by some friend. It said WICHO'S SHIT in marker. It was mostly old-school rap. Stuff he listened to standing in front of the huge mirrors in our par-ents' bedroom. He would put that tape on and dance in front of his reflection, wearing nothing but sweatpants and socks, kicking and jumping all over the mauve carpet, occasionally sparking from the static. This was probably ten years earlier, '92 maybe, and I wouldn't join him, because I was like seven or eight, and the last time I tried, he thought I was being funny and punched a charcoal bruise on my shoulder. This was serious. This was the place he tried new moves before he showed his friends, before he went to the junior high dances. I felt like I was backstage.

Kiana came to our door that night, and when she knocked, I knew it was her. People were always coming over to our place and just peeking in and hollering. Nobody knocked. But from my bedroom, I could hear a thin little rap on the aluminum door, with thin little fingers. This was only about fifteen minutes after Mom told me she was on the phone, when I said I didn't want to talk.

Part of me was glad she was here. Not because I wanted to get lectured again or because I wanted her crying and asking me for help, but because my muscles had been anxious all day. Because I wanted to get this drama over with, get back to relaxed, like yesterday.

The padded sound of feet came to my room. Then she was right there. She looked like hell. Her throat was tensed like someone was poking at the undersides of her jaw with drumsticks. And even though the stress and sadness and all that stuff loomed over everything, I couldn't help being aroused. I couldn't help remembering that night we had sex, at that party. I was pretty drunk and couldn't recall anything else that happened, except her. Those airbrushed forearms and fingertips. Her hipbones and sides of her neck, classically smooth but sharp like the curves of a '67 Eldorado.

"Hey," she said, exhaling.

I nodded her in. She sat on the carpeted floor, and when she did that, I realized how young she really was. Even though she occasionally tried assertiveness over her big cheekbones, it didn't work. She was still a seventeen-year-old kid.

"You okay?" I asked.

She didn't hear anything. She was deep in thought, trying to put together something to say. It looked like she had been doing this all day, this thinking and explaining.

"I know you were there," she eventually said. "This morning."

I reached toward the radio on my dresser, acting like I had something to do.

"Go-Boy is missing," she said. "We can't find him." She looked down at the floor, next to her hip, her pointer finger twisting a loose string in the carpet, her knees pressed tight side by side. "And I know you were there when Sean got hurt."

"Where?" I said.

"I heard you two in his room. I heard my dad."

After she said that, we didn't talk for a while. In my head, that cutting-metal scream sounded different now that I knew she heard it. Now it was more of a feeling than a sound. I pictured her in a closed room, lying in bed, blankets clenched and knotted around her neck. I imagined her eyes being peeled like those fish, ready to dart in any direction. And I still wanted nothing to do with this, but now I wanted somebody to snitch on her dad for me, to get some kind of justice.

"Please don't say anything," she said. She was looking at the floor below my bed. "Don't say anything about what my dad did. He didn't mean to do it. He was drunk. It was an accident."

We heard that noise from Go-Boy's bedroom. He didn't say anything and I didn't either. We just got up and walked out to the living room to see what was happening.

On the floor was Go's brother. I didn't know for sure, but I guessed him to be around three years old. He was wrapped in an orange blanket, like a stork had left him on the front step but then dragged him into the house. He was half asleep, that tired-little-kid daze in his eyes. The carpet around him was matted and full of lint. A New York Knicks cup that was tipped sideways and caked with soda syrup was tucked under the couch.

That's when Go's dad appeared from the kitchen. He was a terror. He raged under his breath, tipping side to side like he was on a boat, and he felt so close to us at that moment, like we could taste the moisture in his panting breath. Then he came swinging, throwing a glass ashtray straight at the little boy on the floor, hitting him in the head. And then he kept throwing more stuff. The ashtray knocked the kid out. It was a lucky shot, because when he randomly threw a wooden napkin holder and the remote control, one ricocheted off the opposite wall and the other flew back into the kitchen. He didn't seem to be aiming at Sean or at anything, just throwing things to throw them.

But the messed-up part was that Go didn't do anything and I didn't do anything. In my memory, the distance between us and Sean — the fifteen feet — seemed close enough for one of us to reach out and block the ashtray. But we didn't. We just watched it happen.

When Kiana and me left my house, Mom gave me one of those looks. I don't know what it meant, it was just one of those distrustful looks.

We walked down the road to the point. Kiana was a half step in front of me, and I looked at the ground and watched the back of her jeans drag on the gravel. There was an old telephone pole lying sideways that we sat on. It overlooked the mouth of the river and the ocean. I wanted to tell her that it was just out there, not even a day ago, that her brother Go floated in a boat and asked a girl to marry him. But I wasn't that type of guy to be yapping. Pop always was telling me not to mess around in other families' business.

She told me that when Go was little, he used to run around the house naked with his arms raised above his head. He'd wear a fireman's hat. She laughed when she said this, even though she hadn't been born when it happened — she just saw pictures. "He was so cute," she said.

And I thought about how tomorrow would come, and how Go would still be missing, and I'd still be the only one who knew what really happened, what really almost killed that little kid. Go-Boy would be gone and Sean would be half dead and their dad wouldn't remember why.

The humpies were still jumping in the river, maybe not as strong as they were that morning, but close. I told her I had watched them swim in. I told her that in thirty minutes the river went from calm to crazy. I was lying a little, but it didn't matter, because she didn't care.

"Man, where do they all come from?" I asked.

She didn't answer.

"I wonder if they swim in from Russia or Hawaii."

Then we were silent again.

Upriver, a boat stopped along the far shore and a lady hopped out, carrying ten-gallon buckets, and walked up to her drying racks. Underneath her miniature gazebo thing, fifty or sixty salmon fillets hung.

"Sorry about yelling at you," she said, shifting, pulling her knee to her chest and then dropping it back down. I could tell it wasn't easy for her to say that. If she didn't have a boyfriend, that would have been the moment to grab her hand or her thigh or something.

We sat a little longer, and I bet her she couldn't count every single humpy that jumped. She didn't try.

"I wasn't really drunk," she told me. "I lied. I wasn't drunk last night."

I picked up a gilly — a chunk of broken glass that had been polished by the ocean into a smooth rock. I massaged it between my fingers. Kiana was sitting on my right side, and I hoped she'd grab at that gilly and pretend like she wanted it. But instead of taking it from me, she would hold my fingers and our hands would drop between us, still locked. Then we'd weave them all together like a zipper, and I'd set them halfway up her lap where both legs met together. Maybe we'd kiss in a few minutes. Maybe not. I didn't care. We could wait. We could just sit there like that, hold hands.

"So," she said. "You promise you won't say anything about my dad?"

I leaned forward, confused, dropping my elbows on my knees. Then I dropped that gilly and pulled my jeans up to keep them from touching the ground.

"Please."

I would later understand how stressful this was for Kiana, how keeping the family together was her only priority, and how it was more important to her than to anyone else. But right then I couldn't see that. I felt used. I felt she was messing with me. Maybe she was being honest, maybe she really was sober the other night and was now sorry. But I didn't feel that way. At that moment I didn't believe her.

"I already told you," I said. "I wasn't there."

"Thank you."

Then she got up and just left me sitting.

*

After that glass ashtray hit Sean's head, just above his ear, it rolled a short half moon and bumped against the leg of the couch. It was emerald green, with floating sparkles, and caked with muddy ash residue. Where it hit Sean's head, it looked like it left a divot the size of a watch battery, for just a split second, before the swelling flared. Go-Boy was standing slightly in front of me. I saw all of it happen around his shoulder. To my right was the entryway and the door.

But we didn't move. Go-Boy's dad threw that napkin holder and remote control, still screaming, and then he tripped a bit and caught himself on a lamp. Then he looked around like he forgot what he was doing.

That's when I left. I grabbed my shoes and went out the door without even putting them on. The front step was muddy and my right sock got wet from my big toe to my arch.

After Kiana left me sitting on that telephone pole, alone, I watched the humpies jump some more. In a few weeks, all of these flapping and wiggling things would be dead. They'd wash up on the beaches and sandbars like all of them before. That's what Go told me, anyway. He said that when they swim into the river from the ocean to spawn, they stop eating. He said the fresh water messes with them. He said after a couple weeks, after they've dropped their eggs and sperm in all the right places, they die. Just like that. These things cruise around the ocean for years, and then when they're ready, when they group up and find their way to some river, they swim right in and die.

I figured I'd sit there on that telephone pole and watch them a little longer. They were right at the mouth of the river. They had swum some long-ass distance and were just happy to flip around. They didn't know what was ahead of them. They didn't know that all of this led to their death. But I imagined that didn't even matter. They'd still swim up this river if they knew what it meant, because it was the only thing they knew how to do.

■

So Long, Anyway

FROM *Epoch*

MY DENTIST DIED a long time ago. We weren't close. I mean we were, inasmuch as he had had his fingers in my mouth, but apart from that, I only knew him as a pleasant man who was good at small talk, who always remembered a comment I once made about becoming a cop.

"What do you think you want to be?" he asked me when I was thirteen.

I considered the point with a pure and recently developed countenance of total objectivity. In the late hours of the night, as I lay in my bed, looking up at the glowing star stickers I had stuck to my ceiling, I had come to understand the implications of my future death, as well as the implications of a burgeoning atheistic materialism.

"I used to want to play for the Brewers," I told him, implying with a wry grin that this was something very young, very stupid people believed, as though we weren't both talking about me from the year before. "But cop's not bad."

"Oh yeah?" he asked, nodding. "How come?"

"I don't know," I said. "I like detective books."

At that point in my life I was wary of dentistry. Four years earlier I had come in for a routine cleaning and been told that I had eleven cavities from drinking Coke, and that I would have to come back to get them filled in a week. I knew that these weren't the teeth I was always going to have. I tried to tell him that it didn't matter if they rotted in my head, that they weren't really my teeth anyway. What was wrong with going six months without any, knowing that the good ones were on the way?

"Trust me," he said. "You don't want to do that."

"Oh," I said. "I think I do."

"For the sake of your social life, Jay."

"I won't smile."

"What about eating?"

"Instant Breakfast."

"What about talking?"

"Through the nostrils."

He crossed his arms, then uncrossed them to remove his glasses. "Have your mom set up an appointment with the receptionist," he said. We walked down the hall, and he gave me a toothbrush and a toy car.

His name was Dr. Fenton. He was tall and husky — he must have weighed 250 pounds — and he had a face like a red apple. He had silver hair that was once brown and liked to wear glasses with small magnifying lenses attached to the frame with a clip. He could flip them up and down, depending on what he was looking at.

"Here we go," he would say to me, storming into the room after I'd spent twenty-five uncomfortable minutes with the dental assistant, trying to answer her questions about my life with a sharp metal scraper crammed up against my gums.

"How are you, Jay?" he'd ask. Then he'd flip down the lenses. *Flip.*

I remember a very long, very white coat, with his name, Dr. Fenton, written in embroidered blue cursive on the chest pocket. I remember rubber gloves pulled with a stretch onto his gorilla hands the first time I ever went to him. Fifth grade. At this point AIDS officially existed, and I was being indoctrinated by competing medical theories at school.

"You get it from trying to blow yourself," said Greg Lumberton, out on the playground.

"You get it from having your sister blow you," said Chris Jones. "And you can get it if you touch somebody who already did it. The only cure is to have *his* sister blow *you*."

"You get it from using public telephones," said Brent Husley. "If you dial the wrong number."

"You get it from falling off of high places," said Neal Benthe. "And not getting up fast enough."

"Now. Listen. One can *only* contract the HIV virus, a precursor to AIDS, from *direct blood contact* with someone who's *already* infected," said the teacher, Ms. Joppster, slapping at a pull-down poster of the human body with her long pointer stick. "Do you all hear me?" She turned to us and crossed her arms. "Nothing else. I've heard what you say to one another, and I'm here to tell you that it just isn't true." She was an old lady. I have to think, in hindsight, that she was often drunk during class. "I have AIDS," I said to my closest friend, Steve Nestor, as we were walking home from school one day. "I woke up this morning coughing blood all over the place."

"That's bullshit."

"I thought it was blood," I said, my voice squeaking. "I was *convinced* it was blood until I looked."

"Then it doesn't count."

"You don't have it," I asked, "do you?"

"No. But I think you might."

"*I know!*" I yelled, nodding. "I *do* think I might have it."

Dr. Fenton didn't have AIDS. Neither did I, but I had a different problem. It wasn't quite hypochondria, it was more just wanting to have something happen. Anything. I spent whole afternoons wishing that my friends would die so I could go to their funerals and deliver a speech from the podium. I knew that I was small and that they would have to adjust the microphone for me. Probably give me something extra to stand on. But being seven would multiply the impact of my words. I knew that the younger you were, the more willing older people would be to inflate the profundity of your statements. I had once been camping with my dad and gone into the bathroom hut with him to pee. Instead of regular urinals, there was one long urinal, like a bathtub. Inside it there were pink cakes and drains, but there was also a salamander. A tiny brown salamander, standing around. My dad and I both peed on it, and while it was happening — the salamander didn't move, it didn't even *blink* — I said, "It's a hard life, isn't it, Dad?" He broke out laughing. He told the story to all of his friends. I never understood why it was so funny, but I could tell by the tone of his voice and the grins that I was on to something big. If Neal Benthe happened to get run over by a semi while chasing a kickball across the street, it would be tragic, but not that tragic. I would get to give my speech. Big things would be *happening*, and I would be at the center of a swirling commotion.

Unfortunately for me, nobody whom I knew died until I was sixteen. Then, of all people, it was Dr. Fenton. When they finally figured out what had happened to him, and published a diagrammed article in the paper, I licked the top row of my teeth and remembered the last time I had seen him.

I had grown cool the summer between my sophomore and junior years of high school. Very withdrawn and blasé about my future, which was the only topic Dr. Fenton was capable of addressing — other than, of course, mouths.

"Still want to be a police officer, Jay?" he asked. "Work as a detective here in town?"

"I don't know," I said, leaning back in the reclining dentist's chair. I put my hands behind my head. "I don't really care how things turn out."

"Oh no?" he said quickly, studying my x-rays. "Let me ask you something, then, Jay. Do you care about plaque, Jay? Tartar? I'd like to think that you'll care a little more how things turn out when you've got a shooting pain back there and you can't take any liquids. How much Coke have you been drinking lately?"

My façade of cool fell apart. "A lot," I said. "I can't stop."

He frowned at the x-rays. I looked over and saw that the assistant was staring at me, shaking her head.

"He says he hasn't been flossing, either," she said.

"Hm?" asked Fenton. His magnifiers were flipped down and he was deeply engrossed in the negatives. He never listened to his assistants. Whenever I came, the last one had been replaced by a new one who looked slightly different.

"I said he hasn't been *flossing*," she repeated, raising her voice.

"You know, Jay," he said, ignoring her, "you have a great set of chompers here, I have to say."

"Really?" I asked.

"Really. But that doesn't mean you're off the hook with the flossing."

"I know," I said. "I know."

"Any gum sensitivity?"

"None whatsoever," I said, desperate to please him.

Dr. Fenton had that magic to him, something fatherly and expert but also kind and harmless. Very simply, he would save you and your mouth if anything bad happened.

My coolness had arrived all at once, as though it had been delivered by the UPS man. Suddenly my hair was a little longer and I wasn't chubby. My voice wasn't high and I had pubic hair and I even had a job at the grocery store. I touched breasts. I learned how to smoke cigarettes and then I learned how to steal my mother's cigarettes and then I learned how to steal whole cartons of cigarettes from the store when there weren't any managers up in the office, doing the books and looking at the video monitors. My dad taught me how to drive and then gave me the Jeep Wagoneer to use. I smoked weed and had a CD player. I sometimes listened to Pink Floyd and explained to my friends how the music related to the meaning of the universe.

"Big," I would say, caught up in the ecstasy of it all. "Space! *Huge!*"

"Listen to this Comfortably Numb solo," my friend would say, very serious. "Just listen. Pure beauty."

I was actually out, being cool, the night Dr. Fenton died. When I read about it in the newspaper a week later, after he had let me down for the first and only time in our well-established professional relationship, the profundity of it shook me and forced me to reevaluate my atheism. I wanted to wrap my coolness up and send it back.

I had been over on the west side of town, driving through the snow, trying to find Chrissy Conlinson's house. Her parents were away, and she was having a few people over. When I finally found the right address, I parked and ran across the street with my hands in my pockets, shivering. Part of my being cool, for some reason I can no longer remember, involved never wearing a jacket.

The party was much more than a few people. It was out of control. There was a girl in the kitchen wearing a bra and a pair of jeans, waving around a bread knife and yelling at a small crowd. There were four or five people upstairs on the balcony, drunkenly singing along to the Brady Bunch song coming out of the stereo. Someone was asleep in the bathtub. My friends were outside on the porch. I said hello to them, then went inside. The girl with the knife had moved away from the fridge, and I opened it, and I made myself a rum and Coke.

Across town, Dr. Fenton was leaving Magnum, a new restaurant beside the river. His friends said he had ordered steak. His wife was in Atlanta visiting their daughter, and Dr. Fenton's buddies had arranged a guy night. They were disappointed when he stood up after just one drink, apologetically explaining that he had heartburn, and hadn't been quite right all week, and felt as though he just needed to get into bed and get some rest. They understood. In reality, it was angina. They said good night and shook his hand one by one. He and Dave Kelly, a local real estate agent, made plans to play tennis.

Dr. Fenton walked across the restaurant with the ticket for his coat held in the palm of his clammy right hand. He gave it to a woman named Martha Pepstein, who later told the newspaper that he had a certain greenish look about him then, not quite pale, but not natural at all.

"His shirt looked too tight," she said. "He looked like he couldn't breathe." She found his coat and he tipped her well. He looked across the dining room one last time and nodded at his friends, who waved and smiled before returning to their conversation.

The road to Magnum ran alongside the river, bending and twisting with the shoreline. To the left, there was the uphill slope of a steep ravine; to the right, the ravine continued down toward shore, where it eventually met the frozen river. The snowstorm had been gaining momentum all night, and now, at around nine-thirty P.M., the plows had fallen behind, and the road was covered in an inch of snow. Since there was a winter storm warning that night, and Brad Spakowitz, the town meteorologist, had broken into *Cheers* reruns to show us all the approaching blob of scattered green light on his radar screen, not many cars were out. The road was lit only by tall amber lights spaced out every quarter mile.

About two hundred yards from Magnum, Dr. Fenton's cream Cadillac DeVille went off the road. It very quietly slipped down the ravine through the woods, knocking into small trees and bushes, plowing very quietly, creating a clear path of speckled whiteness and broken branches leading back up. It whispered away. It made no noise as it descended. It nicked a rock. The car finally came to rest with its hood against an oak tree, its back tires spinning slowly, frictionless, against the drifts of snow.

It didn't take long for the tracks that led from the road to the ravine to be covered up. It's hard to believe that nobody drove by in that small window of time, that the road was empty for fifteen or twenty minutes. But sometimes when you're driving you see curious things and you imagine that whatever has happened, it has been taken care of. You see incredible black marks on the highway that veer left and then right and then left again, implying that a car has sailed off a bridge and exploded, just impossible angles for speeding vehicles, and you somehow convince yourself that nothing extraordinary has happened at all. Or, if something extraordinary truly *has* happened, you believe that the authorities were there to help, they came, and that whoever was driving is now home safe, playing Scrabble in front of a fire.

Back at the party, I was bored. It turned out, like so many parties in high school, to be nowhere near as decadent as it initially appeared. The girl with no shirt had put it back on, slid the knife into a drawer, gone upstairs, and started singing with the Brady Bunch group. I'd stopped drinking. There was a moment with my friends out on the porch when we all stopped talking at once. It was because we had nothing to talk about. I took that as a cue to go home and fall asleep under the glowing green stars on my ceiling. They were still there. I'd tried to peel them off when I turned cool, but the glue had been too strong.

I said good night to the people I liked and vaguely nodded at the people I didn't, then left through the front door, amazed at how much snow had fallen in the few hours I'd been inside. I put my hands in my pockets and just looked at the white sparkling street, the white sparkling street that was actually amber from the lights. There were no tracks. It gave me a giddy feeling. No car tracks, no human tracks. I shoved my hands in my pockets and hopped off the porch, toward the street.

I misjudged where I was. I thought I was going down the driveway, but really, I was in the yard, moving across dead grass instead of concrete. When I came to the curb, I wasn't expecting it, and my right foot went down farther than it should have, and I lurched forward, yanking frantically with my shoulders to get my hands up out of my pockets in time for the fall. The problem with the falling reflex, though, is that your hands try to go *out*, not up, so I was fighting against a few million years of evolution in the space of maybe two seconds. The watch on my left wrist got caught up. I got the right hand out, but not by much; my body, realizing it was the best choice of many bad choices, turned a bit in that direction, and I took most of the fall on my right shoulder and forearm.

Not all of it. My mouth was open for a little yelp of surprise and a quick, bracing inhalation. The snow slowed my face down as it hit, like a strange freezing pillow, but my top right canine nicked the cement underneath. It cracked in half.

I was more mad than hurt, although it did hurt. Blood dripped down into the snow. I reached up gingerly to touch my mouth, and when my finger scraped against the jagged nub of the tooth I yelled, "*Ah!*" and then "*Oh!*" at the silent street. After I got to my feet, I wiped down my shirt and my pants and thought about going back inside for help. Instead I went to my car and found the scraper. While I wiped away the snow and sucked up air and swallowed the blood in my mouth, I thought about how at least something was happening. I would have a story to tell when I got home. I would have something interesting to tell my friends. I would have to make a special visit to Dr. Fenton. And for the rest of my life I would have something artificial in my mouth to go along with the story. Proof. I'd always have something to say to new people.

It's possible that Dr. Fenton also broke off some of his teeth when his Cadillac DeVille went down the ravine, but I doubt it. There are coincidences, and then there are coincidences. Granted, I'm relying on my imagination, but when I see that car sliding down through the trees, it's going as slow as the snowflakes around it; it's just barely moving, this diagonally moving boxy thing that has the density of balsa wood. Inside, as seen through the glass of the passenger window, there is a man breathing heavily, blinking rapidly, holding on to the wheel, and leaning forward into his seat belt.

I took my time driving home. The Wagoneer had four-wheel drive, but it was a monster of a car, and it didn't have antilock brakes, and

I was happy to revel calmly in the emergency of it all: a frantic, wounded trip home through a dangerous storm. I pulled into my driveway behind my dad's car, a bigger, newer SUV. I made sure to walk to the house without my hands in my pockets.

"Lemme see," my dad said when I showed it to him. "Take your hand away."

"Ow," I said when he touched it. "Why would you do that?"

"Have you been drinking?" he asked. "Rum?"

"A little bit."

"Brush your goddamned teeth before your mother smells it."

"I can't."

"Find a spray," he said. "Do something intelligent."

"Should we call the dentist?" I asked. "Should we get Dr. Fenton on the phone?"

"It's eleven o'clock on a Friday night, Jay. Don't you think he has something better to do?"

"Aren't dentists on call?" I asked. "Isn't this a tooth emergency?"

"No," said my dad. "You can make it until tomorrow. They'll fix it like new."

"You say that now," I said. "How humiliated will you be when you find your son has bled to death overnight? From his gums?"

"We're not calling the dentist," said my dad. "Go to bed. Go do something other than talking to me."

"What are you watching?"

"I'm watching *Predator*."

"Can I watch it with you?"

"Fine," he said. "Fine."

"Where's Mom?"

"She's asleep."

"Then why are you worried about her smelling my breath?"

"Because sometimes she wakes up."

"Dad?" I asked.

"What?"

"What will happen with my tooth?"

"They'll fix it. They'll make it look new. Welcome to adulthood, where all your parts are fake or broken and you get sore on certain evenings."

We watched *Predator.* I jealously listened to my father eat his popcorn. When I couldn't stand it any longer, I walked across the living room, took a handful, and ate it piece by piece on the other side of my mouth. The metallic taste of blood mixed with the salt and the butter. I can't say it was very good.

I think Dr. Fenton was probably dead by the time I got into bed and looked at my stars, although the coroner was never exactly sure, since it took eight days to find the body. He might have made it through the night. But his heart attack was of the explosive variety. A full blockage. The atherosclerosis had begun around his twenty-ninth year, shortly after he injured his knee playing basketball with his son. The injury forced him to quit his regular exercise routine, and he gained thirty pounds. His smoking picked up. After the knee surgery, he'd been forced to wear a brace and take two months off work. He was depressed. Back then, a torn ACL was murder. They didn't have lasers.

When I called in the morning they told me that Dr. Fenton wasn't available.

"What do you mean?" I asked.

"He won't be in today," said the secretary. "I'll schedule you with somebody else. We have an excellent cosmetic dentist on staff."

"I want Fenton," I said. "I'll wait until Monday for Fenton." I would wait until the Armageddon. He was my meat-and-potatoes guy, and I was going to stick with him.

"I'm going to schedule you with Dr. Veldspar. We'll have it taken care of in no time."

"Where's Fenton?"

"Well," she said, "we don't know."

She sounded concerned.

Since my dentist was missing, I went to Dr. Veldspar, and he had a weird little nose and contact lenses. He was too young. He had an alternative haircut and talked to me about baseball. He hardly said a word about my tooth, even as he fixed it. He just kept talking about baseball.

"You must like the Brewers, then," he said, responding to nothing I could remember saying. He didn't know me.

I didn't nod or shake my head. I opened my mouth wider and

stared up at the strange black hourglass symbol that is imprinted on every dentist's light I have ever been beneath. I waited for his tools.

As the days passed, and stories about Dr. Fenton's disappearance showed up on the front page of the newspaper each morning, I thought less about my new tooth and more about where he was. Had he left town? Run away with another woman? His poor wife was in agony. There were photos of her crying. I remembered more things from our shared past. Our shared past of ten years probably amounted to two total hours of face time.

"Jay," he'd once said to me as we walked down the hall together, back toward the waiting room. "Are you sure you want to be a police officer? Why not a doctor instead?" He leaned down and opened the cupboard full of free toys. We always made a stop here when I was finished. It was his way, I think, of getting me to take a new toothbrush. He made it look like a toy.

"I don't like science," I said, digging around, looking for a yo-yo. "And I don't like blood. Why would I want to spend time with sick people?"

"Why would you want to spend time with criminals?" he asked. "And don't you think you'll run into blood if you're a police officer?"

"Maybe," I said. I had the yo-yo. I didn't care.

"Blood's not so bad," he said. "Everyone has it. Really, it's small red packages of oxygen."

This made me look up at his round red face. He was enormous, and what he said sounded just as true as anything else I'd ever heard in my life. There are always moments when dentists lock on to something huge, something too true to chuckle away. They ask you about your jaw, and you say that it's sore in the mornings, and they tell you that you've been grinding your teeth. The only way to fix it, they tell you, is to remove the stress. They say it as though your divorce and the death of your parents fall into the category of dental problems, and when they say it, you believe them.

At that angle, I could see up his nostrils. There were black hairs sticking out of them. His face looked like it was miles away. He put his hand on my shoulder, smiled, and handed me a new green toothbrush. "Take this," he said. "Brush regularly."

Dr. Fenton's engine died when he hit the final tree. I haven't been honest about the speed of the descending car. It was going much faster than a snowflake, because when they finally found it — when the sun came out for a whole day and enough of the snow melted to make the cream paint on the roof of the car visible from the road — the whole front end was mashed in. The airbag was deployed. His teeth were probably fine.

Since his car had stopped, all of his lights had gone out. His heater had died. He had some gray light for a half hour, and maybe even the amber glow of the streetlamps back up on the road coming in through his rear window.

But soon it was all blackness inside his car. The temperature dropped. He was half conscious, confused, and weak. Maybe even lying forward with his face in the airbag like a pillow. There was no light. Just a black box, and inside it the sound of a man wheezing. Maybe the sound of a man crying out. Wheezing, and the occasional scrape of a Gore-Tex coat across a leather seat. Panting. There was a vast pain in his chest, but his brain was bathing in endorphins. The death-bath of endorphins, when you feel like you're floating on air, or you see things, or you take your death casually, like you don't care. It was pitch black. It was dark. True, all of space is big, but for a moment it fits inside your mind, and you get to be incomprehensible for a change.

I didn't even finish college. And I'm not cool, I'm definitely not cool, thank God. That ethos, whatever empty, cold planet it comes from, sucks. Because what's the point? Why? There are better ideas.

For example: I don't live very far from where I grew up, and I see lots of old faces around town, each carrying a little added fat and skin, so despite this vast break in time, this embarrassing absence when we see each other's faces and wonder what exactly has happened to us all, I leave. Magnum's gone, but the road is still there, and at night I take slow passes. I go out of my way and drive down there along the river.

If someone had been behind him, Dr. Fenton would have made it home. That's clear. So I see myself that night, behind him in my big Jeep Wagoneer, towering over him on the road, far away from, say, a cocktail party, watching him go home. I just watch him to be sure.

This is important: in this slight fantasy, there is nothing happening. Nothing. I receive no recognition.

He is, after all, only a dentist.

I see nothing happening, and there are absolutely no events to speak of. Everything is, for a moment, as it should be. When he turns on his blinker and stops the Cadillac in his driveway, I keep going and forget about it. I remember that I am busy with other things. I tap the horn once and nod.

He doesn't know I've been behind him, and he doesn't even hear it, but this is just me saying so long anyway.

JOY WILLIAMS

■

Literature Unnatured

FROM *American Short Fiction*

THOMAS PYNCHON, who deemed Nature "loveable and scatter-brained," wrote in *Gravity's Rainbow*, "We are obsessed with building labyrinths where before there was open plain and sky. To draw ever more complex patterns on the blank sheet."

The sheet gets blanker with each day. There's more of us — human beings — and less of everything else. We are living the chronicle of deaths foretold. That we live in a world radically, rapidly decreasing in biodiversity is inarguable. *Biodiversity*. A word as lively as a blown lightbulb. Where's the zing? Where's the Punch and Beauty? It's a word closed to metaphor. The terror, the importance, the huge-ness behind the word is barely implied. Biodiversity is indeed not oxymoronic, like *Wildlife Museum*, but there's a certain contradictory inertness, a deadness about it. We use language to conceal, distort, and subvert the reality of many things, a great many things, and flattened terms like *environment* and *biodiversity* are words thrust in an ever-reductive context of cant. They're words that have lost their juice, their power. Once *Nature* became *Environment* she became se-mantically much diminished, as befitted her humbled station. The grandeur was gone. It became just a matter of politics. The Environ-ment became society, *was* society. It could be friendly or controlled, hostile or unstable, but it was primarily anthropocentric and gener-ously relative in its applicability. Like our state forests, those lands of many uses, many not so ecologically benign — Environment, as a concept, is utilitarian. There's the home environment, of course, the workplace, the school. There's the environment of Wall Street and the CIA. *Natural* becomes one prefix among many. An environment that's "natural" has already sidled away from Nature some. It has come to mean, sort of, not the same thing. It's something to locate between the tennis courts and the condos. Something that hasn't been drilled or mined or dammed yet, but exists, rather, in that wondrous state of pre-becoming — drilled or mined or dammed. It's already on the grid, the graph, but isn't being *used* . . . for now.

In Richard Ford's story "Sweethearts," a petty thief about to go to prison frets that he'll never get to eat seafood there. When his ex-girlfriend tries to assure him that surely fish will be served once in a while, he glumly counters that "fish isn't seafood." He's not a lower-class con, he's a middle-class con, one with certain socioeconomic ambitions. It's hard to argue with his assessment. Fish is to Seafood as Nature is to Environment.

William Gass can say that the word *Nature* is merely a wastebasket and should never be used for anything other than collecting its ambiguities, but the wastebasket itself is on the verge of being tossed. (Nature is to Wastebasket as Environment is to Dump.) Biology has morphed into Biotechnology, which has transmogrified into Nanotechnology. (The Future perhaps finds *bio*, the Greek word for life, to be too restrictive and prefers the sturdier ambiguity of *nano*, dwarf.) As the time shrinks between the use of a product and its dismissal into the waste stream (a blank and telling coinage), so quickens our seemingly boundless ambition to reduce and reconstitute life into something else. As one booster, a director of the AI (artificial intelligence) lab at MIT, puts it, *Our goal is to have such exquisite control over the genetics of living systems that instead of growing a tree, cutting it down and building a table out of it, we will ultimately be able to grow the table.*

Biotech is to Nanotech as a Tree is to a Table.

Significances shift. Things become unnecessary. Literature has pledged its troth to humanity, but much of humanity has found no need for literature. As a necessity, it ranks, in the eyes of much of the world, well below electronics. Still, Literature does try to keep up with humanity's stupidities and desires, its benumbing incomprehensions and inchoate longings. It never quite knew what to do with Nature anyway. Even when Nature was Nature in this country — say, 150, 175 years ago — and her eradication well under way, our writers seemed wary of characterizing her as anything other than, well,

Other. It was the whole Immanence vs. Transcendence thing. God gave us the living world to utilize, not be a part of. Brother Wolf be damned. What could be more un-Christian than that relationship? Still, Nature as theme resulted in three of the monuments of American literature, all written between 1836 and 1854: Emerson's *Nature,* Melville's *Moby Dick,* and Thoreau's *Walden.*

Henry Thoreau's Nature was homey, messy, and modest. All of Nature was swell to him and made him so content he wanted to build a little house right in the middle of her, and did. He died of a chill while counting tree rings, poor fellow. He was always trying to codify things, Henry was. One of his lesser-known pronouncements was *Wildlife is a civilization other than our own.* And what does that mean, exactly? It's just crazy talk.

As for Emerson, his Nature was completely a mental fabrication. It had no real substance, no reality, its ever-mutating appearances no more than pretty or somber playthings to entertain in the mind. It was the surrealistically detached *transparent eyeball* of the observing self that was important to Emerson. When Thoreau came upon Nature, a pleasant glade in the woods, say, he might describe it *as if I had come to an open window. I see out and around myself.* Both writers were startlingly disengaged from the very Nature they professed to be addressing, enlisting her primarily for literary and philosophical purposes. Melville was the greatest grappler of the three, and *Moby Dick* showed that not only was Nature unamenable to reasoned inquiry, she was a super-reality to which the irreality of language could never adhere. The book was one thing, the whale quite another. Man and Nature are mutually exclusive. After the leviathan brilliance and permutability of *Moby Dick,* writers reduced an intransigent Nature to a more or less comprehensible style — naturalism — and found an earnest, if somewhat squalid and solidly humanistic, resting place there for many years.

When exactly did *Nature* become *Environment?* It's a matter of style, of course, as well as diminished expectation. The frontier closes, so we change the definition, if not the meaning, of *frontier.* Frontier never meant anything anyway, except the demolishment of the Indians. If by making Nature irrelevant the suspicion only deepens that we're irrelevant too, let us burrow deeper into the vernacular, away from that scarily empty, blank, and open plain and sky. Environment is something we can work with. And it's willing to work with us. User-friendly, open to interpretation, compromise, and readjustment. Nature, in the sense of wildness, wilderness, has collapsed. The Environment is only making signs, albeit very large ones — species extinction, global warming — that it might.

So far, Environment has proved itself to be not nearly as literary as Nature used to be. It's hard to imagine Faulkner getting himself worked up over it, lavishing it with his favorite words — *tremendous, primeval, looming, musing* . . . Ike McCaslin could regret the wilderness's passing but could comfort himself with the notion that there was "exactly just enough of it," because he saw the two of them, himself and the wilderness, as "coevals with the two spans running out together, not toward oblivion, nothingness, but into a dimension free of both time and space." He didn't think of the wilderness as being conquered or destroyed so much as he saw it *retreating* before the onslaught of ax and saw and log lines and dynamite and tractor plow, retreating "since its purpose was served now and its time an outmoded time, retreating southward through this inverted apex, this triangle-shaped section of earth between hills and river until what was left of it seemed now to be gathered and for the time arrested in one tremendous density of brooding and inscrutable impenetrability at the ultimate funneling tip."

A graceless, certainly nonholistic image, that funnel. Man, comic, puny, redundant as he may be, fills up all available space. Everything else is pushed out and drains away. Nature is gone — deswamped, denuded, and deriverd — and man is the lesser for it, morally corrupt and now forever unworthy, but he endures, he will endure, you can bet on that, though much diminished. And this, in Faulkner's view, is the ruined wilderness's revenge on the people who have destroyed it — this diminishment. William Burroughs put it all a little more sourly when he wrote about the destruction of the forests and their creatures: *All going, to make way for more and more devalued human stock, with less and less of the wild spark, the priceless ingredient with the result being a vast mudslide of soulless sludge* . . .

The only Nature man has now to confront is his own — the seemingly endless varieties and vagaries of *human* Nature in the seemingly limitless environments he creates. Why, we can live in *sterile* environments. Sterile environments are, in fact, the preferred locus of much of contemporary writing. But even if we've buried Nature and crave, with somewhat unseemly impatience, closure on the matter — the let's-get-past-the-mourning-period-and-on-with-things attitude — Environment, now that we're comfortable with this unmothering matrix of a word, isn't going to be quite so submissive. The demise of Environment would be quite the dead end, for without it the whole show closes. *Environmentalism* and *environmentalist,* on the other hand, refer to a movement and an attitude — negative, obstructionist, unpatriotic — much derided in political circles. While the word *environment* can be used pretty much in any way one chooses, *environmentalist* is a word with a singular signal, limning a creature who lacks even the status of the individual, so herd-like is he in his thinking, so technologically fearful, so culturally unhip. Unheroic, whining, and warning, an environmentalist is someone preposterously *not on man's side.*

We must look at the human family as it is, one character graciously concedes in Saul Bellow's novel *A Theft.* Could this become a problem? As the screen shrinks, could this obsessional looking at the human bring about the death of literature? Is this all there is? Might we ever weary of it? Will X find love? Or hold on to love? Or his way? His will? What about Daddy? What will we do about Daddy? Or Mummy, for that matter. God, that Mummy and her crippling ways. Oh, they're getting old and batty. As for X, love's gone but left all those kids, none of whom could exactly be considered normal, and one's way not normal at all. Sad. Let us pray. Or not pray. Let us get into the car and go. Take off. Light out. Or let us stay, and withdraw into our minds, our endlessly fascinating minds. And twiddle there.

When did Nature *retreat* from Literature? When did she become *outmoded?* It was sometime after Faulkner's bear and Hemingway's marlin. The great man's bear had somehow transmogrified into the lustful lubricated sow of Stanley Elkin's "The Making of Ashenden." The other great man's great fish had become the scabrous, sickly trout in Raymond Carver's "Nobody Said Anything." Robinson Jeffers was employing his solemn if somewhat hysterical tremolo in Nature's honor, but Beckett was showing the fun that could be had in a world reduced to sand and rubbish bins. Flannery O'Connor was still drenching her South in mad-God sunsets, but her Nature — the mules and fields, bulls and tree lines — was just so much weedy backdrop for her grace-starved characters. It took a William Gaddis to pollute the very river where the witless faithful drowned at the moment of baptism. Nature had become Emerson's bauble with a vengeance — a crumpled dove kicked down an autumnal suburban street by nasty boys. Annie Dillard's inquisitive Pilgrim set off considerable rhetorical fireworks on Nature's behalf, but John Cheever had quietly withdrawn from any larger engagement. In *Oh What a Paradise It Seems,* his last, subdued book, Nature couldn't even be counted on to be refreshing in an Episcopalian sort of way. She had become a poor puddle of a pond about to be sacrificed to a highway. Though still linked to the human — the individual's — melancholy trudge through time, she was becoming a matter of literary indifference. Donald Barthelme pronounced even *weather* off-limits to his writing students. Rain, heat, winter, lightning, it was all boring; it showed a lack of imagination on the writer's part. We were bored, we were complacent, we were scared. We added up the things we owned. We added up the things we wanted to own. In a world of glut and waste, we stripped the language down to sticks. Then, because we lived in a world of glut and waste, we cranked it up again. When did Literature opt for Environment over Nature? Maybe it was when Ray Carver's hapless child ran down that fish in a poisoned creek, holding just enough runoff to cover it, and brought it into the house. Or rather, Cloud of Unknowing's promise had turned into the secular toxic drift of *White Noise.* Emerson's transcendental *Alone is heaven* had turned on itself like a snake and was Don DeLillo's cave dweller, totally sensorily deprived and exulting that he *had never been less bored in his life.*

Sartre, in "What Is Literature?," posited three words that indicated different relationships between literature and society. These were *ceremony, complicity,* and *contestation.* In the first, the writer blandishes the reader with generally accepted and cherished commonplaces. Reading becomes a ceremony of approval. *Complicity* involves a degree of conscious or unconscious bad faith on the part of the writer as he simply confirms society's more or less congratulatory, always forgiving self-image: *We must look at the human family as it is . . .* With *contestation,* however, the writer breaks the cozy contract, for the desire is to confront, disturb, even alienate the reader as he seeks not to entertain but to shame. He shakes the reader mockingly, angrily. *You must wake up!* The writer becomes increasingly at odds with his society, his times. Such literature moves increasingly toward negation until it consumes itself. And falls silent.

To save Literature, to rescue it just short of the dangerous, even terminal, obligations of confrontation, the critic Tony Tanner, by way of the critic Michael Bakhtin, posits a fourth method by which the writer may honorably pay witness. He calls it *carnivalization.* A retreat, of sorts, certainly. For a carnival, too, needs its admiring, complicitous confederates to succeed. The writer dazzles. The reader admires. A game is created, and in the endless environment of the game, both romp in giddy comity. Nature becomes a lexical construct, she falls before the juggernaut of language. The world is words, nothing but words, which adhere to it like flies to a sticky strip (Emerson updated for these ruder times). It's phenomenology vs. ontology all over again.

But carnivalization is its own dead end. Fat Tuesday can't go on forever. It exists only for what comes after, the demands of newer and graver realities. In a diminished world, wanting more seems an unimaginative response. But what does imagination have to do with wanting? More *is* what we want. More words, more writers wanting words. November has been deemed NaNoWriMo by its founder, one Chris Baty. NaNoWriMo stands for National Novel Writing Month, and people are urged to write a fifty-thousand-word novel in thirty days. Ten thousand human souls completed the challenge last year. There are no prizes. Still, gratification can be had. One woman who showed her accomplishment to a friend was much pleased when the friend reported back, "This does not suck." Fine, fine. Why should university writing programs get all the respect? There will always be words, and people enjoy fooling around with them and making them do funny things. When the last California condor — a soaring being whose wingspan engulfs the puny shadows of great eagles — has been shot or poisoned or simply permitted, despite every good intention of the world, to fall into extinction, words will still be with us, doing the darnedest things. While we patiently adjust to the indignities, bland replications, and awesome heartlessness of the new totalitarianism that is our Environment, words will tarry along with us, wittily scolding and gently deriding and amusing and defending us. Actually words, just words, might be far better suited to our Pop-Tech Environment than Literature will prove to be. Now that Nature has been allowed to float away from the needs of fiction, much like the flensed whales were from the "mother" factory ships of *Moby Dick*'s time, all that's left is our obsessive renderings.

With some exceptions, most notably in the works of Peter Matthiessen and Cormac McCarthy, particularly McCarthy's work of brutal mysticism, *Blood Meridian,* Nature has dried up as literary übersource. She is addressed today most frequently in the environmental essay, though her last redoubt may be the modest, unthreatening haiku. The environmental essay, creaking with good intentions, fairly shouts itself hoarse in exhortation, but is relegated to a shelf or two in the world's virtual library. The ecosophy of Deep Ecology is too abstruse and self-conscious to ignite the soul's fire. Emerging only in the 1980s, its language is already exhausted. The days of the great lyrical Arcadians are past. The merely good Arcadians are falling sorrowfully sanguine or are content to exclaim politely over chickens, crows, and coyotes. How movingly tenacious Nature is! With what dignity does the shot goose fold her wings and . . . die. Edward Abbey, that fabulous scold, is no longer with us. Nor is the more academic Aldo Leopold. Of his gracefully argued land ethic, many would respond: What's that, who's he? Today's essayist considers the rant to be in poor taste. It wins no hearts and minds. The reasoned argument, it is well known, is a magnet for inattention. The spiritual ecologists — Berry, Toolan — have their own shining shelf, but are not to everyone's taste. So the contemporary, secular essayist has chosen a middle ground, championing civilization while adopting an air of aggrieved melancholy — mature, personal — as she bears her ailing charge — Nature — toward the gates.

The Novel, which has, or certainly should have, considerable responsibilities toward the world, continues to roam across the sociological, psychological desert, occasionally visiting the only water hole that Nature's replacement, the Environment, offers: a sense of place.

*

Even here the bones have been pretty much picked clean. In an America *heavily thickening into empire* — Robinson Jeffers's words, Wyoming's no more than a firecracker string of tall tales in Annie Proulx's clever hands. The South has ceded its claim to the grotesque to — everywhere. The great soft American middle has no room in its amoebic sprawl for the sensibility of a Willa Cather. Florida has long been colonized by the crime and thriller writers. The most environmentally informed of them, Carl Hiassen, is forgiven his advocacy by adoring critics because his case against those despoiling Florida's landscape is so funny, so fabulously funny. His readers love the satire, but that doesn't mean they're going to forgo their powerboats for the sake of the manatee. As for Texas, large and colorful as it may be, where's the locus if the Trans-Texas Corridor becomes real? This wet dream is a megahighway that, in the words of its boosters, will make an ordinary interstate look like a cow path. Six lanes for cars, four for trucks, plus a rail line. They don't know the route yet, but they know they want *it*. Ground will be broken. Thousands of miles of ground. And broken good. Estimated time of completion: half a century. Is Literature up to the task of addressing the human spirit's thirst for more infrastructure? Will the word *infrastructure* replace the word *Environment* in our social-ecological consciousness? Or, if not replace, come to mean the same thing? Infrastructure . . . *Literature and the Infrastructure of Growth and Continuance. Literature and the Infrastructure of Humanism* . . . well, yes, possibly. Literature makes every effort to be adaptable. Lifeless rivers can still drown us, the real and the not real alike. What Literature might not be able to adapt to is the age of *post*humanism, an age ecocentric rather than anthropocentric. If Literature is showing signs of starvation, it is because it is feasting solely on the human — the individual — celestial junk food. For much of the world's meaning is an inhuman meaning, as Kafka was only one of many to realize.

The early reaction to the devastating tsunami in the waning moments of 2004 was that if an early warning system had been in place, many thousands of lives would have been saved — as though that massive underwater earthquake in the Indian Ocean were not dissimilar from the launching of a clutch of nuclear-tipped warheads by some unfriendly power. Without technology, humans were sorely dis-

advantaged. Only the elephants and birds sensed the forthcoming calamity and fled. It wasn't long before conservative commentators es-
pied the inappropriateness of this and declared that the real enemy of
humankind was still . . . NATURE. And the Outrage began. David
Brooks of the *New York Times* was left almost speechless. Almost. He
called Nature *genocidal, amoral,* and *viciously cruel,* comparing her
dark and unmerciful ways to those of man, whose temperament he
described as *upbeat and romantic.* "This is not the Nature we tell ourselves about when we visit a national park or an organic grocery
store," he wrote, puzzled. The tsunami allowed us to forget for a moment the gruesome cruelties man inflicts on man, on animals, on the
earth. It allowed us to feel sentimental about ourselves yet again.
Steve Chapman of the *Chicago Tribune* was even more indignant: *Moments like these mock the notion that human beings should live in harmony with nature. When did nature ever live in harmony with us? Nature
is the greatest mass killer in history, dwarfing the most bloodthirsty tyrants
the world has ever seen.*

And they told us we were safer once Saddam Hussein was captured. Even safer when we saw him in his underwear, doing his pathetic laundry.

But now the real enemy, Nature, has shown her face, dared to show
her face again! Nature, the cowardly bitch. The Environment would
never do this to us. The Environment is not indifferent to man; it
knows how to serve our needs, unnecessary as many of those needs
may be. As for any mischievously berserk surprises this new ser-
vant of ours might have in store, they can be corrected technologically. This thinking took a hit from Hurricane Katrina, a hybrid beast
whose hour had come around at last. Nasty Nature was acting up
again, but it was the built environment — the sloppily built environment — that delivered us into such ruin. We were flabbergasted. This
new beast, who will visit us increasingly in the future, may in a
crude, cruel, paradoxical way usher in the very biocentric, integrated,
posthumanist age we've been so desperate to avoid. This is reaction-
ary thinking, of course; it's barely thinking at all. Clearly, an integrated, dynamic, biocentric, posthumanist age will not be ushered in
without resistance.

Susan Sontag spoke of the *inadequacy of response* to great suffering and destruction. And perhaps the resources of language will never be adequate to our comprehension of the world and our place in it. But was it only a dream that Literature was once dangerous, that it had the power to awaken and change us? Surely it must be, become, dangerous now. Modernism brought the novel off the streets and into the mind. Postmodernism invited the psych-op troops in as occupiers, and they moved in with shrieks and holographs and unguiding lights. Orientation was out. Disorientation was in. Oh, it's been fun, sort of. Indulgence always is. But it's time to climb out of the sandbox. When Nature became Environment it was more than just a semantic shift and the blunting of our species' most significant tool: language. Spirit was lost. We lost just that much more of the sense of *Behold*. *Behold* the mystery, the mysterious, undeserved beauty of the world, the extraordinariness of myriad beings, not only of the human kind. There are more birds in this country than there were one hundred years ago, but only a few species — starlings, sparrows — are in the big numbers. So might our vocabulary swell in a de-Natured world, but unexceptionally, without luster.

Without the delivering words, Literature dies. Though in the future, the *future environment,* you can call it something else, I suppose.

CONTRIBUTORS' NOTES

Jonathan Ames is the author of three novels, *I Pass Like Night, The Extra Man,* and *Wake Up, Sir!,* and three collections of essays, *What's Not to Love?, My Less Than Secret Life,* and *I Love You More Than You Know.* His first graphic novel, *The Alcoholic,* with illustrations by Dean Haspiel, will be published in 2008. He is the winner of a Guggenheim fellowship and a sometime amateur boxer, fighting as "the Herring Wonder." His website is www.jonathanames.com.

Alison Bechdel is the creator of the long-running comic strip *Dykes to Watch Out For.* Her graphic memoir, *Fun Home,* published in 2006, was nominated for a National Book Critics Circle Award. She lives in northern Vermont, where she is working on another memoir.

D. Winston Brown is a native of Birmingham, Alabama, where he currently lives and works.

Scott Carrier is an independent radio producer and a freelance writer. His work has been broadcast on *All Things Considered* and *This American Life* and has appeared in *Esquire* and *Rolling Stone.*

Joshua Clark, founder of Light of New Orleans Publishing, has edited several books, most recently *Louisiana: In Words,* an anthology of 120 Louisiana writers depicting a day in the life of the state. He contributes travel pieces, essays, fiction, and photographs to many publications, including the *Los Angeles Times*, the *Chicago Tribune*, the *Miami Herald*, *Poets & Writers*, *Louisiana Literature*, *Time Out New York*, and the Lonely Planet anthologies. He covered New Orleans in Hurricane Katrina's aftermath for *Salon* and National Public Radio, and he is the author of *Heart Like Water*, an oral history and memoir on surviving Katrina and living in the disaster zone.

Edge Foundation, Inc., was established in 1988 as an outgrowth of a group known as the Reality Club. Its informal membership includes some of the most interesting minds in the world. The mandate of the Edge Foundation is to promote inquiry into and discussion of intellectual, philosophical, artistic, and literary issues, as well as to work for the intellectual and social achievement of society.

Jennifer Egan is the author of three novels, *The Invisible Circus*, *Look at Me* (a finalist for the National Book Award), and the best-selling *The Keep*, and a short story collection, *Emerald City*. She has published short fiction in *The New Yorker*, *Harper's Magazine*, *McSweeney's*, and *Ploughshares*, among others, and her journalism appears frequently in the *New York Times Magazine*. She lives with her husband and sons in Brooklyn, New York.

Stephen Elliott is the author of six books, including the novel *Happy Baby*. His most recent book is a collection of erotic stories, *My Girlfriend Comes to the City and Beats Me Up*. Elliott's website is www.stephenelliott.com.

Kevin A. González was born in San Juan, Puerto Rico. His stories have appeared in *Playboy*, the *Virginia Quarterly Review*, *Indiana Review*, and *Best New American Voices 2007*. He received his M.F.A. from the Iowa Writers' Workshop and is currently a Carol Houck Smith Fellow at the University of Wisconsin at Madison.

Miranda July is a filmmaker, writer, and performing artist. Her work has been presented at sites such as The Kitchen, the Guggenheim Museum, and two Whitney Biennials. She wrote, directed, and starred in her first feature-length film, *Me and You and Everyone We Know*, which received a Special Jury Prize at the Sundance Film Festival and a Caméra d'Or at the Cannes Film Festival. July's short fiction has been published in *The New Yorker, Paris Review, Harper's Magazine,* and *Zoetrope: All-Story,* and she is the author of the story collection *No One Belongs Here More Than You.* Raised in Berkeley, California, she lives in Los Angeles.

Matthew Klam is the recipient of an O. Henry Award, a Whiting Writers' Award, and a PEN/Robert Bingham Award, and has received grants from the National Endowment for the Arts and the Fine Arts Work Center in Provincetown. He was also honored as one of the twenty best American fiction writers under forty by *The New Yorker.* He is the author of *Sam the Cat,* a finalist for the Los Angeles Times Book of the Year and a New York Times Notable Book. He is a contributing writer to *GQ* and the *New York Times Magazine.*

Lee Klein helped his high school baseball team win the 1990 New Jersey State Prep Championship before going on to pitch two unremarkable seasons for Oberlin College. He has edited Eyeshot.net since 1999, and graduated from the Iowa Writers' Workshop in 2006. His writing has appeared in the *Black Warrior Review, Barcelona Review, Pindeldyboz, Hobart,* and other publications. He lives in Philadelphia, where he primarily roots for his fantasy baseball team, the Humble Moths.

Nam Le was born in Vietnam and raised in Australia. He has received fellowships from the University of Iowa Writers' Workshop, the Fine Arts Work Center in Provincetown, Phillips Exeter Academy, the MacDowell Colony, and Yaddo. His work has won the Pushcart Prize and appeared in several publications, including *Zoetrope: All-Story, A Public Space,* and *Harvard Review.* His debut collection, *The Boat,* will be published in the summer of 2008.

Jen Marlowe spent the past six years facilitating conflict transformation programs with youths from Palestine and Israel, Afghanistan, and Bosnia-Herzegovina. **Aisha Bain** is a human rights activist and served as deputy director of the Center for the Prevention of Genocide. **Adam Shapiro** is a human rights activist and founding member of Incounter Productions, which produced the documentary film *About Baghdad.*

David J. Morris grew up in San Diego and went to college in Texas. His work has appeared in the *Virginia Quarterly Review, Salon, Etiqueta Negra,* and *Rock and Ice.* He teaches at the University of California at Irvine.

Conan O'Brien has been combining his talents as writer, performer, and interviewer on NBC's popular and critically acclaimed *Late Night* since 1993. In 2009, O'Brien will take over the reins of the network's venerable late-night television franchise *The Tonight Show.* A two-time *Harvard Lampoon* president, he honed his writing skills at HBO's *Not Necessarily the News* before becoming a staff writer for *Saturday Night Live,* for which he won an Emmy Award in 1989. He went on to become a writer/producer for *The Simpsons* in 1991. O'Brien lives in New York City with his wife and two children.

Mattox Roesch ran a T-shirt-printing business from a basement in Minneapolis before moving to rural Alaska. Before that, he played the drums. His fiction has appeared in the *Missouri Review, Redivider,* and *Agni Online.* The author is grateful to *Agni* for first publishing "Humpies," his debut story, which is from a project titled *Sometimes We're Always Real Same-Same.* Roesch has received a Loft Mentor Series Award and a Minnesota State Arts Board grant. "Humpies" is dedicated to Luis.

Patrick Somerville's first book of fiction, *Trouble,* came out in September 2006. He lives in Chicago, where he teaches creative writing at the University of Chicago's Graham School. You can read more of his work at www.patricksomerville.com.

Joy Williams is the author of four novels — the most recent, *The Quick and the Dead,* was a finalist for the Pulitzer Prize in 2001 — and three collections of stories, as well as *Ill Nature,* a book of essays that was a finalist for the National Book Critics Circle Award in criticism. Among her many honors are the Rea Award for the short story and the Strauss Living Award from the American Academy of Arts and Letters. She lives in Key West, Florida, and Tucson, Arizona.

THE *BEST AMERICAN*
NONREQUIRED READING
COMMITTEE

Chris Bernard is a graduate of Raoul Wallenberg Traditional High School and in the fall of 2007 will be enrolled at the Academy of Art College in San Francisco. He will be studying 3-D digital animation and visual effects, in hopes of someday working at Pixar, and if not Pixar, somewhere like Pixar. His tenure on the *BANR* Committee was long and distinguished, serving as the group's film expert, most-prompt and most-iPod-wearing member, and undisputed non sequitur king.

 Having grown up in the Bay Area's finest city (San Francisco), and having marveled from afar at the *Best American* Committee's derring-do, **Josh Freydkis**, seventeen, is thrilled that he has finally been able to join the *BANR* action. When not spending his Tuesday nights in the dimly lit basement of the *McSweeney's* office, Josh enjoys surfing, art, death metal, and playing music with the TNT crew.

Daniel Gumbiner hails from the more sensitive side of the Golden Gate: Marin County, where he attended Redwood High School. He has an abiding love of hummingbirds, the soft-spoken-nerd lisp, and most fluffy things. This was his first and last year on the committee, and by the time you read this, he will be at Wesleyan University, probably wearing plaid.

Katie Henry is a junior at Berkeley High School, where she was named the editor in chief of her school newspaper for the 2007–2008 school year. In her free time, she enjoys psychoanalyzing literary characters, working for the SPCA (Society for the Prevention of Comma Abuse), and writing self-indulgent bios. She dedicates this self-indulgent bio and all her work on *BANR* to her teacher Matt Carton.

 In the fall of 2007, **Arianna Kandell** will be a senior at Berkeley High School. When she's not wandering the streets of San Francisco singing the played-out verses of Gershwin's "Summertime" a half-step out of tune, you can find this gal playing the trumpet and making use of the Bay Area's transportation system while she postulates the nature of life's existential realities. If you see her tucked in the back table of North Beach's historic Café Trieste, stop and stay awhile; she'll undoubtedly have a coffee-shop epiphany she'd like your advice on.

During **Anna Kong**'s *BANR* tenure, she was a senior at Mission High School and is now attending UC Berkeley. Anna's top three, most time-consuming activities of the year are badminton, Dragonboat, and Mock Trial. She is widely known around school as the loud, studious Chinese girl whose every word drips with sarcasm. In her free time, there is nothing Anna enjoys more than reading, journaling, and enjoying herself at the latest blockbuster hit.

 Bora Lee lives in Berkeley, California, with her family and two turtles. She attends Lick-Wilmerding High School, where she is an avid badminton player, and where she enjoys welding, reading, and eating candy. She will eat anything with hot sauce.

Belinda Man, a San Francisco native, attended Galileo High School and will, by the time you read this, be at Evergreen State College in Washington State. A workaholic when it comes to the arts, Belinda is a playwright and photographer, and plans to one day write and direct her own films. She loves Ben & Jerry's vanilla ice cream, because who needs complicated flavors when life is already complicated enough?

Nina Moog is a sixteen-year-old San Franciscan with green eyes and dazzling kneecaps. Now a senior in high school, Nina can often be found acting, meandering in the sewers beneath Oakland, or indulging in a game of bumblepuppy. Nina hopes to one day find the yeti, kiss her elbow, bake the most delicious apfelstrudel the world has ever seen, and be able to pogo-stick to school (aprox. 3 miles).

After a long three years as a committee member, **Felicia Wong** will be leaving the School of the Arts and joining the *Best American Nonrequired* Sulking Committee. Wherever she is, Tuesdays will seem awfully empty without stories of brownies, Stephen Gaghan, and prom night. Next year she will be at- tending the University of Microwaved Ramen and will sorely miss the sunny Mission, with its delightful coffee, swing sets, taxidermy, and, of course, 826 Valencia.

Vast assistance was also provided by **Maxwell Klinger,** who served as this volume's Guy Friday and intern. He attended every meeting, mentored the committee members when asked, and helped to find many of the best pieces in the collection.

Great and appreciated help was provided down the stretch by the always sharp, always quick, always resourceful *McSweeney's* staff member called **Michelle Quint.**

We are also indebted to **Tanea Lunsford, Fiona Armour,** and **Ike Ekah,** three students who began the year as regular members of the committee but, due to jam-packed schedules, had to postpone their tenure until 2007–2008.

NOTABLE
NONREQUIRED READING
OF 2006

MARTIN CENDREDA
  La Brea Woman, *MOME*
JAI CLARE
  The Sweetest Skin, *Consumed*
BROCK CLARKE
  What Is the Cure for Meanness?, *One Story*
MARTHA CLARKSON
  Memory Vats, *Nimrod International*

RAMOLA D.
  The Next Corpse Collector, *Green Mountain Review*
GUY DELISLE
  Shenzhen (graphic novel)
STEPHEN DIXON
  Winter, *New England Review*

ANNE ELLIOTT
  Three Lessons in Firesurfing, *Hobart*
STEPHEN ELLIOTT
  The New New Middle East, *The Believer*

TOM FARLEY
  The Case for HGH, *ESPN*
ERIC FEEZELL
  Water Buffalo Outsourcing, *The Big Jewel*
RONALD FRAME
  The Click, *Sewanee Review*
SETH FRIED
  Logic Puzzle #232: The Descending Bicycle, *Ninth Letter*

WILLIAM H. GASS
  A Little History of Modern Music, *Conjunctions*
SHARI GOLDHAGEN
  It's Really Called Nothing, *Small Spiral Notebook*
TYLER C. GORE
  A Sketch of My Childhood in the Country, *Opium*
PAUL GRIFFITHS
  Music in the Modern Postmodern Labyrinth, *New England Review*
KELLE GROOM
  Oprah and the Underworld, *Swivel*
XIALU GUO
  Winter Worm, Summer Weed, *Ploughshares*

DANIEL HANDLER
Naturally, *Zoetrope: All-Story*
ANTONIA HARRISON
The Bones in Her Face, *Water-Stone Review*
JENNIFER HIGGIE
Please Release Me, *Frieze*
JESSICA HOHMANN
The Mr. Sperm Donor Pageant, *Brainchild*
TRAVIS HOLLAND
The Archivist's Story, *Michigan Quarterly Review*
TREVOR J. HOUSER
Piranha-Otter, *Zyzzyva*
JAMES HUGHES
Separating the Warriors from the War, *Stop Smiling*
SANDRA HUNTER
Blessed Are the Meek, *Glimmer Train*

NATHAN IHARA
Lobster Is Tender Meat, *Opium*

GISH JEN
Amaryllis, *Paris Review*
BETSY JOHNSON-MILLER
What Gets Buried, *Agni Online*

MICHAEL KIMBALL
Excerpts from the Suicide Letters of Jonathan Bender, *Post Road*
MICHAEL KIMMELMAN
Seeing Red, *New York Times Magazine*

JHUMPA LAHIRI
Once in a Lifetime, *The New Yorker*
JASON LARSON
Explain the Diagram, *Lilies and Cannonballs Review*
ALLEN LEARST
The Blood of Children, *Water-Stone Review*
MATTHIAS LEHMANN
Hwy 115 (a Fantagraphics book)
JOHN L'HEUREUX
Devotions, *Epoch*
DOUGLAS LIGHT
Wedding Factory, *Hobart*

SAYERS, JOE
Your New Religion (chapbook)

JENNIFER SEARS
Slight Change in Tuesdays, *Fence*
DAVID SEDARIS
Road Trips, *The New Yorker*
NICHOLAS SHAXSON
What Caring Neighbors Do, *Virginia Quarterly Review*
HUGH SHEEHY
Harold Plays the Pauper, *Southwest Review*
DAVID SHIELDS
DS, *from* Reality Hunger: A Manifesto, *Willow Springs*
DAVID SHUMWAY AND HEATHER ARNET
Playing Dress-Up: Dave Bowie and the Roots of Goth, *Goth*
JULIEANNE SMOLINSKI
Travels with Joe Mundt, *Swivel*
SCOTT SNYDER
The Star Attraction of 1919, *Epoch*
MANIL SURI
The Tolman Trick, *Subtropics*

SONYA TAAFFE
Notes Toward the Classification of the Lesser Moly, *Zahir*
MICHELLE TEA
Charming Deformities, *The Believer*

JOSH WEIL
Good at Quiet, *West Branch*
MIKE WHITE
Attack of the Killer Dwarves, *River Styx*
MARTIN WONG
New Traditions, *Giant Robot*
SUSAN WOODRING
Inertia, *Isotope*

TIPHANIE YANIQUE
The International Shop of Coffins: Simon Peter, *American Short Fiction*

SILAS ZOBAL
The Bellwether, *Shenandoah*
LENI ZUMAS
Dragons May Be the Way Forward, *Open City*

THE B·E·S·T AMERICAN SERIES®

THE BEST AMERICAN SHORT STORIES® 2007. STEPHEN KING, editor, HEIDI PITLOR, series editor. This year's most beloved short fiction anthology is edited by Stephen King, author of sixty books, including *Misery, The Green Mile, Cell,* and *Lisey's Story,* as well as about four hundred short stories, including "The Man in the Black Suit," which won the O. Henry Prize in 1996. The collection features stories by Richard Russo, Alice Munro, William Gay, T. C. Boyle, Ann Beattie, and others.

> ISBN-13: 978-0-618-71347-9 • ISBN-10: 0-618-71347-6 $28.00 CL
> ISBN-13: 978-0-618-71348-6 • ISBN-10: 0-618-71348-4 $14.00 PA

THE BEST AMERICAN NONREQUIRED READING™ 2007. DAVE EGGERS, editor, introduction by SUFJAN STEVENS. This collection boasts the best in fiction, nonfiction, alternative comics, screenplays, blogs, and "anything else that defies categorization" (*USA Today*). With an introduction by singer-songwriter Sufjan Stevens, this volume features writing from Alison Bechdel, Scott Carrier, Miranda July, Lee Klein, Matthew Klam, and others.

> ISBN-13: 978-0-618-90276-7 • ISBN-10: 0-618-90276-7 $28.00 CL
> ISBN-13: 978-0-618-90281-1 • ISBN-10: 0-618-90281-3 $14.00 PA

THE BEST AMERICAN COMICS™ 2007. CHRIS WARE, editor, ANNE ELIZA-BETH MOORE, series editor. The newest addition to the Best American series— "A genuine salute to comics" (*Houston Chronicle*)—returns with a set of both established and up-and-coming contributors. Edited by Chris Ware, author of *Jimmy Corrigan: The Smartest Kid on Earth,* this volume features pieces by Lynda Barry, R. and Aline Crumb, David Heatley, Gilbert Hernandez, Adrian Tomine, Lauren Weinstein, and others.

> ISBN-13: 978-0-618-71876-4 • ISBN-10: 0-618-71876-1 $22.00 CL

THE BEST AMERICAN ESSAYS® 2007. DAVID FOSTER WALLACE, editor, ROBERT ATWAN, series editor. Since 1986, *The Best American Essays* has gathered outstanding nonfiction writing, establishing itself as the premier anthology of its kind. Edited by the acclaimed writer David Foster Wallace, this year's collection brings together "witty, diverse" (*San Antonio Express-News*) essays from such contributors as Jo Ann Beard, Malcolm Gladwell, Louis Menand, and Molly Peacock.

> ISBN-13: 978-0-618-70926-7 • ISBN-10: 0-618-70926-6 $28.00 CL
> ISBN-13: 978-0-618-70927-4 • ISBN-10: 0-618-70927-4 $14.00 PA

THE BEST AMERICAN MYSTERY STORIES™ 2007. CARL HIAASEN, editor, OTTO PENZLER, series editor. This perennially popular anthology is sure to appeal to mystery fans of every variety. The 2007 volume, edited by best-selling novelist Carl Hiaasen, features both mystery veterans and new talents. Contributors include Lawrence Block, James Lee Burke, Louise Erdrich, David Means, and John Sandford.

> ISBN-13: 978-0-618-81263-9 • ISBN-10: 0-618-81263-6 $28.00 CL
> ISBN-13: 978-0-618-81265-3 • ISBN-10: 0-618-81265-2 $14.00 PA

THE B·E·S·T AMERICAN SERIES®

THE BEST AMERICAN SPORTS WRITING™ 2007. DAVID MARANISS, editor, GLENN STOUT, series editor. "An ongoing centerpiece for all sports collections" (*Booklist*), this series stands in high regard for its extraordinary sports writing and topnotch editors. This year David Maraniss, author of the critically acclaimed biography *Clemente*, brings together pieces by, among others, Michael Lewis, Ian Frazier, Bill Buford, Daniel Coyle, and Mimi Swartz.

ISBN-13: 978-0-618-75115-0 • ISBN-10: 0-618-75115-7 $28.00 CL
ISBN-13: 978-0-618-75116-7 • ISBN-10: 0-618-75116-5 $14.00 PA

THE BEST AMERICAN TRAVEL WRITING™ 2007. SUSAN ORLEAN, editor, JASON WILSON, series editor. Edited by Susan Orlean, staff writer for *The New Yorker* and author of *The Orchid Thief*, this year's collection, like its predecessors, is "a perfect mix of exotic locale and elegant prose" (*Publishers Weekly*) and includes pieces by Elizabeth Gilbert, Ann Patchett, David Halberstam, Peter Hessler, and others.

ISBN-13: 978-0-618-58217-4 • ISBN-10: 0-618-58217-7 $28.00 CL
ISBN-13: 978-0-618-58218-1 • ISBN-10: 0-618-58218-5 $14.00 PA

THE BEST AMERICAN SCIENCE AND NATURE WRITING™ 2007. RICHARD PRESTON, editor, TIM FOLGER, series editor. This year's collection of the finest science and nature writing is edited by Richard Preston, a leading science writer and author of *The Hot Zone* and *The Wild Trees*. The 2007 edition features a mix of new voices and prize-winning writers, including James Gleick, Neil deGrasse Tyson, John Horgan, William Langewiesche, Heather Pringle, and others.

ISBN-13: 978-0-618-72224-2 • ISBN-10: 0-618-72224-6 $28.00 CL
ISBN-13: 978-0-618-72231-0 • ISBN-10: 0-618-72231-9 $14.00 PA

THE BEST AMERICAN SPIRITUAL WRITING™ 2007. PHILIP ZALESKI, editor, introduction by HARVEY COX. Featuring an introduction by Harvey Cox, author of the groundbreaking *Secular City*, this year's edition of this "excellent annual" (*America*) contains selections that gracefully probe the role of faith in modern life. Contributors include Robert Bly, Adam Gopnik, George Packer, Marilynne Robinson, John Updike, and others.

ISBN-13: 978-0-618-83333-7 • ISBN-10: 0-618-83333-1 $28.00 CL
ISBN-13: 978-0-618-83346-7 • ISBN-10: 0-618-83346-3 $14.00 PA

 HOUGHTON MIFFLIN COMPANY www.houghtonmifflinbooks.com